SURVEILLANCE, PRIVACY, AND THE GLOBALIZATION OF PERSONAL INFORMATION

Surveillance, Privacy, and the Globalization of Personal Information

International Comparisons

Edited by

ELIA ZUREIK, L. LYNDA HARLING STALKER,

EMILY SMITH, DAVID LYON,

AND YOLANDE E. CHAN

McGill-Queen's University Press

Montreal & Kingston · London · Ithaca

ISBN 978-0-7735-3707-1

Legal deposit second quarter 2010
Bibliothèque nationale du Québec

Printed in Canada on acid-free paper that is 100% ancient forest free
(100% post-consumer recycled), processed chlorine free

This book has been published with the help of a grant from the Canadian
Federation for the Humanities and Social Sciences, through
the Aid to Scholarly Publications Programme, using funds provided
by the Social Sciences and Humanities Research Council of Canada.
Funding has also been received from the Surveillance Studies Centre,
Queen's University.

McGill-Queen's University Press acknowledges the support
of the Canada Council for the Arts for our publishing program.
We also acknowledge the financial support of the Government of
Canada through the Canada Book Fund for our publishing activities.

Library and Archives Canada Cataloguing in Publication

Surveillance, privacy, and the globalization of personal information :
international comparisons / edited by Elia Zureik ... [et al.].

Includes index.
ISBN 978-0-7735-3707-1

1. Privacy–Cross-cultural studies. 2. Electronic surveillance–Cross-
cultural studies. 3. Globalization–Cross-cultural studies. I. Zureik, Elia

JC596.S97 2010   323.44'8   C2010-900487-6

This book was typeset by Interscript in 10.5/13 Sabon

Contents

Preface

Not long ago, a bibliographic search for available academic work on surveillance and privacy would yield a limited number of scholarly sources. Existing research tended to be confined to case studies that dealt mostly with privacy in the workplace, legal challenges to government eavesdropping on citizens, and online transactions of one kind or another. What the public at large thought of privacy and issues of surveillance was left largely unexplored. The accelerated diffusion of information and communication technology in social, economic, and political life in the past two decades has led to a more serious examination of the impact of the technology affecting individual privacy in areas involving, among other things, the flow of personal information, the mobility of people, policing, and the collection and sharing of personal information by government and private sectors.

Research on public opinion, an established area of social science research, dealt with privacy issues in an episodic fashion. Driven mainly by commercial and media interests, surveys of what the public thought of privacy usually came in reaction to so-called big events such as the terrorist attacks of 11 September 2001, which triggered government moves to combat terrorism through various pieces of legislation that were interpreted by scholars and privacy advocates as posing a threat to citizen privacy.

To narrow the research gap, the Globalization of Personal Data (GPD) project at Queen's University decided at the outset to conduct an international survey on surveillance and privacy using a single instrument and set of questions. The entire survey process was led by Elia Zureik. Prior to the launch of the quantitative phase of the survey, focus group interviews of a qualitative nature were carried out in each of the eight participating countries. All of the qualitative focus group findings and background country reports, as well as a summary of the overall quantitative survey findings and information on how to access the dataset, can be found online at http://www.sscqueens.org/research/intl_survey. The purpose of the qualitative data was to fine-tune the questionnaire that was eventually used to collect data cross-nationally from a total of 9,090 respondents in Brazil, Canada, China, France, Hungary, Mexico, Spain, and the United States in the summer of 2006. In December 2007 Japan was added to the list, using an online sample of 516 respondents. Analysis of the Japanese data is not included in this volume due to the specific nature of the sample and its date of completion.

The collection of original papers in this volume reports the analyses of these surveys. The GPD project convened an international workshop at Queen's University in November 2006, at which experts from several countries presented the findings of their data analysis.

Because of the large amount of data available to the contributors, we asked them to be parsimonious with regard to their texts and to place most of their tabular results on the website of the GPD. The relevant tables, figures, and appendices available online are referred to in each chapter accordingly. The interested reader can access these at http://www.sscqueens.org/book_tables.

This volume is the culmination of group efforts that started in the early part of 2004 following the receipt of a grant from the Social Sciences and Humanities Research Council of Canada under its Initiative on the New Economy program. Two workshops, in 2004 and 2005, were organized to deal with conceptual and methodological issues related to the international survey.

The editors would like to acknowledge their gratitude to a host of researchers and institutions that facilitated the successful completion of this project. Foremost, we would like to thank the Social Sciences and Humanities Research Council for its generous support of this research. Queen's University is gratefully acknowledged for providing an enviable environment in which to house the GPD project. The cooperation and support of the Office of Research Services at Queen's University played a major role in providing advice and guidance throughout the period of the project. Within Queen's University, the following researchers offered their expert advice throughout the project: Yolande E. Chan (business), Arthur J. Cockfield (law), David Lyon (sociology), Vincent Mosco (sociology), David Skillicorn (computing science), and Jane Webster (business).

It was always an aim of the project to involve students in the design, formulation, and analysis of the data. Assisting in this task were Queen's sociology students in the master's program Athena Elafros, Chen Luo, Wei Liu, Midori Ogasawara, Emily Smith, and Daniel Trottier. Martin French and Jason Pridmore, doctoral candidates in sociology, provided input throughout the preparation phase of the study. Similarly, Stephen Marmura in sociology worked in the GPD project as a postdoctoral fellow, as did Kathleen Greenaway from the School of Business. Doctoral candidate Andrey Pavlov (mathematics and statistics) was responsible for providing statistical advice during the data analysis phase. L. Lynda Harling Stalker was invaluable as the GPD postdoctoral fellow deeply involved in the construction of the survey questionnaire.

Outside Queen's, our thanks go to Professors Colin Bennett (University of Victoria), Andrew Clement (University of Toronto), Charles Raab (University of Edinburgh), and Gary King (Harvard University), the latter of whom gave us access to the software that was used to analyze the vignettes in the survey.

Under the guidance of Andrew Grenville and assisted by researchers Jennifer Bridge, Ciela David, and Michelle McAvoy, the international survey was fielded by Ipsos Reid, an international public opinion firm operating from Toronto. The Chinese survey was ably carried out by Millenriver Marketing Research in Beijing under the supervision of Guo Liang of the Chinese Academy of Social Sciences and with the assistance of Chang Huili. In Japan the online survey was carried out by Macromil Inc. with assistance from Midori Ogasawara and Yasuhiko Tajima.

The focus group interviews in Canada and the United States were conducted by Malcolm Saravanamuttoo on behalf of EKOS Research Associates from Toronto. Ipsos Reid was responsible for the focus group interviews in Brazil, China, France, Hungary, Mexico, and Spain. The focus group summary reports and background papers in the eight countries were prepared by Ipsos Opinion do Brasil, Ipsos China, Ipsos Insight France, Ipsos Szonda Hungary, Ipsos North America, Ipsos Bimsa Mexico, Ipsos Spain, and EKOS Research Associates for Canada and the United States. GPD researchers Emily Smith and Shannon Yurke wrote supplementary background papers for Brazil, Canada, Hungary, Mexico, Spain, and the United States. François Fournier of the Centre for Bioethics, Institut de recherches cliniques de Montréal, prepared the paper for Quebec. The focus group summary reports are available at http://www.sscqueens.org/intl_survey_background.

Special thanks also go to Jeffrey Moon and Alexandra Cooper at the Maps, Data and Government Information Centre, Queen's University Stauffer Library, who meticulously archived all of the survey findings Stauffer background materials in the ODESI system. We appreciate their expertise and enthusiasm for this process. Researchers interested in obtaining access to all of the survey materials and findings should contact Jeffrey Moon at moonj@queensu.ca.

We are grateful for the financial support in the publication of this volume from Queen's University Office of Research Services, Queen's University Department of Sociology, Ryerson University Privacy and Cyber Crime Research Institute, Office of the Privacy Commissioner of Canada, Queen's School of Business, and the Canadian Federation for the Humanities and Social Sciences. Thank you also to Don Akenson and Kyla Madden at McGill-Queen's University Press for their continued support throughout the lengthy review process and to Robert Lewis for his expert copyediting of the manuscript.

Joan Sharpe, the project's administrative manager, provided much-needed support. We extend our thanks to her, to Sarah Withrow of Queen's News and Media Services, who worked tirelessly to make sure the media were informed about the results of the international survey, and to Anna Dekker, who rendered with much appreciation her usual, efficient editorial services.

Finally, the editors express their thanks to two anonymous reviewers whose comments significantly improved the quality of the manuscript.

Elia Zureik, L. Lynda Harling Stalker, David Lyon, Emily Smith, and Yolande E. Chan

SURVEILLANCE, PRIVACY, AND THE GLOBALIZATION OF PERSONAL INFORMATION

INTRODUCTION

David Lyon

This book about surveillance, privacy, and public opinion is situated in two contexts. The first is the field of surveillance studies, and the second is the Globalization of Personal Data (GPD) project located at Queen's University within the Surveillance Studies Centre (formerly the Surveillance Project; see http://www.sscqueens.org/projects/gpd). The first connects to a number of key issues for social and political analysis in an era of advanced communication and information technologies that both help to constitute and at the same time throw up numerous challenges for the world understood as globalized. As Zygmunt Bauman (2000) cannily observes, today's social relations are in a state of liquidity. Among other causes of this state, new softwares and hardwares, unimaginable less than a generation ago, now enable a general social disengagement, a melting of things once thought solid, and a radical shifting of power relations to an "*extraterritorial*" (Bauman 2000, 11, original emphasis) dimension, no longer bound or even slowed down by the resistance of space. Surveillance studies is in part a concerted attempt to trace some of the extraterritorial power relations of the present, visible in all manner of devices and systems, from cell phones to Web 2.0, from security cameras to biometric passports, and from credit cards to national ID cards.

This brings me to the second context, which is much more specific: a research project aimed at understanding some of the key dimensions of this emerging reality. The GPD project was an international collaborative endeavour that focused attention on key processes of surveillance, such as border security (Zureik and Salter 2005), airport security and surveillance (Salter 2008), national identification cards (Bennett and Lyon 2008), and location tracking (Lyon, Marmura, and Peroff 2005), as well as attention on how to explain these theoretically (Lyon 2006). Each of these has a strong bearing on personal data and its constant and chronic globalization. However, as the authors of this book are skeptical of views that start with "technologies" and examine their supposed "impact" or that try to explain surveillance without ever grappling with the question of how ordinary people interact with it or ever acknowledging that it cannot in fact work without their involvement, witting or unwitting, the present series of studies attempts to explore that interaction. Although many avenues exist for such analysis, these studies try to gauge public opinion. Let me enlarge on the two contexts.

The towering figure of mid-twentieth-century studies of surveillance is George Orwell. No one has yet matched his achievement of supplying the concepts that have dominated at least Western understandings of the watchful state. Most occur in the bestselling novel – Orwell was an author and an activist, not an academic – *Nineteen-Eighty-Four*, and the most (in)famous is "Big Brother." If one sought a sociological parallel, it would probably be Max Weber, whose explorations of bureaucracy show that it spawns surveillance in every organization touched by its rules and processes. Weber wrestled with the reality that bureaucracy represents at once a highly efficient means of getting things done and also an insidious threat to human liberties and indeed to the human spirit. Whatever he intended by his "iron cage" metaphor, it was not meant to sound inviting or pleasant (Weber 1958).

Although much may yet be learned from both Orwell and Weber – the latter reminds us forcibly that surveillance is Janus-faced and not simply sinister – it has to be said that the surveillance landscape has altered dramatically since the mid-twentieth century. Simply put, the state is no longer the main player, and bureaucracy is no longer its main instrument. Since the 1980s, political-economic restructuring has helped to make all sorts of institutions, companies, agencies, and groups part of the process of governance alongside more formal government, and the chief tool in these processes is networked computer-based communications. These two factors work with and through each other and at the same time foster the sorts of globalization in which space becomes less of a barrier, not only to trade and production but also to organizational surveillance. Travellers, workers, consumers, and citizens all find that their personal data are of interest to numerous agencies, and those agencies depend on tracking, monitoring, and profiling them for their marketing, employment, entitlement, and service strategies.

Surveillance studies (see the online journal *Surveillance and Society*, Surveillance Studies Network 2006, Goold 2009, Goold and Neyland 2009, Hier and Greenberg 2009, Hier and Greenberg 2007, Lyon 2007, Lyon 2002) examines this newer world in which all manner of agencies using all manner of technologies (or none at all) are involved in surveillance practices. In the earlier period of bureaucratic surveillance when Orwellian and Weberian insights reigned, the main challenge, ironically, was couched in terms of "privacy." This was ironic because neither Orwell nor Weber had much time, if any, for "privacy," which emerged from a complex tangle of legal and cultural milieux. This notion, especially when understood socially (Regan 1995) and in terms of broader human rights, is indeed important, as is spelled out in several chapters of this book. But although necessary, it is not sufficient for understanding and responding to the challenges of surveillance today. Scholars in the field have instead turned to other ideas, such as "social sorting," to consider the real meaning of surveillance today.

The clues came from some classic studies undertaken in the 1970s and 1980s, notably James Rule's *Private Lives and Public Surveillance: Social Control in the Computer Age* (1974), Gary Marx's *Undercover: Police Surveillance in America* (1988), and Oscar Gandy's *The Panoptic Sort: A Political Economy of Personal Information* (1993). They each commented insightfully on the "privacy" implications of their analyses – of bureaucratic, policing, and consumer realms – but each also pointed forward to the classificatory capacities of new technology surveillance, which depends on searchable databases (Lessig 1999) and has enabled the massive rise of "social sorting" (Lyon 2003).

It should be said that the kind of study mounted at Queen's University in the Surveillance Project is heavily dependent on these scholars. The reason I have already mentioned several collections of papers edited by team members is that they reveal the extent of our reliance on research conducted in collaboration with many of the scholars I have been situating here. Our attempt to grapple with the pressing questions thrown up by the "new surveillance" (Gary Marx's phrase; 1988) includes this present study of the GPD project – the second context of the book. Although some of the explorations in this field are theoretical – notably but not exclusively debating the ideas of Michel Foucault and Gilles Deleuze – others are decidedly empirical in emphasis, as is the GPD project, which has attempted to understand the ways that personal data – particularly from travellers, consumers, citizens, and workers – are processed.

As Bauman says, in many ways modernity today is "post-panoptic" (2000, 11; see also Boyne 2000). Surveillance is no longer found merely in spaces of engagement, such as the prison, the factory, or the office. Jeremy Bentham's Panopticon prison design depended on the inmates believing that at any time the "inspector" could be in the control tower watching them. In Bauman's post-panoptic power relations, the "people operating the levers of power on which the fate of the less volatile partners in the relationship depends can at any moment escape beyond reach – into sheer inaccessibility" (2000, 11). In our words, personal data are globalized – they flow freely within today's liquid modernity – and we have made several attempts to explain why this happens, how the flows are channelled, and what its consequences are. We have traced data trails through airports and marketing companies, examined how locations technologies using global positioning systems (GPS) or cell phones enable further overcoming of space, and considered how government departments, commercial enterprises, and groups dedicated to protecting the public interest have responded to the new surveillance.

The largest single research effort of the current GPD project has been to investigate a further dimension of surveillance: the roles and responses of the subjects of surveillance, be they travellers, workers, consumers, or citizens, and how far "privacy" is relevant to such groups. Other studies of surveillance also look at offenders, children, patients, and so on. We do not pretend that our study is in any way exhaustive, but we did choose to focus on some categories of people whose data are most obviously amenable to globalization. To this end, the participating countries were chosen to reflect different histories, political cultures, and levels of socio-economic development. The survey was also motivated by a lack of international comparative data on crucial issues related to the surveillance and privacy of personal information.

This research is done in the conviction that such surveillance subjects actively and often knowledgably participate in their own surveillance and that this, not merely the activities of corporations and governments or the power of new technologies, is what both constitutes and in some circumstances may reconstitute surveillance today. Hearing from such subjects is a vital part of acting on that conviction. The chapters that follow tell the story.

PART 1

Methodological Considerations

INTRODUCTION

Elia Zureik

Public opinion research has become a standard staple in academic work and media reporting of topical events. The origins of public opinion research, at least in Western societies, can be traced back to the early part of the twentieth century, particularly in the United States, where behavioural and applied social sciences took roots. The rise in public opinion research was in no small measure stimulated by the spread of statistical and sampling techniques and eventually by computerization, mass political participation and with it means of communication, and the need on the part of governments and the private sector to monitor the public's views.

The widespread use of public opinion research brought with it several policy- and research-related issues that continue to dog this field.[1] The basis of such criticism is the extent to which public opinion taps informed decisions on the part of the public. Equally important, commentators referred to the role played by polling organizations and academic researchers in the sampling and designing of public opinion surveys and in the wording of the questions. The role of the media in shaping public opinion comes under scrutiny as well. It is argued that the media are not a neutral institutional sector but play a role in framing public issues and the debate about such issues. These and other problems are magnified when the research itself is concerned with abstract and complex concepts such as privacy, surveillance, and national security, among others.

The two chapters in this section address these and other issues from different angles. The chapter by Elia Zureik and L. Lynda Harling Stalker focuses on the myriad conceptual and methodological problems encountered in the study of privacy and surveillance – nationally as well as cross-nationally. Andrey Pavlov's chapter applies a statistical and modelling technique to show how the use of vignettes makes it possible to estimate variations in cross-cultural understandings of privacy concerns and to correct for these variations for the purposes of cross-country comparisons.

Privacy, it is pointed out, has two aspects: (1) the way we manage our interactions with others so as to protect our personal privacy through what Erving Goffman (1959) calls dramaturgical role playing; and (2) our having to safeguard against state and private-sector incursions into the private domain. Largely, the focus in this volume is on the latter.

One way to get around the abstract nature of concepts is to contextualize the questions by tapping the experience of respondents in various roles, such as travellers, workers, citizens, and consumers. We probed respondents' main sources of information, whether they personally withheld information for privacy reasons, and their experiences with government and private-sector initiatives to collect information about them and to share this information with third parties.

The crux of cross-national surveys is the issue of the validity and reliability of the data. The chapter by Zureik and Harling Stalker discusses how the obstacle of cultural relativity has been dealt with by using vignettes that correspond to specific questions in the survey that contain abstract concepts. The basic idea of the vignettes is to give respondents a universal set of hypothetical scenarios against which it is possible to compare their self-assessment with regard to the same concepts.

The comparison of the self-assessment and the vignette scenarios across cultures is taken up in the chapter by Pavlov, who applies a modelling technique developed by Gary King and colleagues (2004). The vignettes provide an invariant tool against which to compare answers to the self-assessment questions. The scores on the scales in the self-assessment questions and vignettes are computed and averaged for the respondents in each country. For example, in comparing answers to the self-assessment question and the vignettes with regard to France, Hungary, and China, the self-assessment answers show that France has the highest ranking, followed by China and then Hungary. To what extent do these answers reflect real situations in terms of one's having a say over his or her personal information? The answer to this question is provided by examining the responses whereby Chinese participants ranked the three hypothetical persons in the vignettes as having "complete say" or "a lot of say" over their personal information. The statistical model corrects for the discrepancy between the self-assessment and vignette responses and places China in a lower rank compared to France. Pavlov interprets the high ranking given by the Chinese respondents to all the vignettes, even when it is clear that the person in the vignette has no control or little control over personal information, to mean that the standards in China of judging what it means to have control over one's personal information are very different from what they are in either France or Hungary.

NOTE

1 See Harper and Singleton (2001). The authors point to the bias in the wording of questions, the use of so-called "push" questions that prompt respondents to provide anticipated answers, the presence of contradictory results emanating from competing surveys, and a lack of knowledge among respondents regarding privacy-related laws. They compare attitudinal and behavioural data, concluding that behaviour is a better indicator of consumers' intentions when it comes to privacy and online transactions. For these reasons, they question the relevance of privacy surveys to policymaking.

1

The Cross-Cultural Study of Privacy: Problems and Prospects

ELIA ZUREIK AND L. LYNDA HARLING STALKER

INTRODUCTION

Investigating public opinion is by now a deeply entrenched tradition in Western democracies, and attempts are increasingly being made to extend this practice to non-Western societies (Telhami 2003). As Walter Lippmann pointed out nearly a century ago, there is no consensus over the stability of public opinion; however, in times of national crisis, public opinion seems to cohere: "The symbols of public opinion, in times of moderate security, are subject to check and comparison and argument. They come and go, coalesce and are forgotten, never organizing perfectly the emotion of the whole group. There is, after all, just one human activity left in which whole populations accomplish the union sacrée. It occurs in those middle phases of a war when fear, pugnacity, and hatred have secured complete dominion of the spirit, either to crush every other instinct or to enlist it, and before weariness is felt" (1945, 11).

Public opinion is believed to be an indispensable barometer of democracy (Osborne and Rose 1999). C. Wright Mills (1959), writing in response to the onslaught of mass society after the Second World War, cautioned against slippage into abstracted empiricism in which the study of public opinion is severed from its historical and social structural contexts and thought of solely as the domain of aggregated and privatized attitudes. He called for the establishment of a connection between "personal troubles" and "public issues" in the study of public opinion. It is thus important to be cognizant of the processes that shape and mould public opinion and of the extent to which public opinion reflects informed choice.

Gary Marx, a keen writer on social control and surveillance, sounds a familiar cautionary note regarding survey research in general. He regards commercial surveys, but less so academic public opinion surveys, as having the potential to be "a form of surveillance." Who designs the surveys and writes the questions that make up the surveys are central aspects of survey research. Marx asks, "Does everyone have an equal chance to determine what the questions are, who gets questioned and how the data will be used?" (2008, 254). These and other ethical questions are not new. They have been raised since survey research and polling were inaugurated in the early part of the twentieth century.

Oscar Gandy (2003) makes the point that at times public opinion surveys about privacy have been driven by corporate and special interests, whose framing of the questions (with the aid of academics and privacy experts) has depicted a concerned but fragmented public who are willing to trade personal privacy for utilitarian benefits offered by polling organizations. From a policy angle, he argues, public opinion surveys about privacy have played an important, and at times insidious, role in framing the debate among policymakers.[1]

As we will show in a subsequent discussion, in addition to these ethics- and policy-related questions, important methodological issues must be addressed when carrying out public opinion research. For example, Kevin Haggerty and Amber Gazso (2005), in their discussion of public opinion research on privacy and surveillance, caution that we should be conscious of nonresponse rates and the likelihood of overrepresentation of "pro-surveillance" respondents, as those who are "anti-surveillance" are most likely to have unlisted telephone numbers and to screen incoming calls or simply to refuse to particpate in the survey. They advocate that researchers should be upfront with the response rates, both for the no-contact numbers and for those who refuse to participate. In order to ameliorate this problem, Haggerty and Gazso propose using weighting to compensate for the underrepresentation of anti-surveillance respondents. In this survey, we asked one-quarter of those contacted who were not willing to participate why they did not wish to take part. Very few cited privacy as a reason (see appendix 1.1 below).

From the perspective of our multicountry project, there are other vexing aspects to studying public opinion cross-culturally, particularly in cases where the subject of investigation involves abstract concepts such as privacy, surveillance, and control of information. There is a need therefore to heed Mills's concerns and those of others by devising an attitudinal study that is contextualized and sensitive to larger structural events – such as those of 11 September 2001 in our case – and to the role that the government and media play in shaping public attitudes to privacy and surveillance, particularly in times of national crisis.[2]

This chapter discusses the conceptual and methodological issues encountered in the cross-cultural study of public opinion, with special focus on surveillance and privacy. It highlights (1) the definition of privacy (or lack thereof) across cultures, (2) the importance of studying privacy, (3) dimensions of privacy, (4) methodological considerations and problems, (5) what questions to ask, and (6) triangulation of privacy determinants.

WHAT IS PRIVACY?

Defining privacy is not a straightforward exercise. In fact, there is no universal definition of privacy (Aiseu et al. 2004). Instead, privacy has to be understood in terms of culture, privacy for whom, under what conditions, and where. In Western countries with a tradition of privacy debates, the definition of privacy seems to cluster around the following six dimensions: (1) the right to be let alone, (2) limited access to the self, (3) secrecy, (4) control of personal information, (5) personhood, and (6) intimacy. This definition extends the original four-way definition (i.e., solitude, intimacy, anonymity, and reserve) provided by Alan Westin more than forty years ago:

> Viewed in terms of the relation of the individual to social participation, privacy is the voluntary and temporary withdrawal of a person from the general society through physical or psychological means, whether in a state of solitude or small-group intimacy or, when among larger groups, in a condition of anonymity or reserve. The individual's desire for privacy is never absolute, since participation in society is an equally powerful desire. Thus each individual is continually engaged in a personal adjustment process in which he balances the desire for privacy with the desire for disclosure and communication of himself to others, in light of the environmental conditions and societal norms set by the society in which he lives. The individual does so in the face of pressures from the curiosity of others and from the process of surveillance that every society sets in order to enhance its societal norms. (1967, 7)

As remarked by Anthony Giddens, privacy has two aspects: "privacy as the 'other side' of the penetration of the state, and privacy as what may not be revealed" (1991, 153). Erving Goffman's (1959) dramaturgical exploration of privacy, it can be said, belongs to the second aspect of Giddens's definition. In social settings, we are all actors playing roles (such as worker, citizen, traveller, and consumer) on a front stage, which is the outward presentation of ourselves; it is the back stage where our private realm exists. The first aspect of Giddens's notion of privacy is related to modernity and the rise of the nation-state and civil society. Although civil society has provided protection against encroachment by the state on the private domain, the state and civil society continue to exist in a state of tension, particularly in times of national crisis, such as the events of 9/11. Westin (2003) seems to be in agreement with Giddens. For Westin, privacy ought to be considered within the political and the socio-cultural/organizational spheres.

This Western, individual-centred approach to privacy poses problems for anyone investigating traditional and collectivist societies. In the case of our multicountry survey, this is especially true of the research on Brazil, China, and Mexico, where collectivist values predominate. Even in Western countries such as France and Spain, privacy is not a dominant issue in public discourse, as it is in Canada and the United States. Hungary, an eastern European country that is covered by our survey, exhibits altogether a different attitude to privacy as influenced by communist party rule during the latter half of the twentieth century. The varied national experiences dictate a nuanced approach to studying privacy as a value, an approach that must recognize the political culture of the societies concerned.[3] In a subsequent section of this chapter, we propose a model in which we triangulate attitudes to privacy, national values, government regulations regarding privacy, and demographic characteristics.

WHY STUDY PRIVACY?

Barry Schwartz writes, "Guarantees of privacy, that is, rules as to who may and who may not observe or reveal information about whom, must be established in any stable social system. If these assurances do not prevail – if there is normlessness with respect to privacy – every withdrawal from visibility may be accompanied by a measure of espionage, for without rules to the contrary persons are naturally given to intrude upon invisibility" (1968, 742). Here, Schwartz makes clear that privacy serves to stabilize the social system. But privacy serves personal ends as well. In seeking an answer to the question "why privacy?" Lucas Introna invokes ontological and existential arguments. Not only does privacy define the "context" in which people interact, but it is also linked to intimacy by providing "moral capital" for sustaining human relationships. Borrowing from Goffman (1959), Introna locates the possibilities of enactment and management of social roles in "our ability to control who has access to us, and who knows what about us" (1997, 267). This is why many writers consider privacy to be a requisite of autonomy: "without privacy there would be no self" (269).

In highly individualistic societies such as those in Canada and the United States, privacy is linked to individual rights, sometimes at the expense of collective and communitarian rights. In the case of the latter, the exercise of privacy has to be weighed against societal needs and the common good, which is why privacy can never be absolute (Etzioni 1999).

The task facing policymakers is to balance individual needs for privacy against societal requirements, bearing in mind, as Charles Raab points out, that the "balancing process" is fraught with problems (1999, 79). It is difficult to establish a balance in which privacy values are able to counter legislative and bureaucratic attempts to limit the introduction of privacy protection measures. What is needed, he argues, is "steering" rather than "balancing," with steering reflecting a multifaceted approach to privacy protection that relies on a combination of "regulation and self-regulation" and that aims to educate the public and to make use of privacy-enhancing technologies (88–9). Priscilla Regan (1995) argues forcefully that privacy is not only an individual attribute but also a common good on three counts: privacy is a "common value" to which each of us subscribes in varying degrees; privacy is a "public value" since it is a requirement for democratic practices at the political system level; and privacy is increasingly acquiring a "collective value" due to the pervasive influence of technology on the community as a whole.

Thus privacy is a means to an end: at the socio-cultural and psychological level, it is the means for self-realization and ontological security; at the political level, it is promoted as an antidote to state interference. In referring to Westin's pioneering work, Stephen Margulis (2003a, 2003b) cites four functions of personal privacy. It provides for (1) personal autonomy and the desire to avoid being manipulated, (2) emotional release and management of psychological and physical stress, (3) self-evaluation, which refers to one's need to integrate experience meaningfully, and (4) a certain amount of protection of communication, which in turn defines boundaries both for interpersonal relations and for sharing information with others whom we trust.

DIMENSIONS OF PRIVACY

Privacy with Regard to What?

Privacy violation, Gary Marx (2001) argues, implies transgressing four borders: (1) natural borders, (2) social borders, (3) spatial and/or temporal borders, and (4) ephemeral or transitory borders. This is akin to the definition provided by Robert Smith, editor of the online *Privacy Journal*, who sees privacy as "the desire by each of us for physical space where we can be free of interruption, intrusion, embarrassment, or accountability, and the attempt to control the time and manner of disclosures of personal information about ourselves" (quoted in Privacy International and EPIC 2003, n.p.). These, in turn, are equivalent to the four dimensions of privacy that are listed in the annual report of the advocacy group Privacy International.[4] According to the report, the study of privacy encompasses information privacy, bodily privacy, privacy of communication, and territorial privacy.[5] Although these are different facets of privacy and involve separate methods of data collection, they all can be cross-referenced through data mining and the convergence of information and communication technologies to construct profiles of people. Thus through data mining techniques, bodily, territorial, informational, and communicational data can be converted and merged to construct digitized persona of individuals (Maden 2003). Whether practised by the private or public sector, this merging of data is the basis for social profiling, which is considered by some to constitute privacy violation on two counts: first, personal information that was collected for one purpose is being used for another, the so-called function creep; second, data are merged from various sources to construct or infer behavioural patterns of subjects.

Because of the pervasive nature of privacy concerns, analysts agree that privacy considerations can emerge at any of the following levels: individual (as in everyday encounters), group membership (as in medical research or in ethnic, national, and racial profiling), organizational (as with members of organizations and workplaces), and global (as in transborder flows of personally identifiable information).

What to Look for in Studying Privacy?

Margulis (2003a, 2003b) makes the point that although secrecy and privacy differ in certain respects, both revolve around controlling access and processes (of how information, possessions, and space are managed), and both operate as types (of privacy) and as functions (of privacy). The main difference between secrecy and privacy is that the management of secrecy is invested with greater emotional and cognitive efforts than is the management of privacy. Secrecy is propelled by intentions to keep certain individuals, groups, and organizations from penetrating the boundaries of the self. Our interest is mainly in the study of privacy, at both the individual and group levels.

The current empirical and legal study of privacy has expanded significantly to include (1) awareness of existing technological, legislative, and organizational means in the private and public sectors to protect/enhance privacy, (2) reaction to and experience with specific privacy- and surveillance-related technologies, (3) the impact of so-called big events on privacy issues, (4) an increase in the articulation of privacy and national security, (5) attempts at harmonization of national, regional, and international standards of privacy, and (6) the importance of privacy for commerce and individual users of electronic communication and transactions.[6]

The globalization of commerce, travel, and communication has also meant the globalization of privacy issues (Bennett and Raab 2003). Comparative analysis of privacy legislation in various countries is examined in several chapters of this volume.[7] There is, however, a dearth of systematic information that deals with cross-national attitudes to privacy. Not only is the cost of such a comparative approach prohibitive, but the methodological and conceptual issues involved in researching cross-national attitudes to privacy are also substantial. We hope that this project will shed light on this matter.

METHODOLOGICAL CONSIDERATIONS

Why Conduct Cross-National Studies?

There are two main reasons for studying privacy cross-culturally. First, it is our desire to fill a glaring gap in the emerging literature on an important topic of investigation. More than a decade ago, Colin Bennett remarked, "the lack of reliable cross-national data on citizen attitudes toward privacy would suggest a pressing need to commission surveys that allow more comprehensive and reliable inferences to be drawn. There is surely an unjustifiable imbalance in the survey data currently available" (1996, 17). With the possible exception of small-scale comparative case studies, whose focus is Internet experience with e-commerce, the main shortcoming of comparative research on privacy in the past decade remains that it does not address the same phenomenon across countries using *standardized* research instruments, such as the one carried out by us in the Globalization of Personal Data (GPD) survey. Survey research on privacy is most developed in North America – particularly in the United States. However, we have seen in the past decade a constant expansion of privacy studies covering various facets and countries (which are mostly Western). In large measure, this increase has been due to the promotion of human rights and good governance and to the establishment of privacy ombudsman offices in several countries. More significant, however, the spread of globalization has spurred cross-national interest in privacy. State reactions to terrorism have been accompanied by national legislation to counter terrorist activities. These political initiatives triggered reactions from the public and from privacy advocacy groups that saw in excessive government intrusion ominous threats to privacy protection. Recent public opinion surveys that examined citizen attitudes to antiterrorism legislation focused on privacy in the context of national security (Zureik 2004). The sheer magnitude of transmission of financial and personal data across and within borders has led to calls for developing proper means to safeguard informational privacy. Several public opinion surveys that dealt with the spread of electronic commerce concluded that, as seen by consumers, for e-commerce to be successful, adequate privacy protection of personal data is a basic requirement. More of the European than the American public tend to leave it to government rather than business to regulate citizen privacy. In a world that is becoming increasingly connected, privacy ceases to be the exclusive concern of individuals, or even single governments, and becomes the global concern of regional, supranational, and international organizations – for example, the European Union and the Organization for Economic Cooperation and Development (OECD).

A second reason to study privacy cross-culturally is highlighted by Ronald Inglehart and Christian Welzel (2004), researchers with the University of Michigan-based World Values Survey.[8] Although their concerns are admittedly with cross-cultural research in general, their arguments are valuable for our research questions. When countries are units of analysis, representative surveys are needed to measure the motivational and behavioural patterns of entire countries. This is especially so when analyzing the links between values and social institutions/systems. This means that questions need to focus on social values and beliefs, not on mere opinions. This also makes possible the comparability of beliefs over time and space. Cross-cultural surveys consider culture to be a variable, thus allowing us to see how cultural traditions shape economic, social, and political spheres. Cross-cultural surveys allow for the creation of field-tested theories that are interdisciplinary and integrate subfields of a discipline (Inglehart and Welzel 2004). Aggregate measures allow for theoretically far-reaching analyses of social phenomena. This methodology complements surveillance studies, an emerging transdisciplinary field that includes sociology, political science, criminology, law, business, and geography.

How to Study Privacy Attitudes

More than a decade ago, in his stocktaking of privacy legislation and public opinion surveys, Bennett (1996) located public opinion surveys carried out with varying frequency and using different samples in Australia, Hong Kong, Hungary, Japan, the Netherlands, New Zealand, Sweden, the United Kingdom, and West Germany. He confined his search to items dealing with informational privacy and excluded so-called "single privacy" issues, such as people's feelings about the invasiveness of census questions, the introduction of ID cards, and direct marketing. Our focus in the chapters in this volume extends beyond informational privacy to include territorial, communicational, and bodily (or physical) privacy. As well, we are concerned with what consumers think of direct marketing/ profiling and its implications for privacy and with how they regard the use of surveillance technologies, such as closed circuit telelvision (CCTV), in public places. Bennett supplemented his public opinion surveys with an inventory of privacy legislation in twenty-five other countries, the overwhelming majority of which were Western.

Although the bulk of published surveys use telephone and, to a lesser extent, face-to-face interviews that are based on national samples, there is a discernible increase in combining various methodologies given the widespread interest in privacy (MORI 2003). Qualitative studies (usually comprised of small samples, such as focus groups) are used to test and develop questions for use in quantitative surveys. They are also used in a follow-up manner to examine policy implications emanating from quantitative results. Academics interested in issues pertaining to employee and consumer attitudes to privacy have made important contributions to developing privacy scales and indices that are based on small-scale quantitative methods in an organizational setting. It should be noted, however, that the bulk of large-scale privacy surveys are quantitative in nature and that they tend to be national in scope. In most cases, such surveys are conducted by public opinion firms, some of which operate internationally. Unless commissioned for specific purposes, these omnibus surveys tend to react to salient issues of the day. In the case of recurring issues of public concern (and privacy is such an issue), similar questions appear over time in omnibus surveys. Several polling organizations, particularly those affiliated with academic institutions, make data sets containing longitudinal privacy items available for secondary analysis.

As well, websites themselves have become common research sites, permitting online collection of data from respondents and carrying out content analysis of privacy seals (LaRose and Rifon 2003). The Internet has also been used as a source to study privacy policies of websites. The sampling of websites for the purpose of content analysis of privacy statements has become a major undertaking in consumer and privacy studies. What's more, the Internet can become a basis for drawing samples of consumers and administering surveys. Interest in the Internet has spilled over into the methodological domain. Most public opinion firms carry out so-called interactive, or online, polling by tapping into Internet users to study privacy attitudes, whether for marketing, political campaigning, or the study of social movements. The advantage of Internet-based sampling is the speed with which questionnaires are answered and their cost-effectiveness compared to other forms of face-to-face or telephone surveys. The disadvantage in using the Internet for opinion surveys is the inherent bias of the samples. Online respondents tend to be educated, predominantly male, urban, and frequent users of the Internet.

OPERATIONALIZING THE CONCEPT OF PRIVACY

The study of privacy spans nearly a half-century of empirical research. Systematic analysis of public opinion polls dealing with privacy and surveillance date back to the mid-1970s.[9] In carrying out such research, investigators made various attempts to develop operational definitions of privacy. It may be argued that the pioneering work of Alan Westin, in association with several public opinion firms in the United States, has furthered the study of privacy more than any other research. Oscar Gandy's comment, cited above, concerning the danger that these surveys will be used to confer legitimacy on political and corporate agendas by influencing the ongoing privacy debate makes it all the more important to pay close attention to the types of questions used by pollsters when assessing public reaction to privacy issues as well as close attention to the context in which the questions are asked.

As summarized by Margulis (2003a, 412), Westin's (1967) dimensions of privacy regarding personal lives have remained influential. He posits that privacy can be understood under three categories. First, one can see privacy as *solitude*, whereby one is "free from observation by others." Next, privacy can be understood in terms of *intimacy*, where there is "small group seclusion for members to achieve a close, relaxed and frank relationship." Subsequently, he argues that there is privacy as *anonymity*, which allows one to enjoy "freedom from identification and from surveillance in public places and public acts." Last, Westin puts forth privacy as *reserve*, the "desire to limit disclosure to others," which "requires others to recognize and respect that desire." As demonstrated by Elia Zureik elsewhere (2004), public opinion surveys have operationalized these and other privacy components so as to give us a longitudinal view of attitudes to privacy.

To build on these understandings of privacy, Westin provides a classification of "ideological positions" of consumers regarding informational privacy – referred to as the "privacy dynamic" (Harris and Westin 1991, 6–12).[10] This typology includes *fundamentalist* consumers (25%), who generally distrust consumer organizations regarding personal information stored about them; *pragmatists* (60%), who believe that privacy regulation laws and oversight are in place to guarantee protection of personal information; and the *unconcerned* (about 20%), who are willing to render personal information with little concern for privacy as long as they receive commercial benefits. In essence, what surveys can set out to investigate is citizen awareness, not just consumer awareness, regarding data protection measures.

Privacy surveys tap not only into respondents' awareness of various issues but also into the assessment of threats to privacy. These include threats emanating from law enforcement agencies, other government agencies (through the use of technologies such as ID cards, CCTV, and biometrics), online and offline business transactions, healthcare systems, educational institutions, employers, and marketers. One can also set out to see how people come to rank personal data (financial, health, etc.) in terms of sensitivity. This could then be followed up with respondents' experiences with attempts to secure information about one's self.

WHAT PROBLEMS TO EXPECT IN CROSS-NATIONAL PRIVACY SURVEYS

The pitfalls in carrying out global research on privacy were highlighted by an international panel that published its findings in the volume *Information Privacy in a Globally Networked Society: Implications for Information Systems Research* (Davison et al. 2003). Davison and colleagues note that problems spanned two general areas. First, one can see quality challenges in attitudinal surveys in general. These would include measurement bias and response bias, nonresponse bias, proxy sampling frames, and unjustified assumptions about Likert scales. Second, quality challenges can arise in privacy-related research in particular. These would include problems with nonresponse levels and biases, situational relativities, cultural relativities, and rigour versus relevance to strategy and policy.

Challenges of a general nature should be familiar to students of survey research. Questions regarding the reliability and validity of the items in cross-national research are important in controlling for measurement bias. Sensitivity in formulating the topic and in phrasing the questions is crucial here. How does one get honest responses from participants in a survey if they feel that their answers might compromise them? This is crucial in societies where the respondents are not accustomed to revealing intimate data about themselves, such as eastern European countries and other authoritarian regimes. A nonresponse bias due to nonrandomness among those who do not respond may lead to biased samples that do not cohere with the population composition originally envisaged in the sample design. Also, bias can be generated in relation to the extent of nonresponse to certain questions in the survey.

For the sake of convenience and/or cost, researchers sometimes choose proxy samples to carry out their research, assuming that they are representative of a given population. The Likert scale problematic is a familiar one. How does one ensure that the ordinal scales used in questionnaire items are actually ranked meaningfully in an equidistant fashion cross-culturally? One should also keep in mind that Likert scales are not generally used in qualitative data.

Quality challenges that are specific to privacy-related surveys must consider privacy as an intervening or confounding variable (Haggerty and Gazso 2005). A low response rate can in itself be an indicator of people's privacy concerns. Can one assume that attitudes to privacy among those who answer a questionnaire are similar to attitudes among those who do not respond, even when the latter's refusal is due at least in part to placing a high value on privacy? Because privacy means different things to different people and spans several domains, it is important that respondents be told by the interviewer the context of the attitudes to privacy that are being sought. For example, Roger Clark (in Davison et al. 2003) suggests that researchers should distinguish between behavioural privacy, privacy of the person, communicational privacy, and privacy of personal data.

In addition to addressing cultural relativism, which weighs heavily in cross-national investigations of privacy, Clark makes a connection between the media and their influence on public attitudes to privacy, a point that was raised by Gandy, cited above. According to Clark, "Media reports (which for the most part reflect propaganda, public relations campaigns and controlled information flows from governments, government agencies, and corporations) are likely to condition responses during the days and weeks that follow their publication. An extreme case of this bias is evident in the enormous politicization of privacy-related matters in the U.S.A., the U.K., and a few other countries following the assault on civil rights unleashed since 12 September 2001, and justified as responses to the terrorist assaults on New York and Washington D.C. the previous day" (in Davison et al. 2003, 345).

An equally useful study of cross-national research is written by the president of Market and Opinion Research International (MORI), Robert Worcester, in collaboration with Marta Lagos and Miguel Basanez (2000). The paper is very useful because it is written by individuals who have substantial experience in carrying out international surveys. The paper speaks to the nitty-gritty problems faced in cross-cultural public opinion research. The authors highlight the problems encountered in drawing up representative samples in regions where a reliable frame for a population count (such as a census) is not available, where within-country population heterogeneity (such as in Brazil) poses sampling problems, and where there are serious problems of language and questionnaire translations across cultures. Here, the problem of meaning and lack of language equivalence across cultures becomes challenging. In our case, for example, we must consider the extent to which the word "privacy" is salient in eastern European countries, Brazil, Mexico, and China compared to Canada and the United States. Does "privacy" mean the same thing to people from different cultures? Worcester and colleagues suggest using reverse translation (i.e., in our case, explaining what the word "privacy" means in so many words) to make sure that the researcher is tapping equivalent meaning, even though a given word may not be part of the vocabulary of the country. Here is how they put it: "In those cases [cross-cultural contexts] the word is translated into a phrase, and has to be analyzed as such. Back translations of question-naires is a fundamental part of multinational, multilingual studies; many mistakes are made when this is not done, even when working in the same language" (8).

Worcester and colleagues raise two additional problems: one concerns the use of semantic differential scales, and the other refers to the assumptions of cross-cultural comparability of socio-demographic indicators. We alluded to the first problem above, but the authors add an interesting dimension to the relationship between culture and placement on a Likert-type scale. They note that in Latin America it is culturally more comfortable for people to take a middle position so that they do not appear to be partisan. Thus a four-point scale produces higher nonresponse rates than a scale with uneven choices. It is also the case, however, that some would prefer a midpoint on the scale so as to "hide" their true location. With regard to socio-demographic indicators, the problem raised by cross-cultural research is best illustrated when comparing income, education, and occupational data cross-nationally. In many societies, ranking data on income is problematic. Is a middle-income position in one country equivalent to a similar position in another country? What about those countries with thriving informal economies? How does one deal in a meaningful fashion with the comparative distribution of income? Similarly, when ranking people by education level, can one assume that the quality of education is comparable cross-nationally? In societies undergoing extensive political and economic transitions, such as in eastern Europe and certain developing countries, the meaning of socio-demographic differentiation and ranking changes quickly over time. This change is also evident in regions within one country.

WHAT QUESTIONS TO ASK

Researchers in business schools have been pioneers in cross-national studies of privacy from consumer and corporate perspectives. For example, Steven Bellman and colleagues hypothesize that "cross-cultural values will be associated with differences in concern about information privacy" (2004, 214). Drawing on Colin Bennett's (2003) research, on the work of Bellman and colleagues (2004), and on our own investigation, among that

of others, we can make the following observations in the form of questions, which the GPD survey addressed to some extent.

At the outset, we were interested in how demographic variables pan
out in cross-national surveys of privacy. Do we expect to find that cross-
national variations will remain when controlling for various demographic variables, such as education, gender, race, age, income, and so
forth? How will cross-national variations in attitudes to privacy compare to within-country variations? What is the extent and nature of the
relationship/correlation, if any, among the four components of privacy
to which we refer above, namely informational, territorial, bodily, and
communicational privacy? Is the saliency of these privacy components
the same cross-nationally?

This led us to wonder about the extent to which one can explain
variations in responses to privacy items on the basis of national culture variables. In other words, is the attitude to privacy shaped by the
unique historical experience of the country in question? This would include the socio-political structures that developed over time. Is it the
case that people living in countries that have experienced authoritarian regimes orient themselves differently to privacy than those living in
liberal-democratic states, and in what ways? How familiar are citizens
with privacy legislation? To what extent are they likely to make use of
such legislation? Similarly, how will the cultural distinction between collectivist and individualist orientations at the societal level manifest itself
in terms of attitudes to privacy?

As a basic component of culture, societal values give an indication of
what is considered important. How then do individuals in cross-national
surveys rank privacy as a value relative to other values, including the
value of human rights? Is the attitude to privacy, as a social value, contingent upon orientations to technology generally, such that the more
individuals understand the technology the more likely they are to endow
technology with elements of trust in terms of protecting their privacy?

Building on this, one comes to questions of awareness. Do people
know, and do they care to know, what happens to the information that
is routinely collected about them? Or, alternatively, does their concern
directly correlate to the type of personal information discussed (health,
financial, etc.)? Are Internet users aware of privacy policies (so-called
privacy seals) that are posted on the websites of various public- and
private-sector organizations? What do users think of these policies? Do
they consider them adequate means of ensuring privacy protection?

The media have great influence on public attitudes to key issues in the public domain, and since privacy is one of them, we set out to ask respondents about their sources of information on privacy issues? Privacy is often linked to security in policy and media discourse. Do people in various countries perceive it in this manner, or do they consider it to be a uniquely American concern that is less relevant to their situation?

Since our concern in this project is with four different types of actors (i.e., citizens, travellers, employees, and consumers), do people in different countries orient themselves differently to privacy depending on the role(s) they occupy? In particular, how do consumers and citizens come to understand privacy? Does the extent to which consumers are willing to trade information about themselves in return for material or non-material personal benefits vary cross-nationally? What do consumers think of fair information practices as they relate to the three main justice perspectives discussed in the literature, namely distributive, procedural, and interactional? What do citizens think of the practice of governments providing the United States with advance information on travellers destined for the United States? To what extent could this be considered a sign of compromising individual privacy and national sovereignty? For a detailed discussion of how the GPD survey questions were devised, see L. Lynda Harling Stalker's background paper, "Every Word Counts: Writing the International Survey on Privacy and Surveillance" (2007).[11]

TRIANGULATION OF PRIVACY DETERMINANTS

Any cross-national study of attitudes has to start with culture as a variable. We provide below one example from the GPD survey in which we triangulate the data so as to highlight the role of culture and regulatory policies regarding attitudes to privacy.

We start off by referring to the work of Geert Hofstede (2001) and his classification of culture according to four main indicators. Hofstede's work has been used in cross-national comparisons of individual concerns about privacy,[12] although most of these studies originated in the business research community.

A second approach is wider in scope, and we are not aware that it has been used in a direct fashion in the study of privacy. We are referring to the above-mentioned international World Values Survey, which is routinely carried out in various countries using the same instrument. This approach relies on locating relevant items in the World Values Survey

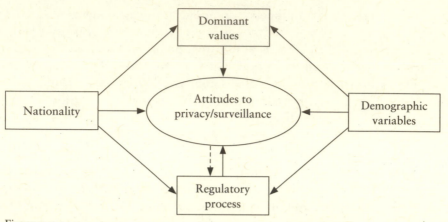

Figure 1.1
Relationships between values, nationality, demographic variables, regulatory process,
and attitudes to privacy/surveillance
Note: This model is a modification of the one proposed by Sandra Milberg and colleagues (1995).

that would give us indicators of the political/cultural framework of a
society as delineated through questions dealing with authority, equality,
tolerance, trust, risk, and so on[13] and then relating these cross-national
values to attitudes about privacy.[14]

A third perspective in the triangulation process that is directly connected to our concerns first examines the extent to which privacy is in-
stitutionally regulated through legislation in the various countries under
discussion and then relates the regimes governing privacy in each country to the findings of our public opinion survey (see figure 1.1). The
assumption here is that experience with and awareness of privacy legislation play an important role in shaping people's attitudes to privacy
and in people's being shaped by these attitudes. Take, for example, the
recent use by Privacy International of thirteen institutional measures to
rank countries on a scale from 1 to 5 according to whether the country
in question has endemic surveillance (score 1.1 to 1.5) or protects the
human rights of its citizens (score 4.1 to 5.0).[15]

Another distinguishing feature of our approach to privacy research
is that it analyzes on a country basis the relationship between attitudes
to privacy and demographic variables such as age, gender, and education to see whether within-country differences using these variables are
confirmed cross-nationally. Very few studies on privacy have carried out
cross-national comparisons using age, gender, and education as variables.

Table 1.1
Scores of the four main indices in Hofstede's (2001) cultural values inventory as they relate to the eight countries in the GPD sample

Index	Brazil	Canada	China	France	Hungary	Mexico	Spain	US
UAI	76	48	40	86	83	82	86	46
IDV	38	80	15	74	55	30	51	91
PDI	69	39	80	68	45	81	57	40
MAS	49	52	55	43	79	69	42	62

UAI = Uncertainty Avoidance Index; countries with high UAI exhibit a low level of tolerance to ambiguity and are low risk takers.
IDV = Individualism Index; countries with high IDV exhibit loose societal bonds and are more self-reliant.
PDI = Power Distance Index; countries with high PDI exhibit acceptance of unequal balance of power in society.
MAS = Masculinity Index; countries with high MAS exhibit assertiveness in contrast to caring values

Table 1.2
IDV index scores grouped into low, medium, and high ranges

Low (score 1–40)	Medium (score 41–80)	High (score 81–120)
China (15)	Hungary (55)	US (91)
Brazil (38)	Spain (51)	Canada (80)
Mexico (30)		France (74)

THE EXAMPLE

For the purpose of demonstrating the use of culture as a variable, we have chosen question 17 from the GPD survey,[16] which dealt with the extent to which respondents thought that laws enacted after the events of 9/11 to protect national security were intrusive.

Relying on Hofstede's (2001) cultural values inventory, table 1.1 presents the scores of the four main indices in the inventory as they relate to our sample of eight countries.

Using the above country scores, we are able to divide our sample into three groups of low, medium, and high range by IDV index, as shown in table 1.2.

Each respondent in the survey received a score from 1 to 4 on question 17. We excluded "not sure" responses from the analysis. We calculated the mean score for every respondent on this question and carried out a means test to see whether the differences between the three ranges were statistically significant. Low scores denote perceptions that the laws are highly intrusive and high scores that they are not intrusive at all. If the

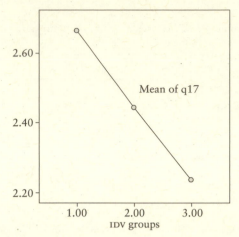

Figure 1.2
Mean distributions of responses to question 17 of the GPD survey by IDV index

relationship between responses to this question and the imported score values from Hofstede's index are to be confirmed theoretically, we expect an inverse relationship between IDV scores and responses to question 17. Individuals who fall in the low range on Hofstede's index (i.e., individuals who are not competitive and self-reliant) tend to welcome laws and don't feel that laws are intrusive.

There are statistically significant differences between the means of the three groups in the answers to question 17. Figure 1.2 takes the analysis one step further and displays the relationship between the scores for each group on Hofstede's index and the responses to question 17. We can see from the figure that there is an inverse relationship in the expected direction between the scores for cultural values obtained from Hofstede's index and the responses to question 17. In estimating the regression line for linearity between the dependent variable (i.e., attitudes toward laws) and the independent variable (i.e., IDV scores), we obtain the following equation, in which both the correlation and the constant are significant at p. 000, thus rejecting the null hypothesis of no association: attitudes to government laws = 2.881 − 0.167 (IDV scores).

CONCLUSIONS

This chapter presents an overview of conceptual and empirical approaches to the study of privacy and provides a road map to the construction of the questionnaire. The pitfalls in carrying out public opinion surveys are legion. We have attempted a summary of the problems, particularly as they pertain to a cross-national study such as ours.

As pointed out in the chapter, other studies of national and even multinational scope have examined privacy attitudes. The national surveys are mainly North American in origin, and they tend to focus on attitudes to specific events, particularly the attacks of 9/11. Multinational surveys are limited in scope and sample size, and they have primarily been driven by privacy concerns over electronic commerce. To our knowledge, this is the first study of its kind that uses the same instrument in a cross-national context to study surveillance and privacy attitudes among the general public. Although no study is completely immune to methodological and conceptual problems, care was taken to minimize such shortcomings. We operated on several levels. First, we ensured that the existing national samples representing the main demographics of a country (with the exception of China and countries such as Brazil whose rural populations had low access to telephones for the purpose of interviewing) were adequate to allow us to carry out multivariate analysis of the data. Second, through back-translation, we ensured that the wording of the questionnaire conveyed similar meanings to respondents. Third, we used a limited number of vignettes to ensure comparability in meaning across cultures. Fourth, through recourse to national cultures, we were able to triangulate attitudes to privacy and surveillance with cultural values as revealed in existing cross-cultural studies.

The data collected in the GPD survey are rich in scope and national representation. The chapters in this volume skim the surface of what the data can offer. We hope that in the future, researchers will make full use of the data.[17]

CONTACTS AND RESPONSE RATES BY TYPE OF RESPONSE

Contacts and response rates	Brazil	Canada	China	France	Hungary	Mexico	Spain	US
Total contacts	3,830	20,599	17,546	16,992	34,122	3,204	20,928	36,081
Response rate[a]	26.1%	4.8%	11.6%	5.8%	2.9%	31.2%	4.7%	2.7%
Total contacts with qualified respondents	1,046	5,998	2,038	n/a	1,136	1,431	8,235	1,728
Total disqualified	2,001	2,487	36	15,990	10,334	111	0	2,152
Total refusals	783	11,356	15,508	4,729	18,080	1,662	12,693	22,953
Refusal rate[b]	20.4%	55.1%	88.3%	27.8%	52.9%	51.8%	60.6%	63.6%
Total refusal reasons recorded	783	2,726	7,505	1,216	2,939	1,662	264	2,310
Percentage of refusals asked[c]	100%	24%	48.3%	25.7%	16.2%	100%	2%	10%
Reasons for refusal[d]								
Don't have time	403	29	4,329	322	1,247	1,245[e]	99	17
Not interested	380	44	911	582	917		121	44
Hung up phone			1,655					
Unfamiliar with topic			242	16	65		8	
Privacy concerns			61	15	28	28	4	3
No match with sample requirements			255					
Language			38					
Too old					153			
Can't hear properly					26	36		
Illness					69			
It's the weekend					12			
Not in tune for it					9	12		
Not willing to answer a research company					8	70		
Not willing to answer on phone					6			
Don't want to talk about the government						271		
Other		2,653	14	278	399		23	2,246
Don't know/not sure				3			9	

a Calculated by dividing the total sample size by the total contacts.
b Calculated by dividing the total refusals by the total contacts.
c Calculated by dividing the total responses by the total refusals. Note from Ipsos Reid: In France and Mexico 2.5% of refusals were asked, and in Brazil, Hungary, and Spain 100% of refusals were asked.
d Possible responses to question D, "It would be helpful for us if you could briefly explain why you are not interested in participating in this interview": (1) Don't have the time, (2) I am not interested, (3) Unfamiliar with the topic, (4) Privacy concerns, (5) Other (specify), (6) Don't know/unsure (not read).
e In the case of Mexico, this figure is a combined count for "don't have time" and "not interested."

NOTES

1 Roger Clarke (in Davison et al. 2003), another key researcher on privacy, concurs with this assessment.

2 Governments are accused of tapping into public sentiments of fear in times of crisis to justify the use of illegal means to obtain citizens' personal information; see Ireland and Howell (2004) and Amoore and De Goede (2005). Regarding the role of government trust by citizens and willingness in times of crisis to trade off civil liberties for security, see Davis and Silver (2004).

3 A series of background papers dealing with privacy and Internet use covering each of the eight countries in the sample was commissioned prior to designing the questionnaire for the GPD survey. The purpose behind these papers was to assist the research team in preparing the questionnaire and to contextualize the findings of the survey. The background papers are available at http://www.sscqueens.org/intl_survey_background (accessed 9 November 2009).

4 See http://www.privacyinternational.org/survey/phr2003/overview.htm#The Right to Privacy (accessed 9 November 2009).

5 In our cross-cultural study of privacy, we collected questionnaire data that tap people's experiences in their roles as workers, travellers, citizens, and consumers.

6 These and other facets of privacy played a key role in the design of the questionnaire used in the GPD survey. The various themes covered by the questionnaire are elaborated upon in a subsequent section of this chapter.

7 See, for example, Arthur J. Cockfield's chapter in this volume, in which he examines in detail various privacy regimes pertaining to the eight countries covered by the GPD survey.

8 The World Values Survey entails public opinion polling on key questions that relate to various value statements. This research started in 1981 and includes data from more than seventy countries. See http://www.worldvaluessurvey.org (accessed 9 November 2009).

9 See the review by Katz and Tassone (1990).

10 It is important to note that Westin's "privacy dynamic" and the labels he used triggered criticism from privacy advocates. For example, the Electronic Privacy Information Centre (EPIC) has noted with concern that these surveys are sponsored or commissioned by business and that a segment of the public is identified as comprising "fundamentalists" even though the concerns of those in this segment could be genuine (Privacy International and EPIC 2003).

11 Available at: http//www.sscqueens.org/book_tables (accessed 9 November 2009).

12 Applications of Hofstede's work by various researchers are available at http://www.geert-hofstede.com/ geert_hofstede_resources.shtml (accessed 9 November 2009).

13 See http://www.worldvaluessurvey.org (accessed 9 November 2009).

14 World Values Survey results that deal with Mexico and Brazil are addressed by Nelson Arteaga Botello in this volume.

15 See http://www.privacyinternational.org/article.shtml?cmd[347]=x-347-545269 (accessed 9 November 2009).

16 See the appendix to this volume.

17 The survey data are available for public use; for more information on how to access them, please see http://www.sscqueens.org/research/intl_survey (accessed 9 November 2009).

Application of the Vignette Approach to Analyzing Cross-Cultural Incomparabilities in Attitudes to Privacy of Personal Data and Security Checks at Airports

ANDREY PAVLOV

INTRODUCTION

A key problem in opinion research across cultures is comparability of meaning. Of the various methodological innovations employed in public opinion research to overcome this hurdle, researchers have resorted to the use of anchoring vignettes in interviews (King et al. 2004). Cheryl Alexander and Henry Becker point out that "A major problem in public opinion and survey research is the ambiguity that often arises when survey respondents are asked to make decisions and judgments from rather abstract and limited information. The use of vignettes helps to standardize the social stimulus across respondents and at the same time makes the decision-making situation more real" (1978, 103).

By varying the social characteristics of the situation as described in the vignettes, one can study the effects of factors such as age, gender, ethnicity, and in our case country on respondents' attitudes. Thus respondents are less likely to be biased in their responses if given a standardized, contextualized situation in which they are asked to express their views regarding the behaviour of neutral persons other than themselves.

The use of anchoring vignettes increases the reliability and validity of cross-cultural survey research. This is especially necessary when dealing with sensitive topics such as health or with abstract concepts such as, in our case, privacy. As is shown in this volume, privacy can have different meanings in different cultures. Corresponding to self-assessment questions asked early in the Globalization of Personal Data (GPD) survey, a set of vignettes was presented in which the respondents were requested to assess the various proposed scenarios. As the vignettes were the same for each respondent and were constructed to approximate the varying degrees of the response scale, it is argued that one can compare responses across cultures with more certainty. A minimum of 25% of surveyed respondents should be asked anchoring vignettes to establish a baseline for cross-cultural comparison. This allows for the development of thresholds for comparing the self-assessments. Gary King and colleagues (2004) suggest that utilizing vignettes with one-quarter of a survey sample is considerably less costly than doing so with the whole sample, and it is still possible to maintain the increased reliability and validity for which we strive.

For our survey, we decided on two anchoring vignettes, one dealing with control over personal information and the other with respect accorded to travellers at airports.[1] The vignettes were then presented to half of the respondents in each country. Although we would like to have done more – ideally one set of vignettes for each of the four actors (i.e., consumers, workers, travellers, and citizens) – cost in terms of time and money was a deciding factor.

Initially, three sets of vignettes were constructed and pretested. Each set was devised to address abstract issues related to different actors (see below). Once the results from the pretest were analyzed, and through consultation with the polling firm, we settled on two sets. The first asked about the extent of "say" over personal information. The second asked about the "respect" people receive from airport officials. The pretest showed that our other vignette did not evoke any new findings of significance.[2] Further, to do more than two would have been expensive in terms of both time and money. Each respondent got one or the other of the vignette sets, so we ended up with 50% of the sample for each.

Anchoring vignettes are a novel modelling technique using parametric data in order to correct for the problem of comparability. As indicated, respondents are asked to assess their personal stance with regard to the concept at hand and to compare this assessment to a hypothetical situation involving the same concept as depicted in a series of vignettes. Unlike self-assessment, the vignettes provide an invariant tool against which to rank the respondent's self-assessment and, at the same time, provide us with means of comparing the rankings among respondents in the sample. Based on the results, it is then possible to correct for incomparability in meaning. This chapter explores the use of this technique in the GPD international survey.

Table 2.1
Raw response frequencies for question 2 of the GPD survey (%)

	Brazil	Canada	China	France	Hungary	Mexico	Spain	US
No say	27.3	17.0	10.3	9.5	31.0	9.3	15.3	16.7
Some say	37.2	51.0	17.3	30.3	41.4	50.4	52.0	53.7
A lot of say	18.2	22.0	50.5	24.5	13.4	21.9	13.4	17.5
Complete say	17.3	9.9	22.0	35.7	14.2	18.4	19.3	12.1

WHY DO WE NEED TO CORRECT RESPONSES?

To make it easier for the reader to appreciate the problem, it will be explained within the framework of question 2 of our survey: "To what extent do you have a say in what happens to your personal information?" There are four possible responses to this question, with "refused" and "don't know" responses being dropped from analysis: "complete say," "a lot of say," "some say," and "no say." The results of the survey for question 2 are given in table 2.1.

This table shows the frequencies of responses in each category by country. We see, for instance, that France has a high percentage of "complete say," China has a frequency for "a lot of say" that is at least twice as high as in other countries, while Hungarians reported mostly "no say" and "some say." Does this mean that, compared to other countries, French and Chinese people have much more say in what happens to their personal information and that Hungarian people have little say? We should be very careful in interpreting these figures since what the table actually shows is people's opinion, based on their intuition, rather than verifiable facts.

It is clear that the concept being measured, as well as the suggested categorical scale, is abstract and can be understood by people very differently depending on their cultural background and perhaps other factors, such as age or gender. This creates inconsistencies in responses, and we cannot compare them directly.

OUTLINE OF THE MODEL

The statistical model suggested by King and colleagues (2004) is an attempt to measure this incomparability. To do this, respondents are asked a series of vignettes. In the vignettes, they answer the same question but with regard to hypothetical people as presented in short stories.

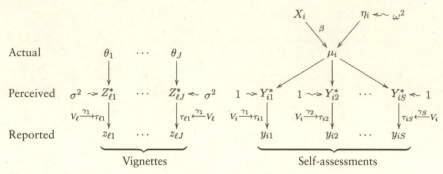

Figure 2.1
Statistical model for estimating actual response with anchoring vignettes

Respondents give their assessment on the same categorical scale. Using the answers to the vignette questions, the model corrects the answer for self-assessment, as shown in figure 2.1.

It is assumed by the model that there actually exists a variable (call it μ), measured on a continuous scale, that represents one's "amount of say" over what happens to one's personal information. We do not observe this variable, of course, but we can perceive it and categorize it under one of the four responses. The perception is modelled by a normal error, and categorization is done by means of three thresholds (τ's), which divide the real numbers into four segments corresponding to the four answers. Both the actual amount of say (μ) and the thresholds depend on one's cultural background.

The vignettes, thought of as people, have their own "true" amount of say (θ's in the figure). When these θ's are assessed by a respondent, we can estimate his/her thresholds and then use them to estimate the respondent's μ.

PRELIMINARY ANALYSIS

Before we consider the model for question 2, let's once again look at the raw responses, summarized in table 2.1. To make the comparison of countries easier, and following the ideas of the model, we have developed a score that represents how much say an average citizen of each country has in what happens to his/her personal information.

As in the model, assume that the "amount of say" is measured on a continuous scale and that the four responses are equidistant on that scale. Assign values for the responses in the following way: "no say" = 0, "some

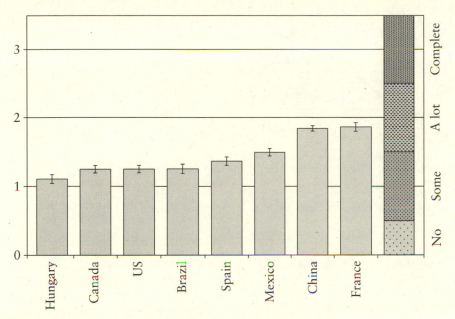

Figure 2.2
What we might get without correcting incomparability for question 2 of the GPD survey

say" = 1, "a lot of say" = 2, and "complete say" = 3. Now compute the mean of these values for each country. If we want to classify the resulting means into one of the four categories, we may take the midpoints between our codes as thresholds – that is 0.5, 1.5, and 2.5 – giving us the outcome shown in figure 2.2.

The error bars in figure 2.2 represent 95% confidence intervals for the estimated scores. As we have already observed, France and China received the highest score, while Hungary had the lowest score. Also, if we look at our conventional categorical scale, we see that all countries are at least in the "some say" region, with China and France scoring high in the "a lot of say" region, followed by Mexico, which is on the boundary. It is worth noting at this point, to be discussed further, that the response values were chosen somewhat arbitrarily, so the heights of the bars are not very informative. Rather, we should look at the differences. For instance, we can note the big gap between China and Hungary or conclude that the Canadian score is not significantly different from that of Brazil.

Now take a look at the vignette responses. We did not use the model at this point; we merely looked at how people rated the four vignettes, as shown in table 2.2.

Table 2.2
Vignettes response frequencies for question 2 of the GPD survey (%)

	Brazil	Canada	China	France	Hungary	Mexico	Spain	US
MIKE								
No say	46.1	42.0	50.2	60.1	35.0	12.2	16.7	42.7
Some say	27.8	22.2	17.0	23.3	21.6	29.4	27.8	21.7
A lot of say	12.9	8.8	18.9	11.9	8.4	26.7	11.2	11.4
Complete say	13.3	26.9	14.0	4.7	35.0	31.8	44.3	24.2
JAMES								
No say	45.5	46.5	42.7	60.0	30.9	11.7	17.3	42.3
Some say	28.7	21.7	16.4	21.6	29.3	27.5	25.2	33.1
A lot of say	15.0	13.0	28.0	13.6	13.2	26.4	14.0	9.6
Complete say	10.9	18.8	12.8	4.9	26.6	34.5	43.5	15.0
MARY								
No say	35.8	13.5	7.9	21.4	14.5	7.9	13.7	16.7
Some say	19.0	10.4	10.6	12.6	10.2	21.9	22.2	15.9
A lot of say	18.4	13.1	26.8	29.7	10.0	36.0	12.9	14.4
Complete say	26.8	63.0	54.7	36.3	65.4	34.2	51.2	53.0
RITA								
No say	34.7	27.6	20.7	39.3	33.5	8.8	14.0	31.9
Some say	37.4	41.1	23.1	41.6	27.3	26.0	35.8	39.6
A lot of say	14.4	13.4	38.9	15.4	12.9	29.4	12.5	11.3
Complete say	13.6	18.0	17.3	3.7	26.3	35.7	37.7	17.2

By simply looking at these frequencies, we see that those for "complete say" and "a lot of say" were low with respondents from France. Coupled with the fact that the French people rated themselves very high on the say scale (35.7% reported "complete say"), we may in fact expect that they will have the greatest μ estimate. The situation is somewhat different with China. Although its self-assessment score was as high as that of France, we see that Chinese respondents tended to give considerably more "complete say" and "a lot of say" ratings to all vignettes. This may mean that people in China have lower standards for what it means to them to control their personal data. We expect the model to correct for this and rank China's μ lower than France's. Another interesting change is expected with Mexico and Spain, both of which had a rather high self-assessment score but gave a lot of "complete say" and "a lot of say" responses to persons in the vignettes.

FITTING THE MODEL AND DISCUSSION OF RESULTS

The statistical model that we are going to use predicts one's amount of say (μ) and classification thresholds (τ) based on a group of variables

Table 2.3
Regression coefficients for μ for question 2 of the GPD survey

	"Amount of say" of respondents	
	Coefficient	Standard error
Gender	-0.0178	0.0368
Log-age	-0.0883	0.0491
White	0.02	0.0609
Education: high school	0.1367	0.0567
Education: postgraduate	0.326	0.0552
Brazil	0.4973	0.09
Canada	-0.1626	0.0788
France	1.3037	0.0816
Hungary	-0.4373	0.0829
Mexico	-0.7069	0.0936
Spain	-0.7688	0.0807
China	0.3738	0.0848

that account for differences in cultural background. In the case of the GPD survey, we are mostly interested in carrying out a cross-country comparison, but along with country we also include respondents' age, gender, race (i.e., white or nonwhite), and education (i.e., less than high school, high school, postsecondary). Income might be an important variable, but it is very difficult to measure on a single scale for all countries.

Table 2.3 shows the results of fitting a model with the mentioned explanatory variables.

As noted above, the location and the units of the continuous scale on which we define μ have no meaning and are chosen arbitrarily. (The model is identifiable for having no intercept and for fixing the variance of the random error at 1.) Thus the coefficients of the model cannot be assigned their usual interpretation. However, we can still say which variables make a significant contribution to the model and in which direction they influence the value of μ. For example, gender and race (white indicator) do not significantly differ from zero; negative log-age means that older people have, on average, less say than younger people; French people have, on average, more say than Americans (the United States is the reference country because its indicator is not in the regression). Also, the amount of say grows with education.

The four vignettes are assumed to have fixed values of θ's, whose estimates are given in table 2.4.

Table 2.4
Amount of say in the vignettes (θ's) for question 2
of the GPD survey

	"Amount of say" of vignettes	
	Value (θ)	Standard error
Mike (q29)	-0.5839	0.2174
James (q30)	-0.5601	0.2167
Mary (q31)	0.8718	0.2187
Rita (q32)	-0.2442	0.2161

Table 2.5
Regression coefficients for thresholds (θ) for question 2 of the GPD survey

	Thresholds		
	No/some	Some/a lot	A lot/complete
Intercept	-2.6242	-0.3862	1.0135
Gender	-0.0708	-0.016	-0.0032
Log-age	0.495	0.1816	-0.0574
Education: high school	-0.1203	-0.072	-0.0268
Education: postgraduate	-0.0938	0.0685	0.1058
White	0.019	0.205	0.2631
Brazil	0.493	0.3261	0.4391
Canada	-0.0662	-0.2138	-0.1433
France	0.6815	0.4679	0.7332
Hungary	-0.0673	-0.3704	-0.4982
Mexico	-1.1992	-1.0499	-0.733
Spain	-0.8374	-0.8092	-0.9786
China	-0.0835	-0.6936	0.0413

It is difficult to see from this table how the vignettes compare to the respondents, but we clearly see how the vignettes are ordered. In particular, we may notice that Mike and James are almost identical, so the analysis results would not change if one of these two vignettes were missing. However, the situation may change if we add more background variables to the model.

The last component of the model is the thresholds (τ), shown in table 2.5, which people use to categorize their perception of μ.

This table can be useful for comparing standards of classification between different strata. For example, white people have slightly higher

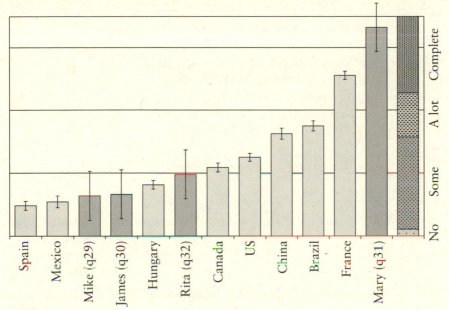

Figure 2.3
Country comparison with the vignette technique for question 2 of the GPD survey

standards than nonwhites; Mexicans and Spanish have considerably lower standards than Americans (that is, if an average American judges someone to have "a lot of say," an average Mexican may classify the same person as having "complete say").

To visualize the estimated mean "amount of say" between countries, we fix other parameters of the model, thus picking a reference group, and calculate μ's from the model for that reference group across countries. We can also calculate the thresholds for that reference group and see how each country would be classified by an average representative of the reference group. Note that it is not important how we choose this group when we compare just the respondents since it will affect only the location of estimated μ's, not the differences between them. However, if we want to compare respondents with vignettes, the reference group is important because vignettes are fixed values.

Figure 2.3 uses the following reference group: age = thirty years old, race = white, gender = male, and education = postsecondary. The thresholds shown are those of the US part of the reference group.

We see that, as was intuitively expected in the preliminary analysis, France remains at the head of the list. China is still high, but it differs significantly from France compared to its former near exact alignment. Another big change has occurred with regard to Mexico, which exhibited very low standards for having much say, and we now see it at the tail of our ranking. The same applies to Spain. We still observe that all countries would be classified as having at least "some say." However, we now have to add that this is according to American standards (thresholds). If we picked extreme thresholds, like those of Mexico or France, we might see a very different classification picture.

WHICH RESPONSES TO USE

After establishing the vignettes model, we can calculate the estimated "amount of say" (μ) for each respondent. These values are supposed to provide a score on how much say respondents have in what happens to their private information, consistent in the cross-cultural context. The reader may now wonder whether to use the original or the corrected responses in any subsequent analysis involving question 2. It also becomes a point of argument whether the other questions, where vignettes were not available, provide a valid picture of the concepts they address.

The answer is that both original and corrected responses may be appropriate to use depending on what interpretation the results are given. When we use raw responses, we really work only with people's opinions, and therefore all findings should be classified accordingly. For example, we have seen that 18.4% of 1,071 Mexicans reported having "complete say" over what happens to their personal data. It would be incorrect to infer from this that 18.4% ± 0.47% of the people in the population of Mexico have "complete say"; this is rather an estimate of how many people in Mexico would rank themselves in this category. After we have reanalyzed the responses with reference to the vignettes, we can obtain objective results. For example, we can quantify the difference in the "amount of say" between Mexico and other countries or compute correlation of "amount of say" with other variables.

ANALYSIS OF QUESTION 23
AND ITS SET OF VIGNETTES

Another set of vignettes used in the survey deals with how much one's privacy is respected at airports. The base question is number 23 of the GPD survey: "To what extent is your privacy respected by airport and customs officials when traveling by airplane?" The four categorical

Table 2.6
Raw response frequencies for question 23 of the GPD survey (%)

	Brazil	Canada	China	France	Hungary	Mexico	Spain	US
No respect	18.1	7.9	2.4	2.5	4.7	11.4	6.3	10.9
Some respect	36.8	45.1	59.0	8.5	19.8	39.3	28.3	51.7
A lot of respect	26.1	29.9	16.1	63.6	33.3	29.4	27.5	21.2
Complete respect	19.0	17.1	22.4	25.4	42.2	19.9	37.8	16.2

answers to this question are: "completely respected," "a lot of respect," "somewhat respected," and "not respected at all." Table 2.6 gives the raw percentages of responses to question 23.

France shows a remarkable difference from the rest of the countries, reporting mostly in the two upper categories. Hungary and Spain have the highest percentages in the "complete respect" category. On the other end of the scale, the United States and Canada have heavy percentages in the "some respect" group, and Brazil has a significant portion of "no respect" opinions.

Figure 2.4 compares the countries against a one-dimensional score, which now reflects the "amount of respect" people feel they have at an airport. The score is obtained in the same way as for question 2, namely by averaging the response codes in each country.

The countries in this figure clearly break into two groups: European (including Hungary, France, and Spain) and non-European. Within each group, there is no significant difference in the average "amount of respect," but the European group is somewhat higher on the scale than the other countries. This is the picture of people's opinion, without correction of vignettes.

The four vignettes that correspond to question 23 are Magda (Q33), Shekeel (Q34), Mohammad (Q35), and Hanna (Q36). Table 2.7 gives the percentage breakdown of the responses to these questions.

Based on these figures, we may expect that the model will change the picture. Mohammad is a very extreme vignette, presumably having very little respect at the airport. This was generally recognized by most respondents from France, but as many as 13.4% of Hungarians thought Mohammad's privacy was completely respected. This indicates that the standards of Hungary may be lower than those of France, and we may see Hungary drop on the corrected ranking. On the other hand, Brazil and China have been somewhat more critical in their judgment of Mohammad than France, which may bring their "amount of respect" score up. The same observations can be made with regard to Shekeel.

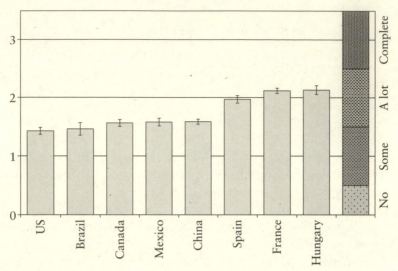

Figure 2.4
What we might get without correcting incomparability for question 23 of the GPD survey

Table 2.7
Vignettes response frequencies for question 23 of the GPD survey (%)

	Brazil	Canada	China	France	Hungary	Mexico	Spain	US
MAGDA								
No respect	49.4	18.8	25.2	38.4	37.6	27.6	39.1	24.6
Some respect	27.8	50.4	50.8	30.9	35.4	36.7	24.6	48.3
A lot of respect	10.4	15.8	11.4	22.5	9.7	21.4	17.7	9.7
Complete respect	12.4	15.0	12.6	8.2	17.3	14.3	18.6	17.4
SHEKEEL								
No respect	57.0	36.0	44.1	40.5	32.7	48.4	45.1	34.5
Some respect	24.2	41.0	40.7	31.8	34.8	27.5	20.0	40.9
A lot of respect	9.7	11.2	8.0	18.5	12.7	16.4	19.0	10.4
Complete respect	9.1	11.9	7.3	9.2	19.8	7.6	15.8	14.1
MOHAMMAD								
No respect	68.4	53.9	71.4	58.5	47.7	54.6	61.1	44.6
Some respect	20.2	32.9	21.2	26.5	29.6	22.9	18.5	35.7
A lot of respect	7.1	5.8	3.2	11.5	9.2	15.5	11.8	9.3
Complete respect	4.4	7.4	4.2	3.4	13.4	7.0	8.6	10.4
HANNA								
No respect	11.4	2.3	8.3	2.6	2.6	3.7	3.1	4.9
Some respect	17.3	19.8	34.3	2.8	8.7	16.3	7.8	26.2
A lot of respect	31.2	27.1	14.8	37.5	21.1	30.0	26.8	22.6
Complete respect	40.1	50.7	42.7	57.1	67.7	50.0	62.3	46.3

Table 2.8
Amount of say in the vignettes (θ's) for question 23 of the GPD survey

| | "Amount of respect" of vignettes | |
	Value (θ)	Standard error
Magda (q33)	-1.0989	0.2535
Shekeel (q33)	-1.4365	0.2545
Mohammad (q34)	-2.1894	0.2569
Hanna (q35)	0.5356	0.2526

Table 2.9
Regression coefficients for μ for question 23 of the GPD survey

| | "Amount of respect" of respondents (μ) | |
	Coefficient	Standard error
Gender	0.2922	0.0431
Log-age	-0.3119	0.0581
White	0.0815	0.0698
Education: high school	0.0113	0.0754
Education: postgraduate	-0.0632	0.0717
Brazil	0.4582	0.1196
Canada	0.1998	0.0838
France	0.843	0.0895
Hungary	0.5062	0.1
Mexico	0.1168	0.1032
Spain	0.4177	0.0847
China	0.702	0.095

Tables 2.8, 2.9, and 2.10 give the estimated parameters of the model.

The results suggest that more respect is given to females than males. The model reveals no significant race-based difference in respect and (not surprisingly) no education-based difference. Interestingly, older people are less respected by airport customs officials, and the gap between "no respect" and "complete respect" shrinks with travellers' age.

The difference between countries is summarized in figure 2.5, which shows the average estimated "amount of respect" for the reference group (same as for question 2) and the vignettes.

As was expected, Brazil and China appear to have a higher corrected "amount of respect" score. Otherwise, the picture hasn't changed very much. There are no clear groups anymore; rather, the countries change gradually on the scale. According to the American thresholds, all people

Table 2.10
Regression coefficients for thresholds (τ) for question 23 of the GPD survey

	Thresholds		
	No/some	*Some/a lot*	*A lot/complete*
Intercept	-2.6242	0.6311	1.504
Gender	-0.0708	0.2273	0.1627
Log-age	0.495	-0.3315	-0.4312
Education: high school	-0.1203	0.0211	0.1553
Education: postgraduate	-0.0938	-0.0659	0.1424
White	0.019	-0.1366	0.0565
Brazil	0.493	0.1559	0.4509
Canada	-0.0662	-0.1144	0.0779
France	0.6815	-0.5104	0.3415
Hungary	-0.0673	-0.4878	-0.3867
Mexico	-1.1992	-0.3285	0.0275
Spain	-0.8374	-0.4052	-0.2815
China	-0.0835	0.5265	0.4611

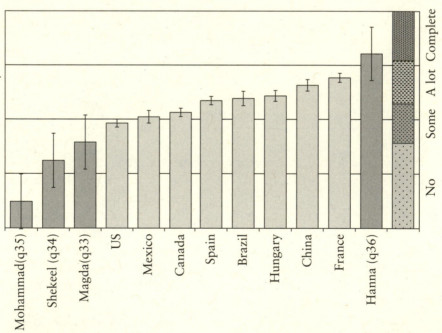

Figure 2.5
Country comparison with the vignette technique for question 23 of the GPD survey

have at least "some respect" and some countries typically have "a lot of respect." This agrees with the distribution of our default score shown in figure 2.4.

CONCLUSION

In this statistical-methodological chapter, we have analyzed two questions that deal with concepts with no precise meaning, where respondents' answers were based on their own understanding of the concepts. Along with the main questions, a series of vignettes had been presented. We have seen how these auxiliary questions helped us to understand the cultural differences that biased the responses. If these differences are strong, some implications can be seen with bare eyes, as in the case of question 2. However, for a more delicate analysis, we need a quantitative tool, such as the model developed by King and colleagues (2004).

The anchoring vignette approach demonstrates that there are cultural differences in understanding the concepts of control over information and respect while travelling, and the models presented correct for these differences. The model helped us to measure the cultural differences and to compare the bias-corrected answers. Country was the main factor accounting for these differences, and we have observed significant changes between reported and corrected scores, especially for question 2.

On the downside, we have been unable to include in our analysis some presumably important background variables, such as income and occupation. This was due mainly to inconsistency of scales or categories across countries as well as to missing values.

NOTES

1 See the appendix to this volume for self-assessments and anchoring vignettes. Question 2, control over personal information, is the self-assessment for group A (questions 29 to 32), and question 23, respect from airport officials, is the self-assessment for group B (questions 33 to 37).
2 The eliminated question was: "How much electronic monitoring do you experience in the workplace?"

PART 2

Privacy Regimes and Resistance to Surveillance

INTRODUCTION

L. Lynda Harling Stalker

As we have seen so far, notions of privacy and surveillance are neither clear nor concise. This is true within cultures or nations, and the complexity increases when cross-cultural comparisons are added to the research mix. In this section of the book, we present two chapters that provide different ways of approaching questions about privacy and surveillance using cross-cultural comparisons. The first is a legal analysis of countries' privacy laws pertaining to personal data; the second uses statistical modelling to determine how individuals in different nations react to surveillance mechanisms and infringement of the privacy of personal data.

In the first chapter, Arthur Cockfield takes us through the privacy legislation from the eight countries under investigation. In particular, Cockfield looks at the national privacy laws that govern, or impact, the flow of data across international borders. He uses Canada's Personal Information Protection and Electronic Data Act (PIPEDA) as the central comparison. PIPEDA is "An Act to support and promote electronic commerce by protecting personal information that is collected, used or disclosed in certain circumstances, by providing for the use of electronic means to communicate or record information or transactions and by amending the *Canada Evidence Act*, the *Statutory Instruments Act* and the *Statute Revision Act*."[1]

Using the Canadian results from the Globalization of Personal Data (GPD) survey to support his argument, Cockfield sets out to demonstrate

that those in business (i.e., Canadian business) need to be aware of
privacy legislation when conducting transactions in other countries. He
argues that, for the most part, privacy laws tend to be underdeveloped,
always playing "catch up" to emerging information and communication technologies and an increasingly globalized marketplace. In his
concluding remarks, Cockfield divides the countries along three lines
based on similarities of legal protection offered to data privacy: (1)
Canada and Europe, (2) the United States, and (3) developing countries
(i.e., Brazil, China, and Mexico). Cockfield further provides a synopsis
of how legislation varies and can be used as a key factor in our understanding of public opinions on privacy.

The subsequent chapter is Andrew Grenville's analysis of the GPD
survey data across seven of the nine countries.[2] Grenville's key research
objective is to try to understand how and why people traverse what
he calls the "path of resistance." That is, why do some people resist
surveillance mechanisms (e.g., by refusing to give personal details to
a business or by lying to the government) whereas some do not, and
how do those who resist enact their resistance? Using various statistical
tests, Grenville develops a model that has a continuum between resistance to surveillance and inaction. This model is mitigated by variables
of trust, knowledge, experience, and control drawn from various questions in the GPD survey. He uses this model to run comparisons across
countries and demographic factors. He then segments his continuum
to identify three groups of respondents: informed resisters, status quo
satisfied, and alienated skeptics. His analysis demonstrates the importance of looking not only among countries but also within countries to
grasp the nuances of public opinion on an abstract concept like privacy.

Together, these two chapters make us question how we understand
privacy as a value and surveillance as a social norm. Cockfield squarely
identifies privacy as a value that has been formalized through such
enactments as PIPEDA. He reminds companies of the importance of
recognizing how this social value is interpreted differently in different cultures. There cannot be an a priori assumption that Canadian
companies, and by extension their customers, are protected when data
flow across political borders. Grenville demonstrates statistically how,
through their actions, different cultures exhibit their understanding of
privacy as a social value. Those cultures that are more likely to resist
surveillance understand privacy differently from those that are more
likely to be complacent.

What ties these two chapters together is that cross-cultural, or at least cross-country, research is still important in today's globalized world. Political and economic structures, history, and culture are all critical to the ways people express their opinions on privacy. Furthermore, both authors in this section urge not only governments – which some might argue have a fiduciary responsibility to their citizens – but also businesses and private-sector organizations to be informed and to inform people about surveillance and privacy issues.

NOTES

1 Bill C-6, http://www.parl.gc.ca/PDF/36/2/parlbus/chambus/house/bills/government/C-6_4.pdf (accessed 30 September 2007).
2 The results of the Chinese and Japanese surveys were not available when Grenville, a senior vice-president of IPSOS Reid, carried out his analysis.

3

Legal Constraints on Transferring Personal Information across Borders: A Comparative Analysis of PIPEDA and Foreign Privacy Laws

ARTHUR J. COCKFIELD

INTRODUCTION

Technological developments such as the Internet and other information technologies make it less costly and more efficient for industry to monitor, collect, store, exchange, cross-index, and retrieve digital information. These developments have led to an increase in cross-border transfers of personal information by governments and businesses. Often, this information can provide detailed information concerning an individual's identity.

This chapter explores the relationship between Canadian federal private-sector privacy laws and their interaction with foreign laws that govern private-sector information collection practices. The Personal Information Protection and Electronic Documents Act (PIPEDA) is the Canadian federal legislation governing commercial transfers of personal information. The statute came into full effect on 1 January 2004. The goal of this chapter is to assist in gauging whether the personal information of a Canadian resident is subject to legal protections similar to those found in PIPEDA when it is transferred to seven other countries: the United States, three European Union countries (i.e., France, Hungary, and Spain), Mexico, Brazil, and China.[1] The analysis is summarized at the end of the chapter in appendix 3.1.

The international survey of the Globalization of Personal Data (GPD) project provides a helpful guide to many of the cultural differences surrounding privacy issues. To supplement the legal analysis within this chapter, the Canadian summary reviews GPD survey results for questions about issues such as attitudes toward private-sector sharing of customers' personal information with foreign governments and other third-party private-sector organizations.

At the outset, it is important to note several limitations with the analysis in this chapter. First, the study draws in most cases from primary sources of foreign privacy law, such as statutes. At times, however, English translations of these foreign laws were unavailable (this is particularly true with respect to Mexico, Brazil, and China), so it was necessary to resort to secondary sources that describe foreign laws.

Second, privacy laws have been introduced in recent years in all of the countries under scrutiny, and this nascent legal regime is subject to review and change. These potential changes may alter the analysis and conclusions concerning interaction between Canadian privacy laws and foreign privacy laws.

Third, although privacy laws can be very complex, this chapter ignores many of these complexities, some of which may have important impacts on cross-border transfers of personal information. For example, the study concentrates on federal laws that regulate a given country's private-sector information collection practices; however, in most countries an increasingly complex patchwork of additional laws, administrative practices, and judicial decisions govern privacy issues. Privacy regimes also include subnational (e.g., provincial, state, or municipal) laws, Constitutional protections for privacy in certain cases, criminal laws, and common-law privacy protections (e.g., invasion of privacy torts).[2] A fuller accounting of these complexities would be necessary to assist in understanding the legal implications of cross-border transfers of personal information from Canada to foreign countries.

Fourth, the chapter does not consider the gap that may exist between privacy laws and the compliance with and enforcement of these laws by individuals, businesses, and government. For example, the study reveals that the limited sectoral regulation of private-sector transfers by US laws may not afford the same level of privacy protection as Canadian laws, but it may be the case that the US Federal Trade Commission enforces privacy laws in a more rigorous manner in comparison to the Canadian federal privacy commissioner. In other words, a nation may have what appear to be strong privacy laws on its books, but these laws may have little impact to the extent they are not enforced. Similarly, cultural or other conditions may encourage firms in certain countries to be more concerned that their goodwill will be diluted to the extent their customers are unhappy with their privacy practices, which could lead to heightened privacy sensitivity on behalf of the firms and encourage consumer-oriented information collection practices (even if these practices are not mandated by any laws).

The chapter begins with a summary of some of the principles under PIPEDA that govern cross-border data flows to businesses based in foreign countries. A comparison is then offered between PIPEDA and the main federal privacy laws of the countries noted above. The chapter concludes by summarizing the degree of comparability between PIPEDA and the privacy regimes of the other countries under scrutiny (see appendix 3.1).

CANADA

Overview of PIPEDA Third-Party Transfer Provisions

In 2004 PIPEDA came into full effect and covered all organizations, including foreign companies, that collect, use, or disclose personal information during the course of their commercial undertakings. PIPEDA also applies to transactions that would normally fall under provincial jurisdiction unless a provincial government has passed substantially similar legislation.[3] To date, Quebec, Alberta, and British Columbia are deemed to have passed substantially similar legislation by the federal government and thus are exempt from PIPEDA with respect to the collection, use, or disclosure of personal information within these provinces.[4]

PIPEDA applies only to organizations that collect "personal information" in the course of "commercial activity" (PIPEDA, s. 4[1][a]). Personal information is defined as "information about an identifiable individual," not including the "name, title or business address or telephone number of an employee of an organization" (PIPEDA, s. 2[1]). "Commercial activity" is defined as "any particular transaction, act or conduct that is of a commercial character, including the selling, bartering or leasing of donor, membership or other fundraising lists" (PIPEDA, s. 2[1]).

PIPEDA was modelled on the Canadian Standard's Association (CSA) Model Code for the Protection of Personal Information. This Model Code contained ten fair information practices principles, which were transplanted directly into PIPEDA as schedule 1. The principles are thus binding under Canadian law (PIPEDA, s. 5[1]). This section briefly introduces a few of the relevant principles surrounding transfers of personal information to third parties.

Principle 1 encourages accountability by mandating data collector responsibility for the personal information of a data subject. Further, organizations that collect data must designate an individual to be accountable for their collection practices (e.g., a chief privacy officer) (PIPEDA, s. 4[1]). Importantly, this principle also indicates that "An organization is responsible for personal information in its possession or custody, including information that has been transferred to a third party for processing. The organization shall use contractual or other means to provide a comparable level of protection while the information is being processed by a third party" (PIPEDA, s. 4[1]).

However, an organization might not always be bound by the accountability principle, depending on how the information transfer to a third party is characterized. A distinction has been made by the privacy commissioner of Canada between situations where information (1) has been transferred by a principal organization to an external service provider/agent ("processor"), whose use and manipulation of the information are regulated by contractual agreement; and (2) has been disclosed outright to a third-party organization. In cases where information has been transferred for processing according to a contractual agreement, the Office of the Privacy Commissioner (2004) has taken the view that such transfers may be performed without the consent of the individual to whom the information pertains, as long as the contract between the principal organization and the processor contains the following provisions:[5]

- naming a person to handle all privacy aspects of the contract;
- limiting use of the personal information to the purposes specified to fulfil the contract;
- limiting disclosure of the information to what is authorized by the principal organization or required by law;
- referring any people looking for access to their personal information to the principal organization;
- returning or disposing of the transferred information upon completion of the contract;
- using appropriate security measures to protect the personal information;
- allowing the principal organization to audit the third party's compliance with the contract as necessary.

As a result of this stipulation, firms operating within Canada that transfer personal information outside of the country for processing must seek contractual assurances from any third party that the information will be treated in the ways mandated by PIPEDA.[6] The checklist, however, would also appear to suggest that the Canadian firm may need to conduct an audit of the foreign firm to ensure that it has the resources, privacy practices, and policies in place to fulfil PIPEDA requirements; documentation of this audit could assist the transferor organization in minimizing its liability for the actions of a third party. If this view is accurate, it could force Canadian firms to incur significant compliance costs when they transfer personal information to foreign firms where the legal regime is not substantially similar to PIPEDA. As touched on below in the section on the United States, it may make sense for the Canadian government to negotiate a safe harbour agreement with the United States to reduce compliance costs for US and Canadian firms. For example, if a US firm was to self-certify under some type of Canada-United States safe harbour agreement, the Canadian firm would likely not have to conduct an audit of this firm's privacy practices.

With respect to other types of transfers of personal information across borders (i.e., transfers to third parties that do more than mere processing), the general approach of PIPEDA is that the consent of an individual must be obtained before certain personal information can be collected, used, or disclosed (see principle 3). However, consent need not be explicit in many circumstances. Rather, the expectations of a "reasonable person" determine whether consent must be explicit or may be implied based on the circumstances. Explicit consent is always required when the personal information is particularly sensitive, such as with medical and financial records (PIPEDA, s. 5[3]). Because the "reasonable person" consent provisions within PIPEDA require context-based analysis, it is likely that courts will have to discern the scope and applicability of these provisions to particular fact patterns.

For instance, in *Englander v. Telus Communications Inc.*, an individual brought a complaint under PIPEDA against a national telephone company because the company did not disclose that it was selling customer information in electronic form to third-party marketing companies. The company maintained that it did not need to seek consent because the information was already publicly available in phone books and through directory assistance. The Federal Court of Appeal disagreed, however, and held that the company must provide disclosure at the time of enrolment to its customers concerning all of the purposes for which the information was collected. The court noted that "There are, therefore, two competing interests within the purpose of [PIPEDA]: an individual's right to privacy on the one hand, and the commercial need for access to personal information on the other. However, there is also an express recognition, by the use of the words 'reasonable purpose,' 'appropriate' and 'in the circumstances' (repeated in subsection 5(3)), that the right of privacy is not absolute" (*Englander* 2004, para. 38).

In balancing the customer's right to privacy against industry needs, the court held that first-time customers must be told, before their information becomes publicly available, that they can choose not to be publicly listed and thereby prevent this information from being sold to third parties (creating, in other words, an "opt-in" regime for the collection, use, and disclosure of this type of personal information).

Because the law concerning the need for explicit or implied consent for disclosure of personal information to related and unrelated third parties is in its early developmental stage, Canadian businesses should proceed with caution and consider implementing policies that encourage an opt-in regime for cross-border transfers of personal information, especially if it can be determined that this information is sensitive in nature.

Discerning How Canadians View Transfers of Personal Information and the Laws that Govern These Transfers

As mentioned at the outset of this chapter, the ways that citizens view the collection and sharing of personal information by industry can shape privacy laws, privacy policies developed by firms, and enforcement activities by governments. The GPD survey promotes insight into this process. With respect to Canadian survey results, 41% of the respondents claim they are somewhat or very knowledgeable about the laws that deal with the protection of personal information in government departments and private companies. For this group of respondents, 51% believe that laws are somewhat or very effective at protecting personal information held by government departments and private companies.

Moreover, 47% of the respondents have a reasonable or very high level of trust that private companies will protect personal information. Relatedly, 31% of respondents have a lot or complete say in what happens to their personal information. Finally, when asked about the extent to which they think it is appropriate for a private-sector organization to share or sell its customers' personal information with foreign governments, 19% say, "yes, if a customer is suspected of wrong-doing," 25% say, "yes, with expressed consent of customer," and 45% say, "no." When asked about such sharing with third-party companies (which could be construed as domestic and/or foreign third-party companies), 12% say, "yes, if customer is suspected of wrong-doing," 31% say, "yes, with expressed consent of customer," and 49% say, "no."

The GPD survey results show that a majority of Canadians continue to have significant concerns about the collection, use, and disclosure (including transfers to third parties) of their personal information by industry and raise questions about the efficacy of the business community and government response to these issues thus far. Due to complex ongoing technology/legal changes with respect to privacy issues in Canada and abroad, Canadian policymakers need to develop flexible and responsive policies and laws to support important values and interests (such as the ability to maintain control over our own personal information) while ensuring that the legislative/policy framework does not unduly impede the needs of businesses to efficiently direct their goods and services at their target audiences.

With this overview in mind, the analysis in this chapter will now focus on whether the foreign privacy laws of the previously mentioned countries contain private-sector data collection principles similar to those found in PIPEDA.

UNITED STATES

The Interaction between the US Sectoral Approach and PIPEDA

Unlike Canada, the United States has chosen not to pursue a comprehensive federal legislative framework to govern private-sector information collection practices. Rather, the US federal government has legislated privacy protection on a sectoral basis in areas of perceived sensitivity, such as financial, health, and children's privacy. The sectoral protections are often promoted under market efficiency rationales: one view suggests that the market will do a better job at reaching a balance between commercial needs and privacy interests because it is simply good business to align a business's collection practices with customer needs.[7]

Appendix 3.1 summarizes how the main US federal statutes that govern private-sector collection practices compare with PIPEDA, including a review of:

- the Fair Credit Reporting Act, which regulates certain privacy practices with respect to credit reporting;
- the Videotape Privacy Protection Act, which regulates the treatment of personal information maintained by video stores;
- the Health Insurance Portability and Accountability Act, which establishes minimum standards for the treatment of healthcare information by healthcare providers and related entities;

- the Children's Online Privacy Protection Act,
- which was passed in 1998 to protect children's personal information from collection and misuse by commercial websites.

Of particular interest is the Gramm-Leach-Bliley Act (GLBA), which regulates privacy practices in the financial sector. The Act permits an "opt-out" regime where customers must themselves take proactive steps to contact their financial institutions and request constraints on the sharing of their personal information with unrelated third parties (GLBA, title 5, §502[b]). This feature can be contrasted to PIPEDA, which instead appears to mandate an "opt-in" regime with respect to sensitive personal data such as financial information, the result being that PIPEDA encourages companies to seek express consent prior to the collection, use, and disclosure of this information. This encouragement seems to be lacking in the US legislation, the result perhaps being that the different approaches may lead to some problems with respect to legal compliance with the Canadian statute.

Consider the following hypothetical example. James is a Canadian citizen who has resided in the past in the United States. When a resident of the United States, James receives a credit card from a US credit card company with operations around the world. The company provides James with disclosure concerning its privacy practices. In accordance with the GLBA, the company tells James that he can "opt out" of its information sharing practices with third parties if he calls a toll-free number.

In addition, the credit card company strives to comply with relevant US state laws by disclosing to James that, if he is a resident of Vermont, he must "opt in" to information sharing practices by providing the credit card company with authorization to do so (Vermont law with respect to this issue is similar to PIPEDA). James moves back to Canada, and the US credit card company switches his address to the new Canadian one for recordkeeping purposes.

Once back in Canada, James makes credit card purchases. The credit card company collects information on these purchases and sells this information to unrelated third parties for marketing purposes. The credit card company, which is now operating a business in Canada by providing credit to James, would seem to be in violation of the consent provisions of PIPEDA and potentially subject to PIPEDA sanctions. Due to the highly integrated economies of the United States and Canada, it is likely that these sorts of legal violations have taken place.

The only way that the US credit card company would be in compliance with PIPEDA would be to alter its privacy policy to follow PIPEDA's requirements, then make a determination concerning which customers reside in Canada, and finally adopt an alternate information collection, use, and disclosure policy for these customers. Moreover, the credit card company would have to ensure that its privacy policy respected *all* privacy laws of foreign locales where its customers may reside, potentially imposing significant compliance costs on the firm (which, in theory, could be passed on to customers in higher interest rates).

Another possible way for US companies to reduce legal exposure and reduce compliance costs would be to enter into a Canadian-supported "safe harbour" agreement, if available. Due to the provisions within the European Union's Data Protection Directive that restrict transfers to third countries that do not have adequate privacy protections (subsequently discussed below in the section on the European Union), the United States and Europe entered into a Safe Harbour Agreement in 2000. Under the agreement, US companies self-certify with the US Department of Commerce that they are adhering to specified privacy principles (which roughly parallel the Data Protection Directive's principles).

The Canadian government could explore the development of its own "safe harbour" agreement with the United States. Such an agreement could also lower compliance costs for Canadian firms, as they would not have to conduct audits of self-certifying firms to ensure that these firms have the resources and policies in place to comply with PIPEDA. More research is needed to clarify whether such an agreement would materially lower compliance costs for US firms with operations in Canada or for Canadian firms that transfer personal information to US firms. Concerns have been expressed, for instance, that the safe harbour agreement between the United States and the European Union has not been fully embraced by multinational firms operating in these countries.

Access to Personal Information by US Government Authorities

The US Patriot Act was enacted following the terrorist attacks of 11 September 2001.[8] It gives the US government new powers to review information banks of private and public businesses in an effort to locate and arrest terrorists. Although the analysis in this chapter focuses on comparing Canadian laws to foreign laws governing private-sector information collection practices, the Patriot Act provides an example of the ways that foreign laws governing *government* collection practices may also have a significant impact on the way that personal information about Canadians is treated after it crosses a border.

The privacy commissioner of British Columbia, David Loukidelis, concludes in a report that the Patriot Act allows US authorities to access the personal information of Canadians if it ends up in the United States through outsourcing or is held by Canadian companies that are affiliates of US companies. The report notes that once personal information about British Columbians crosses a border, it is subject to the laws of the new jurisdiction, regardless of any provisions within an outsourcing contract (Loukidelis 2004). The report issues a series of recommendations to promote privacy protections when personal information is transferred across borders to foreign third parties.

The Patriot Act raises an issue of legal exposure for Canadian companies that transfer personal information across the border to US firms. As discussed previously, principle 1 of PIPEDA's collection principles encourages accountability by stating that companies are responsible for personal information even after it has been transferred to third-party processors, including unrelated foreign companies. A Canadian company cannot contractually oblige a US company to prevent access to this information if doing so would be a violation of the Patriot Act. Hence it is at least arguable that the Canadian company would be in violation of principle 1, as it has not ensured that the personal information is subject to a comparable legal regime that exists within Canada. On the other hand, PIPEDA provides exceptions to the need for consumer consent, such as "lawful purposes," and under this view, access to personal information by US authorities is permissible as long as the information is accessed for a lawful purpose. In order to reduce legal exposure, Canadian companies should disclose the fact that transferred personal information may be accessed by US authorities.

THE EUROPEAN UNION
(HUNGARY, FRANCE, AND SPAIN)

Similarities between the EU Data Protection Directive and PIPEDA

The European Union and its member countries are often considered to be leaders in the development of laws to protect consumers' right to privacy. In 1981 the Council of Europe adopted the Convention for the Protection of Individuals with Regard to the Automatic Processing of Personal Data (1980), which sets out fair information collection practices that resemble the ones in place today within PIPEDA.[9] The Organization for Economic Cooperation and Development's *Guidelines on the Protection of Personal Privacy and Transborder Flows of Personal*

Data (1980) are similar to practices set out in the European convention. Both documents proved influential in the development of the Canadian Standard Association's subsequent privacy guidelines. Hence it is not surprising that Canadian and European private-sector privacy laws are similar in many respects.

The major instrument of EU data protection law is the EU Data Protection Directive (1995), often referred to as simply "the General Directive." Adopted on 24 October 1995, the General Directive was to have been incorporated by all EU member-states into their national legislation by 1998; however, several states failed to meet this deadline. Nevertheless, as of 2004, France, Hungary, and Spain had all passed national legislation that adequately implemented the General Directive. The General Directive has two main purposes: first, to allow for the free flow of data within Europe; and second, to achieve a harmonized minimum level of data protection throughout Europe.

Passage of the General Directive motivated in part passage of PIPEDA, as Canadian regulators were concerned that cross-border information flow from Canada to Europe might be impeded by the comparatively weak privacy protections that were in place in Canada prior to PIPEDA. The General Directive requires member-states to allow personal data to be transferred only to those third countries that provide an "adequate level of protection" of such data. Article 25(6) of the directive empowers the European Commission to determine whether the legal protection afforded in a particular third country fulfils the necessary requirements. In 2002 the commission recognized that PIPEDA provides adequate protection for certain personal data transferred from the EU to Canada, permitting this information to flow freely from the EU to recipients in Canada subject to PIPEDA without additional safeguards being needed to meet the requirements of the General Directive.

As noted, the General Directive contains provisions that are substantively similar to PIPEDA's fair collection principles.

Differences between PIPEDA *and the* EU *Data Protection Directive*

Although PIPEDA and the General Directive offer highly equivalent provisions governing private-sector collection practices, the two laws also differ in some circumstances, as outlined below. Appendix 3.1 notes some of the EU provisions that are either highly equivalent or moderately equivalent to the Canadian provisions.

With respect to transfers to third parties, there are notable differences surrounding the consent provision as well as the third-party transfer provision.

For instance, article 7 of the General Directive declares that "Member States shall provide that personal data may be processed only if: (a) the data subject has unambiguously given his consent." The article goes on to list permissible disclosures where such consent need not be sought. The General Directive, therefore, does not address consent in the way that PIPEDA does but rather states when consent is and is not necessary, depending on the specific action (e.g., information processing) under consideration. In contrast, the "reasonable person" test under PIPEDA, discussed previously, appears to offer more flexibility in determining when express consent needs to be sought. Under PIPEDA, express consent appears to be mandated only for sensitive forms of personal information such as financial or health information.

In addition, the European approach incorporates a more comprehensive legal provision with respect to third-party transfers. Article 26 of the General Directive states in part,

> Member States shall provide that a transfer or a set of transfers of personal data to a third country which does not ensure an adequate level of protection within the meaning of Article 25 (2) may take place on condition that:
> (a) the data subject has given his consent unambiguously to the proposed transfer; or
> (b) the transfer is necessary for the performance of a contract between the data subject and the controller or the implementation of precontractual measures taken in response to the data subject's request.

PIPEDA does not contain similar prohibitions for transfers to foreign third parties, although, as previously discussed, transferors must take steps to ensure that third-party transferees provide adequate protection in certain cases, such as processing. Nevertheless, PIPEDA contemplates contractual assurances so that both PIPEDA and the EU General Directive arrive at the same end result: personal information can be transferred to countries where adequate legal protection for privacy is not provided as long as consumers are informed of this fact and consent to the transfer.

MEXICO

Overview

The Mexican legislature has attempted to pass omnibus privacy legislation in recent years, but these efforts have proved unsuccessful. As a result, there is no comprehensive privacy legislation governing commercial
organizations in Mexico. However, some protections can be found in
other existing statutes. For example, provisions in the Federal Consumer
Protection Law (1992) place restrictions on direct marketing and credit
reporting agencies. As well, on 7 June 2001 the Mexican E-Commerce
Act took effect. The law amended the Civil Code, the Commercial Code,
the Rules of Civil Procedure, and the Federal Consumer Protection Law.
Although the legislation pertains only to electronic communications, it
nonetheless created several provisions that deal with consumer privacy.

Mexican Privacy Law and PIPEDA

Mexican law does not appear to offer equivalent legislation in many
circumstances when compared to PIPEDA. Data collection principles,
such as those found in Canada that deal with accountability, identifying
purposes, limits on collection and use, accuracy, and challenging compliance, are not present at this time in Mexican law. Similarities between
PIPEDA and Mexican law exist in certain cases.

BRAZIL

Overview

Article 5(10) of the 1988 Constitution of Brazil provides that "the privacy,
private life, honor and image of persons are inviolable, and the right to
compensation for property or moral damages resulting from their violation
is ensured." As well, article 5(72) establishes the concept of "habeas data,"
a modern-day version of the habeas corpus guarantees found in many
other constitutions around the world. This article guarantees Brazilians the
right to access their personal information contained in government records
or data banks and permits them to correct any errors in the data.

The scope of the constitutional right to habeas data was clarified with
the passage of additional procedures and definitions in 1997. Under the

Habeas Data Law (1997), an individual has a right to petition for rectification of incorrect data. However, if the maintaining organization disputes or chooses not to make the correction, the petitioner has the right only to annotate the data with an explanation, not the right to force a correction.

Brazil's constitutional guarantees to privacy and data protection have since been augmented with additional statutory protections. Although there is no comprehensive Brazilian legislation that regulates private-sector information collection practices, broad consumer rights in data collection were created under the 1990 Consumer Defence Code, article 43 of which provides that consumers must have access to personal data, to consumer files and other information stored in files, and to databases both about themselves and about the sources of this data.

In addition, a number of other statutes regulate aspects of consumer privacy. Bill 1589/99 establishes that any supplier of products/services on the Internet may collect personal information on a data subject to the extent such data is necessary for the transaction. This personal information must be maintained in secrecy, except when its owner expressly authorizes disclosure and/or transfer. Bill 84A/99 creates penalties for businesses that transfer personal information via computers to third parties without authorization from the data subject. According to Bill 268/99, the owner of any personal data who has given his/her authorization to include such information in a proprietary database is entitled to restrain the use and dissemination of the data for purposes that differ from the ones that have motivated the delivery of the data. In addition, the Informatics Law of 1984 protects the confidentiality of stored, processed, and disclosed data as well as the privacy and security of physical, legal, public, and private entities. Citizens are entitled to access and correct their personal information in private or public databases.

Brazilian Privacy Law and PIPEDA

Due to the lack of any kind of omnibus legislation that governs privacy, it appears that Brazilian privacy laws do not offer protections similar to those afforded by PIPEDA in many circumstances. Data collection principles relating to accountability, limits on collection, safeguards, accuracy, and challenging compliance are not present at this time in Brazilian law. Areas where Brazilian legislation offers some comparison to the principles set out in PIPEDA are noted in appendix 3.1.

CHINA

Overview

There is no comprehensive data protection statute in force in China. Various reasons for this reality have been proposed, such as the long tradition in China of valuing the good of the collective over the good of the individual, the tight governmental and administrative control of citizens' records and recordkeeping, and even the crowded living environment. Nevertheless, privacy protections can be found in different Chinese statutes, including the Constitution and criminal laws.

The Constitution of the People's Republic of China does not contain an explicit "right to privacy." Article 38, however, describes the inviolability of a citizen's personal dignity, which includes that libel and false accusations are forbidden by any means. Articles 37 and 39 also provide for the protection of freedom of the person and residence. Article 40 protects the privacy of communications in general, except in criminal investigations and public security matters.

Article 30 of the Law on the Protection of Minors (1991) provides that "no organization or individual may disclose the personal secrets of minors" and that "with regard to cases involving crimes committed by minors, the names, home addresses and photos of such minors as well as other information which can be used to deduce who they are, may not be disclosed, before the judgment, in news reports, films, television programs and in any other openly circulated publications."

There are other laws in place as well that deal with privacy in one way or another. Article 39 of the Law on the Protection of Rights and Interests of Women (1992) provides that "women's right of reputation and personal dignity shall be protected by law. Damage to women's right of reputation and personal dignity by such means as insult, libel or giving publicity to private affairs shall be prohibited." Article 33 of the Law on Lawyers (1996) requires lawyers to protect the personal secrets of their clients. Article 14 of the Law on Statistics (1983) provides that data collected from investigations shall not be disclosed without the consent of data subjects. Article 47 of the Provisional Regulations Relating to Bank Management (1986) provides that all information concerning the savings of clients shall not be disclosed.

As a whole, the above provisions do provide a minimum level of protection for the privacy of citizens. However, the above privacy protections are not geared primarily toward data protection. As noted, no general data protection law exists in China, and there are very few laws that limit government interference with the collection, use, and disclosure of personal information. Furthermore, there are no laws or regulations that limit the ability of Internet service providers (ISPS) to use and distribute personal data gathered through the Internet.

Importantly, China is considering the implementation of comprehensive data processing legislation and continues to participate in the Asia-Pacific Economic Cooperation (APEC) privacy initiative. In February 2003 the APEC Data Privacy Subgroup was established under the auspices of the Electronic Commerce Steering Group (ECSG) with the mandate to develop the APEC Privacy Framework (APEC Data Privacy Subgroup 2004, Tang 2004). All twenty-one member-countries are represented on the ECSG, and eleven countries participate in the Privacy Subgroup, including China.

CONCLUSION

Four main conclusions can be derived from the above discussion.

First, the European Union had previously passed legislation that is highly equivalent to PIPEDA, so cross-border transfers of personal information from Canada to one of the European Union nations will be governed by similar legal regimes.

Second, the United States has adopted a different approach in comparison to Canada, as it regulates only private-sector collection practices for certain sectors, such as the financial and healthcare industries. This sectoral legal regime offers laws that are moderately equivalent to PIPEDA in some circumstances. Nevertheless, cross-border transfers of personal information from Canada to the United States will generally not be subject to the same legal protections. In particular, legislation passed in the wake of the 9/11 terrorist attacks, such as the Patriot Act, enables US intelligence officials to access personal information without resort to traditional safeguards generally available under Canadian law. Due to the difficulties that US firms may encounter when attempting to comply with PIPEDA, Canada should explore the development of a "safe harbour" agreement (similar to the one negotiated between the European Union and the United States) to simplify compliance.

Third, the three developing countries under scrutiny – Mexico, Brazil, and China – have not passed legislation that is equivalent to PIPEDA, raising the risk that transfers of personal information to these countries will not be offered a level of legal protection similar to what is available in Canada. Canadian firms that transfer personal information on Canadians to firms within any of these countries should seek contractual assurances that this information will be handled in the ways mandated by PIPEDA.

Fourth, as discussed in the Canadian summary, the GPD survey results suggest that a majority of Canadian respondents worry about a loss of control over their personal information, including when this information is transferred across borders to third parties. The message for Canadian businesses is that they need to maintain a high level of sensitivity to the privacy needs of their customers or risk alienating their customer base, especially in light of technology changes that make it less costly to collect, use, and disclose personal information.

APPENDIX 3.1

COMPARING PIPEDA TO FOREIGN PRIVACY LAWS

Country	*PIPEDA principles 1 to 5*				
	1 Accountability	*2 Identifying purposes*	*3 Consent*	*4 Limiting collection*	*5 Limiting use, disclosure, and retention*
United States	Gramm-Leach-Bliley Act, s. 6802(2)	Fair Credit Reporting Act, s. 607(a) Gramm-Leach-Bliley Act, s. 6802(a), s. 6803 Children's Online Privacy Protection Act, s. 1(A)(i)	Fair Credit Reporting Act, s. 604(o), s. 604(1), s. 619 Children's Online Privacy Protection Act, s. 1(A)(ii) Gramm-Leach-Bliley Act, s. 6802(b)(1)(A)(B)(C) Video Privacy Protection Act, s. 2(A)(B)	Children's Online Privacy Protection Act, s. 1303(a)	Video Privacy Protection Act, s. 2710 Children's Online Privacy Protection Act, s. 1303(a) Health Insurance Portability and Accountability Act
France Hungary Spain	Directive 95/46/EC, arts 10, 17, 19, 21, 25 Directive 2002/58/EC, art. 4	Directive 95/46/EC, arts 6, 10, 11, 19, 21 Directive 2002/58/EC, art. 5	Directive 95/46/EC, arts 2, 7, 8, 26 Directive 97/66/EC, arts 5,6, 11, 12, 14 Directive 2002/58/EC, arts 5, 6, 9, 10, 12, 13	Directive 95/46/EC, art. 6 Directive 2002/58/EC, arts 6, 9, 12	Directive 95/46/EC, arts 6, 11 Directive 97/66/EC, art. 6 Directive 2002/58/EC, art. 6
Mexico	No equivalent legislation	No equivalent legislation	Federal Consumer Protection Act, art. 76(I)	No equivalent legislation	No equivalent legislation
Brazil	No equivalent legislation	Bill no. 268/99	Consumer Defense Code, art. 43(2) Bill no. 84A/99 Bill no. 1589/99	No equivalent legislation	No equivalent legislation

PIPEDA principles 6 to 10

Country	6 Accuracy	7 Safeguards	8 Openness	9 Individual access	10 Challenging compliance	Law on the Protection of Minors	Regulation related to Bank Management
China						No equivalent legislation	No equivalent legislation
United States	Fair Credit Reporting Act, s. 623(2)(A)(B) Health Insurance Portability and Accountability Act	Children's Online Privacy Protection Act, s. 1(D) Gramm-Leach-Bliley Act, s. 6801 Health Insurance Portability and Accountability Act, s. 1173(d)	Fair Credit Reporting Act, s. 609(a)(c) Children's Online Privacy Protection Act, s. 1(A)(i) Gramm-Leach-Bliley Act, s. 6803	Fair Credit Reporting Act, ss. 609, s. 611 Children's Online Privacy Protection Act, s. 1(B)(i)(ii) Health Insurance Portability and Accountability Act	Fair Credit Reporting Act, s. 617, s. 621 Health Insurance Portability and Accountability Act, s. 1176 Video Privacy Protection Act, s. 2710(c)	No equivalent legislation	No equivalent legislation
France Hungary Spain	Directive 95/46/EC, art. 6	Directive 95/46/EC, art. 17 Directive 97/66/EC, art. 4 Directive 2002/58/EC, art. 4	Directive 95/46/EC, arts 10, 11 Directive 2002/58/EC, arts 9, 12	Directive 95/46/EC, arts 10, 12, 14	Directive 95/46/EC, arts 22, 28		
Mexico	No equivalent legislation	Federal Consumer Protection Act, art. 76(II)	Federal Consumer Protection Act, art. 76(II)	Federal Consumer Protection Act, art. 16	No equivalent legislation		
Brazil	Consumer Defense Code, art. 43(1)	No equivalent legislation	No equivalent legislation	Consumer Defense Code, arts 43(3), 44(1)	No equivalent legislation		
China	No equivalent legislation	No equivalent legislation	No equivalent legislation	No equivalent legislation	No equivalent legislation		

Legend:

No equivalent legislation   Moderately equivalent legislation   Highly equivalent legislation

NOTES

1 France, Spain, and Hungary, as members of the European Union, must (and do) conform to existing EU data protection legislation. The discussion will focus on the overarching EU legislation without going into detail about each country's national data protection regime.

2 For discussion of the legal concepts of privacy within the workplace in all countries surveyed, see Avner Levin's chapter in this volume.

3 For a more detailed discussion of PIPEDA, see Perrin (2001) and McIssac et al. (2005).

4 Quebec has passed the Loi sur la protection des renseignements personnels dans le secteur privé, RSQ c. P-39.1; Alberta has passed the Personal Information Protection Act, SA 2003, c. P-6.5; British Columbia has passed the Freedom of Information and Protection of Privacy Act, RSBC 1992, c. 165.

5 For an example of a case where the privacy commissioner accepted a nonconsensual transfer of personal information to a service provider pursuant to the terms of a contract, see PIPEDA Case Summary #145 (2003).

6 See also Office of the Privacy Commissioner of Canada, "Privacy Commissioner Findings," including PIPEDA Case Summary #35 (2002) (noting that the processing contract should be extended to any subcontractor retained by the service provider) and PIPEDA Case Summary #277 (2004) (holding a company responsible for an error by its e-mail distributor because it remained liable for personal information transferred to the third-party processor). Case Summary #35 is online at http://www.priv.gc.ca/cf-dc/2002/cf-dc_020110_02_e.cfm (accessed 15 January 2008), and Case Summary #277 is at http://www.priv.gc.ca/cf-dc/2004/cf-dc_040902_02_e.cfm (accessed 15 January 2008).

7 For discussion, see Cockfield (2001).

8 The official name of the statute is the Uniting and Strengthening America by Providing Appropriate Tools Required to Intercept and Obstruct Terrorism (USA PATRIOT) Act of 2001.

9 For background, see Swire and Litan (1998).

4

Shunning Surveillance or Welcoming the Watcher? Exploring How People Traverse the Path of Resistance

ANDREW GRENVILLE

Ordinary people find myriad ways of coping with surveillance – resigning themselves to it, finding modes of settlement that retain some dignity or freedom, or, on occasion, openly objecting to the gaze in whatever shape it takes. (Lyon 2007, 159)

Surveillance and a lack of privacy are a fact of everyday life for most people. Some actively watch for watchers and bristle at being monitored. Others just shrug off surveillance, if they even notice it.

This chapter is concerned with trying to understand why and how people vary so widely in the ways they navigate a world of surveillance and infringement of privacy. Working within the confines of the Globalization of Personal Data (GPD) survey, I posit a model to explain why some resist surveillance, whereas others accept or ignore it.[1] Then, using the elements of the model, I create a segmentation of people that provides some insight into the mindsets we see as people trip lightly along, stumble aimlessly across, or stride fiercely down the path of resistance.

WHAT PEOPLE DO: METHODS OF RESISTANCE

Resistance can take many forms. An extreme example is the protagonist in the film *Minority Report*, who "goes so far as to modify his body to subvert the surveillance system, having his eyes replaced to subvert the coding system, which reads retinal patterns" (Shapiro 2005, 30). On the social level, there is also mainstream advocacy, exemplified by the national and local campaigns to emphasize the "right of poor and homeless people to use public spaces," which Joe Doherty and colleagues (2008, 305) cite in their study of homelessness, exclusion, and the regulation of public space. These types of resistance are dramatic and notable, but the more common forms of resistance are "the ordinary weapons of relatively powerless groups: foot dragging, dissimulation, false compliance, pilfering, feigned ignorance, slander ... and so forth" (Scott 1985, xvi).

John Gilliom (2005) studied this type of personal resistance among a group of "welfare moms" in Ohio and found "a dense pattern of unconventional and seldom-noticed politics [that] ... advanced the interests of those families and thwarted the mission of the surveillance regime" (72). Their efforts, he found, "produce tangible improvements in their families' lives" (72). He reported that, among the "welfare moms," resistance also importantly "marks and maintains a zone of autonomy and self-determination" (77). Clearly, these less organized or dramatic forms of resistance are worthy of further study.

It is these more individualistic forms of resistance that surveys are particularly useful for measuring. In the GPD survey, people were read a list of eight things they might have done to protect their personal information – from refusing to give personal details to a business to lying to the government. Gary Marx (2003) has delineated "eleven behavioral techniques of neutralization intended to subvert the collection of personal information" (369). The GPD survey's resistance items represent a subset of four of Marx's "eleven easy moves," with half of the survey items being "refusal moves" (374).

Refusal moves were the most commonly practised type of resistance in all countries. There was tremendous variation from country to country in the prevalence of these practices, with Canadians and Americans being the most resistant and Mexicans and Brazilians the least. The pattern of response, however, was similar across most nations. Mexicans do stand out, however, in that they are most likely to feel the need to resort to blocking moves. The prevalence is especially notable in that not too many Mexicans tend to engage in other types of resistance.

The question that jumps out at me is why do some resist whereas others comply, and why does the rate of resistance vary so much by country? There are obviously hosts of reasons relating to national culture, class, technological development, political views, and identification with or alienation from the dominant culture.

Table 4.1
Methods of resistance: "Have you ever done the following for the purpose of protecting your personal information?" (%)

Type of move	Resistance item	Canada	US	France	Spain	Hungary	Mexico	Brazil
Refusal	Refused to give info to a business because you thought it was not needed	77	77	57	52	33	48	26
Refusal	Asked a company not to sell your name and address to another company	66	73	39	32	38	17	9
Refusal	Asked a company to remove you from lists it uses for marketing	71	77	32	31	22	19	8
Refusal	Refused to give info to a gov't agency because you thought it was not needed	33	34	36	10	8	30	12
Discovery/counter-surveillance	Asked a business you were thinking of dealing with about its policies on the collection of consumer info	28	37	12	16	11	13	5
Blocking	Purposefully gave incorrect information about yourself to a marketer	20	22	15	12	6	29	7
Avoidance	Asked a company to see what personal info, besides billing info, it had about you in its records	18	24	6	8	8	13	6
Blocking	Purposefully gave incorrect information about yourself to a gov't agency	5	9	3	2	1	11	1

But are there some basic underlying factors that are common to all cultures? Is there a primary process that we can discern? Using elements measured in the GPD survey, I put forward and test a model of how people come to their position of resistance or acquiesce to surveillance.

FOUR STEPS ON THE PATH TO RESISTANCE

The path to resistance, I suggest, can be mapped out in four basic steps: knowledge of surveillance, recognition of the experience of being monitored, trust (or mistrust) of the monitors, and finally, the sense of whether or not one has any control over his or her personal information.

Let us consider this model in more detail, with some examples. The first step is knowledge: one must know how surveillance and monitoring happen. For example, if you travel by subway in Toronto and don't know that there is a closed circuit television (CCTV) camera lurking behind those curved mirrors in the dark corners of the Toronto Transit Commission's subterranean hallways, you cannot be aware that you are under surveillance.

Second, only once you are aware of the possibility of surveillance can you come to notice that you are experiencing it. Once you know that CCTV exists, for example, you can make a conscious choice to accept, avoid, or subvert it.

Third, only once fully aware of what is happening can you chose to trust or not trust that the information is being used to an end that you are in agreement with. So, if you think CCTV is helping to keep you safe, you might be happy to be observed.

Fourth, there comes the question of control. You may not trust how CCTV data is being used, but if you want to get on the subway and the only entrance has CCTV, you may feel you have no choice but to give up control over your bodily image.

TESTING THE MODEL: MEASURES AND METHODS

The survey included items measuring each of these four concepts: knowledge of surveillance, awareness of the experience of being monitored or invaded, trust in monitors, and control over one's data. Summated ratings scales were created to measure each of the concepts – except for control – where a single measure was used.

Knowledge of surveillance was assessed based on people's answers to the question "In general, how knowledgeable are you about each of the following: Internet; Global Positioning System (GPS) used in automobiles; Radio Frequency Identification (RFID) Tags on consumer products;

Closed Circuit Television (CCTV) in public spaces; Biometrics for facial and other bodily recognition; and Data mining of personal information?"[2] This list is technologically oriented and therefore fails to comprehend many types of surveillance and monitoring. The methodologies it does cover, however, represent powerful advances in the potential of surveillance. Thus it addresses a selection of essential tools of which informed citizens should be cognisant.

Awareness of being monitored or of having one's privacy invaded was calculated based on the responses to the question "Have you personally, to the best of your knowledge, ever experienced any of the following: Detention at a border checkpoint resulting in a search; Detention by airport officials resulting in not being able to board the airplane; Detention by airport officials resulting in being denied entry into a country; Victim of identity theft (e.g. someone uses your name); Victim of credit card fraud; Your personal information monitored by a government agency; Your personal information monitored by an employer; Your personal information sold by a commercial business?"[3]

Trust was assessed based on the response to the questions "When it comes to the privacy of personal information, what level of trust do you have that the (country of interview) government is striking the right balance between national security and individual rights?" and "What level of trust do you have that private companies, such as banks, credit card companies and places where you shop, will protect your personal information?"[4]

Control was measured using the single available item: "To what extent do you have a say in what happens to your personal information?"[5]

Resistance was measured using people's answers to the eight items covering active resistance that are detailed in table 4.1. Despite the fact that these items measure multiple types of Marx's resistance moves, an analysis of scale reliability suggests that, taken together, they do a good job of representing a single underlying concept: resistance.[6]

Testing a model is always problematic. There is no statistical technique to actually prove causal order, but we can see whether the data seems to support the theory (Davis 1990).

We can expect each of the four steps to be predictive of people's level of resistance or acquiescence – independently and in combination with each other. And we can anticipate where a person stands on one step to be predictive of where they are on the next.

Shapley Value regression was used to test whether each step made an independent contribution and to measure the strength of the relationship.[7] Correlations were used to look at the relationship between each step.

Table 4.2
Strength of relationship between steps and resistance: Results of Shapley Value regression overall and by country

	Overall	Canada	US	France	Spain	Hungary	Mexico	Brazil
Awareness	A	B	B	B	A	A	D	B
Experience	A	B	B	B	C	A	B	A
Trust	D	C	C	C	C	C	D	D
Control	D	D	D	B	D	D	D	B

A Very strong relationship $R^2 > .10$ B Strong relationship $R^2 > .05 = <10$
C Moderate relationship $R^2 > .01 = < .05$ D Weak or no relationship $R^2 = < .01$

MIND THE STEP ...

The Shapley Value regression results indicate that all four steps predict resistance or acquiescence. It also reveals that the first two steps – awareness of surveillance and knowledge of being monitored – are big steps, the most important predictors of resistance.[8] The correlations between each step were also significant and in the direction expected.

The measure of control had the weakest relationship overall, and it was not a statistically significant predictor in all the countries. It is quite possible that a sense of control is simply not realistic – particularly among the well-informed. As David Lyon (2007, 164) has suggested, "it is simply impossible to know all that happens using our personal data, let alone respond intelligently or imaginatively to it." So perhaps, although we can expect a sense of control to make a difference, we cannot expect a sense of control to be a deciding factor for all people. Or it may be that the single measure just did not capture the concept fully and adequately. Most likely, both hypotheses are true.

Although we know that the world is a messy place and that people are not completely understood through simple models, these data do support the idea that these are at least some of the steps along the path of resistance. So with this evidence in mind, let us examine where people are along this path and how positions on these steps combine to provide evidence of divergent schools of thought on surveillance and resistance.

MINDSETS: A CITIZEN'S SEGMENTATION

We identified segments, or schools, of thought based on how people answered questions on the elements of the model:

- knowledge of surveillance;
- experience of being monitored;
- trust in the watchers;
- a sense of control over one's personal information; and
- the resistance in which one has engaged.

We used these inputs in a k-means clustering algorithm. This type of analysis uses people's patterns of response to these items to identify and define the segments.

After comparing and testing many alternatives, we found a three-segment solution to be the most meaningful and reliable.[9] We have named these segments informed resisters (26% of total usable sample), the status quo satisfied (41%), and alienated skeptics (33%).

Informed resisters do not trust either government or corporations to protect their information. They are relatively knowledgeable about surveillance technology and are more likely to be aware their privacy has been invaded. As a result, they are actively engaged in avoiding surveillance and in controlling the flow of their personal data. Most feel they have only "some" control over their information – the amount they obtain through their resistance, one assumes.

Alienated skeptics do not trust that government or private companies will use their private information appropriately. They also lack a sense of control over their information. And they do not have much knowledge of surveillance technology. They seem to have largely given up hope of being able to have control over their information and are not active in resistance.

The status quo satisfied are more trusting that business and government will protect their personal information. Somewhat knowledgeable and somewhat resistant, with a sense of control over their privacy, they are the least concerned about sharing their personal information.

KNOWLEDGE, EXPERIENCE, TRUST, AND CONTROL

As the model would suggest, the segments knowledge, experience, trust, and sense of control shape responses to surveillance. It is clear from the informed resisters that knowledge brings heightened awareness of the experience of surveillance, reduces trust, and reveals a lack of control. For the alienated skeptics, ignorance breeds fear and a sense of powerlessness. The status quo satisfied seem to know enough to be comfortable that their

Table 4.3
Levels of knowledge, experience, trust, and control by segment* (%)

	Measure	Status quo satisfied	Informed resisters	Alienated skeptics
Knowledge	Very/somewhat knowledgeable	44	70	19
Experience	Invasions experienced	8	18	5
Trust business	Very high/reasonable level of trust	76	24	6
Trust gov't	Very high/reasonable level of trust	84	16	11
Control	No/some say over info	51	59	80

* The knowledge and experience data are averages for the knowledge and experience scales.

information is safe. The path to resistance is not a straight one. Each segment travels it in its own way.

Now let us look at how the segments differ in terms of some of the other aspects of the survey.

The knowledge and trust findings are echoed in responses to questions specifically about knowledge of the laws that deal with the protection of personal information and belief in the effectiveness of those laws. Alienated skeptics are less likely to claim to be knowledgeable about the laws, and the status quo satisfied are much more likely to believe these laws will protect them. This trust-mistrust axis extends also to reaction to national ID cards. The status quo satisfied are much more comfortable with this concept.

Most informed resisters are engaged citizens: 66% have contacted some branch of government in the past six months. In contrast, 76% of alienated skeptics and 55% of the status quo satisfied have had no contact with local, state, or national government, either face to face or online, in the past six months.

The sharing of personal information is another topic on which the segments show notable differences. Alienated skeptics are more likely to take the stance that under no circumstances should government or private-sector organizations or employers ever share information with anyone. Informed resisters have a similar but slightly more nuanced approach. They are a bit more likely to be adamantly opposed to sharing information with private organizations and are somewhat more permissive when the information is shared between governmental agencies. Monitoring by employers is, likewise, least likely to be opposed by the status quo satisfied and most likely to be completely unacceptable to the alienated skeptics.

A sense of respect for privacy was another telling point of difference between the segments. When travelling by airplane, the status quo satisfied are more likely to feel their privacy has been respected. Alienated skeptics who have travelled by plane, meanwhile, are less likely to feel they have been afforded the appropriate respect.

When it comes to commercial use of information, knowledge and trust seem to make a difference. Alienated skeptics – despite their discomfort with their personal information being shared or used – tend to belong to more customer rewards programs. If they had a better understanding of how personal information is used, one suspects they might be less open to using such programs. The status quo satisfied, who have greater trust that businesses use information appropriately, are more comfortable with being targeted by commercial enterprises based on analyses of their personal data.

There are, of course, other telling differences, but these data tell a pretty clear story: the status quo satisfied are relatively comfortable with others using their personal data. The alienated skeptics are the most upset about what they see as invasions of their privacy – but they lack knowledge and a sense of control. Informed resisters, on the other hand, know more, are less comfortable, and are acting to gain some control.

ACTS OF RESISTANCE

Informed resisters, as their name would suggest, are much more likely to have used a whole host of resistance moves. The status quo satisfied, trusting that most uses of personal information are acceptable to them, have chosen to be less resistant. But there is a large gap between alienated skeptics' discomfort with sharing their personal information and their lack of resistance. It would appear either they do not know how to resist or they believe resistance is futile – or both.

WESTIN PLUS MARGULIS, POPE, AND LOWEN

The segments, at first blush, share some clear commonality with Alan F. Westin's (2003) fundamentalist, pragmatist, and unconcerned segments. I suspect there is considerable correspondence between the fundamentalist and informed resister segments and between some of the status quo satisfied and the unconcerned. The alienated skeptics do not fit into this scheme so obviously, suggesting this GPD segmentation takes into account some dimensions not covered by Westin's scheme.

Table 4.4
Relationship between acts of resistance and each segment (%)

Type of move	Resistance item	Status quo satisfied	Informed resisters	Alienated skeptics
Refusal	Refused to give info to a business because you thought it was not needed	47	89	35
Refusal	Asked a company not to sell your name and address to another company	36	75	15
Refusal	Asked a company to remove you from lists it uses for marketing	33	74	14
Refusal	Refused to give info to a gov't agency because you thought it was not needed	16	46	16
Discovery/ counter- surveillance	Asked a business you were thinking of dealing with about its policies on the collection of consumer info	15	38	4
Blocking	Purposefully gave incorrect information about yourself to a marketer	13	32	8
Avoidance	Asked a company to see what personal info, besides billing info, it had about you in its records	9	27	4
Blocking	Purposefully gave incorrect information about yourself to a gov't agency	4	9	2

In the current volume, Stephen Margulis, Jennifer Pope, and Aaron Lowen offer some indices that are inspired by Westin's work. Working from a pool of items analogous to ones used by Westin (see Smith 2006), they created indices based on factor analysis. They limited their analysis to the United States and Canada and found three different factor solutions in each country.

In Canada the first factor concerned the appropriateness of invasions of privacy. The status quo satisfied were least concerned, and the other two held similar, more concerned positions. The second factor was about personal concern. Not surprisingly, the alienated skeptics had the greatest level of concern, and the status quo satisfied had the least. The third factor, in Canada, assessed perceptions of intrusiveness. Informed resisters were more likely to see intrusions, and the status quo satisfied were the least likely.

Table 4.5
Prevalence of the segments by country (%)

	Canada	US	France	Spain	Hungary	Mexico	Brazil
Status quo satisfied	45	37	41	45	56	39	26
Informed resisters	41	50	34	26	16	13	10
Alienated skeptics	15	13	24	29	29	48	64

In the United States the first factor also assessed feelings about appropriateness of invasions of privacy, and the pattern was very similar to the Canadian one: the status quo satisfied were least concerned, and the other two were more so. The second factor concerned perceptions about the government threat. The status quo satisfied scored the lowest and the alienated skeptics the highest. The third US factor related to having control versus no control. As might be expected, the alienated skeptics felt the least control and the informed resisters the most.

To make the segments a little more concrete, let us consider who these people are and where they live.

WHO ARE THESE PEOPLE AND WHERE IN THE WORLD DO THEY LIVE?

The national differences in segment membership are stark. This reveals, at a glance, just how different the path is that each nation has taken. It also highlights, for me, concerns and opportunities.

Differences of this magnitude – given their pattern – immediately bring to mind questions of income, education, employment, and class. Unfortunately, it is a fact of global research that you simply cannot create clear and precise equivalent measures of income and education that cut across diverse nations. The economic systems are too varied and the educational standards too distinct for us to be able to chart these things for each segment. But the pattern is obvious: informed resisters are better educated and wealthier; alienated skeptics are poorer and less well informed; and the status quo satisfied, for the most part, are relatively comfortable middle-class citizens.

Perhaps not surprising is that informed resisters and the status quo satisfied are computerized (91% and 72% used computers in the past six months), whereas most alienated skeptics are not (61% nonusers).

Demographically, there are other differences, but they are not as glaring. Informed resisters are somewhat more likely to be men (55%).

Alienated skeptics are somewhat more likely to be women (57%) and to be a bit older on average (age forty-four on average versus forty-three for informed resisters and age forty-one for the status quo satisfied).

These socio-demographic differences tell us a great deal about how each segment has arrived at its place along the path of resistance. But demographics are not destiny – a theme to which I will return at the end of the chapter. Before we do that, however, let's wander back to the path of resistance.

BACK ON THE PATH

Thinking again of the model of how one moves toward a position of resistance or acquiesce to surveillance, we can approximate where each of these segments stands along the path to resistance.

If we think of the path as a journey, we can say that informed resisters have travelled its length and that their knowledge, experience, and lack of trust have led them to be resistant. Alienated skeptics have travelled the path in a very different way. They are aware that what they don't know can hurt them, but they don't know much more than that. And they feel powerless to change their circumstances. The status quo satisfied know enough to feel secure trusting government and business with their information. Their ease of consent gives them a greater sense of control.

So the segmentation gives some support to the model. But it also directs us to consider some questions about how the segmentation and the model can help us to think about what this means.

With that in mind, I now move to the concluding portion of this chapter: a brief discussion of implications for government, business, privacy advocates, and, yes, workers, travellers, consumers, and citizens.

THE IMPLICATIONS

Surveillance is an exchange of information between actors. The gatherer obtains data from the subject. These data feed back to the provider of the information. There is an action and a reaction in this exchange.

Another way to think of surveillance is to liken it to a conversation. A good conversation has an agreeable back and forth. Both parties are engaged and enriched. In a bad conversation, either the exchange is typically one-sided or there is disagreement or confusion as to the objective. A bad conversation is anything but beneficial to both.

As a citizen, worker, consumer, and traveller, I want exchanges and conversations that are mutually beneficial. For there to be mutual benefit, both parties must agree on and understand what they are talking about; there must be informed consent.

So if this is my aim and that of my fellow travellers, consumers, workers, and citizens, what do these data tell me and those who share the objective of mutual benefit based on informed consent?

First, there is a dire need to increase people's level of understanding of surveillance technology and how it is used. Without this, there is tremendous potential for exploitation and alienation. As we have seen, there are currently society-crippling levels of resignation and despair, especially in some countries.

Once people understand the benefits and risks of providing personal data, they can give their informed consent. This is essential to effective communication. Without informed consent, the interaction is exploitative in nature and, as a result, very limited functionally.

Building trust is the next step. Trust can be built only on a foundation of understanding. Communicators who believe they can sell warm and fuzzy feelings of trust without first creating awareness and knowledge are fooling just themselves (and perhaps their clients).

With understanding and trust, a sense of control is possible and informed consent can be given.

The problem these data reveal is that too many people – watchers and the watched – are talking past each other. Actors are settling for a face-off between exploitation and resistance – both relatively ineffective – when greater communion between watcher and watched is well within their grasp. It is in the best interests of government, privacy advocates, and business to engage in a concerted effort to educate people about surveillance and resistance. All it takes are four simple steps.

NOTES

1 This chapter is based on the seven countries in the survey carried out by Ipsos Reid from June to August 2006: Brazil, Canada, France, Hungary, Mexico, Spain, and the United States. China was not included because this analysis was carried out before the China survey was undertaken from August to October 2006.
2 To create the scale, I summed the responses to the "very knowledgeable, somewhat knowledgeable, not very knowledgeable, or not at all knowledgeable" scale (scored 1 to 4) for question 1 and transformed the sum into a number between 0 and 100, with 0 being no knowledge of anything and 100 being very knowledgeable about everything. Factor analysis revealed a single factor,

suggesting this is truly measuring just one underlying concept. The scale – despite consisting of only five items – had good internal consistency (Cronbach's alpha of .80) and, by extension, reliability.

3 The scale was the sum of the "yes" answers for question 8, rescaled to 0 through 100, where 0 is yes to none and 100 is yes to all. The scale had three main subthemes: detention (questions 8 and 1 to 3), theft (questions 8, 4, and 5), and personal information (questions 8, 6, and 7). The reliability of the scale is relatively weak (Cronbach's alpha of .52), but this can be traced to floor problems arising from the fact many people had little or no awareness of these types of monitoring/invasion.

4 The scale was created by summing the answers to the "very high level of trust, reasonably high level of trust, fairly low level of trust, very low level of trust" scale (scored 1 to 4) and transforming the sum into a number between 0 and 100. Zero represents no trust, and 100 equals complete trust. This scale is moderately reliable (Cronbach's alpha of .62), which is not bad considering it is only a two-item scale.

5 The response categories were "complete say," "a lot of say," "some say," and "no say."

6 The Cronbach's alpha was a respectable .72, indicating good internal consistency, and the score was not improved by removing any of the items.

7 Shapley Value regression was used because it does a better job of dealing with multicollinearity and provides a better estimate of the independent contribution of each item in the model. See, for example, Jane Tang and Jay Weiner, "Multicollinearity in CSAT Studies," http://www.ipsos-ideas.com/library/IpsosInsight_WP_Multicollinearity.cfm.

8 Shapley Value regression measures each item's contribution to the overall R^2 – a measure of the predictive value of the model. The R^2 for the overall model was .14 for awareness, .11 for experience, .05 for trust, and .02 for control.

9 With the k-means algorithm of the Statistical Package for the Social Sciences (SPSS), there is a stability issue. Since the algorithm starts from the first few respondents in the file and then iterates from there, the resulting segmentation may not be reproducible when run with a different start point or within a subsample. So as part of our testing, we routinely randomize the start point and repeatedly resegment. If a cluster analysis is not very stable, this is usually because the number of segments one is seeking does not really fit the data. I tried a range of numbers of segments (three through ten), and only the three-segment solution was stable. In fact, it was so stable that it reproduced almost exactly time after time. This suggests that the three-segment solution represents the data very well.

North America, Europe, and Developing Countries

The United States and Canada

INTRODUCTION

Emily Smith

As discussed in part 1, national cultural values and social factors significantly influence public opinions on issues of privacy and surveillance. Part 2 has furthered this analysis by providing an overview of the different privacy regulations within countries that also greatly impact concerns about privacy as well as by exploring why people resist surveillance within and across cultures. The chapters in part 3 have been grouped together based on a deeper examination of survey results within particular countries. Part 3.1 deals with results from the United States and Canada.

Although the Globalization of Personal Data (GPD) survey seeks to move beyond only questions of privacy in order to inquire about the flows of information and about the consequences of these flows for the subjects of surveillance, national public opinion polling tends to focus on social attitudes toward privacy. This type of polling is prevalent in the United States and has grown in Canada in the past fifteen years. Surveys on privacy issues are conducted by various organizations, such as advocacy groups, government agencies, businesses, think-tanks, research centres, media outlets, and commercial polling organizations, which all have an interest in the outcome of the findings. Despite concerns raised about the varying quality of these polls (Harper and Singleton 2001, Gandy 2003), they are often used by a range of interest groups within policy debates about privacy and data protection legislation. Overall, these polls tend to show that citizens have high levels of concern about personal information privacy in Canada and the United States, with variations being based on demographics such as gender, age, and race.[1] Changes have also been demonstrated in public opinions on privacy over time, influenced largely by the terrorist attacks of 11 September 2001 and by subsequent increases in the levels of government and private-sector surveillance.[2]

Some of the most well-known and respected studies on privacy, primarily in the United States but also in Canada, have been conducted by the Louis Harris and Associates polling organization under the direction of Dr Alan F. Westin from 1978 to the present. These surveys are published by Privacy and American Business, a project of the Center for Social and Legal Research, which is supported by major banks, airlines, credit reporting agencies (e.g., Equifax), and credit card companies. The Harris-Westin public opinion surveys track US consumer concerns about privacy and have found that there are two main driving factors in privacy attitudes: individual levels of distrust in institutions; and fears of technology abuse (Westin 2000). In 1990 Westin created an index of general concern about privacy, called the Privacy Dynamic, which is used to group respondents into three categories of concern, which he refers to as the privacy fundamentalists, the privacy unconcerned, and the pragmatic majority (Harris and Associates 1991). Despite the criticisms of the Harris-Westin surveys (EPIC 2005), they can be credited for breaking data down into socio-economic, demographic, and other factors that help to explain variations in attitudes by context, thus providing a more complex breakdown of results (Bennett and Raab 2006).

The three chapters in part 3.1 compare previous public opinion polling with the GPD survey results in Canada and the United States and move more specifically to particular issues within each country. First, Stephen Margulis, Jennifer Pope, and Aaron Lowen take on the challenging task of conceptually replicating the Harris-Westin General Concern about Privacy Index, mentioned above, using the GPD survey question items for data in the United States and Canada. Although these authors were not able to directly replicate the Harris-Westin instrument, as this was not the original intention in creating the GPD survey, their complex statistical analysis makes a useful connection both between these two surveys and to the study of privacy within and across cultures. Although Canada and the United States are culturally similar, Margulis, Pope, and Lowen's findings reveal significant differences between national structures of privacy concerns. These differences are related to attitudes and beliefs about whether, and to what extent, privacy is protected by government and private-sector organizations in each country.

In the second chapter, Stephen Marmura delves into specific GPD survey results within the United States on the issues of security and privacy in relation to public trust in government, state policies, and media messages. He focuses on two main areas of the survey results in the United States: whether citizens perceive that state surveillance policies encroach on individual rights; and public perceptions of media attention paid to surveillance, terrorism, security, and privacy. To situate the GPD findings in a more complex picture, findings from other surveys dealing with related issues are used throughout. Highlighted is the dichotomy between, on the one hand, a growing public concern about government surveillance of citizens and, on the other hand, the willingness of citizens to defend the government's right to employ special powers to prevent terrorism since 9/11. Marmura takes a critical look at the shift in the United States to a national security state model both of governance and of conduct as a global superpower, at citizen trust in government, and at the role of the media in shaping public opinions and in exploiting public anxieties over the real or perceived threats of terrorism as set by government agendas.

Finally, from the Canadian angle, François Fournier examines the survey results for the province of Quebec compared with the rest of Canada (ROC). This comparison is made in order to uncover the impact of social, political, and cultural differences within the country between French and English Canadians.[3] Fournier provides a detailed breakdown of survey results in three categories: (1) perceptions of individual control, knowledge of laws, and proactiveness regarding personal information; (2) trust in public- and private-sector practices in the collection and sharing of personal information; and (3) the balancing of national security, feelings of insecurity and privacy, and perceptions of government policies and practices in a post-9/11 world. He emphasizes translation and language issues that arise on a number of questions that affect results as well as uses some previous poll results regarding public opinion in Quebec on privacy and personal information issues.[4] His analysis reveals a few significant differences in responses, such as that more Quebecers favour the implementation of a national identity card (which is tied to larger national identity issues within the province), but he shows that ultimately there are no sharp contrasts between these groups.

NOTES

1 For a more comprehensive analysis of previous public opinion poll findings on privacy in the United States and Canada, see background reports by Emily Smith, François Fournier, and Shannon Yurke at http://www.sscqueens. org/intl_survey_background (accessed 20 November 2009).

2 Immediately following 9/11, polls showed a greater willingness by Americans and Canadians to accept more invasive police surveillance technologies, such as biometric and facial recognition technologies, and a decreased concern over privacy, along with greater trust in government. This initial support for increased surveillance after a large event has now subsided, and concern over privacy is again increasing.

3 The GPD survey was oversampled in Quebec to allow for further analysis in this province, and samples were weighted in proportion to the rest of the country when comparing results.

4 See the background paper by Fournier at http://www.sscqueens.org/intl_survey_background (accessed 20 November 2009).

The Harris-Westin Index of General Concern about Privacy: An Exploratory Conceptual Replication

STEPHEN T. MARGULIS, JENNIFER A. POPE, AND AARON LOWEN

Louis Harris and Associates and Alan Westin developed the Index of General Concern about Privacy, which they have used to analyze survey data on privacy-related issues from several national US samples. The index was used to classify respondents, and more important, the items in the index had value in organizing and interpreting survey results. Because of the apparent value of this index, we attempted a conceptual replication of the index using the Globalization of Personal Data (GPD) survey questions. It was a conceptual replication because the GPD survey did not include the Harris-Westin privacy concern items. Therefore, we could not directly replicate the Harris-Westin measure. However, Emily Smith (2006) and we believed that the GPD survey included questions that could provide a basis for a conceptual replication of the index. Our goal was to create another index of privacy concern and to examine its correlates in GPD survey data, much as Harris and Westin had done with Harris's survey data (e.g., Harris and Westin 1991). We also wanted to assess the cross-national generality of the index and drew on Canadian and US data from the GPD survey for this purpose.

THE HARRIS-WESTIN INDEX OF GENERAL CONCERN ABOUT PRIVACY

Alan Westin, among the most influential theorists on privacy, uses a classificatory approach as a central feature of his research (see Margulis 2003 for a description and review). A prime example is his classification of privacy's forms and functions. Another example is a classificatory approach to an individual difference measure of privacy concern that he and Louis Harris and Associates introduced in a 1990 Harris-Equifax poll of privacy opinions of US residents (Harris and Westin 1991). Harris and Westin called their measure an Index of General Concern about Privacy.

The index is based on four items. For each item, one specific response is used to indicate high concern. One question asks respondents about their concern "about threats to their personal privacy today"; the high concern response is "very concerned." A second question asks respondents whether they agree "business organizations seek excessively personal information from consumers"; the high concern response is "strongly agree." A third question asks respondents whether they agree "that the [US] Federal government since Watergate is still invading the citizen's privacy"; again, the high concern response is "strongly agree." The fourth question asks respondents whether they agree "consumers have lost all control over how personal information about them is circulated and used by companies"; the high concern response is "agree." Whether "agree" means "strongly agree," as in the aforementioned items, or both "strongly agree" and "agree somewhat strongly" is unclear (Harris and Westin 1991, 6–30).

Harris and Westin classify respondents into three categories based on how often respondents express high concern. Those classified as high concern respondents have expressed high concern on three or four of these items; moderate concern respondents have expressed high concern on two of the four items; low concern respondents have expressed high concern on one or none of the four items (Harris and Westin 1991).

When Harris and Westin examined the relationship between their three privacy concern groups and the groups' responses to other polling questions on business and governmental aspects of personal privacy, they found that "[i]n a majority of these [analyses], the index worked as a direct predictor – people in the High General Concern About Privacy group were the most concerned about privacy interests on specific questions; people in the Moderate Concern group were next in their privacy concern; and people in the Low Concern group were the lowest in privacy concern" (Harris and Westin 1991, 6).

Westin (see Harris and Westin 1990, 6) appears to equate privacy fundamentalists with the high concern group. Privacy fundamentalists "rejected consumer-benefit or societal-protection claims for data uses and sought legal-regulatory privacy measures" (Westin 2003, 445). Westin appears to equate the privacy unconcerned with the low concern group.

The privacy unconcerned "were generally ready to supply their personal information to business and government and rejected what was seen as too much privacy fuss" (445). Westin appears to equate privacy pragmatists with the moderate concern group. Westin regards privacy pragmatists as holding a more balanced view of privacy because they "examined the benefits to them or society of the data collection and use, wanted to know the privacy risks and how organizations proposed to control those, and then decided whether to trust the organization or seek legal oversight" (445). The pragmatic position is consistent with Westin's own position on privacy (see Westin 1970).

A COMPARISON OF HARRIS-WESTIN AND GPD PRIVACY CONCERN INDEX ITEMS

As noted above, we attempted a conceptual replication of the Harris-Westin index of privacy concern using data from the GPD survey. The goal was to create an index of privacy concern and to examine its correlates in GPD survey data. The GPD survey did not include the Harris-Westin privacy concern items. However, as noted, Smith (2006) and we believed that the GPD survey included questions that could provide a basis for a conceptual replication of the index. That is, there are GPD survey questions that reasonably fit the items/issues that are the basis for the Harris-Westin index.

The GPD survey questions that we and Smith (2006) believe are comparable to the four items in the Harris-Westin Index of General Concern about Privacy – namely concern with threats to personal privacy, loss of control over how personal information is circulated and used by companies, whether organizations seek excessively personal information from consumers, and whether respondents agree the US government since Watergate is still invading the citizen's privacy – are included in table 5.1. Although we agreed on the assignment of six items (they are the questions in italics in table 5.1), we differed from Smith on which GPD questions were consistent with the Harris-Westin items. These differences point to the judgmental problems researchers face when attempting a conceptual replication in lieu of a direct replication. The latter was impossible because the Harris-Westin items were not included in the GPD survey instrument.

The GPD survey questions and our interpretation of the degree of general concern implied by the GPD questions' response alternatives are shown in table 5.2.

Table 5.1

A comparison of questions from the GPD survey identified as comparable to the four
items in the Harris-Westin Index of General Concern about Privacy

Harris-Westin	This chapter	Smith (2006)
Concern about threats to your personal privacy	6, 10, **11**	11
Consumers have lost all control	**2**	2
Business organizations seek excessively personal information from consumers	**19**	6, 19
Government still invading citizen's privacy	**5**, **17**, **18**, 23	5, 17, 18

Note: Questions in bold are those that GDP researchers agreed are consistent with the Harris-Westin items.

Given presumably comparable questions, we next addressed whether
to follow the Harris-Westin classificatory approach to privacy concern.
We did not follow the Harris-Westin approach for several reasons. First,
their approach reduces ordinal or perhaps interval response scale data
to nominal data, thereby eliminating potentially useful behavioural variance in the responses to these items. Second, if these items are multifactorial, then combining items across factors into a single scale measuring a
single concept would be methodologically problematic (W. Rogers, personal communication, 22 September 2006). As we shall report, the items
are multifactorial. Third, it was not clear how Harris and Westin treated
respondents who had answered any of their four items with a "not sure"
response. Harris and Westin (1991) report not sure rates for two of the
four items in their index. For their item on concern about threats to
respondent privacy, the not sure rate was 1% in 1990 and 1991 (Harris
and Westin 1991, 6, table 3). For their item on loss of control over personal information, the not sure rates were 3% and 4%, respectively, in
the 1990 and 1991 polls (Harris and Westin 1991, 9, table 6). We believe
that respondents with a "not sure" response to any of the four general
concern items would have been eliminated. Otherwise, the classification
rules have the potential of misclassifying respondents. We treated "do
not know/not sure" responses as missing data. Fourth, we did not know
Harris and Westin's explanation for choosing the cut-offs for their three
levels of concern (e.g., why are three high concern responses considered
high concern whereas two high concern responses are considered moderate concern?). Because the criteria were not known, meaning that we
were not able to directly replicate their technique, we opted for a parametric approach to scaling privacy concern.

Table 5.2
Interpretation of the degree of general concern implied by the GPD questions' response alternatives

GPD question and author interpretation	Response category 1	Response category 2	Response category 3	Response category 4
2[a]	"No say"	"Some say"	"Complete say"	"A lot of say"
Interpretation	High concern	Somewhat lower concern	Lower concern	Even lower concern
5[b]	"Very high level of trust"	"Reasonably high level of trust"	"Fairly low level of trust"	"Very low level of trust"
Interpretation	The least concern	Intermediate concern	High concern	The most concern
6[c]	"Very high level of trust"	"Reasonably high level of trust"	"Fairly low level of trust"	"Very low level of trust"
Interpretation	Low concern	Intermediate concern	High concern	The most concern
10[d]	"Very effective"	"Somewhat effective"	"Not very effective"	"Not at all effective"
Interpretation	Low concern	Intermediate concern	High concern	Higher concern
11[e]	"Very worried"	"Somewhat worried"	"Not very worried"	"Not worried at all"
Interpretation	High concern	Intermediate level of concern	Intermediate concern	Low concern
17[f]	"Highly intrusive"	"Somewhat intrusive"	"Not very intrusive"	"Not intrusive at all"
Interpretation	High concern	Intermediate concern	Lower concern	Lowest concern
18[g]	"Yes, it is the government's right under all circumstances"	"Yes, if the citizen is suspected of wrong-doing"	"Yes, as long as the government has the expressed consent of the citizen"	"No, under no circumstances should government share information about citizens"
Interpretation[h]	Low concern	Moderate concern[i]	Moderate Concern	High concern or, alternatively, high commitment to personal privacy

Table 5.2
Interpretation of the degree of general concern implied by the GPD questions' response alternatives (*Continued*)

	"Yes, it is the organisation's right under all circumstances"	"Yes, if the customer is suspected of wrong-doing"	"Yes, as long as the organisation has the expressed consent of the customer"	"No, under no circumstances should organisations share information about citizens"
19j				
Interpretation[k]	Low concern	Moderate concern[l]	Moderate Concern	High concern or, alternatively, high commitment to personal privacy
23m	"Not respected at all"	"Somewhat respected"	"A lot of respect"	"Completely respected"
Interpretation	High concern	Intermediate concern	Low concern	Lower concern

a "To what extent do you have a say in what happens to your personal information?"

b "When it comes to the privacy of personal information, what level of trust do you have that the government is striking the right balance between national security and individual rights?"

c "What level of trust do you have that private companies, such as banks, credit card companies and places where you shop, will protect your personal information?"

d "In order to put national ID cards into use, the government would need to have a national database containing personal information on all citizens. This information could include address, gender, race, and tax information. How effective do you feel efforts to protect this type of information from disclosure would be?"

e "When it comes to privacy, how worried are you about providing personal information on websites, such as your name, address, date of birth, and gender?"

f "The government has enacted laws aimed at protecting national security. To what extent do you believe laws aimed at protecting national security are intrusive upon personal privacy?"

g "To what extent do you think it is appropriate for a government agency to share a citizen's personal information with a third party, such as other government agencies, foreign governments and the private sector?" For each sector, the respondents were asked, "Which of the following best describes your beliefs?"

h In our analyses, we focused on other government agencies and the private sector (Q18a and Q18c) as targets. We treat questions 18a and 18c as separate items.

i What Westin would consider moderate concern because of the justifications for sharing.

j "To what extent do you think it is appropriate for a private sector organisation to share or sell its customers' personal information with third parties, such as the national government, foreign governments and other private sector organisations?" For each sector, the respondents were asked, "Which of the following best describes your beliefs?"

k In our analyses, we focused on the national government and other private-sector organizations (Q19a and Q19c) as targets. We treat questions 19a and 19c as two separate items.

l As stated above, this and the next response are likely what Westin would call moderate concern because of the justifications for sharing.

m "To what extent is your privacy respected by airport and customs officials when traveling by airplane?"

THE USE OF US AND CANADIAN DATA

Despite the large amount of GPD data available, we chose to analyze US data because the Harris-Westin polls are based on US samples. Canadian data contrast well because, socio-political differences notwithstanding, Americans and Canadians are culturally similar but not identical. Specifically, although the United States and Canada are culturally similar, having a 0.272 cultural distance ranking (Pope 2003), the UK (0.110 cultural distance ranking) and Australia (0.021 cultural distance ranking) are more culturally similar to the United States than is Canada. There is enough distance between Canada and the United States, as well as differences in national and corporate security issues, to justify examining them separately in this study. Distinguishing between the two countries allows us to examine different perceptions of privacy issues between the two countries.

Jennifer Pope's (2003) examination of cultural distance is based on Harry Barkema and Freek Vermeulen's (1997) updated cultural distance index. The index is based on Geert Hofstede's (1993) five dimensions of culture (i.e., power distance, individualism-collectivism, masculinity-femininity, uncertainty avoidance, and long- versus short-term orientation). However, Barkema and Vermeulen substituted Russel Reed's (1993) Scale of Marginal Propensity to Save for Hofstede's long-term orientation dimension because Hofstede did not gather data on the long-term orientation of many countries. This substitution differentiates Pope's (2003) scale from the original cultural distance index developed by Bruce Kogut and Harbir Singh (1988) based on the other four Hofstede dimensions.

ANALYSIS OF THE DATA

The sizes of the initial samples were 1,001 respondents in the Canadian sample and 1,000 respondents in the US sample. GPD tables 5(a) (Canada) and 5(b) (US) (available online)[1] contain the correlations between the privacy concern items (independent variables) in table 5.1. Although none of the correlations for either country is greater than 0.5, many of the independent variables are significantly correlated. It is also interesting to note that the significant correlations are not the same in the United States and Canada. For example, question 2 in Canada is significantly correlated with the other variables only in factor 2, whereas in the United States question 2 is correlated with items from all three factors (i.e., correlated with questions 5, 6, 10, 11, 17, and 18c; see also table 5.3). Furthermore, other variables in the Canadian sample follow the same pattern, showing significant correlations only with other variables in their respective factors. In the US sample, on the other hand, the correlations are more random.

Descriptive statistics, separated by country, are included in GPD table 5(c) (online). Interestingly, despite the differences in the results of the Canadian and US factor analyses, there are few significant differences between Canadian and US means of the selected GPD questions that were the dependent variables in our regression analyses. The mean differences between the two countries range from approximately 0.01 to 0.27. A number of the questions had statistically significantly different means, but only question 9, related to government ID cards, had a practical as well as statistical difference, with a difference in means of 0.27, with the US showing higher concern about ID cards (3.03) than Canada (2.77).

THE STRUCTURE OF PRIVACY CONCERN

As our first step, we ran three statistical tests to determine the appropriateness of conducting a factor analysis of the GPD survey's eleven privacy concern questions (see above and table 5.2). The anti-image correlation matrix for the items yielded no correlations above 0.3, the Kaiser-Meyer-Olkin (KMO) Measure of Sampling Adequacy was .720 (p = 0.000), and the chi-square for Bartlett's Test of Sphericity measure was 1177.3 (df = 55, p = 0.000). All three tests indicated these questions are appropriate for factor analysis.

As noted above, we treated "don't know/not sure" responses to any of the eleven questions as missing data. We also recoded the questions so that "4" represented high concern on all eleven questions. We used a principal components analysis extraction method to generate an un-rotated component matrix and used a Varimax Rotation, employing a Direct Oblimin Rotation with Kaiser Normalization, to generate a rotated solution. We report the results of the rotated components analysis because it was more straightforward to interpret than was the unrotated solution. Table 5.3 summarizes the results. All factors loading near or above 0.5 are in italics. Included in table 5.3 are the Cronbach's alphas for these factors. First, we will describe the factors. Then we will discuss the stability of the factors.

Table 5.3
Factor loadings for US and Canadian samples

GPD question	Canada, factor 1	Canada, factor 2	Canada, factor 3	US, factor 1	US, factor 2	US, factor 3
2	-.090	.699[a]	-.216	-.052	.122	**.518**
5	.130	**.702**	.199	.134	**.757**	.318
6	.117	**.718**	.151	.100	.326	**.580**
10	.199	**.533**	.387	.298	**.502**	.362
18a	**.661**	.098	.105	**.596**	.408	-.095
18c	**.683**	-.034	.001	**.690**	.148	-.017
19a	**.743**	.114	.171	**.715**	.195	.045
19c	**.731**	.080	-.038	**.764**	-.203	.180
11	-.067	.032	**.623**	.060	-.115	**.711**
17	.083	.124	**.653**	-.010	**.662**	.081
23	.108	.040	**.523**	.109	.487[b]	-.040
Cronbach's alpha[c]	.694	.564	.265	.675	.506	.306

a All factors loading near or above 0.5 are in bold.
b This is the strongest loading for question 23 in the US sample.
c Alphas were tested using Hotelling's T-Squared Test. All p-values, except two, were 0.003 or higher. The two nonsignificant p-values were the alphas for US factors 2 and 3.

Both the US and Canadian samples have three factors. However, the factors are relatively different. Additionally, the factors are "cleaner" in the Canadian than in the US data. For that reason, we will describe the Canadian results first.

DESCRIPTION OF FACTORS

Canada

Questions 18a, 18c, 19a, and 19c load 0.66 or higher on factor 1. Each asks about the appropriateness of governmental and private-sector sharing of personal information of citizens or customers, respectively. Factor 1 addresses the *appropriateness* of invasions of privacy.

Questions 2, 5, 6, and 10 load above 0.53 on factor 2. These questions address the extent of one's say about what happens to personal information (Q2), level of trust that the government (Q5) and private-sector organizations (Q6) will protect individual rights/personal information, and the effectiveness of governmental protection of personal information in a national database (Q10). Factor 2 seems to address *personal concern* about possible invasions of personal information privacy.

Among all of our Canadian and US factors, this one comes closest to the Harris-Westin General Concern about Privacy Index.

Questions 11, 17, and 23 load above 0.52 on factor 3. These questions address worry about providing personal information to websites (Q11), the perceived intrusiveness of national security laws on personal privacy (Q17), and whether airport and customs officials respect the privacy of those travelling by airplane (Q23). The questions in factor 3, especially questions 17 and 23, seem to share a concern about the possible *intrusiveness* of invasions of privacy.

The United States

As with the Canadian sample, questions 18a, 18c, 19a, and 19c load 0.59 or higher on factor 1. Each asks about the appropriateness of governmental and private-sector sharing of personal information of citizens or customers, respectively. Factor 1 addresses the *appropriateness* of invasions of privacy.

Factor 2 has three, perhaps four, questions. Questions 5, 10, and 17 load 0.50 or higher on factor 2, while question 23 loads 0.487 on factor 2. Although the question 23 loading does not achieve the 0.5 level, this loading is higher than question 23's loading on factors 1 and 3. The questions measure trust in the government to strike a proper balance between national security and individual rights (Q5), governmental efforts to protect a national database of personal information (Q10), the intrusiveness on privacy of governmental laws protecting national security (Q17), and respect for the privacy of airplane travellers by airport and customs officials (Q23). The common element seems to be a concern about invasions of privacy by the government or its agents. Factor 2, then, addresses *the government* as the possible threat to personal privacy.

Questions 2, 6, and 11 load above 0.51 on factor 3. These items assess having a say about what happens to one's personal information (Q2), trust in private-sector organizations to protect customers' personal information (Q6), and worries about providing personal information on websites (Q11). The items in factor 3 can be interpreted as concern about *the private sector* as a possible threat to personal information privacy, which is explicit in question 6 and implicit in questions 2 and 11, *or* it can be interpreted as a concern about *having versus not having control* over how one's personal information is used, which is explicit in question 2 and implicit in questions 6 and 11. Because question 2 shows the most significant relationship with the dependent variables, we believe that *having versus not having control* probably best fits the description of the factor.

THE STABILITY OF FACTORS

A visibly significant difference between a question's factor loadings on a factor it defines compared to the other extracted factors is taken to indicate a strong factor loading, and a Cronbach's alpha of at least 0.6 indicates a factor's stability. These rules of thumb lead to two conclusions. First, the Canadian factor structure is more stable than the US factor structure. The differences in loadings of questions *across factors* for the Canadian sample are in the 0.5 to 0.6 range for all questions except question 10 (see table 5.3 above). Moreover, the Cronbach's alphas for the three Canadian factors are all statistically significant, and two are at least 0.5. The exception is factor 3 (see table 5.3).

By comparison, there is a relative lack of clean separation of factors for two of the three US factors. In factor 1, question 18a cross-loads on factor 2, unlike the Canadian sample. Moreover, for factor 2, two of the three questions that loaded above 0.5 cross-loaded on at least one other factor. In fact, question 10 cross-loads on the two other factors. In this regard, question 10 also cross-loads on two other factors in the Canadian sample. In factor 3, two of the three questions (Q2 and Q6) cross-load on factor 2. The Cronbach's alphas for these factors are also problematic. Only one is statistically significant and large (over 0.6), and that is for factor 1. Although we have described a cross-national difference in factor stability, we cannot explain it.

Second, question 10, about governmental protection of personal information in a national database, is unusual. It is the only question of the eleven that cross-loads on the two other factors in the Canadian and US samples. We do not know why this is the case.

Using the factor scores as independent variables in regression analyses, we found a number of the dependent variables were substantially correlated with the factor scores at the $p = 0.1$ level or higher. However, because factor scores do not allow us to determine directional movements of variables, we regressed each of the dependent variables that showed the predictive power of factors against each of the questions in the factors (our independent variables). Since the use of factors makes interpretation "ambiguous" at best (Greene 1997), ordinary least squares (OLS) regression is used in subsequent analyses to examine each individual independent variable against the dependent variables. Multicollinearity

Table 5.4
Summary of significance of regression results for Canada

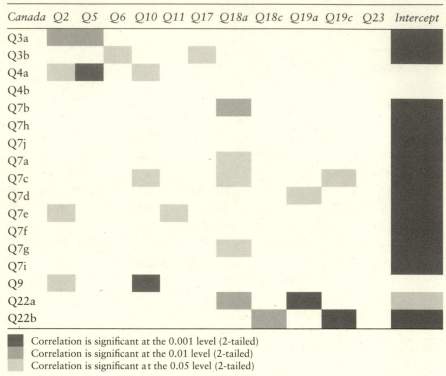

Canada	Q2	Q5	Q6	Q10	Q11	Q17	Q18a	Q18c	Q19a	Q19c	Q23	Intercept

■ Correlation is significant at the 0.001 level (2-tailed)
■ Correlation is significant at the 0.01 level (2-tailed)
□ Correlation is significant at the 0.05 level (2-tailed)

in the independent variables, which is assumed in factor analysis, may lead to the appearance of individually insignificant coefficient estimates.

THE PREDICTIVE POWER OF FACTOR QUESTIONS

We present regression results for each question in turn, comparing results for the two countries; results are in GPD tables 5(d)-(k) through 5(d)-(k) (online). Table entries include coefficient estimates with t-statistics below in parentheses. Significance is indicated at the 0.1% level, at the 1% level, and at the 5% level. The tables include the p-value of an F-test of all explanatory variables (prob>F), adjusted R-squared terms (Adj R²), and the number of observations used in that regression (N). We used heteroscedasticity-robust standard errors in all regressions. Tables 5.4 and 5.5 summarize GPD tables 5(d)-(k) through 5(d)-(k) (online), showing which variables are significant at what level.

Table 5.5
Summary of significance of regression results for the United States

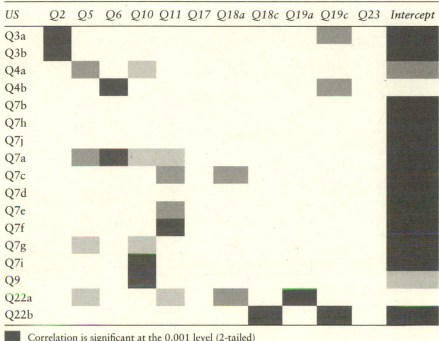

US	Q2	Q5	Q6	Q10	Q11	Q17	Q18a	Q18c	Q19a	Q19c	Q23	Intercept
Q3a												
Q3b												
Q4a												
Q4b												
Q7b												
Q7h												
Q7j												
Q7a												
Q7c												
Q7d												
Q7e												
Q7f												
Q7g												
Q7i												
Q9												
Q22a												
Q22b												

Correlation is significant at the 0.001 level (2-tailed)
Correlation is significant at the 0.01 level (2-tailed)
Correlation is significant at the 0.05 level (2-tailed)

Question 3, which gathered self-reported knowledge of laws concerning personal information protection, had explanatory variables that were statistically significant as a group (F-test p-values at or below 2%) but showed little predictive power overall (adjusted R-squared values at or below 5%). For question 3a, on protection of personal information by government departments, both Canadian and US respondents' answers were predicted by respondents' belief in their own control over their personal information (Q2). Canadians with low levels of trust in government (Q5) were those with low self-reported levels of knowledge about laws that protect personal information (Q3a), a result that does not hold for US respondents. There is also a significant negative relationship with question 19c (on the appropriateness of private organizations selling data to other private organizations) for US respondents; those who report high levels of knowledge about laws pertaining to government department handling of personal data find business-to-business information sharing to be less appropriate. Although self-reported knowledge levels are not the same as actual knowledge levels, the tendency for consumers who are better informed about laws that affect government agencies to disapprove of private-sector information sharing may reflect a failure of the private sector to signal competence and/or trustworthiness in their data handling techniques in the United States. However, their level of knowledge about laws affecting private companies' control of information (Q3b) had no relation to question 19c. We cannot explain this or other counterintuitive results (presented later in the chapter).

Interviewers elicited attitudes toward effectiveness of these laws pertaining to the protection of personal data by government departments in question 4a but only for respondents who had claimed, in question 3a, that they were very or somewhat knowledgeable about these laws. This accounts for the substantially smaller number of respondents in question 4 compared to question 3. However, in both Canada and the United States, the independent variables used to explain question 4a have substantial explanatory power, namely adjusted R-squared values of 13% to 15%. For Canadian and US respondents, there is a significant relationship between high levels of trust and the belief that personal information protection laws are effective. Again, for Canadians but not Americans, there is a positive association between the perceived effectiveness of "privacy" laws and belief in one's ability to control personal information (Q2).

Question 3b, on knowledge of laws governing private company handling of personal information, finds for US respondents that low levels of knowledge are associated with the belief that one has little control over personal information (Q2). This relationship does not hold (is not significant) for Canadians, for whom low knowledge levels are associated with low trust in private companies. Returning to question 17, and another counterintuitive result, high levels of self-reported knowledge about privacy laws concerning private companies are associated with a higher likelihood of having the attitude that national security laws are intrusive upon personal privacy.

With respect to the perceived efficacy of personal information protection laws for private companies (Q4b), the regression analysis provides no individually significant relationships for Canadians, although question 6 is "nearly" significant with a coefficient estimate of 0.209. The interpretation is that consumers with a high level of trust that private companies will protect personal information are more likely to believe that personal information protection laws are effective. The marginal statistical significance *might* be due to collinearity among the predictors suppressing the level of significance. US respondents who believed that laws pertaining to private company handling of personal information were effective held attitudes that private companies would protect their private information (Q6) and that data sharing between private companies was appropriate (Q19c).

The ten subparts of question 7 examine behaviours of respondents that protect their personal information. For convenience, we first consider behaviours directed at government agencies, subparts b, h, and j (see GPD table 5(f/g) online). The explanatory variables considered here were not jointly significant for question 7h, concerning deceit, and question 7j, on pursuing knowledge about government policies. Question 7b, on resistance to sharing (what is perceived as) unnecessary information, shows some significance for both countries according to the F-test (p-values less than 0.1). However, there is a weak relationship between the independent variables (factor questions) and actual behaviours directed at government departments (Q7b, h, j). For US respondents, adjusted R-squared terms are low and there is a lack of both statistical and real significance, as measured by the magnitude of the coefficient estimates. For Canadian respondents, only question 18a is statistically significant; the belief that a government agency should not share information with other government agencies is associated with higher refusal to provide information that is perceived as "not needed" (Q7b).

GPD table 5(h/i) (online) contains regression results for seven business-related behaviours. Canadians show little relationship between the independent variables and business-related personal information behaviours. Although F-test p-values reject the hypothesis that all coefficient estimates are equal to zero for questions 7a, 7d, and 7i, each of the seven adjusted R-squared values is less than 2.5%, indicating little real significance. Even for those three items, there is little consistent relationship. There is an increased incidence of information-protecting behaviours against the private sector: refusing to give information (Q7a), asking to be removed from marketing lists (Q7d), reading online privacy policies (Q7i), and attitudes approving the appropriateness of government information sharing with other government agencies (Q18a). This peculiar result indicates that those more trusting of government personal data handling are less trusting of, and more willing to take actions protecting themselves against, the private sector.

For US respondents, on the other hand, there are significant F-test p-values for all but one business-related behaviour (Q7g, on giving false information to a marketer). The behaviours of refusing to give information (Q7a), asking to be removed from marketing lists (Q7c), asking about policies (Q7e), and asking for revelation of held information (Q7f) are all more common among those who express high concern about websites (Q11). The belief that government would not be effective in controlling information used on national ID cards (Q10) is associated with higher incidence of refusing to give information (Q7a), of giving incorrect information to a marketer (Q7g), and of reading online privacy policies (Q7i). This set of attitudes and the results reported below are consistent with the idea that certain groups of Americans are what Harris and Westin call privacy fundamentalists. These are people who dislike sharing their private information, regardless of the public or private nature of the data-controlling agency.

Perhaps most interesting is the relationship between question 7a, on whether a respondent has refused to give information to a business, and the level of trust that government (Q5) and private companies (Q6) will protect personal information. In particular, as trust in government increased, the respondent was more likely to have declined to provide information to a business (and, it should be pointed out, was more likely to have provided false information to a marketer). The result, stated another way, is that decreased trust in government was associated with a lower rate of declining to provide and/or providing false information to a business or marketer. Further, as trust in private companies declined, respondents were more likely to have refused to provide information to companies.

GPD table 5(j/k) (online) provides perhaps the most direct test of the internal consistency of the attitudes and behavioural information elicited by the GPD survey. In particular, note that all F-test p-values are zero to the fourth decimal place and that adjusted R-squared values are all above 18%, some as high as 25%. Question 9, on approval of national ID cards, is associated with the belief that the government would be effective in protecting the information from disclosure for respondents in both countries. For Canadians, support for national ID cards is also associated with the perception of no control over personal information (Q2).

Question 22 deals with the appropriateness of employers sharing employee personal information, and Canadian and US responses were similar in their relationships with the independent variables. In particular, the view that it is inappropriate for government (Q18a) and private companies (Q19a) to share information with government agencies is associated with the view that it is inappropriate for employers to share information with government (Q22). Similarly, the belief that it is inappropriate for government (Q18c) and private companies (Q19c) to share information with private companies is associated with the view that it is inappropriate for employers to share information with private companies. This seems to provide positive evidence that the responses given were internally consistent across attitudes, and it supports the validity of the results. Additionally, US respondents who believed it is inappropriate for employers to share information with the government also had little trust the government was striking the right balance between national security and individual rights (Q5) and were more likely to worry about providing information on websites (Q11). These results also support the idea that there are respondents who may be privacy fundamentalists in the Harris-Westin sense.

DISCUSSION AND CONCLUSIONS

This study contributes to the body of literature in several ways. First, not only do we examine privacy issues within a culture, as Harris and Westin (1991) did for the United States, but we also extend the examination of privacy concerns across cultures, to both Canada and the United States. We found significant differences between cultures in the structure of privacy concerns. Interestingly, the Canadian factors were cleaner, stronger, and more stable than the US factors. We cannot explain this finding to our own satisfaction. We found that national differences in how privacy concerns are structured, in turn, are related to respondents' attitudes and beliefs about whether and to what extent personal information privacy is protected by governmental and private-sector organizations.

These results provide some support for the validity of the factors (i.e., the results are often consistent with what the factors "mean"). Specifically, we found more privacy concern factors than Harris and Westin (1991) proposed. We believe our factor 2 for Canada is roughly equivalent to Harris and Westin's "general concern about privacy" construct. However, we also discovered that privacy concerns are more than simply a general concern about privacy. Privacy concerns are multifactorial. They also include how much we feel we can control our private information as well as our beliefs about the appropriateness of governments and private businesses invading our privacy. Put differently, Canada and the United States provided five different "privacy concern" factors. One factor crossed national boundaries; four did not. This finding strengthens our supposition that privacy concerns are culturally specific.

We found that the structure of privacy concerns is related to respondents' attitudes and beliefs about whether and to what extent personal information privacy is protected by governmental and private-sector organizations. We conclude that our results, in spite of some counterintuitive outcomes, provide support for the validity of the factors (i.e., the results are often consistent with what the factors "mean"). Specifically, respondents in both countries who express feelings of a low level of control over their personal information tend to have a low level of knowledge about personal information privacy laws. As regards Canadian levels of knowledge about laws pertaining to how government departments handle data, those with higher levels of knowledge have more trust in the government balance between national security and individual rights. Further, in both countries, high levels of trust in the government balance between national security and individual rights are associated with the belief that privacy protection laws are effective. Moreover, for Canadians, there is a positive association between their perceived effectiveness of these laws and their belief in their ability to control their personal information. The correlation between high levels of self-reported knowledge about privacy laws and attitudes toward privacy data is striking in that those who claimed to be well informed also distrusted private-sector data sharing and found national security laws to be intrusive with regards to personal privacy.

When considering past privacy-protecting behaviours related to government departments, we found little relationship between attitudes and behaviour. One exception, for Canadian respondents, is the association between the belief that a government agency should not share information with other government agencies and a higher rate of refusing to provide information that is perceived as "not needed."

On the other hand, past privacy-protecting behaviours related to private companies show substantial cross-cultural differences. In particular, US respondents, but not Canadian respondents, were likely to take actions to protect their private information (although the actual US and Canadian means are similar), and Americans' greater likelihood of taking action was significantly related to their attitudes about websites and national ID cards. With the exception of asking a company to remove the respondent from marketing lists, the relationship between attitudes and behaviours aimed at private companies was weak or nonexistent for Canadian respondents.

Questions 9 and 2, in particular, show internal consistency of the information gathered by the GPD survey. In particular, approval of national ID cards is associated with the belief that the government would be effective in protecting the information from disclosure for respondents in both countries. For Canadians, respondents who support national ID cards also tend to believe they have less control over their personal information. This relationship does not hold for US respondents. Further, the view that it is inappropriate for government agencies to share information with other government agencies and private companies (Q18a and Q18c) is associated with the view that it is inappropriate for employers to share information with government agencies and private companies (Q19a and Q19c). This is true for respondents in both countries.

We were disappointed that our adjusted R-squared measures never exceeded 0.3. This suggests that although the GPD survey data highlight some of the issues that are important to privacy concerns, the issue is more complex than what was captured by the data. Another concern, not discussed above, is the number of respondents who answered "do not know/not sure" to multiple questions. Although we treated these answers as missing data, it was unclear why these data occurred (e.g., ignorance of the topic, selection bias, distrust of the interview process. Uncovering the reasons for the nonresponses is critical to understanding public attitudes on privacy, and we recommend that future replications of this survey explore this issue.

NOTES

1 The authors wish to thank Emily Smith and William Rogers for their help with this chapter. Please address all queries about the chapter to Dr Stephen T. Margulis at margulis@gvsu.edu.
2 All of the GPD tables cited in this chapter are available at http://www. sscqueens.org/book_tables (accessed 30 November 2009).

6

Security vs Privacy: Media Messages, State Policies, and American Public Trust in Government

STEPHEN MARMURA

INTRODUCTION

This chapter considers two interrelated sets of issues addressed by the Globalization of Personal Data (GPD) survey as they pertain to public attitudes in the United States. The first concerns trust in government,[1] specifically whether state surveillance policies implemented to counter the threat of terrorism are perceived by citizens to impinge unduly upon their individual rights. The second related area concerns public perceptions about the amount of media attention regularly given to various aspects of surveillance, terrorism, security, and privacy. Analysis proceeds from the premise that the GPD survey findings dealing with both sets of issues, along with any potential relationships between the two, may be better appreciated if America's dual character as both a "security state" and the sole global superpower is held firmly in view. Popular attitudes toward the role of the state are considered in light of this dual character, as is the role traditionally played by the media with respect to real or perceived threats to the state and its citizens. The findings of other surveys and studies dealing with these and related issues are addressed throughout. Attention to these areas enables a more comprehensive approach to the subject matter, allowing for greater insight when assessing the GPD survey findings.[2]

THE SURVEY FINDINGS

Public Trust in Government

American public trust in government with respect to the state's implementation of "appropriate" national security measures is a primary concern of this chapter. The findings for question 5 of the GPD survey indicate that a small majority, 52.7% of US citizens, do not trust the government to strike the right balance between maintaining national security and protecting individual rights. Twenty-five per cent (24.7%) indicate a fairly low level of trust in this regard, while 28% have a very low level of trust. By contrast, 28.6% indicate a reasonably high level of trust and 9.9% a very high level of trust. Eight per cent (8.3%) are not sure. The survey results for question 17 indicate that a majority of the public, 57.2%, feel that government laws aimed at protecting national security are intrusive. Fifteen per cent (15.1%) of respondents view such laws as highly intrusive, while 42.1% see them as somewhat intrusive. By contrast, 18.1% believe government laws are not very intrusive, and 8.4% believe that they are not intrusive at all. Sixteen per cent of respondents were not sure.

Related Findings of Other Surveys

The GPD survey results for questions 5 and 17 do not indicate whether revealed levels of public mistrust stem primarily from the fear that the state has implemented national security polices that are too invasive and hence that the government is not committed enough to protecting individual rights or, alternatively, from the belief that the government is not being assertive and/or intrusive enough in terms of safeguarding national security. To clarify this issue, attention will be directed to the results of two public opinion polls conducted for the *Washington Post* and ABC News (henceforth, ABC polls) by TNS Telecoms of Horsham, Pennsylvania.[3] These surveys, which were conducted on 10 January and 12 May 2006, deal directly with public attitudes toward government terrorism/security policies versus privacy rights, with some questions focusing attention on the specific issue of warrantless wiretapping by the National Security Agency (NSA).[4] The results from four Pew Research polls, designed to measure public concerns with respect to the broader category of "civil liberties," are also deemed significant.

According to the ABC poll conducted in January (ABC News/ *Washington Post* 2006a), 3 in 10 Americans feel that the government is making unjustified intrusions into personal privacy as it investigates terrorism. Significantly, however, the same poll indicates that 51% of the public consider the use of warrantless wiretaps by the NSA to be an acceptable way for the federal government to investigate terrorism (further discussed below). Forty-seven per cent deem them unacceptable. Similar results appeared in the ABC poll conducted in May (ABC News/

Washington Post 2006c). This survey indicates that just under half of Americans (45%) believe the government is not doing enough to protect Americans' rights as it investigates terrorism. This concern is considerably higher than in 2002 and 2003, the two years following the attacks of 11 September 2001, according to earlier ABC polls. Annual surveys conducted from 2001 to 2004 by the commercial polling organization Harris Interactive reveal a similar pattern with respect to changes in public attitudes on this issue. Both the January and May ABC polls indicate that 65% of the public believe it is more important for the government to investigate possible terrorist threats even when this intrudes on personal privacy than it is for the government to avoid such intrusions even if they limit its investigative ability.

The ABC poll findings could be interpreted as indicating a higher level of public trust in government and/or tacit support for its surveillance practices than the findings of the GPD survey. However, other results from the January ABC poll suggest that this is not the case. This poll indicates that 42% to 48% of Americans say that as the government investigates terrorism, it is doing enough, rather than not enough, to protect the rights of citizens. Eight per cent say it is doing too much. Furthermore, as many Americans (48%) were worried that the administration of President George W. Bush would not do enough to investigate terrorism as were worried that it would go too far (44%). Similar results were obtained for four surveys conducted by Pew Research between 2004 and 2006 that probed public concerns about civil liberties. These polls asked respondents whether they had a "bigger concern that the government had not gone far enough to protect the country" from terrorism or whether they thought the government had "gone too far in restricting civil liberties." The results for the polls as stated in terms of responses to the first versus the second option were as follows (see Pew Research 2006): 49% vs 29% (July 2004); 52% vs 31% (July 2005); 48% vs 34% (October 2005); 46% vs 33% (January 2006).

In light of the findings cited above, it seems unwise to interpret the comparatively high level of public mistrust indicated in responses to question 5 of the GPD survey as fully equivalent to a belief that the government is not doing enough to protect citizens' privacy rights. It also seems likely that a portion of those respondents for question 17 who indicated that government security laws are either somewhat intrusive or highly intrusive might still view such laws as desirable in light of the threat of terrorism. When these points are taken into account, the ABC and Pew Research poll results do not appear to conflict with those of the

GPD survey on the matter of public trust. Taken together, they portray a citizenry that is growing increasingly uneasy about intrusive government security practices, but a substantial majority of this citizenry remain willing to tolerate threats to privacy in the name of greater security.

Perceptions of Media Messages

Roughly one-third of respondents for question 14 indicate that the media gives more attention to terrorism than to government violations of personal privacy, while 10.9% feel that more coverage is given to the latter. A small majority (53.2%) indicate that they do not know or are not sure. In the case of question 15, 44.5% of respondents perceive a bias toward greater coverage of stories about terrorism, while only 7.1% believe that more media attention is given to stories about private-sector violations of the personal privacy of consumers. An additional 23.5% indicate that equal coverage is given to both, while 24.8% are not sure. The results for question 13 indicate that 29.1% of Americans believe that a lot of media coverage is given to stories about the safety of personal information, while 46.6% feel that "some coverage" is provided. Thirteen per cent indicate "not much coverage," 2.4% selecte "no coverage at all," and 8.9% are not sure. Overall, public perceptions appear consistent with what is likely to be the reality in terms of actual levels of news coverage for these topics, a point that will be taken up later in the analysis.

THE LARGER CONTEXT: AMERICA AS A GLOBAL POWER AND SECURITY STATE

Public attitudes toward recent US government surveillance initiatives conducted in the name of homeland security have clearly been influenced by the events of 9/11, a fact borne out by numerous polls conducted from 2001 onward. However, it should also be kept in mind that America's drift toward a national security state model of governance was already well underway before the 9/11 attacks, dating back to at least the 1980s (Lyon 2003). Similarly, achieving military as well as economic and communicative global dominance has been central to US foreign policy since the end of the Second World War (Johnson 2001, 2004; Schiller 1998; Wallerstein 2003). These larger realities should be taken into account when assessing the survey findings, as they hold potentially significant implications with respect to both citizens' trust in government and the media's role in shaping relevant public attitudes. The latter two issues will be considered in turn with some necessary overlap.

"Trust" in Context: American Attitudes toward the role of the State

Popular distrust of the federal government has a long history in the United States. At the same time, it should be recognized that widespread, grassroots skepticism toward the notion of "big government" has traditionally had less to do with the size of government per se than with widespread sentiments concerning those areas in which it is considered appropriate for the state to invest financial, technological, and human resources. Significantly, the rapid growth of America's military-industrial complex after the Second World War, its open-ended War on Terror, and a related expansion of surveillance and policing powers at home do not *necessarily* conflict with such sentiments. And numerous polls indicate broad public support for state powers introduced or expanded after 9/11. These points hold importance in relation to the GPD survey findings. They suggest that despite growing public concern about government monitoring of citizens, political leaders may still be able to rely on high levels of patriotism and/or nationalist sentiment when attempting to gain support for domestic surveillance practices. As with the case of military actions abroad, it is the ability to link relevant policies to questions of national security that appears critical.

Before we proceed further, it should be noted that the terms "welfare state" and "security state" are being employed here for heuristic purposes, namely to designate a general shift toward a mode of governance less concerned with an equitable distribution of public resources and more oriented toward reducing risks to state and corporate interests – particularly those risks associated with participation in the global economy. The two concepts need not be understood as mutually exclusive and refer primarily to changes in emphasis in government policymaking. Significantly, this shift in emphasis gained momentum in 2001. As David Lyon (2003, 4) makes clear, the 9/11 attacks provided the opportunity for those with an interest in expanding the state's surveillance capacities to integrate and exploit "existing ideas, policies, and technologies" in the name of the War on Terror. Both the Patriot Act, which was passed into law on 26 October 2001 (after virtually no political debate), and the Department of Homeland Security, created in 2002, now provide the federal government with unprecedented "preventive" powers to combat potential threats to the state and its citizens (EPIC 2006; Lyon 2003).

Arguing that privacy is a concept "whose time has come and gone," Calvin Gottlieb (1996, 162) cites the general lack of attention devoted to privacy issues by politicians in Western democracies during election time. Gottlieb attributes this lack of attention to the high likelihood that politicians have a better sense of what is important to voters than do academics, lawyers, and journalists. Putting aside for the moment the question of whether journalists are doing an adequate job of keeping the public informed about privacy issues – a matter that may in turn have implications with respect to attitudes – it is certainly worth heeding Gottlieb's larger point. This concerns the persistence of a general trend whereby consumers/citizens have proven ready and willing to sacrifice personal information for perceived benefits, especially in the commercial sphere. Although the intrusive state measures introduced in the wake of 9/11 may or may not represent a special case in this regard, the rhetoric of "tradeoffs" is certainly worth holding in mind for present purposes. The equation of less privacy with greater security is virtually the sole formula invoked by policymakers and industry leaders when attempting to rationalize such initiatives as the Patriot Act. At the same time, the causes – and hence potentially more effective solutions – to the problem of foreign-inspired terrorism are typically ignored. The latter point will be returned to in the next section.

Americans arguably have been more culturally predisposed to (further) abandoning the welfare state model of government than have the citizens of other Western liberal democracies. Ulrich Beck (2000, 111–12) cites the results of a 1992 poll conducted by the *Economist* in this regard. The poll in question was designed to survey value attitudes in Western democracies around such notions as "freedom" and "equality." One salient finding of the poll was that although 60% of Germans and 80% of Austrians felt that the state should intervene to bring about greater income equality in the face of the free market, 80% of Americans were opposed to the idea. In like vein, a recent study by William Epstein (2004) suggests that the American public has long been skeptical of the idea that the state should be proactive in the area of social welfare. In addition, the study found that pronounced differences in outlook among various groups in society, particularly blacks versus whites, have decreased markedly over the past few decades.

Epstein's (2004, 470) research involved the examination of numerous polls, including the General Social Surveys (1972–98), the National

Elections Surveys (1948–98), and the CBS/*New York Times* polls (since 1976). He concluded that a general consensus, one cutting across categories such as race, class (including the rich and very poor), and union versus nonunion households, has long characterized popular attitudes toward social welfare. This consensus is one "which has cemented a position quite a bit to the right of center, ideologically centered on voluntary civic participation and good character – 'compassionate conservatism': communitarianism rather than communalism" (Epstein 2004, 475).

Findings such as those cited above may help account, at least in part, for the results of an ABC poll conducted in January 2002. ABC's polling director, Gary Langer, designed a survey to reassess what appeared to be a dramatic upsurge in public trust in government after 11 September 2001. This upsurge was widely interpreted by politicians, as well as by the foreign and domestic press, to be a direct consequence of the 9/11 attacks. The poll in question took the form of a split-survey. Half of the respondents were asked the first of the two questions shown below, and the other half were asked the second:

> Question: When it comes to handling national security and the war on terrorism, how much of the time do you trust the government in Washington to do what is right? Would you say just about always, most of the time, or only some of the time?

> Question: When it comes to handling social issues like the economy, health care, Social Security and education, how much of the time do you trust the government in Washington to do what is right? Would you say just about always, most of the time, or only some of the time? (Langer 2002, 8–9)

Significantly, whereas 68% of respondents indicated that they trusted government to handle national security issues "just about always" or "most of the time," only 38% said they trusted it to handle social issues "just about always" or "most of the time" (Langer 2002, 9).

It seems plausible that the low level of public trust indicated in responses to the second split-survey question may be a reflection not only of the contentious nature of the social welfare issues listed, a possibility noted by Langer (2002, 9), but also of deep-seated populist ideals holding that the role of the state should remain limited, as suggested above. Traditionally, this "limited" role has often been understood in libertarian terms, referring to the state's obligation to maintain law and order and defend property rights at home while protecting its citizens from foreign threats. At the very least, the results for the ABC poll suggest that what changed after the 9/11 attacks was not public trust in government as such but rather "the context in which that trust was being evaluated and expressed" (Langer 2002, 9). More specifically, the poll results lend support to the idea that the high levels of public trust widely reported after the events of 9/11 primarily signified both American patriotism as expressed by a willingness to rally behind the president in a time of national crisis and approval of the state's military role in the face of foreign (or foreign-inspired) threats. Broader changes to attitudes concerning other functions, institutions, or policies of government were likely negligible or nonexistent (Chanley 2002; Langer 2002).

As suggested earlier, poll results dealing with public attitudes toward government may be strongly influenced not only by how survey designers utilize such terms as "trust," "mistrust," or "confidence" but also by the particular institutions, branches of government, policies, politicians, or incidents that respondents are likely to have foremost in mind at the time they are interviewed (Chanley 2002; Cook and Gronke 2005). Langer (2006) suggests that this tendency may help to account for differences in attitudes toward NSA wiretapping as measured by an ABC poll taken on 12 May 2006 versus one conducted by *Newsweek* on 10 and 11 May 2006. Both polls were administered shortly after the NSA phone-record logging program was disclosed to the public by USA *Today* on 10 May 2006. The key questions for each poll, ABC and *Newsweek* respectively, were as follows:

It's been reported that the National Security Agency has been collecting the phone call records of tens of millions of Americans. It then analyses calling patterns in an effort to identify possible terrorism suspects without listening to or recording the conversations. Would you consider this an acceptable or unacceptable way for the federal government to investigate terrorism? Do you feel that way strongly or somewhat?

As you may know, there are reports that the NSA, a governmental intelligence agency, has been collecting the phone call records of Americans. The agency doesn't actually listen to the calls but logs in nearly every phone number to create a database of calls made within the United States. Which of the following comes CLOSER to your own view of this domestic surveillance program? It is necessary to combat terrorism. [Or] It goes too far in invading people's privacy. (Cited in Langer 2006)

In the case of the ABC poll, 63% said the program was "acceptable," while 35% indicated it was "unacceptable." By contrast, only 41% of respondents for the *Newsweek* poll said the program was "a necessary tool," while 53% said that it "goes too far" (Langer 2006).

Langer (2006) argues that several differences between the two news polls probably had an impact on the responses for each. For example, he notes that the ABC poll asked two general preliminary questions: whether the American government, as it then stood, was doing enough to protect Americans' rights; and which was more important at the time, investigating terror or preventing intrusions on privacy. He argues that these questions may have inspired respondents to think about "the tradeoffs between these two, highly desirable aims" (Langer 2006). He also suggests that the term "necessary tool" may represent a higher bar in the minds of respondents than "acceptable." Most notably, Langer (2006) points out that the ABC poll describes the rationale for the NSA practices, whereas the *Newsweek* poll does not. Unlike the ABC poll, which states that the NSA analyzes calling patterns to identify possible terrorism suspects, the *Newsweek* poll doesn't explain what the NSA is doing with collected phone records. Hence "it may be harder to say something like this is OK without knowing its purpose" (Langer 2006).

Interestingly, Langer (2006) appears to find the ABC poll (which he oversaw) as the better measure of public attitudes than the *Newsweek* poll, due to the fact that it explicitly connects NSA wiretapping to the goal of preventing terrorism. Consequently, he chooses to overlook that the surveillance practices in question could very well be used for other purposes, such as spying on antiwar activists, environmentalists, or others critical of state policies. Significantly, however, that the ABC poll might be "biased" in this respect may actually make it a more meaningful measure of relevant public attitudes. This is the case not because the ABC poll necessarily describes reality more accurately, as Langer (2006) implies, but rather due to the reflexive nature of public opinion. More specifically, the context within which American attitudes are being shaped is one in which the mass media regularly and uncritically collapse the issues of terrorism and security/surveillance into a single problematic. This issue will be given further attention in the next section.

When viewed against the findings of earlier polls, the GPD survey results for questions 5 and 17 indicate that there has in fact been growing public

concern about government surveillance of citizens, even when such practices are held up against the need for greater security. However, that
most citizens continue to defend the government's "right" to employ special powers to prevent terrorism may be more telling. It should be noted
that many or most recent polls measuring public attitudes toward state
surveillance practices have drawn specific attention to the contentious
issue of the NSA's warrantless wiretapping program, news of which was
first broken by the *New York Times* on 16 October 2005. Although the
NSA program was not declared unconstitutional until 17 August 2006,
debates and questions concerning its legality were already being widely
circulated by the media. Such issues were almost certainly on the minds
of many respondents to the GPD survey, which was conducted in the
United States between 27 June and 28 July 2006. This was not long
after 10 May 2006, when *USA Today* revealed that AT&T, Verizon, and
BellSouth had been providing the NSA with the domestic phone records
of millions of Americans since 2001. Hence widespread acceptance of
such a controversial program may indicate even greater public tolerance
for less conspicuous, ostensibly legal forms of state surveillance.

Media Messages and Public Opinion

Discussion in this section proceeds from two basic premises. The first,
by now well established in mass media research, is that "in all political
and economic systems, news 'coincides with' and 'reinforces' the definition of the political situation evolved by the political elite" (Murdock
1973, 172). The mechanisms, both direct and indirect, through which
this situation is sustained within democratic societies have been well
documented in the work of various media researchers, including James
Curran (2000), Ben Bagdikian (2004), Edward Herman and Noam
Chomsky (1988), and Robert McChesney (2004), and will not be re-
viewed here. However, references to specific influences on media content
will be made where relevant. The second premise informing this discussion is that the media represent one of the most important forces shaping public opinion. Although they are by no means the only significant
influence on human attitudes, and even though the media reflect as well
as shape popular sentiments and beliefs, it is also clear that the mass
media hold a privileged position in information-based societies such as
the United States. As Greg Philo and Mike Berry (2004, 94) remark,
the media "are central to the exercise of power in society" and "can set
agendas in the sense of highlighting some news stories and topics, but

they can also severely limit the information with which we understand events in the world."

To begin, it should be noted that the GPD survey results for questions 13 to 15, which deal with public perceptions of media messages, do appear to be relatively consistent with what most of the media studies literature would predict, and with what recent evidence suggests, concerning actual media content. That is, public perceptions concerning the *proportion* of media coverage in the areas of privacy/security versus terrorism appear to reflect what the media likely are disseminating on a regular basis. For example, the survey results for questions 14 and 15 indicate that the public feels the media are devoting relatively more attention to governmental as opposed to corporate violations of privacy. This seems probable in light of recent media attention to the NSA wiretapping program. The survey findings for questions 13 to 15 also suggest that although most of the public (75.7%) believe that some coverage (46.6%) or a lot of coverage (29.1%) is being given to stories about the safety of personal information, roughly one-third of Americans also feel that more media attention is being devoted to stories about terrorism than to stories about either governmental or corporate violations of privacy.[5] That the subject of terrorism makes for press at least as sensational as the issue of information privacy should be fairly clear. That terrorism also represents a much "safer" news topic, one readily made compatible with state propaganda concerning the War on Terror, is a point that will be returned to shortly.

News media criticism of governmental and corporate conduct, as it occurs within democratic societies such as the United States, rarely strays beyond the range of debate visible within mainstream political circles and/or state- and corporate-sponsored think-tanks (Herman and Chomsky 1988; McMurtry 1998). One consequence is that the very presence of such criticism tends to make the press appear far more "free" with respect to both its willingness and its ability to play the role of watchdog than is indicated by its actual ties to, and dependence upon, state and corporate goodwill. News reports dealing with foreign and domestic policies implemented in the name of the War on Terror provide a good example. As Ian Lustick (2006, 14) observes, the American media are now "filled with arguments, including criticism of how the War on Terror is prosecuted, that nonetheless establish its rationale and scale as unquestionably appropriate." Hence, rather than being the target of extensive media critique, the War on Terror has become the background narrative against which definitions of problems, categories of analysis, and the boundaries of acceptable opinion are framed (see Lustick 2006, 8–28). In this sense, widespread media attention to such necessarily controversial issues as the NSA's warrantless wiretapping program may arguably serve to mask the more far-reaching implications of an underlying elite consensus. This consensus is reflected in the broad bipartisan support for the expansion of state powers – enabled by private-sector tools and services – in the areas of law enforcement and surveillance after 9/11.

The Patriot Act of 2001 was unprecedented in granting new surveillance and investigative powers to the state (Lyon 2003). Sweeping changes were made to US law, including amendments to the following: Wiretap Statute (title 3), Electronics Communications Privacy Act, Computer Fraud and Abuse Act, Foreign Intelligence Surveillance Act, Family Education Rights and Privacy Act, Pen Register and Trap and Trace Statute, Money Laundering Act, Immigration and Nationality Act, Money Laundering Control Act, Bank Secrecy Act, Right to Financial Privacy Act, and Fair Credit Reporting Act (EPIC 2006). Yet despite its tremendous scope and obvious import, evidence suggests that the public have not been well informed about the nature of this Act. A survey conducted by the University of Connecticut in August 2005 found that although 64% of Americans said they support the Patriot Act and 57% said they are familiar with its contents, only 42% were able to identify its primary intent of "enhancing surveillance procedures for federal law enforcement agencies."[6] The study also found that the more citizens knew about the Act, the less likely they were to support it. Fifty-seven per cent of those who knew the intent of the legislation indicated support, compared to 70% of those who could not identify its intent.

Although Americans appear ill-informed about the scope and scale of their government's new surveillance activities, a relentless stream of media stories about the threat posed by international terrorism has underscored their apparent necessity (Arsenault and Castells 2006; Kellner 2005). Politicians and government spokespersons have been quick to exploit public anxieties in this regard, frequently positing a direct link between the need for greater surveillance at home ("homeland security") and ongoing military operations abroad (the "war on terror"). One example concerns statements made by President Bush during a Washington news conference in August 2006, in which he defended his administration's policies in Iraq. While criticizing a federal judge's ruling of 17 August 2006 that the NSA's warrantless wiretapping program was both unconstitutional and in violation of the Foreign Intelligence Services Act, Bush tied both the NSA program and US policies in Iraq directly to the War on

Terror: "Those who heralded the decision not to give law enforcement the tools necessary to protect the American people just simply don't see the world the way we do. They see maybe these kind of incidents. These aren't isolated incidents; they're tied together. There is a global war going on ... A failed Iraq in the heart of the Middle East will provide safe haven for terrorists and extremists" (CNN.com 2006).

More often than not, such statements are circulated endlessly by the media with little in the way of relevant background information, appraisals concerning the accuracy of specific claims, or critique of underlying policies (Philo 2002; McChesney 2004).

A recent investigation conducted by the Center for International and Security Studies at Maryland (CISSM) concerning American media coverage of "weapons of mass destruction" (WMD) for the periods 5–26 May 1998, 11–31 October 2002, and 1–21 May 2003 revealed a persistent distortion of key facts and a general lack of balance in news reporting on this topic (Moeller 2004). Much of this imbalance was attributed to the "inverted pyramid" approach to news writing. Ironically, this convention is closely related to a journalistic concern with "objectivity" – the idea that facts and statements should be presented "just as they are" without interpretation by reporters. Greatest weight is given to the statements of "key players" such as political leaders, with (any) criticism left to rival politicians or establishment experts (Moeller 2004; Schudson 2003). The end result in this case was that the White House set the news agenda (Moeller 2004, 7). For example, the media followed the administration's lead by lumping together unrelated forms of weaponry and warfare under the broad category of WMD and, even more significant, by consistently associating WMD with terrorism. With respect to the latter tendency, the report states, "That is undoubtedly an accurate reflection of common fears, but is not an accurate representation of established fact. No terrorist organization has yet demonstrated the capacity to perform an act of mass destruction under a strict definition of that term. There is an important difference between common fears, however prudent they might seem, and actionable threat. It is extremely important that those who wield American power understand the difference. Media coverage did not acknowledge that distinction during the periods examined, and that is an evident defect" (Steinbruner 2004, iii).

In light of the above, it is worth noting that a Harris poll conducted on 21 July 2006 found that 50% of Americans continue to believe that WMD were uncovered in Iraq after US troops invaded that country in March 2003 (Harris Interactive 2006).[7]

Numerous surveys indicate that negative public perceptions of Arabs and Islam increased markedly in the years following 9/11. Although this development is perhaps unsurprising, it should also be recognized that the demonization of Arabs and/or Muslims has a long history in the US news and entertainment media, a trend closely tied to America's material and strategic interests in the Middle East (see Karim 2003, McAlister 2001, Said 1994, 1997). Significantly, negative public attitudes have not been restricted to views about specific leaders, organizations, or terror suspects and include widespread perceptions about the nature of the Islamic faith. According to Pew Research, a growing number of Americans (25% in 2002 versus 44% in 2003) believe that Islam is more likely than other religions "to encourage violence among its believers" (Pew Research 2003). Similarly, a poll conducted by ABC in March 2006 found that 58% of the public believe that there are "more violent extremists in Islam" than among the followers of other faiths, compared to 38% of the public in 2002. The same poll found that 46% of Americans hold a generally unfavourable opinion of Islam (ABC News/*Washington Post* 2006b).

The GPD survey reveals that the American public, like the publics of most of the other countries polled, is generally uncomfortable with the idea of increased security checks for certain visible minorities in potential risk situations such as the boarding of airplanes.[8] However, a survey commissioned by Cornell University's Department of Communication indicates that a significant minority of Americans do favour differential treatment for some individuals and groups with respect to government surveillance practices. More specifically, a direct link was found between negative perceptions of Islam and of Muslim Americans and attitudes toward restrictions on civil liberties proposed or initiated after 9/11. A brief summary of the study's key findings is presented in *Cornell News* (2004):

> About 27 percent of respondents said that all Muslim Americans should be required to register their location with the federal government, and 26 percent said they think that mosques should be closely monitored by U.S. law enforcement agencies. Twenty-nine percent agreed that undercover law enforcement agents should infiltrate Muslim civic and volunteer organizations, in order to keep tabs on their activities and fund raising. About 22 percent said the federal government should profile citizens as potential threats based on the fact that they are Muslim or have Middle Eastern heritage. In all, about 44 percent said they believe that some curtailment of liberties is necessary for Muslim Americans.

Significantly, the Cornell study also revealed a direct correlation between television news watching habits, a respondent's fear level, and attitudes toward restrictions on civil liberties for *all* Americans. Those who watched the most news were also the most likely to favour state restrictions on civil liberties, such as greater authority to monitor the Internet. Interestingly, these findings resonate with a large body of survey research conducted by George Gerbner and his associates, suggesting a positive correlation between the time Americans spend watching television and their fear of violent crime. A central premise advanced in Gerbner's "cultivation theory" research is that in comparison to light or moderate viewers, heavy television viewers are generally more inclined to perceive the world as a violent and dangerous place and to harbour unrealistic fears about threats to their personal safety. Gerbner's work also has direct implications with respect to the issue of trust in political institutions. Like the Cornell study, it suggests that harsh law enforcement policies are more likely to be perceived by heavy television viewers as necessary for the maintenance of public safety and social order (see Gerbner 1998, Gerbner et al. 1994).

It is important to emphasize that both the actual threat posed by foreign-inspired terrorism on the American mainland and the efficacy of measures enacted to prevent it have been grossly exaggerated by political leaders, commercial advocates of surveillance technologies, and the popular media. For example, John Mueller (2006, 5) notes that intelligence estimates from 2002 held that as many as five thousand al-Qaeda terrorists and supporters were living in the United States. Yet a secret FBI report from 2005 revealed that after more than three years of well-funded investigation, no true al-Qaeda sleeper cells had been located anywhere in the country. Likewise, the NSA's massive wiretapping program has not led to a single indictment on any charge (Mueller 2006, 5). Even assuming the presence of a serious terrorist threat within US borders, wiretapping and other forms of surveillance, such as those associated with ID cards, biometrics, or closed circuit television (CCTV) face-recognition technologies, appear poorly suited for coping with it (see Lyon 2003, 62–87).

It seems doubtful that the character of news coverage given to the issues of terrorism, state surveillance, and/or homeland security will change significantly in the foreseeable future. And the US government remains committed to influencing public attitudes toward both foreign and domestic policies implemented as part of the War on Terror. For example, in late 2002 Secretary of Defence Donald Rumsfeld created the new position of deputy undersecretary of defence for special plans. The "special plans" in question include managing and restricting public information and controlling news sources (Johnson 2004, 298–300; Lustick 2006, 159). In January 2003 the White House created the Office for Global Communications to influence public opinion both domestically and abroad (Johnson 2004, 299). There has also been mounting pressure on universities to eliminate curriculum deemed "unpatriotic." On 31 October 2003 Congress passed a bill (HR 3077) that could require international studies departments to show greater support for American foreign policy or risk losing their federal funding (see Goldberg 2003, Roy 2005). A main target of the bill was the influential body of post-colonial theory developed by Edward Said from 1978 to 2003. Much of Said's work critically examines the relationship(s) between popular media and news representations of Arabs, Islam, and the Middle East, on the one hand, and US foreign policy, on the other.

CONCLUDING REMARKS

The GPD survey results for questions 5 and 17 suggest that American attitudes toward government surveillance have not remained static since 2001. When held against the results of earlier polls, they indicate that the public has grown more concerned about the intrusive nature of state surveillance practices initiated or expanded after the 9/11 attacks. However, when the survey results are considered in conjunction with credible evidence obtained elsewhere, they also suggest that a majority of the public will continue to demonstrate tolerance for such practices, even when faith that the government will safeguard individual privacy rights remains low. Such tolerance cannot be adequately appreciated without attention to the role played by the mass media in shaping public opinion.

Considerable evidence suggests that public support for state surveillance practices is greatest when the threat of terrorism and the need for national security are strongly associated in the minds of citizens. The survey results for questions 13 to 15, in addition to numerous studies of media content, make it clear that both the quality and quantity of relevant news stories are contributing strongly to this association. At the same time, the media tend to obscure the systemic and pervasive nature of state surveillance policies, to accept uncritically the official rationales provided for their implementation, and to provide a misleading picture of the threat posed by terrorism. It appears fairly certain that the media will continue to contribute to a mindset, already widespread among the American public, whereby the state's expanding surveillance powers are understood as the necessary, if unattractive, price for greater security.

NOTES

1 Unless otherwise indicated, all references to "government" and/or "(the) state"
   should be understood as references to the US federal government.
2 See the appendix to this volume for the complete text of the relevant survey
   questions. The findings of interest here pertain to public trust in government
   as indicated in responses to questions 5 and 17 of the GPD survey and pertain
   to public perceptions of media messages as measured by responses to questions 13, 14, and 15.
3 TNS Telecoms and its predecessor, Chilton Research Services, have been ABC
   News's primary fieldworker provider since 1979. ABC News closely oversees
   the sampling and fieldwork procedures of TNS Telecoms (see Langer and
   Merkle 2006).
4 The January poll was conducted shortly after the *New York Times* (see Risen
   and Lichtblau 2005) revealed on 16 December 2005 that the NSA had been
   authorized to eavesdrop without warrants on international phone calls and
   e-mails involving American citizens. The May poll was conducted almost immediately after *USA Today* (see Cauley 2006) disclosed on 10 May 2006 that
   major US telecommunications companies were providing the NSA with the
   domestic phone records and e-mails of countless Americans.
5 The GPD survey also found that roughly one-third of the public in France believed more attention was given to stories about terrorism than either corporate or governmental violations of privacy. By contrast, approximately half of
   the public in Canada, Mexico, and Brazil held this view.
6 The other options from which respondents could choose were as follows: supplying body armour and higher combat pay for soldiers in Iraq; the procedures
   for interrogating suspected terrorists in foreign countries; and the security of
   airliners and other forms of transportation.
7 This was long after United Nations (UN) inspectors (2002–03) and an independent American survey (2004) concluded that any previous biological,
   chemical, and nuclear arms programs had been dismantled in 1991 under UN
   supervision (see Johnson 2004, 302–6).
8 The notable exceptions were Mexico and Spain, where the public was much
   more comfortable with this idea. See Summary of Findings (November 2008)
   p. 33 at http://www.sscqueens.org/research/intl_survey (accessed 24 February
   2010).

Quebec, the Rest of Canada, and the International Survey: A Case of Two Solitudes? A Comparative Analysis of Perceptions about Privacy and Personal Information Issues

FRANÇOIS FOURNIER

INTRODUCTION

In 2006 the Globalization of Personal Data (GPD) project team responsible for the international surveillance survey expressed its interest in carrying out a comparative analysis of survey results between Quebec and the rest of Canada (ROC). Preliminary analyses suggested significant differences between these two national groups with respect to attitudes toward privacy and the confidentiality of personal information.[1] Looking for and studying social, political, and cultural differences between Quebecers and the ROC have been part of the fabric of Canada practically since its foundation in 1867. The GPD team's request for a paper comparing Quebec and ROC attitudes reflects its interest in cross-cultural comparisons on issues related to privacy and surveillance in the context of the global flow of personal information.

Comparing Quebec with the ROC may suggest that the ROC is considered a homogeneous sociological, political, and cultural entity. This is clearly not the case. Indeed, where seemingly significant differences appear between Quebec and the ROC, one can also observe where other individual provinces or regions stand on these particular issues. This process will help to better identify true variations between Quebec and ROC respondents.

Clearly, any public opinion poll captures only a fraction of the reality it is intended to examine. But the GPD survey represents both a unique and valuable initiative to encapsulate public opinion in today's world on matters of privacy and personal information. It does not tell the whole story on these matters – for example, there were no questions with respect to personal *health* data of electronic nature – but it certainly enlightens important dimensions that should nourish public debate and policy.[2]

The survey questions I have chosen to scrutinize fall under two headings: (1) comparative perceptions of individual control, knowledge of laws, and proactivity regarding personal information; and (2) comparative perceptions of trust in public- and private-sector practices with respect to the collection and sharing of personal information. I present the results with an analysis of possible significant differences and, further, highlight where apparent differences may not be as significant as the numbers make them appear. This begs the questions what is the state of Canadian opinion on these issues, and what are the meaningful differences between the Quebec and the ROC public opinions?

COMPARATIVE PERCEPTIONS OF INDIVIDUAL CONTROL, KNOWLEDGE OF LAWS, AND PROACTIVITY REGARDING PERSONAL INFORMATION

In this first section, I examine respondents' sense of control over their personal information, their perceived knowledge about the laws, and how they react when faced with situations in which their personal information may appear to be at risk. These questions measure respondents' general awareness with respect to their personal information (PI).

Sense of Control over One's Personal Information

The question reads, "To what extent do you have a say in what happens to your personal information?" This pertains to the degree of control, or level of influence, citizens feel they experience with respect to their PI.

- Overall, 80% of Canadians feel they have some sort of say, but mostly partial, over their PI.
- Compared to Quebecers, a significantly higher proportion of other Canadians believe they have at least some degree of control – *Some, A lot*, or *Complete* – over their PI (85% and 66%, respectively).
- More respondents from Quebec are inclined to consider they have *No say at all* (24% compared to 14%). In addition, more of them are likely to have refused to answer or to have answered that they don't know (10% compared to 1%).

Table 7.1
Responses regarding perceived degree of control over PI (%)

To what extent do you have a say in what happens to your personal information? Would you say you have...	Quebec	Rest of Canada	Difference
Complete say	12.1	8.8	+3.3
A lot of say	23.8	20.6	+3.2
Some say	30.0	55.5	-25.5
No say	23.8	14.3	+9.5
Refused/Don't know	10.4	0.8	+9.6
Total	100.0	100.0	Significant p = 0.000[a]

a All answers with p < 0.05, where p is the significance level, are considered to express statistically significant differences between our two national subgroups. For example, p = 0.000 means that it is extremely unlikely that observed discrepancy is due only to randomness in sampling. The statistician of the survey team has calculated the significance level for each question and has established the cut-off point to be 0.05. If the p-value points to differences that *may* be significant, it is ultimately the interpretation of the results that either gives real socio-cultural meaning to these statistical differences or in some cases deflates them.

· Whereas 23% of interviewees from British Columbia and the Atlantic provinces responded *No say at all*, this feeling of alienation from one's own PI drops to 11% or 12% in Alberta, Ontario, and Manitoba/Saskatchewan.

If 80% of all Canadians feel they have at least some control over the handling and circulation of their PI, another way of reading the numbers is to conclude that two-thirds of respondents answered that they do not have a lot of say – only *Some say* or *No say at all* – over their PI. This leaves open the question are citizens alarmed by such a situation, or do they feel this is inevitable in today's world, characterized by widespread circulation of PI?

The comparison between Quebec and the ROC shows clearly that more ROC respondents feel they have some sort of control over their PI.[3] This difference is congruent with a 1998 EKOS survey showing that 60% of Quebecers and 51% of Canadians from the ROC felt they had less personal privacy in their daily life than had been the case ten years prior.[4]

This question was the second question put to respondents. One can speculate as to whether the total percentage of those who feel they have *Complete*, *A lot*, or *Some* say would have been lower if the question had been asked closer to the end of the survey; indeed, over the course of the survey people may have grown more reflective or skeptical about their actual degree of control over their PI.

Awareness of Laws on Personal Information in Canada

The next question refers to the level of knowledge or awareness that Canadians perceive they have of Canadian laws affecting personal information: "How knowledgeable are you about the laws in Canada that deal with the protection of personal information in government departments, and in private companies?"

- Government departments: A slight majority of Canadians from the ROC (51%) feel *Very* or *Somewhat knowledgeable*, whereas this is the case for only 35% of Quebecers. Almost twice as many Quebecers as other Canadians feel *Not at all knowledgeable* (26% compared to 15%). If one includes the responses for the category *Not very knowledgeable*, the margin diminishes but remains significant at 64% compared to 49%.
- Private companies: The same trend appears here in that 44% of Canadians from the ROC, compared to 30% of Quebecers, feel *Very* or *Somewhat knowledgeable*. Twice as many Quebecers feel *Not at all knowledgeable* (32% compared to 16%). Again, if one adds the answers for the category *Not very knowledgeable*, the margin decreases but is still sizable at 70% compared to 56% (see GPD table 7(a) online).[5]

The numbers show a discrepancy between Quebec and the ROC for PI laws pertaining both to government departments and to private-sector companies.

One possible explanation for this discrepancy relates to how Quebec respondents reacted to the framing of the question itself. More specifically, how was the "laws in Canada" part of the question understood by Quebecers and especially by francophones? Could this have been interpreted as laws *outside* Quebec, or federal laws? To anyone familiar with Canadian politics, this is not far-fetched: the fact is that surveys have shown over and over again how francophone Quebecers, even if Quebec is part of Canada, perceive Quebec and the rest of Canada as two quite distinct entities and display less interest in federal institutions.[6] One element that may reinforce such a speculation is that, within the Quebec sample, and with respect to laws pertaining to government departments, 54% of the English respondents felt *Very* or *Somewhat knowledgeable* compared to 33% of the French respondents, and conversely, 46% of the former felt *Not very* or *Not at all knowledgeable*, with 67% for the latter. Similarly, for the laws pertaining to the private sector, the figures for *Very* or *Somewhat knowledgeable*, respectively, are 47.2% and 27%, and those for *Not very* and *Not at all*, respectively, are 53% and 73%.

Another potential interpretation, complementing the previous one, is that although Quebec has extensive – and even cutting-edge – PI laws, governments, consumer groups, and media have faired poorly in explaining them to citizens. In 1997 an EKOS express survey among 550 Quebecers showed that the vast majority of the sample had no knowledge whatsoever of the existence of the Quebec Information and Privacy Commission (CAI) and that two-thirds did not know that there was an Act protecting their privacy applying to private-sector companies (EKOS 1997). More encouraging, in 1999 a survey conducted by the Quebec Statistical Institute (ISQ) asked 2,004 Quebecers, "Are you aware that there are in Quebec laws to protect your personal information and your privacy when you make transactions (e.g., purchase and payment of goods, receipt, etc.)?" Seventy-one per cent answered "yes" (Gouvernement du Québec 1999). In other words, Quebecers seem to be aware that there are general laws protecting personal information, but they do not know the specifics and, possibly, how to make use of them.

Proactivity of Respondents Regarding Protection of Their PI

Other survey questions revolve primarily around actions respondents may or may not have taken to protect their personal information: to what extent do respondents choose to exercise control over their PI in real-life situations? The answers to these questions are also informative of the trust people have in government agencies as opposed to private-sector companies. In other words, they reveal in which context – with the government or with private companies – respondents choose to exercise either more or less control.

Results show that *more* respondents from the ROC take diverse initiatives to protect their PI in interactive contexts with the *private sector*, such as requiring a company to remove them from marketing lists (+19%), refusing to give PI to a business (+18%), asking a company not to sell their PI to another company (+15%), deliberately giving incorrect PI to a marketer (+12%), and enquiring about a business's policies on collection of PI (+11%). However, ROC and Quebec respondents are at par on other proactivity-related issues and in particular with respect to government: refusing to transmit PI to the government, communicating incorrect information to the government, reading online policies of private companies and of government when providing them with PI over the Internet, and asking a company to see what PI they have in their records (see GPD tables 7(b) to (i) online).

Main Findings of the First Section

Three matters have been dealt with in this first section: sense of control over one's PI, knowledge of Canadian PI laws, and proactivity in protecting one's PI. The numbers show that more respondents from the ROC:

- say they are aware of Canadian PI laws relevant to the public and private sectors (+15%);
- feel they have *Some, A lot,* or *Complete* say over their PI (+19%); and
- take diverse initiatives to protect their PI in interactive contexts with the private sector.

It is tempting to try to draw meaningful connections between the results of this first section. For example, the more knowledge of laws there is, the more sense of control one may feel over one's PI, and the more sense of initiative one may expect. If one follows this line of reasoning, it may mean that in Quebec, as compared to the ROC, less information circulates on citizens' rights and practical recourses with regard to their PI and/or that there is less civic education on these issues.

Quebec has the well-deserved reputation in Canada of being *à l'avant-garde* with its PI laws. Does this mean, then, that in Quebec the government, consumer and rights groups, media, and the education system could do better – much better – in terms of informing its citizens about their rights and how to exercise these rights in the context of PI protection? At this point in the analysis, it would certainly be premature to interpret the differences between Quebec and the ROC as the expression of a "cultural trait" of Quebecers that would make them more frivolous with their PI. It appears essentially to be an educational issue, one that should be addressed.

All in all, the survey results show that the majority of ROC and Quebec respondents follow the same patterns and that this majority is simply larger in the case of the ROC (ranging from 10% to 20%). If one takes into account the translation and language issues that I raised for a certain number of questions as well as the relation of Quebecers to Canadian federal institutions, this difference may be even less pronounced.

COMPARATIVE PERCEPTIONS OF TRUST
IN PUBLIC- AND PRIVATE-SECTOR PRACTICES
WITH RESPECT TO THE COLLECTION AND
SHARING OF PERSONAL INFORMATION

The questions under scrutiny in this section involve multiple forms and contexts of as well as reasons for collection, handling, and sharing of personal information: creation of an ID card and of an ID database; PI circulation among and between government agencies, foreign governments, and private-sector interests (businesses, employers, websites); and collection of PI for surveillance purposes. Through these questions, I will examine, directly and indirectly, in whom respondents put greater trust (public versus private sector) and at what level, while continuing to identify significant differences between Quebec and ROC perceptions.

Agreement with and Trust in Governmental Initiatives and Practices

This first subsection addresses respondents' level of agreement with the idea of an ID card and, further, the degree of acceptability of government sharing of personal information with other government agencies, foreign governments, and private-sector organizations.

ID CARD AND DATABASE
The first question to consider is: "Some have suggested that everyone should have a government-issued national ID card that they must carry on them at all times and present it when asked by police or other security forces. To what extent would you agree or disagree with this idea?"

- Over half of all Canadians (53%) *Strongly* or *Somewhat agree* with the idea of a national ID card, while 38% *Somewhat* or *strongly disagree*.
- More Quebecers than other Canadians *Strongly agree* (28% versus 21%). Closest to Quebec on this matter are the Atlantic provinces (26%) and Manitoba/Saskatchewan (25%). When *Strongly* and *Somewhat agree* are added up, both Quebec and the ROC average 50% or more (62% and 50%, respectively). The Manitoba/Saskatchewan region is just behind Quebec with 59%, followed by the Atlantic provinces with 56% (see GPD table 7(j) online).

This is not the first survey to show the relative popularity of an ID card in Quebec (Sondagem 1999, Gouvernement du Québec 1999, Léger et Léger 2000). The idea of creating an ID and/or a voter's card, whether mandatory or optional, has surfaced periodically in Quebec and with special intensity from 1995 to 2001. In 1995 many public actors were voicing their interest in creating such a card: Quebec's chief electoral officer was calling for a mechanism of identification for voters; the Secrétariat d'Inforoute Québec (Quebec Infoway Secretariat) was promoting a multiservice microprocessor card – a "citizen card" – that would give access to governmental services and electronic transactions and that could replace many different existing "nonintelligent" cards; the Régie d'assurance maladie du Québec (Quebec Health Insurance Board) was pushing for its own electronic health card; and Quebec's registrar of civil status also had projects linked to identity. There seemed to be, at that time, a widespread push toward the creation of some sort of a multiuse card. These projects did not succeed, partly because of the joint opposition from the protecteur du citoyen (Quebec ombudsman), the Commission des droits de la personne du Québec (Quebec Human Rights Commission), and the Commission d'accès à l'information du Québec (Quebec Privacy Commission).

Nevertheless, the notion of an ID card remains relatively popular in Quebec and, as previous surveys show, specifically within the francophone population. Until further analysis can be undertaken, I make the assumption that where "national identity" is an issue (i.e., its definition and characterization, whether within minority or majority nations), a national ID card may take on a subjective appeal that outweighs privacy issues. If one follows this line of thought, it could mean that a segment of francophone Quebecers feel that an ID card, no matter how "individual" it is, could somehow protect, reinforce, or validate their collective identity. However, it remains to be seen whether such a card would still be popular among francophone Quebecers if the project was pan-Canadian in scope and piloted by the Canadian government.

The next question addresses issues of the efficiency, as opposed to the legitimacy, of a database containing detailed ID card-related personal information: "In order to put national ID cards into use, the government would need to have a national database containing personal information on all citizens. This information could include address, gender, race, and tax information. How effective do you feel efforts to protect this type of information from disclosure would be?"

This question measures the level of respondents' confidence in government handling of such information. Implicitly, respondents were being asked to indicate their level of comfort with the idea of a central database: will the security measures against potential breaches, or hackers, be adequate, and will the government be tempted to use this information for purposes other than identification?

- Overall, Canadians are divided: 43% feel that government efforts to protect the PI contained in the database from disclosure would be *Very* or *Somewhat effective*, compared to 38% who think the opposite (*Not very* or *Not at all effective*). Another 20% refused to answer or did not know what to answer, suggesting perhaps that the question was long and involved too many issues.
- There is no real significant difference here between Quebec and the ROC. Forty-five per cent of Quebecers and 43% of Canadians from the ROC (Atlantic provinces 49% and Manitoba/Saskatchewan 45%) think government efforts would be *Very* or *Somewhat effective*. However, skepticism – implicit in answers such as *Not very* and *Not effective at all* – is higher among other Canadians than among Quebec respondents (39% compared to 33%). The lowest level of skepticism can be found among respondents from Atlantic provinces and Manitoba/Saskatchewan, with 28% and 29%, respectively (see GPD table 7(k) online).

The small difference between Quebec and the ROC may be due to the fact that some Quebecers are so in favour of an ID card that they are perhaps inclined to accept a trade-off of loss or potential loss of privacy and confidentiality.[7]

GOVERNMENT SHARING PI WITH THIRD PARTIES
The GPD team sought to measure respondents' attitudes on the appropriateness of a government agency sharing citizens' PI with (1) other government agencies, (2) foreign governments, and (3) private-sector entities. Interviewees had to choose one answer out of four: *Always, Never, Yes if citizen is suspected of wrongdoing*, or *Yes if citizen has consented*.

This is the first of a series of three questions: "To what extent do you think it is appropriate for a government agency to share citizens' personal information with other government agencies?"

- Two-thirds of Canadians think it is acceptable for the government to share their PI with another government agency in specific circumstances: 37% if a citizen is suspected of wrongdoing and 30% if the citizen has previously consented. Only 9% of respondents think it is appropriate in any given situation; at the other end, 16% think it is unacceptable in any circumstance.

- A lower percentage of Quebecers than other Canadians would find it appropriate when a citizen is suspected of wrongdoing (32% compared to 38%; 28% for Manitoba/Saskatchewan). Conversely, more Quebecers, as well as respondents from Manitoba/Saskatchewan, would be comfortable in a situation where the citizen has consented to government sharing his/her PI (33% versus 28%) (see GPD table 7(l) online).

Very few Canadians – around 10% – give *carte blanche* to intra-governmental sharing of PI. This result is very informative for public policy, and it invites governments to be transparent with citizens about the contexts in which PI sharing occurs within government.

The second question in this series reads: "To what extent do you think it is appropriate for a government agency to share citizens' personal information with foreign governments?" I will compare the results for this question with the answers given to the previous question.

- Fewer Canadians than was the case in the preceding question think it is acceptable for a government to share its citizens' PI with foreign governments when subject to the same conditions (citizen alleged of wrongdoing or with citizen consent) (59% versus 66%).
- The *Yes under any circumstance* category shrinks by more than half, from 9% to 4%, while the *No under no circumstances* category jumps from 16% to 26%. One Canadian out of ten either refused to answer or didn't know.
- Here again, more Quebecers than ROC respondents would be willing to share PI with foreign governments if the citizen has consented (25% compared to 20%), while more Canadians from the ROC than Quebecers would find it appropriate if the citizen is suspected of wrongdoing (39% compared to 33%).
- Twice as many Quebecers than other Canadians would grant sharing permission to the government in any situation, but the numbers remain quite small (7% versus 3%). And while 27% of the ROC respondents (23% in Ontario) would say *No in any situation*, 24% of Quebecers would offer the same answer (see GPD table 7(m) online).

There is even less enthusiasm than above for *carte blanche* practices with foreign governments. A majority of Canadians are ready to reconsider when they feel good reasons are provided by their government (criminality or citizen consent), but this majority is trimmed by 7%, from 66% to 59%.

The third and last question of this series asks: "To what extent do you think it is appropriate for a government agency to share citizens' personal information with the private sector?"

- In the context of government sharing of PI with the private sector, over one-third of Canadians (39%) would not accept such a practice under any circumstance. This is 20% higher than with another government agency and 13% higher than with a foreign government.
- The percentage of those respondents who would accept government sharing their PI in any situation with the private sector falls to 2% from 9% with other government agencies and from 4% with foreign governments.
- Only half of all Canadian respondents would consider accepting such a sharing with the private sector in the same contexts as above, down from 66% with other government agencies and down from 59% with foreign governments.
- Whereas 48% of respondents from the ROC would accept context-based sharing (i.e., with wrongdoing or consent), 55% of Quebecers would accept such sharing.
- Compared to Canadians from the ROC, more Quebecers (along with Atlantic province respondents) would grant government sharing permission respecting the private sector in any situation, but the numbers are even smaller here (4% compared to 1%). Fewer Quebec respondents would refuse in any given context (35% versus 40%) (see GPD table (7n) online).

With respect to the legitimacy of government sharing PI with third parties, Canadians' level of trust is at its lowest with the private sector. Answers from the ROC and from Quebec follow the same general pattern, with a fraction of Quebecers being more likely to trust government sharing citizens' PI with third parties in any circumstance.

Agreement with and Trust in Private-Sector Initiatives and Practices

This subsection illustrates respondents' degree of faith in private corporations' practices regarding PI – first, in general and including scenarios of PI sharing with third parties and, then, more specifically in the work-place and on the Internet.

GENERAL LEVEL OF TRUST IN PRIVATE COMPANIES
The following question is probably the one that most directly measures, although in a generic fashion, respondents' degree of trust in private-sector handling of PI: "What level of trust do you have that private companies, such as banks, credit card companies and places where you shop, will protect your personal information?"

• Canadians' trust in private companies handling and protecting their PI is evenly split: 47% have a *Reasonably* or *Very high* level of trust, while 51% have a *Fairly* or *Very low* level of trust. Manitoba/Saskatchewan respondents have the highest level of trust (*Reasonably high* or *Very high*) with 59%, while Albertans have the least trust (*Fairly low* or *Very low*) with 57.4%.
• There is no significant difference between Quebecers and other Canadians (see GPD table 7(o) online).

The most significant data here are, perhaps, the very low percentage of Canadians having a very high level of trust in private-sector protection of PI (6%), compared to the 20% who say they have a very low level of trust. The proportion of undecided respondents is relatively low.

PRIVATE SECTOR SHARING PI WITH THIRD PARTIES
A previous set of questions dealt with *government* sharing citizens' PI with third parties (i.e., other government agencies, foreign governments, and the private sector). The questions under study here are exactly the same, except that respondents were now asked their opinion with re-spect to a scenario where *private-sector organizations* would share PI with, and even sell PI to, public or other private third parties.
    The first question reads: "To what extent do you think it is appropriate for a private sector organization to share or sell its customers' personal information with the national government?"

• Seven times more Canadians think it is not appropriate, under any circumstance, for a private-sector organization to share or sell the PI it holds to the government (28% versus 4%). However, almost 60% would accept such sharing with or selling to the government under par-ticular circumstances (i.e., alleged wrongdoing or customer consent).

- A fraction more Quebecers, compared to the ROC, believe it is the organization's right to share PI with the government under any circumstance (6% compared to 3%). In the case of the Manitoba/Saskatchewan region, this percentage rises to 9%, while British Columbia is at 5%.
- More Canadians from the ROC than Quebecers feel that a private-sector organization should never share or sell PI to the government (29% compared to 25%) (see GPD table 7(p) online).

The second question probes sharing with foreign governments: "To what extent do you think it is appropriate for a private sector organization to share or sell its customers' personal information with foreign governments?"

- The gap between the number of Canadian respondents who feel it is always acceptable for a private organization to share PI with or sell PI to a foreign government and those who say the contrary is very significant: only 2% compared to 45%. Forty-four per cent of Canadians say they would consider such actions favourably but only in specific contexts (i.e., customer wrongdoing or with consent).
- Here again, 5% more respondents from the ROC feel this should never happen (46% compared to 41%) (see GPD table 7(q) online).

When one compares perceptions of scenarios with regard to the circulation of PI from government to foreign government versus from the private sector to foreign government, it is shown that considerably fewer Canadians would accept the latter situation, even under specific circumstances. In other words, if a private-sector organization circulated customer PI to foreign governments, this would have considerably less legitimacy than if the national government did the same thing.

The third and last question of the series is: "To what extent do you think it is appropriate for a private sector organization to share or sell its customers' personal information with other private sector organizations?"

- The figures in GPD table 7(r) (online) are quite similar to the ones found in GPD table 7(q) (online). Only 1% of all Canadians answered that a private organization should have the right to share customer PI with or sell customer PI to another private organization under any circumstance, compared to 49% who would never accept this. Forty-three per cent were ready to consider such a practice to be legitimate under certain circumstances (i.e., customer wrongdoing or with consent).

- Here again, more Canadians from the ROC than Quebecers would find sharing between private organizations unacceptable under any circumstance (51% versus 42%).
- Also, there is a difference between Quebec and the ROC with respect to accepting the sharing or selling of PI under specific circumstances: fewer respondents from the ROC would accept PI selling or sharing even under certain circumstances (41% compared to 48%) (see GPD table 7(r) online).

All in all, Canadians are least trusting of PI sharing or selling between private organizations and between a private organization and a foreign government: 49% and 45%, respectively, would oppose it in any circumstance. This decreases to 25% in the case of sharing between a private organization and a national government. This illustrates once more that Canadian respondents have more confidence in government's versus private companies' custodianship and handling of their PI.

There is a small, but consistent, difference between Quebec and ROC respondents throughout the three subquestions: some Quebecers tolerate relatively more sharing of PI by private organizations. Indeed, more Quebecers (+1% to 3%) accept such practices under all circumstances. At the opposite end, more Canadians from the ROC than Quebecers would never accept private-sector sharing of PI with or selling of PI to third parties (+4% to 9%).

EMPLOYERS COLLECTING AND SHARING EMPLOYEES' PI
The next questions relate to the workplace. They measure respondents' opinions regarding surveillance technologies (e.g., surveillance cameras, e-mail checks), and they probe interviewees' feelings on scenarios where employers would share employee PI with the national government or other private-sector organizations.

With regard to surveillance technologies in the workplace, there is no striking difference between Quebec and the ROC. The only difference is that a few more Quebecers would never accept video surveillance or e-mail monitoring (+4%).

Although Quebec and ROC respondents are on the same wavelength regarding the suggestion that employers may share employee PI with the government (conditional agreement, with 67% compared to 70%), the ROC maintains more forcefully than Quebecers that it would never accept such sharing with other private-sector organizations (43% compared to 31%) (see GPD tables 7(s) and 7(t) online).

TRUST IN WEBSITES

The last two questions of the current section relate to Internet perceptions: what is respondents' level of confidence in supplying PI on websites, and who do they think should have the most say over how companies use their websites to track people's activities and PI online (i.e., the website owners, the government, or the individuals)?

With respect to trust in websites when providing PI, the level of concern is high in both national groups but with more worried respondents in the ROC (71% compared to 61%). And when asked who should have more say over how companies use their websites, more Quebecers answered that the government should have the most say (39% versus 23%), whereas other Canadians answered that it is the people using the websites who should have the most say (27% compared to 14%). This contrast may reflect that more Quebecers are ready to put their trust in government, whereas more ROC respondents prefer placing their trust in the individual. This may, however, be a hasty conclusion considering the unusually high percentage of undecided interviewees for that question (40%) (for detailed numbers, see GPD tables 7(u) and 7(v) online).

Main Findings of the Second Section

One consistent finding throughout this section is that Quebec and ROC respondents display more faith in government and public agencies than in private-sector organizations with regard to the handling and use of PI. Recall, for example, that although about 15% of Quebecers and other Canadians find it inappropriate, under any circumstance, for the government to share PI with other public agencies, this proportion soars to over 40% when such a scenario concerns PI sharing between private organizations and remains over 30% in the case of an employer providing PI to a private-sector organization.

As for Quebec and ROC differences, they are not the kinds of discrepancies that reveal completely contradictory tendencies. Differences rarely exceed 10%. Among these differences, mostly minor, with some possibly more meaningful, I have identified that:

- More Quebecers *Somewhat agree* and *Strongly agree* with the development of an ID card (62% versus 50%). The notion of an ID card has always been popular among Quebecers, as previous surveys have shown, but the attempts made by past Quebec governments to set it up have been blocked by a coalition of privacy-related organizations.

The ID card may have a subjective appeal in Quebec and perhaps in other regions in the world where "national identity" is an issue.

- In the scenarios where respondents were asked to judge the appropriateness of government and private-sector organizations sharing PI with third parties, the patterns of response were the same. In most cases, the majority of respondents from the ROC and from Quebec agreed to such sharing but subject to conditions (i.e., in cases of suspected wrongdoing or when consent was previously obtained). A fraction more Quebecers appear to be consistently supportive of the government or private sector sharing the PI they hold with third parties (+1% to 4%), and consequently, a fraction more Canadians from the ROC would always oppose any such sharing (+1% to 7%).

CONCLUSION

I have analyzed over twenty questions throughout this chapter, and about half of the answers appear to display statistically significant differences. On most of these issues, the survey results show that Quebec and the ROC are in tune. The ROC, however, garners wider majorities (from 10% to 20%).

Among the differences that I have identified, more respondents from the ROC:

- feel they have *Some, A lot,* or *Complete* say over their PI (+19%);
- say they are aware of Canadian PI laws relevant to the public and private sector (+15%);
- maintain that they take initiatives to protect their PI when interacting with the private sector: requiring a company to remove them from marketing lists (+19%); refusing to give PI to a business (+18%); asking a company not to sell their PI to another company (+15%); deliberately giving incorrect PI to a marketer (+12%); and enquiring about a business's policies on its PI collection (+11%);
- contend that they would never accept a situation where an employer shared PI of an employee with other private-sector organizations (+12%); and
- are worried about providing PI on websites (+10%).

More Quebecers, on the other hand:

- agree with the notion of setting up an ID card (+12%); and

- would accept the government collecting, in any circumstance, travellers' PI (+10%) and would accept it sharing, in any circumstance, PI with foreign governments (+10%).

Certain aspects of the survey – such as translation and language issues, the high percentage of some *Don't know* answers, and the margin of error for both national groups – may sound warning bells and lead to cautious interpretations.

Also, the identified differences should not detract attention from the many converging answers given by ROC and Quebec respondents. They closely concur:

- on proactivity-related issues: refusing to transmit PI to the government, communicating incorrect PI to the government, reading online policies of private companies and of government when providing PI over the Internet, and asking a company to see what PI it has in its records;
- when they are asked to judge the appropriateness of government and of private companies sharing PI with third parties;
- on their level of trust in private corporations protecting PI; and
- on the issue of employers' surveillance practices (e.g., video surveillance and e-mail checks) in the workplace.

All in all, then, do the mild contrasts between Quebec and ROC responses on privacy and confidentiality issues express a cultural gap between the two groups of respondents? Are Quebecers, for example, asserting specific cultural traits that would make them less aware and less guarded with respect to personal information?

I do think that culture plays a part in some of the differences. For instance, the appeal of an ID card for many Quebecers may have something to do with unsettled "national identity" issues; and the lower level of awareness of PI laws and of related self-initiative may be linked to insufficient civic education on PI and privacy matters in Quebec. I believe, however, that these differences do not reflect clashing values.

There would be grounds to support the idea of a cultural gap if Quebec's privacy institutions and regulations were shaky. This, however, is not the case. In fact, Quebec's leadership in this area is widely recognized throughout Canada. Quebec has strong institutions defending and promoting privacy, such as the Quebec Information and Privacy Commission, the Quebec Human Rights Commission, the Quebec ombudsman, and also active nongovernmental organizations (NGOs) (e.g., La Ligue des droits et libertés). It also has strong privacy legislation, and there is continuous pressure to improve it. The most significant pieces of Quebec's legal framework with respect to privacy, confidentiality, and protection of PI are:

- The Quebec Charter of Human Rights and Freedoms (1982).[8] Section 5 of the chapter on "Fundamental Freedoms and Rights" reads: "Every person has a right to respect for his private life." Section 9 reads: "Every person has a right to non-disclosure of confidential information";
- The Quebec Civil Code, which has seven sections under "Respect of Reputation and Privacy";
- The Act Respecting Access to Documents Held by Public Bodies and the Protection of Personal Information (1982);
- The Act Respecting the Protection of Personal Information in the Private Sector (1994); and
- The Act to Establish a Legal Framework for Information Technology (2001), whose purpose, among others, is to ensure the privacy, integrity, and security of confidential information used to identify individuals, including the use of biometric characteristics or measurements to identify and locate individuals.

The evidence displayed in the comparisons between Quebec and ROC perceptions does not support the case of two solitudes in Canada on matters of privacy and confidentiality. The results of the survey should instead encourage Canadians from all regions to move forward together both toward the reduction of collective insecurities and toward the creative and assertive protection of privacy and personal information.

NOTES

I am deeply grateful to Elia Zureik, leader of the international survey of the GPD project, for inviting me to write this chapter. I am also indebted to Andrey Pavlov, the statistician of the GPD project, who so patiently answered my dozens of requests for information and explanations and who processed the tables I needed. Many thanks to both of them.

1 Indeed, the impression is that Quebecers are, in some aspects, less aware of privacy issues and less guarded with their personal information; see Ipsos Reid 2006.

2 The survey was administered during the summer of 2006 to a Canadian sample of 1,001 respondents: 761 respondents from the ROC (BC, 130; Alberta, 101; Manitoba/Saskatchewan, 69; Ontario, 381; Atlantic provinces, 80) and 240 from Quebec (205 French-speaking and 35 English-speaking). The questionnaire was available in either English or French. Therefore, respondents who did not speak either language were not interviewed. Interviews in Canada were done using Computer-Assisted Telephone Interviewing (CATI) technology, and respondents were screened to ensure nationally representative samples based on gender, age, and regional distribution. In the analysis, one can assume that the variations in perceptions between the two national groups are not the result of biased sampling with regard to respective socio-demographic variables. The margin of error 95 out of 100 times is ±3.55% for the ROC and ±5.57% for Quebec.

3 A translation issue prevents any Quebec-ROC comparison on the sole basis of the first two answers (i.e., *Complete say* plus *A lot of say*). Indeed, the option *A lot of say* was translated for French-speaking Quebecers as *Raisonnablement voix au chapitre*, which, backtranslated, would be *A reasonable say*, quite different from the original English *A lot*. *Raisonnablement* is, in fact, much closer to another possible answer, *Some say*. This inaccurate translation probably accounts for the relatively high Quebec figure for *A lot of say* (24% compared to 21%) and relatively low figure for *More or less say* (30% compared to 56%). It certainly affects previous conclusions based on the addition of *Complete say* and *A lot of say* independently from other answers and suggests that Quebec respondents say they have more control over their personal information than do other Canadians. In fact, the opposite is true. Note that this translation inaccuracy does not apply to the French questionnaire circulated in France, the translation of which was different from the one circulated in Quebec for francophones.

4 It was the third wave of the EKOS Information Highway and the Canadian Communications Household survey that polled 2,201 Canadians (Sciencetech and Gouvernement du Québec 1999).

5 All of the GPD tables cited in this chapter are online at http://www.sscqueens.org/book_tables.

6 For example, a recent Compas poll for the Government of Canada shows that Quebecers, when self-assessing and compared to other Canadians, feel they have less knowledge of federal institutions (De Grandpré 2007).

7 For more discussion of the results on the national ID card in Canada, see Emily Smith's chapter in this volume.

8 The Canadian Charter of Human Rights and Freedoms regulates relations between the citizen and the state, but the Quebec Charter of Human Rights and Freedoms also regulates private relations between citizens.

Eastern vs Western Europe

INTRODUCTION

Elia Zureik

The three chapters in this section deal with two countries in the European component of the Globalization of Personal Data (GPD) survey: France and Hungary. These member-states of the European Union (EU) have in common a centralized state structure in which the national government plays an important role in the regulatory process – more so than in Canada and the United States. The similarity among these European countries ends here, for each country exhibits a different political culture and history that have a bearing on the issues of surveillance and privacy. As pointed out in the chapter on France, privacy is protected by the 1970 Civil Code, understood mainly as the need to protect "private life," with its main focus being the family and personal affairs such as health, love, marriage, and income. In North America, Quebec is an exception. Its 1994 Civil Code is similar to the French Civil Code. Both emphasize a person's dignity and the right to private life.

Until recently, the word "privacy" as understood in Western democracies was not part of the discourse in Hungary, whose experience with surveillance during the communist regime of more than a half-century shaped current attitudes to privacy. Here too privacy centred on family life and intimate affairs rather than on concerns for the protection of personal information in the public and civic domain. Hungary, one of the "new democracies" of central and eastern Europe, has also enacted privacy protection measures in accordance with EU legislation; however, the attitudes of its citizens are coloured by experiences with the ancient regime of Soviet domination. In the chapter on Hungary, Iván Székely compares 1989 public opinion data on privacy to those obtained by the GPD survey. Bearing in mind that the samples and questions used in the two surveys are not identical, he nevertheless finds meaningful comparisons on several privacy issues. A central contribution of the chapter is that it contextualizes the data and explains what appear to be divergent data when comparing Hungary to other Western countries.

When asked in 1989 to indicate which of five main institutions handled personal information "fairly," the workplace and state banks were ranked fairest, while the tax office and bill collectors were rated least fair. Local councils, the fifth institution, occupied an ambiguous place, with a slightly larger percentage rating councils as fair than unfair. With different wording in place, the 2006 GPD survey asked about trust in government and business organizations as handlers of information. Noting the increase in the level of trust over the previous survey, Székely explains that this reflects a general level of increase among EU member-states. But he also points out that this increase in the level of trust is accompanied by a lack of knowledge and awareness of the role of technology. Both surveys indicated disapproval of sharing personal information collected by government agencies and businesses with third parties without the consent of private individuals. With regard to refusal to divulge personal information to government agencies, both surveys indicated that very few were willing to exercise "disobedience," and the majority in both surveys expressed willingness to sacrifice personal information for the sake of safety and national security.

Székely makes the important point that it is not the (invisible) violation of personal privacy by government agencies to which people are opposed but the (visible) appearance that their privacy is being violated. Here he introduces the concept of "threshold of abstraction" to explain that people acquiesce to "invisible" violations of privacy through "abstraction" of data processing and through storage that uses sophisticated technologies beyond the understanding of average citizens. The acquiescence of the younger generation to privacy violations is explained by Székely in the context of wider socio-political changes in Hungary. As part of the "new capitalism" in an environment that is short on social capital, the technocratic generation is willing to tolerate invasion of privacy and to accept limits on individual freedoms and the invisible violations that go with it in order to enjoy economic prosperity.

Several observations from the French data that resonate with the Hungarian data confirm acceptance by the French respondents of the introduction of security technologies, such as closed circuit television (CCTV) and biometrics, in public and private places. Another point at which the French and Hungarian discussions meet is in the contextualizing of privacy, or what Székely calls the "sensitizing context." Privacy is never absolute and has to be understood in terms of place, politics, and culture. Furthermore, in the chapter on France, Ayse Ceyhan stresses the point that there is a need to conceptualize privacy in such a way so as to link it to power. The Foucauldian conception of diffuse power in society is important to bear in mind since it is highly relevant to understanding how privacy violation takes place through invisible technological means and third-party sharing of information. Here, Székely's "threshold of abstraction" meets Foucault's "micropolitics of power."

The French respondents believe there is less privacy nowadays than five years ago, although they know very little about the laws governing privacy protection or about the institutions entrusted with safeguarding privacy. This is in contrast to Canadians, Americans, and Spaniards, who all exhibit a higher level of knowledge. National security and terrorism issues receive extensive media coverage compared to issues of privacy and information protection. Unlike in other Western countries, such as the United States and Canada, the French Labour Code prohibits the collection of data on employees without prior consent, so respondents are opposed to surveillance by employers. With regard to the sharing of information with third parties, the French data show that the majority are opposed to sharing government and private-sector information with third parties. However, 39% believe it is acceptable to share information if the citizen is suspected of wrongdoing, and around one-quarter endorse third-party sharing of information if it is carried out with the consent of the citizen; one-fifth are totally opposed to the sharing of information. There is much less acceptance of the government sharing information with private companies: 45% are totally opposed, 23% believe it is acceptable with the consent of the citizen, but 45% oppose it. Finally, 45% of respondents believe it is acceptable to share information with foreign governments if someone is suspected of wrongdoing; 25% are opposed to such exchanges.

8

Changing Attitudes in a Changing Society? Information Privacy in Hungary, 1989–2006

IVÁN SZÉKELY

INTRODUCTION

Now one of the so-called "new European democracies," Hungary was a communist-led satellite state of the Soviet Bloc from the end of the Second World War to the great political transformation in 1989. These circumstances had a fundamental influence both on the modern evolution of institutionalized privacy protection and on today's public perceptions, knowledge, and attitudes regarding privacy.

Present-day Hungary is a constitutional state with a democratic political system and a well-working market economy, and it is a member-state of the European Union. These political and economic changes have induced a great transformation in society, along with structural changes in people's social status and values. These processes are by no means complete, so in this respect Hungary can still be considered a sort of transitional society.

Along with other more developed, newly democratic countries in the Central and Eastern European region, Hungary was not slow to import new capitalistic methods, including privacy-invasive commercial techniques such as direct marketing and consumer profiling; however, this happened without historical experience or well-developed business ethics. Strong political polarization and the dominance of party politics in the public sphere have also created an environment that invades people's private lives, forcing them to reveal their political views and targeting them as potential voters. This is happening in spite of the fact the country has become a forerunner in institutionalizing informational rights, including information privacy, in its region. Consequently, on the one hand, there is strong institutional protection of information privacy, while on the other hand, people are more vulnerable to practical infringements of their privacy than are their Western fellow citizens.

A DIFFICULT HERITAGE: DISTORTED PRIVACY AND PUBLICITY IN THE SOVIET MODEL

To correctly assess the current situation and the magnitude of the changes, it is essential to understand the Soviet model that dominated the country's politics, law, and social makeup for four decades. Of particular interest are the following attributes of that system:

- The basic informational regime was the exact reverse of expectations in the constitutional democracies. Whereas the Western political ideal was based on the autonomous, self-determining citizen and on the transparent, accountable state, the communist ideal was based on self-determining party-state leadership and on the transparent, accountable citizen.
- Forced collectivism went so far as to bring matters traditionally associated with the sphere of privacy – such as marital disputes – before the local community, which meant the local communist party committee.
- The overriding ideology was intolerant of any form of deviation, with the authorities and party organizations making a point not only of hoarding sensitive data pertaining to dissident behaviour and sentiment but also of publicizing them by way of "instruction" or retribution.
- When the early visions of the cybernetic state and the wired society first emerged, they did not spring from the efficiency principle, as they had in Western democracies, but arose in direct response to the need for a highly centralized administration and surveillance system.
- In the 1970s the universal personal identification code was introduced in Hungary, emulating the Swedish model.[1] This was followed by a system of state population registration based on this code starting in 1974. The personal ID code was used by organizations of all descriptions from retail outlets selling consumer goods to state-run residential banks and the agencies of the Ministry of Interior. In this way, even commercial organizations acquired quasi-administrative powers.
- By keeping the "internal enemies" of the system under surveillance, the secret services and their civilian collaborators perpetuated a situation in which no one could be sure just how much the next person knew about him or her. This constant sense of doubt and distrust massively disfigured human relationships on both the personal and the social levels.

These general tendencies notwithstanding, the regime in Hungary managed to distinguish itself in a positive way from its Soviet Bloc neighbours by allowing a comparatively free flow of Western ideas and the publication of facts and opinion, provided that these were somehow made to fit the conceptual framework of communist ideology. For all these antecedents, the notion of "privacy" is still largely deficient in the Hungarian consciousness, insofar as it is often equated merely with personal intimacies rather than with the private sphere as a whole. The word substituting for the notion of privacy, *magánélet*, means "private life" in English and is associated with family matters, intimate secrets, and the like. This is why the professional literature on informational rights introduced the word "privacy" in Hungarian publications.

THE 1989 SURVEY

In 1989 the State Office for Population Registration (ÁNH), the central authority of communist Hungary responsible for registering citizens' personal data, commissioned a survey by the Hungarian Institute for Public Opinion Research (MKI) of people's opinions about the activities of the ÁNH (see Székely 1991). This was the period of great political changes in the former Soviet Bloc, when the communist system collapsed in countries that are now known as "the new European democracies." The purpose of the survey was to obtain an indirect legitimacy from public opinion in a period when administrative organizations serving the old regime lost political support and had to face the danger of liquidation. The researchers at MKI exploited this opportunity to significantly extend the scope of the original concept: they decided to conduct a comprehensive survey on information privacy and data sensitivity, comparable with existing Western research projects. The result was the first such research of scientific merit in Hungary and the Central and Eastern European region (Székely 1991).

The data on Hungary from the Globalization of Personal Data (GPD) survey (Ipsos Reid 2006) will be used to show longitudinal changes since this earlier study – although not neglecting the limits of comparability – thus examining the question of how stable attitudes are in a changing society or how closely they follow changes in the environment.

The 1989 survey used a nationwide representative sample of 1,000 adult persons according to four major demographic variables: age group, gender, type of place of residence, and education level. Data collection took place through face-to-face interviews, conducted by 153 interviewers, who were directed by fifteen instructors. Data collection was preceded by the preparation and evaluation of in-depth interviews and a smaller-scale pilot survey.

In 2006 a nationally representative sample of 1,005 persons, based on three demographic variables – age, gender, and regional distribution – was used. The interviews were conducted over the telephone. The quantitative survey was preceded by two focus group interviews and the preparation of a background report.

The two surveys used slightly different demographic variables in their sampling frames – year of birth versus age group and region versus type of place of residence (town, village, etc.) – and education level was left out of the demographic variables of the 2006 investigation, although once respondents were chosen they were asked about their education, occupation, and income levels. During the seventeen years that elapsed between the two surveys, the demographic composition of Hungarian society changed; for example, a number of villages received town status, thus the villagers became urban residents, or higher education became de facto mass education, thus the composition of the population regarding education level changed.

In addition, the two surveys applied different ways of conducting the interviews.[2] The composition of the two questionnaires and the formulation of the questions were prepared independently from each other. Finally, one should not forget that the general environment in which researchers tried to measure and interpret people's opinions and attitudes was significantly different in 1989 and 2006. Not only revolutionary developments in information technology but also profound changes in the political system and the society had had a fundamental impact on how people's personal data were processed and used.

All these differences might suggest that the two sets of data cannot be directly compared. However, there are strong similarities between the two investigations: both were intended to explore knowledge about and attitudes toward the existing information practices of their respective historical periods, the questions in both surveys were carefully formulated to avoid either indirect expectations or overly abstract wording, and the degree of detail of the two questionnaires and the expected length of the interviews were similar. Consequently, some results of the two surveys, supplemented with real-life experience, qualitative analyses, and the case law of the data protection (DP&FOI) commissioner,[3] can be indirectly compared and used as points of reference in estimating certain changes or continuities in the minds of the Hungarian public. The following sections present some of the findings of the two surveys that allow comparisons to be made.

CHANGES AND CONTINUITIES, 1989–2006

Trust in Data Controllers

In the first survey, respondents were asked to select from a set of cards, naming various official institutions, the three that handled their data most fairly. Similarly, they were asked to select the three institutions that they considered the least fair. According to the positive and negative "top choices," the fairest data controlling organizations were the workplace, the state banks, and the local councils, while the least fair ones were the tax office, the local councils, and the bill collectors.

In the GPD survey individual organizations were not ranked: a separate question dealt with trust in government data-controlling practices (in the context of striking the right balance between national security and individual rights), and another question was devoted to measuring trust in private companies with regard to the protection of personal information.

When comparing the frequencies of 1989 "top choices" and the 2006 "very" and "reasonably high trust" responses, we can observe an increase in the general level of trust in data controllers. Both 2006 percentages are the highest among the seven countries included in the comparative analysis as of November 2006 (which at the time did not include China). Later in this chapter, possible interpretation of Hungary's characteristics will be provided on the basis of these extreme values, concentrating only on changes or continuities between the two surveys and correlating them with other sociological factors.

These figures seem to confirm the general trend toward increasing trust in data controllers that emerged from surveys conducted in member-states of the EU in the period concerned. The three relevant Eurobarometer surveys conducted in 1996, 2003, and 2008 (International Research Associates 1997, European Opinion Research Group 2003, The Gallup Organization 2008) showed an almost unanimous increase of trust in the fourteen data processing sectors surveyed (with the sole exception of market and opinion research companies, whose acceptance slightly decreased). It might be argued, however, that in the same interval respondents' level of knowledge about data processing presumably decreased; in addition, data processing itself became more abstract and incomprehensible, meaning that a lack of awareness could also have contributed to the increase of trust.

Central Registration and ID Cards

According to the 1989 survey, 73% of the respondents agreed with the introduction of the – at that time still in use – universal personal identification number, or PIN. Another question revealed that only 3% of the respondents did not know what the universal PIN was for.

In 2006 the question was formulated to reveal the level of acceptance of the (universal) ID card. Since in 1989 virtually all respondents were aware of the function of the universal PIN and since this code was printed on the ID document that all Hungarian citizens had been obliged to carry from the end of the Second World War, the connection between the code and the ID card in the system of centralized registration of personal data seems to be evident in the minds of Hungarian respondents.

The figures show an increase in acceptance and indicate the highest level of acceptance (93%) among the countries analyzed in 2006. However, only a part of this difference can be considered a real increase: probably a higher percentage of respondents in 1989 would have accepted the existence of the ID document than accepted the universal PIN. It should be added that in the period of the change of the political system, the universal PIN and the central registration system became symbols of the former dictatorship. Even the abolition of this centralized system came into question. Finally, the system survived, and in today's consolidated period the existence of this system is no longer questioned, especially in view of the earlier abolition of the universal code.

Data Sharing

Among the questions of the 1989 survey, three dealt explicitly with the sharing of personal data among data controlling organizations. At that time, 61% of the respondents opted for the solution that when an administrative body wanted information, it should always have to request the relevant data directly from them, and those data should be used only by that particular body, while 22% thought it permissible for administrative bodies to exchange the personal data in their possession with each other. Replying to another question, 24% approved of the central registry of personal data having access to other registries where other data were kept about people, while 52% disapproved of this possibility. Finally, an overwhelming majority (87%) opposed the central registry giving out personal data to entrepreneurs, and only 7% thought it permissible.

In 2006 one set of questions was designed to measure the extent to which respondents accepted the sharing of personal information in the possession of government agencies in three categories: sharing the information with other government agencies, with foreign governments, and with the private sector. Respondents could choose unconditional answers ("always" or "never") and conditional ones ("yes, if citizen is suspected of wrong-doing" and "yes, with expressed consent of citizen"). The unconditional choices were closer to the 1989 questions, although the 2006 options significantly altered the distribution of the responses.

However, if we combine the "never" and the "yes, with expressed consent of citizen" responses from 2006 – since consent can be regarded as a manifestation of informational self-determination and as the categorical rejection of arbitrary decisions by the data controller – the 2006 results reflect a distribution of opinions that is more or less similar to the 1989 distribution in the "sharing with government agencies" and "sharing with the private sector" categories.[4] Only the option regarding citizens' "wrong-doing" has a significant influence on the distribution of responses; this category will be touched upon separately below.

Disobedience and Resistance

Eight per cent of the respondents in 1989 stated that they were unwilling to provide certain data about themselves at official places; the vast majority (87%) always supplied their personal data when required by administrative bodies. In response to another question, 6% thought it was more in the interests of people that data about them held by official bodies should *not* be precise and complete, and 90% thought it was in the people's interests that registered data be accurate. The general level of disobedience and resistance can be estimated from both questions, although the responses given to the second one instead reflected practical considerations, such as free play for tax evasion.

In the 2006 survey, the counterpart of the first question was: "Have you ever refused to give [personal] information to a government agency because you thought it was not needed?" Here again, 8% responded in the affirmative. This proportion can be directly compared to the 1989 data. Another response figure, namely for those who had deliberately given incorrect information about themselves to a government agency, was less than 1% of the respondents; however, this figure cannot be directly compared to the 1989 opinion on people's interest in the accuracy and completeness of data registration.[5] To sum up, the level of disobedience and resistance does not seem to have changed between the dates of the two surveys.

Fishing in Troubled Waters

Finally, we can indirectly estimate people's attitude toward unlawful activities in 1989 and 2006 by comparing the responses to two differently formulated questions. (Naturally, this does not mean that we can estimate the proportion of lawful behaviour in reality, only people's opinion about others' behaviour.) In the first survey, 46% of the respondents agreed with the following prompt statement: "More data should be registered about people, so that certain people cannot 'fish in troubled waters.'" At that time, "fish[ing] in troubled waters" certainly referred to the activity of the tricksters of the changing political and business environment, to envied representatives of the nouveau riche, or simply to tax evaders. Registration in this context was understood as registration by the state of people's personal data.

In the 2006 survey, the above-mentioned set of questions regarding people's acceptance of the sharing of personal data in the possession of government agencies contained a conditional option: whether data sharing is acceptable in cases where the person concerned is suspected of "wrong-doing." Since the 1989 prompt statement referred to state registration, we can use two categories out of the three asked in 2006: data sharing between government agencies and between a government agency and foreign governments.

Despite the different formulation of the two questions, or question sets, responses to both reflect the level of willingness to sacrifice information privacy (of others, of course) to law and order. In this case, it would be unreasonable to compare exact numbers; however, one may note that the level of this estimated willingness was between one-third and one-half of the respondents in both years.

COUNTRY PROFILE IN 2006 ON GROUNDS OF EXTREME VALUES AMONG THE COUNTRIES SURVEYED

The GPD survey covered a range of countries representing different political models, economic status, regulatory policies, and cultural traditions and values. In this spectrum, Hungary alone represented a whole geographic region and the postcommunist stage of political and social development, as well as a unique cultural context and set of national traditions. It was therefore not surprising that in several categories the Hungarian data represented extreme values in the range of data of the countries surveyed.

It needs to be mentioned in advance that some of these extreme values seem inconsistent with the findings of other quantitative and qualitative investigations. These inconsistencies, however, reveal an important phenomenon and thus reinforce an earlier hypothesis of the author, namely the existence of a "threshold of abstraction" – in short, that it is not the violation of privacy in itself that counts but its perceptibility. In the following analysis, the extreme values will be presented first, their possible reasons explained, and their discrepancies from the expected results noted. The probable reasons for these discrepancies will be discussed later in the chapter.

Knowledge of Laws

Among the seven countries[6] included in the comparative analysis, the level of knowledge about the laws protecting personal information in the public sector is the lowest in Hungary (18%), according to the respondents' judgments of themselves. This percentage is no more than about half of the next lowest value. Similarly, the level of knowledge about laws protecting personal information in the business sector is also the lowest (19%). This is a surprising result in several respects.

To start with, in Hungary a widespread legal and institutional system has been developed for the protection of information privacy since the great political transformation. The level of publicity and the awareness of the population regarding this system are high. Hungary even became a sort of role model for the new democracies of the region in establishing a new system of informational rights and freedoms. The scope of the basic privacy law encompasses both the public and the private sectors. There are numerous sectoral laws and regulations in force: today, nearly 1,000 Acts and regulations contain provisions on processing personal data, so protection of personal information has penetrated the whole legal corpus.

Hungarian printed, electronic, and online media deal with this topic fairly frequently even in comparison with European media practice. A number of well-known landmark cases have been publicized in the press (e.g., see Székely 2008). In addition, both the business sector (with its vested interests in making money out of people's personal data) and the government (with its desire to achieve higher efficiency and controllability by restricting informational rights) often complain about high media coverage and about the overdramatization of the problems of information privacy in the press.

It is worth noting that equally surprising are the data relating to questions about media coverage of privacy, where Hungary shows the second lowest value (after France). Violation of privacy, however, was the most prevalent aspect within this low rating of media coverage. Furthermore, in 1998 Hungary's three parliamentary commissioners[7] ordered a poll about their reputation. The poll results found that the three commissioners collectively constituted one of the most popular public institutions. Forty-three per cent of Hungarians claimed to have heard about the DP&FOI commissioner a mere three years after the post was created (Majtényi 1999, 10).

Resistance

Among the seven countries examined, Hungary exhibits the lowest proportion of active disobedience toward governmental data controllers. As can be seen from the 1989–2006 comparison, this proportion was similarly low even in the turbulent period of the change of the political system, although at that time loyalty toward the government was by no means prevalent; this issue instead divided society. The proportion of those who reported active disobedience toward data controllers in the business sector is again among the lowest in the group of countries surveyed.

Although neither of the surveys contained questions about disobedience toward the respondent's own employer, the assumption is made that this proportion in 2006 would have been among the lowest values too, exceeding the impact of the general phenomenon resulting from the employees' defenseless position.[8] It should also be observed that the level of experienced breach of privacy at the workplace is the highest in Hungary, where 31% of the respondents reported such events. Naturally, this value reflects only the proportion of those breaches of workplace privacy of which the data subjects (the employees) were actually aware. Here, one would need to know whether the absolute number of breaches is that high or the knowledge and perception of Hungarian employees are that developed. One would assume the former since respondents produced relatively low results regarding the knowledge of modern data processing technologies.

The high level of breach of privacy at the workplace, perceived or not, can be regarded as a typical phenomenon in the new European democracies. In these countries, employees are historically unprepared for the sharp practices of new capitalism, as will be discussed later on. Hungarian employees, however, have enjoyed certain advantages thanks to the legal and institutional system of the country: practices like those introduced in a shopping centre in the neighbouring Czech Republic[9] could not be applied in Hungary, not only because of the predictable intervention of the DP&FOI commissioner but also because of adverse publicity in the media. Such cases again support the opinions on public knowledge of laws vis-à-vis the survey results.

Attitudes to Visible Minorities

The only significant minority living in the territory of present-day Hungary are the Roma (about 5% to 7% of the population). The members of this minority bear visible racial characteristics. The social problems regarding the Roma population are far-reaching, well known in public opinion, and regularly publicized in the press. The Roma population has a low standard of living and a low level of assimilation to the majority. Roma people are often victims of racism, prejudice, and discrimination. This situation should be taken into consideration when interpreting the following data on attitudes to visible minorities in Hungary. It should also be borne in mind that the Hungarian sample of the 2006 GPD survey contained only one person who declared him/herself Roma, so Roma people were effectively not represented in the sample. With regard to the methodology of the survey, this is understandable since the majority of Roma people, especially in rural areas, have no land-line telephone and/or have less trust, patience, and interest in surveys than do the rest of the society.

When asked about the media coverage of information privacy of certain social groups, respondents from all surveyed countries, except for Hungary, were of the opinion that celebrities, government officials, and people with high incomes got more media coverage than immigrants and visible minorities. According to Hungarian respondents, media attention was given to the privacy of visible minorities in the highest proportion among the social groups listed in the survey. The percentage of those who expressed this opinion was also the highest among the countries analyzed (43%). This opinion was likely primarily related to national media and the Roma.

Given the widespread prejudice against the Roma, the quoted high percentage presumably reflects a pejorative judgment of the media coverage of the Roma to a considerable degree. A significant part of the respondents must have thought that there was not only *high* media attention given to personal (ethnic, sensitive) information about Roma people but also *too much* attention.

It should also be observed that Hungarian respondents produced the highest percentage regarding media coverage of privacy of personal information among "low income people," "homeless," and "people like you" categories. Pejorative judgments can be hypothesized in the case of the homeless but not in the remaining two categories. The democratically minded reader may be pleased to learn that a certain segment of the population notices these matters in the media, not only the stories about celebrities and paparazzi. It is worth quoting the assessment of the first DP&FOI commissioner from 1995: "The sensitivity of Hungarian society to data protection, and the right to informational self-determination, are more advanced than was previously anticipated. Data protection does not represent a luxury demand of people of higher social standing or educational level, and the sensitivity to data protection cannot be closely attributed to social standing: It spreads across Hungarian society from the unemployed homeless to the highest ranking citizens" (Majtényi 1998, 11–12).

In the light of both positive and negative attitudes toward privacy of personal information of ethnic minorities, another interesting result of the 2006 survey was that Hungarian respondents felt extra airport security checks on visible minorities completely unacceptable in the highest proportion (42%) among the seven countries analyzed. In this result, the impact of three factors may be considered: nationalism and anti-Americanism, the protection of Roma, and the personal experience of tourists from the Central and Eastern European region.

Without going into deeper analysis, anti-Americanism, which is by no means unprecedented in Europe, became the ideology of the right and the extreme right in Hungary. These sectors rhetorically took the side of radical Arab movements – despite their own inclination to discriminate against visible minorities, including Arabs. Although the practical influence of this ideology is low, it may possibly have an effect on the survey results.

As a second factor, the positive attitudes cannot be excluded either, namely the influence of the opinion of those who regard extra airport security checks as unacceptable because of their sympathy toward the Roma and other visible minorities.

Finally, tourists from the Central and Eastern European region, the majority of whom are "white Caucasians," could still have experienced a sort of virtual visible minority treatment in the recent past or, in the case of the older generation, even before the great political changes. These people might have experienced unpleasant or humiliating situations in developed Western countries, not because of their skin colour or racial characteristics but because of their differing language, behaviour, culture, or education. This may be the third factor in people's opinion expressed against discrimination at border crossings or in the case of any other identity checks.

Trust in Data Controllers

The level of trust that respondents have in both governmental and business data controllers is highest in Hungary. If one adds up the number of "very high" trust and "reasonably high" trust responses, governmental data controllers receive 51% and business data controllers 53% of responses. Both findings seem to contradict to a certain extent well-known social phenomena and general public opinion alike. In Hungary (and in most other former communist countries of the region), there has been a tradition of distrust between the governing and the governed – except during the euphoric moments of the change of the political system. Clichés like "all governments are lying" are widespread. There is a traditional gap between "Us" and "Them" – and this is true in relation to successful and prosperous ventures and businessmen too. Stereotypical beliefs such as "You can only get rich if you break the law" or "The wealthy always have something to hide" are popular and often quoted.

This high self-reported level of trust (which is high only in comparison with other countries; otherwise, it represents the opinion of only half of the respondents) seems to be inconsistent also with the constant complaints of both government and business about the low level of trust in data controllers and information services. Finally, the moderate level of average social capital in Hungarian society deserves mentioning: this would make people inclined to put their trust in people they know personally rather than in institutions, opaque systems, and procedures. Current data processing is abstract enough to prevent people from forming their views about trust on the basis of direct contact and experience.

Internet and Profiling

The degree of worry about providing personal information on websites is lowest in Hungary; 42% of the respondents declared themselves "very worried" or "somewhat worried." One might think that this is because of the relatively low Internet penetration and that this result reflects the opinion of the majority of the population, which has no information about the functioning of the Internet. However, if only the subsample of Internet users (48% of the whole sample) is observed, Hungarian respondents still produced the second lowest value (51%), almost sharing the lowest one again. It would be a mistake to attribute this result to people's confidence in technology (or simply to a lack of information) since, as it turned out from another question, the level of acceptance of customer profiling – that is, a practice especially characteristic of internet services – was by far the highest among the seven countries, at 69%.

Extent of Say on What Happens to Personal Information

Despite all the above-mentioned characteristics of the broader environment of data processing – a developed institutional system, a well-working DP&FOI commissioner, a wide range of legal guarantees – the proportion of those who felt that they had a say in what happened to their personal information was the lowest in Hungary, at 45%. A significant level of pessimism is reflected in this result, something to which – according to stereotyped national characteristics[10] – Hungarians are inclined. A general distrust toward the institutional system may also play a part in this result; still, the inconsistency between the amount of legal and institutional protection of personal data and people's opinion is striking.

Data Sharing

The level of acceptance of the government's sharing of citizens' personal information with foreign governments is among the highest in Hungary of the countries analyzed, at 67%,[11] close to a tie for the most acceptance. This high percentage seems to be inconsistent with critical opinions and comments revealed in informal, private circumstances about the transfer of passenger lists to the United States, airport fingerprinting, and the like. It is also possible, however, that a part of the population accepted the strong propaganda in favour of post-9/11 antiterrorist measures, including transborder data checking and matching. One should note that ironically Hungary, together with its capital, Budapest, has always been among the safest countries in the world regarding terrorism.[12] A special historical, social-psychological factor that may well have an impact here can be deduced from Hungary's role as a "border-country." During long and significant periods of its history, Hungary was situated on the edge of empires and alliances: it was the easternmost stronghold of the West against the expansionary Ottoman Empire; later the eastern end of Central Europe under German influence, as a buffer against the Soviets; then after 1956 the western bastion, or rather the shop window of the Soviet Bloc, representing a sort of "soft version" of communism (sometimes called "Goulash-communism"); and after the 2004 enlargement of the European Union, the eastern border of the EU.[13] Living on the political and cultural peripheries and often changing rulers and masters may have resulted in an inclination to "excessive zeal" toward the new master (today the Euro-Atlantic countries and the belated capitalism) and in imbalanced attitudes.[14]

The level of acceptance of employers sharing employees' personal information with governmental agencies is the highest in Hungary. Sixteen per cent of the respondents were of the opinion that such data sharing was appropriate "under all circumstances" and 79% if all positive answers are added up to unconditional and conditional options of data sharing by the employer with the government. Here, this loyalty may be attributed mainly to submission to new capitalist methods and the "Little Brothers" – the decentralized and privatized versions of Big Brother.

Surveillance vs Security

In light of the foregoing results, it is not surprising that among the seven countries the lowest proportion (40%) of people in Hungary believe that laws aimed at protecting national security are intrusive upon personal privacy. Similarly, the proportion of those who accept the idea of national ID cards that people must carry on them at all times and present when asked by the police or other security forces is highest in Hungary in both categories: 77% of Hungarian respondents strongly agreed with this idea and, together with those who somewhat agreed, represented a striking 93% of the population. This proportion is by far the highest among the countries surveyed, higher than in Brazil (79%), where people are also accustomed to carrying national ID cards, and even than in China[15] (77%), where the population has had a long history of centralized control over society. When interpreting the extremely high level

Table 8.1
Privacy attitudes of the Hungarian population by proportions of respondents among the countries surveyed

High or highest proportion	Low or lowest proportion
Privacy invasion at the workplace	Knowledge about privacy laws
Trust in government data controllers	Worry about the Internet
Trust in business data controllers	Judgment of national security laws as
Acceptance of data sharing between the	intrusive upon personal privacy
employer and the government	The impression of having control over
Acceptance of CCTV	what happens to personal information
Acceptance of national ID cards	Activity to protect personal information
Acceptance of customer profiling	

of acceptance of national ID cards, the survival and restored legitimation of the centralized population registration system after the political transformation should be borne in mind.

Closed circuit television (CCTV), however, does not belong to data controlling practices with a long tradition and consequent legitimation. Even so, surveillance cameras monitoring public places are believed to reduce crime by the highest proportion in Hungary (87%), and this proportion is the second highest (86%) in the case of in-store surveillance cameras. These survey results can be attributed to two factors: the strong coalition of the "risk industry" and politics (local and national alike), on the one hand, and significant media support, on the other. Neither of these factors is specific to Hungary, but here they exert a particularly strong influence.

POSSIBLE EXPLANATIONS

If the extreme values mentioned above are summarized, distinct groups emerge, as shown in table 8.1.

The categories listed under both groups and the accompanying survey responses show a rather submissive profile, one in which the public is aware of violations of privacy but accepts them. This profile, at least at the level of stereotyped national characteristics, contradicts the rebellious, freedom-loving image of Hungarians. It also, to a certain extent, contradicts real-life experience, people's interpersonal behaviour, and verbal expression. The first survey can be summarized by stating that whereas in 1989 the majority of the people were moderately well informed, rather suspicious, sometimes "inclined to bluster," *but* obedient data providers, by 2006 they had become uninformed, uninterested, *and* obedient. Naturally, statistical averages and simple distribution of data can easily mask the essential factors. However, this profile deserves a certain interpretation even at this general level.

Similar to other countries of the Central and Eastern European region that fundamentally changed their political systems in the first wave of democratization, the euphoric period of metamorphosis is now over in Hungary. Respect for individual rights and liberties, including the right to information privacy, is decreasing and is significantly lower today than it was in the early 1990s. During the past fifteen years, a young, "new capitalist," more technocratic generation has grown up whose members give precedence to business, political power, and personal career over respect for the rights of other individuals.

Another possible explanatory element is the invasion of new data processing technologies and techniques for which the majority of the population were not adequately prepared and for which they had not accumulated the necessary communitarian and individual experience. A further factor is the expansion of multinational companies in Hungary that, together with the discredited nature of employees' movements and the lack of strong trade unions, has created a workplace environment where the disunited employees feel threatened by dismissal if they try to enforce their rights; moreover, they might believe that their information-al rights can be "sold" to their employers in exchange for their salaries.

Nor should one forget the *morbus hungaricus*, or Hungarian disease, of the present era, namely the overpoliticization of both the public sector and private life. The result of this is that everything must be evaluated with reference to the forced polarization of party politics. A typical, harmful side-effect of this situation is that political powers support the issues of individual rights only when these issues serve their direct interests in daily party politics. In addition, collective rights are often overemphasized at the expense of individual rights and freedoms.

The already-mentioned history of the country – its situation at the periphery of different empires and political and social systems – is certainly in part responsible for the unbalanced nature of popular values and attitudes. The tradition of distrust between government and society and between different social strata may contribute to the level of discrepancy between opinions and actual behaviour. This phenomenon can be observed especially in low-trust societies.[16] One may even risk drawing a parallel between the re-emerging phenomenon of familism[17] and the submissive loyalty to employers and business companies: both are substitutes for the missing social capital that has resulted from a lack of trust in law, institutions, and fellow citizens. These loyal opinions, however, do not necessarily mean loyal behaviour in practice; as opposed to a Japanese-type loyalty to the employer, for example, the average Hungarian employee often tries to outwit his employer, and only a few reveal a real corporate spirit toward the organization itself.

Finally, the low level of civic activities and the unevenly developed nature of present-day civil society may also play a role in the country profile, established on the basis of the Hungarian respondents' extreme values vis-à-vis the other countries surveyed.

One of the main findings of the 1989 survey was the discovery of a privacy-sensitive social stratum. At that time, hardly any demographic or attitudinal specificity of this stratum could be found, which constituted 16% of the population. Again, in 2006 the attempt was made to identify such a stratum, but since then there have not been any coherent subsamples – further analyses are needed to explore these latent correlations.

The Inconsistency between Quantitative and Qualitative Data

Before we accept this rather sombre national profile, it should be pointed out that in a number of cases the quantitative data seem to be inconsistent with other research findings and experience, including the GPD focus group interviews. If the transcripts of the two sets of interviews conducted among Hungarian respondents are analyzed, it may become clear that both the rather solid knowledge and the seemingly stable attitudes are manifested only if there exists a sensitizing context in the discussion. Often a latent awakening to comprehension, a sort of recognition of one's own latent opinion, can be observed. Naturally, this could result from evoking clichés of mass communication, or even from following the moderator's hidden expectations, but in this case the latter possibility can be excluded because of the high professional quality of the conduct of the interviews.

It is observed that asking simple questions characteristic of questionnaires, on the one hand, and leading discussions allowing or even requiring more explanation, on the other, may produce different results. This reinforces the author's earlier hypothesis, drawn from his experience: the existence of a "threshold of abstraction."

THE THRESHOLD OF ABSTRACTION

If a policeman stopped people at every corner and asked them to show their ID cards, soon everybody would protest against the "police state." If, however, the same policeman checked the same people without stopping them – for example, by reading their radio frequency identification

(RFID) passports, using an automatic face recognition system, or simply checking their licence plate numbers through his mobile terminal (which would actually be more efficient) – probably nobody would have objections, for people think they have nothing to hide.

This is a hypothetical but realistic scenario that would take place in a similar manner probably in any developed country but certainly in Hungary. To generalize from this everyday experience, it may be concluded that it is not the violation of personal privacy in itself that counts but its visibility or perceptibility. The more abstract, the less important – no matter how grave the violation is.

However, there exists a threshold: if a sensitizing factor makes an "abstract" violation of privacy visible or understandable, people easily perceive it and react quickly. If we added, "I mean, if your boss read your private e-mails," many would protest against such a practice.

The reader can find striking examples of opposing views emerging from focus group interviews and from the survey data. These opinions seem to contradict the high level of acceptance of data sharing between the government and private-sector organizations as well as the highest reported level among the countries surveyed regarding trust in both governmental and private data controllers.

The insensitivity resulting from a lack of explanation regarding the violation of privacy is exploited by both government and business in Hungary. In a broader context, this raises the social necessity of mediation.

There are different types of social mediators, of which civil organizations constitute an important category. There is however a potential group of professionals who could also play an important role as mediators between data controllers and data subjects: the information technology (IT) professionals. Their present roles and attitudes are however not without contradictions and show significant differences in various regions and among various social and political traditions.

EPILOGUE: ACTORS DESERVING FURTHER
INVESTIGATION – THE IT PROFESSIONALS

A public opinion survey can provide a number of important findings about a representative sample of the population – in other words, about the opinions and attitudes of data subjects. The present analysis concentrates on only two aspects regarding the Hungarian sample – the changes between 1989 and 2006 and the extreme values in 2006 – without analyzing deeper factors and interdependencies. Undoubtedly, there is a need for further analysis of the survey data – among other reasons, in order to search for the present equivalent of the 1989 privacy-sensitive social stratum.

The opinions and attitudes of data controllers (governmental offices, business companies, and other organizations) are also known from various statements and lobbying activities by their leading officials. However, there is a group of players who have a distinguished role in defining the fate of personal data in today's computerized and networked environment and who have not as yet become the subject of specific investigations: the above-mentioned IT professionals. According to the author's experience, the role of these professionals is even more influential in a milieu of underdeveloped or changing values, political transformation, and economic modernization – that is, typically in new democracies.

Whereas the model IT professionals in the Central and Eastern European region are certainly chief information architects of business monopolies or chief information officers of investigative agencies, in North America these people are nonconformist figures, sometimes resembling a sort of modern Robin Hood, who in the new European democracies would be called "hackers" (understood as "crackers").

Although this dichotomy is certainly oversimplified, there might be significant differences in the IT profession in various regions and cultures, despite the evident effect of the globalization of information technology and the expansion of multinational IT companies – developments that certainly influence the attitudes of the professionals working in this environment. Information technologists constitute an unexplored group in privacy research, and both their attitudes and their impact on information privacy deserve further investigation.

NOTES

1 In 1991 the newly established Constitutional Court declared the universal personal identification code unconstitutional. The universal code was later replaced with sector-specific identification numbers.
2 It should be noted that it would have been impossible to use a representative sample for telephone interviews in 1989 since telephone penetration was only 9 lines per 100 inhabitants at that time (in 2006 it was 35 fixed lines plus 95 mobile cellular lines per 100 inhabitants).
3 Parliamentary Commissioner for Data Protection and Freedom of Information.
4 The question regarding the sharing of personal information with foreign governments was not included in the 1989 survey.

5 Level of resistance to marketing and business companies was also measured in 2006, but these questions had no counterpart at all in 1989.

6 Excluding China, which was not covered in the early phase of the survey, the seven countries are: Brazil, Canada, France, Hungary, Mexico, Spain, and the United States.

7 One with general powers (plus his deputy, actually the fourth commissioner), one for the protection of national and ethnic minority rights, and one for the protection of personal data and freedom of information.

8 About the situation of privacy and data protection at the workplace in Hungary, see Szabó and Székely (2005).

9 Cashiers who were menstruating were marked with a red ribbon in order to avoid "abuse" of the "privilege" of the few extra minutes that they were allowed to spend daily in the restroom.

10 See, for example, Miklós Vámos's ironically aphoristic *Xenophobe's Guide to the Hungarians* (1999) or the numerous articles about the famous – or infamous – tune and lyric "Gloomy Sunday" (Fenyo 1997).

11 This figure is derived from adding up the percentages of positive answers to unconditional and conditional data-sharing options.

12 At the time of writing – 17 April 2007 – the head of the Budapest police gave a two-hour online interview on the Government's Portal (http://www.magyarorszag.hu), answering citizens' questions and remarks. The title of the interview was "Budapest Is the Safest Capital of Europe."

13 Since January 2007 two new members have joined the EU, Romania and Bulgaria, thus reducing the length of the eastern borders of Hungary serving as the boundary of the EU. Still, the borders between Hungary and Ukraine, Hungary and Serbia, and Hungary and Croatia remained the borderline of the EU, and this function became further emphasized when Hungary joined the co-called Schengen Region (the group of EU countries with a common policy on external border controls and sharing of travellers' data) in 2007.

14 For an exhausting inventory of interpretations of the last great transformation, see Hankiss (2007).

15 The 2006 GPD survey originally included China; however, due to late provision of survey data and to certain methodological problems, Chinese data were not included in the summary report of November 2006.

16 See the flourishing literature fertilized by Francis Fukuyama's *Trust: The Social Virtues and the Creation of Prosperity* (1995), such as James Bennett's *The Anglosphere Challenge* (2004), especially chapter 3.

17 Familism is an ideology that places the sanctity of family above all, popular in societies where the only trustworthy unit is one's family. The actual behaviour and activities of people in these societies are however often inconsistent with their opinion on the primacy of family.

9

Privacy in France in the Age of Information and Security Technologies

AYSE CEYHAN

For years, France was known to be one of the most reluctant countries to adopt large-scale usage of information and communication technologies (ICT). Even though it invented the Minitel – a small, online, breakthrough computer service connected to the telephone line – in 1981 France, with its state-owned telecom industry, was listed as one of the world's most innovation-averse markets. However, since the end of the 1990s, its ICT industry has grown tremendously, providing consumers with high-speed Internet service that is much faster and cheaper than the Internet services available in the United States. In 2007, 53.7% of the population used the Internet, up by 287.4% compared to 2000 (Internet World Statistics). At the same time, mobile phones have emerged at lightning speed, reaching 83.2% of the population (Observatoire des Mobiles).

France is also one of the world leaders in the production of security technologies such as biometrics used in the law enforcement and identification fields. Among its leading companies, France can proudly cite Sagem, a world leader in the Automatic Fingerprint Identification System (AFIS) that provides more than 50% of the crime fighting biometric technologies in the world and equips nearly 120 police agencies worldwide. Moreover, with companies such as Thales,[1] Oberthur,[2] and Gemalto,[3] France has also become a leader in the production of microchips for personal identification and credit cards. In the past ten years, France has invested heavily in security and antiterrorism technologies and has caught up with its European neighbours, including Germany and the United Kingdom.

The growth of the security technologies sector should be examined in the context of the securitization of the means of identification and the generalization of intensive surveillance of the whole society after the attacks of 11 September 2001 (Lyon 2003, Ceyhan 2006). In this environment, France adopted a "layered security" approach, a practice that combines different security layers, including checking identities, scanning people, tracking their communication, and keeping files on them, among other practices. All these layers rely on high-tech devices that enable security agencies to find networked solutions to security problems. In this approach, France decided to transform its citizens' paper identification documents into biometric ID cards and to create police and surveillance databases to keep files on individuals. It also tightened its antiterrorism and immigration laws[4] and extended the use of biometric technologies and video surveillance both in public places (train stations, ports, airports, stadiums, etc.) and in the private sector (businesses, shopping malls, etc.).

However, the rapid diffusion of ICT and the technologization of security exact a price that is not measurable in monetary terms: a loss of personal privacy. In effect, even if information and security technologies have become part of everyday life, they also contribute to the constitution of virtual surveillance networks that trace individuals' movements and communications and keep their data in thousands of files of which most people are not aware (Marx 1994, Lyon 2003). Indeed, through their connection to databases, identification and surveillance technologies rely heavily on personal information that they gather, store, process, manipulate, and share, making them increasingly intrusive on personal privacy (Lyon 2001, 2003). However, as we can see in table 9.1, compared to other countries examined by the Globalization of Personal Data (GPD) survey,[5] the French public does not seem to be very knowledgeable about privacy laws and is not worried enough about privacy breaches they may bring about.

Moreover, France appears with Hungary among the countries that are least likely to feel that laws aimed at protecting national security are intrusive upon personal privacy. Indeed, as we see in table 9.2, only 41% of the population think these laws are intrusive. In the United States, Spain, and Canada, the proportion of people who believe in the intrusiveness of such laws is considerably higher.

These results are surprising at first glance if one recalls France's sensitivity to the protection of "private life." France's May 1968 motto about personal freedom and its culture of street demonstrations against unpopular political, economic, and social measures seem to create a stark contrast to such indifference. However, this contrast becomes understandable if one looks through a political sociology lens at the French

Table 9.1
Knowledge about laws to protect personal information in government departments and private companies (%)*

	Government departments			Private companies		
	Very knowledgeable	Somewhat knowledgeable	Total	Very knowledgeable	Somewhat knowledgeable	Total
Hungary	3	15	18	3	16	19
France	4	30	34	4	19	23
Paris	4	30	34	4	23	27
Rest of France	4	30	34	4	18	22
Canada	10	38	47	5	35	41
Quebec	8	28	36	6	24	30
Rest of Canada	10	40	50	5	39	44
Spain	7	35	42	7	32	39
US	9	45	54	7	45	52

* Q3. How knowledgeable are you about the laws that deal with the protection of personal information in government departments and private companies in your country?
Source: Ipsos Reid (2006).

Table 9.2
Attitudes toward laws aimed at protecting national security (%)*

	Highly intrusive	Somewhat intrusive	Total
Hungary	8	32	40
France	14	27	41
Rest of Canada	10	37	48
Quebec	12	28	40
Spain	10	44	54
US	15	42	57

* Q17. The government has enacted laws aimed at protecting national security. To what extent do you believe laws aimed at protecting national security are intrusive upon personal privacy?
Source: Ipsos Reid (2006).

notion of the "private life" and examines it in relation to the French political culture founded on a strong centralized state (Tilly 1975, Anderson 1976, Birnbaum 1998).

THE FRENCH CONCEPTION OF PRIVACY

Notion of "vie privée"

French literature does not use the term "privacy," but it does refer to "private life" and/or "personal life." What is private life? It is difficult to define in a straightforward fashion, but the notions that best describe it are domestic life and intimate life. French texts often list health, love, sex, and income as the basic areas of "private life." Intimate life represents the sphere of the private life that should be protected against social and political interference, and its activities – like leisure, travel, and dining – are accepted as sacred. We should point out, however, that this separation and the sacredness of the private life do not mean that the government should not regulate it. In effect, even though everything behind the walls of the domestic life is private, there are some spheres – such as the naming of a child – that are not free from the state's gaze. Indeed, the names of French children must comply with the administratively recognized list, a practice that does not exist in the United States. Such interference would be contrary to the American conception of privacy, which avoids state intrusion in such areas (Levin and Nicholson 1998, 391).

The judicial formulation of the concept of private life is broad and not susceptible to exhaustive definition. According to article 8(11) of the European Convention for the Protection of Human Rights and Fundamental Freedoms, it includes "a person's physical and psychological integrity; the guarantee afforded by Article 8 of the *Convention* is primarily intended to ensure the development without outside interference, of the personality of each individual in his relations with other human beings" (Strasbourg Court of Justice in *Botta v Italy* [1998] 26 EHRR 241 at para. 32).

For the French, "privacy" is a right acknowledged by the Civil Code, which provides that "each person has the right to have his privacy respected," but it has no juridical definition. It is a judge-made concept that covers several aspects of the life of a person (personal life) understood in contrast to public life. Vastly extensive, personal life covers many things. It includes a person's image, personal health and the health of close family members, parental and marital status, romantic attachments and relations with children, political and religious beliefs, and true names and residences (Judgment of 15 May 1970, Cour d'Appel Paris, 1970 DS Jur 466). This means that all information about a specific person is considered personal and therefore deserves protection. If the government wants to interfere with this right, it must do so based on a law that is known to the public and that contains provisions precise enough to curb arbitrary government action. Further, this action must be legitimate as set out in article 8 of the European Convention for the Protection of Human Rights and Fundamental Freedoms. It includes protecting national security, guaranteeing public safety, and preventing disorder and crime.

Historical Outlook: From Personal Dignity to the Protection of Personal Data

The history of privacy protection in France can be traced back to the Revolution. Respect for private life was expressed in the Declaration of Men and Citizens of 1798. Since then the concept has been framed by the interplay of several issues: defence of one's honour and dignity, freedom of the press, the right to one's image, protection of personal life, and data protection. Most of these were products of nineteenth-century French social life and were developed in the Parisian artistic world. It is worth noting that, although contemporary privacy legislation refers more precisely to data protection (a twentieth-century concept), French law is still influenced by the nineteenth-century values of honour, suspicion of the press, and distaste for the disclosure of personal properties and assets (Whitman 2004, 1178–80).

The history of French privacy protection begins with the introduction of freedom of the press, which was recognized in the Constitution of 1791. This document also addressed protections against calumnies and insults relative to private life. However, the idea of freedom of the press was not easily accepted by French politicians and critics, among them the well-known politician Pierre-Paul Royer-Collard, who warned that private life had to be "walled off" against the danger of insult (Whitman 2004, 1173). By the mid-nineteenth century, the question of the "right to one's image" had emerged in the context of political and sexual liberation. Several cases involving celebrities and artists (such as Jean Auguste Dominique Ingres) or parents of artists (like those of Alexander Dumas) dealt with reproductions of their images by photography or in the press.

In the end, the courts restated the absolute right of a person over his life and nullified the photographers' property rights. The courts acknowledged privacy as a property and as a right rather than a value.

These protections continued into and expanded in the twentieth century. Amended in 1970, the Civil Code introduced new protections regarding health, intimate life, and income. In addition, the Penal Code introduced the notion of "offences against personality," which became the principal reference of court cases. This notion includes: (1) offences against privacy, (2) offences against the image of persons, (3) malicious denunciations, (4) breach of secrecy, (5) violations of personal rights resulting from computer files or processes, and (6) offences against persons resulting from examination of genetic characteristics or identification of genetic imprints. In 1978 France adapted its legislation to ICT advances and enacted legislation on data processing, data files, and individual liberties (Loi relative à l'informatique, aux fichiers et aux libertés). Its main aim is to provide a juridical framework for the protection of personal data on the Internet. To oversee it, this law established a data protection authority named the Commission Nationale de l'Informatique et des Libertés (CNIL).

French Citizens' Perception of Privacy

The French participants in the GPD focus groups spontaneously wrote down insights relative to information privacy (data protection, security, confidentiality, etc.) as the first idea that came to mind when they heard the word "privacy" (see GPD table 9(a) online).[6] To a lesser extent, they also wrote down insights relative to intimate life (territorial privacy) and communication privacy. Surprisingly, there was no strong mention of bodily privacy. This is probably due to the fact that this type of privacy covers elements like DNA tests and iris or retina prints that have not been extensively covered by the French media.

French respondents' spontaneous focus on information privacy is understandable in the context of an information society in which the right to privacy and the confidentiality of personal, medical, and life-style-related information obtained by public, private, or transnational actors constitute an important focus of concern. In the virtual world, people have to deal with personal identification numbers (PINs), on-line accounts, e-bays, telemarketing, loyalty cards, and the like, all of which lead them to reveal themselves and their interests on the Internet. With the growth of databases that gather, process, and disseminate their information, people are aware that their actions are being monitored, even if they do not know the full extent of such tracking. This is why they assume that there is less privacy now than there was five years ago.

We have seen that, historically, the most prevalent type of privacy in France was related to "personal matters" such as income, health information, and so forth. This still holds true (see GPD table 9(b) online). However, with the development of the information society, the most threatened type of privacy appears to be information privacy; the least threatened type is territorial privacy. The probable reason for this confidence in the inviolability of territorial privacy is French citizens' trust in existing laws that protect their intimacy, right to their own image, secrets, and the like. By contrast, they express strong concern about the dissemination of their personal data (see GPD table 9(c) online).

Other findings from the presurvey focus groups confirm that French citizens view privacy as both a civil right and a form of property that cannot be exchanged or modified, even for security reasons. On this point, surprisingly, the findings reveal that French respondents did not make a direct association between the current erosion of privacy and the security measures taken after the 9/11 attacks. Rather, they see the increases in security measures as reactions to the social violence that emerged in the 1990s in Paris and Lyon that pitted suburban youth groups against the police. French respondents refer to 9/11 only when they talk about air travel, evoking the tightening of security checks before boarding planes bound for the United States.

A minority of respondents did not personally experience the diminution of privacy as a problem. Some proposed that their personal information was not interesting enough to be used by a third party. This is a common view among French citizens, perhaps because of the association between celebrities and/or wealthy people and the demand for information about them; such people are perceived as "interesting." The majority of citizens feel that the media do not devote much coverage to the personal lives of "ordinary" people (this can be seen in GPD table 9(d) online).

KNOWLEDGE OF PRIVACY LAWS AND ATTITUDES TOWARD SECURITY MEASURES

Knowledge of Surveillance Technologies

As table 9.3 demonstrates, French respondents appear to be fairly knowledgeable about the Internet and about other personal location

Table 9.3
Knowledge of surveillance technologies (%)*

	Internet	GPS	CCTV	RFID	Data mining	Biometrics
Somewhat	34	36	33	16	21	24
Very	34	18	15	4	6	5
Total	68	54	48	20	27	23

* Q1. In general, how knowledgeable are you about each of the following?
Source: Ipsos Reid (2006, 6–7, GPD table 7).

technologies like global positioning systems (GPS), closed circuit television (CCTV), radio frequency identification (RFID), data mining, and biometrics.

Apart from the Internet, the use of which has increased considerably in recent years, French citizens focus on GPS as a technology that enables them to be located easily. This is why GPS has received increasing media coverage. Among surveillance technologies in public places, CCTV cameras have also gained more and more public attention in France. Their number has increased considerably since 2001, reaching nearly 1 million cameras installed mainly in Lyons,[7] Paris, and some cities of the Brittany region. (Compare this to an estimated 4 million cameras in the UK.) Despite this increase, there has been no public debate between citizens and local authorities about the rationales for its adoption and about its effectiveness and limits. Moreover, the national security legislation (the "Sarkozy Laws" – see note 4) adopted CCTV as an essential method of surveillance. This did not generate any reaction from the public, apart from privacy organizations that denounced the violation of privacy facilitated by these cameras in the public sphere.

The extension of the use of surveillance cameras to the private sector (e.g., the workplace) was accepted in recent terrorism laws. Even if France's results appear relatively low compared to other countries' findings (except for Canada), they explain the increasingly widespread belief in the effectiveness of community and in-store CCTV to deter and/or solve crimes in a country that was traditionally hostile to such a technology. As a consequence, the market share of this technology increased at a rate of 45% and is now estimated to make up 35% of the electronic security equipment market (Observatoire de la Sécurité) (see GPD table 9(e) online).

Biometrics, which focus on body parts (fingerprints, iris and retina prints) to identify individuals with certainty, gained public attention after the decision of the Ministry of the Interior (headed at the time by Nicolas Sarkozy) to include biometrics in the French national ID cards.

The decisions of the International Civil Aviation Organization (ICAO) to insert biometric features in passports and of the US Department of Homeland Security to allow entry without visa only to citizens of secure countries (belonging to the visa waiver program) with biometric passports added to popular awareness about this technology.

low Level of Knowledge of Privacy Laws and Data Protection Agency

Even though French citizens have a relatively well developed knowledge of the notion of private life, which they essentially equate with intimate life, and even though they are concerned about infringement on information privacy by public institutions and private companies, they know very little about the laws that protect them. Canadians, Americans, and Spaniards appear to be more knowledgeable than the French about national laws that protect personal information held by government departments and the private sector (see table 9.1 above). French respondents are similarly familiar with technologies of communication and information, and they are comfortable discussing the Internet and personal location technologies such as GPS. However, many are unable to cite the name of the data protection agency – the Commission Nationale de l'Informatique et des Libertés – created to protect their rights. When asked about what to do in case of a serious invasion of their privacy, they list the Ministry of Justice, the Office of the Ombudsman (Médiateur de la République) or the Conciliation Board (Médiateur de la République), and the consumers' association magazine *60 millions de consommateurs*; the CNIL does not spontaneously come to mind.

There is, in fact, a public perception that the CNIL is a government department. The CNIL was created by law in 1978 as the French Data Protection Authority. It lacks independence vis-à-vis the state, however, since the majority of its seventeen members are selected by public authorities. It also lacks financial independence since the Ministry of Finance funds a significant proportion of its budget. Finally, with a staff of 120 permanent people, it is seriously understaffed. The duties of the CNIL include the regulation, supervision, and inspection of public and private data collections and data processing. It thus has an extensive list of responsibilities but a small staff and a lack of nationwide publicity. This explains the respondents' low knowledge of its existence and the widespread lack of confidence in the effectiveness of the laws to protect the personal information held by government departments and private companies.

Near Absence of Privacy Surveys

Unlike other European Union (EU) countries such as the UK, Germany, and Spain, French media coverage about the protection of personal information is low: in 2006 only 18% of media coverage was about privacy questions. Levels reached 59% in Canada, 76% in the United States, and 36% in Spain (Ipsos Reid 2006, 22). This media attention is more prevalent for the government (40%) than for the private sector (37%). France also demonstrates a near absence of surveys on privacy. Apart from very specialized Internet journals and human rights organizations' (like the Federation des Droits de l'Homme) newsletters, popular newspapers do not seem interested in measuring the privacy attitudes of French citizens. The CNIL rarely commissions surveys. In its survey of 2006, the CNIL asked two questions: one about citizens' awareness of the existence of CNIL and the other about citizens' level of knowledge about data protection. To the first question ("Do you know at least the name CNIL?"), only 39% of the respondents answered in the affirmative. To the second question ("Do you feel that you are sufficiently informed about your rights regarding the protection of your personal information?"), 27% answered "yes" and 70% answered "no" (*Notoriété de la CNIL* 2006). The CNIL, however, is not solely to blame for the lack of privacy surveys; other public authorities and universities do not undertake such inquiries either. Public authorities know the language of privacy but seem unwilling to spend time or money measuring it. In the universities, privacy issues have entered the curricula very recently and are largely approached through a juridical angle, leaving aside crucial sociological, philosophical, and political inquiries.

Unlike media coverage about the safety of personal information, security issues and terrorism receive the most media attention. The reason for this is twofold: first, France's two-decade terrorism experience (Middle Eastern-based terrorist attacks in the 1980s and Algeria-bound terrorist attacks in the 1990s) (Bigo 2000); second, the transformation of internal security issues into a hot-button topic since the 1980s and the conflation of immigration, organized crime, and terrorism.

Little Personal Experience of Breach of Privacy but Relatively High Level of Detention at Border Check Points Resulting in a Search

As the focus group findings and the survey results reveal, few people have experienced a real violation of their privacy (Ipsos Reid 2005, 12).

Table 9.4
Detention at a border checkpoint resulting in a search (%)*

Hungary	France	Canada	US	Spain	Mexico	Brazil
23	22	18	13	7	7	2

* Q8. Have you personally, to the best of your knowledge, ever experienced any of the following: detention at a border checkpoint resulting in a search?
Source: Ipsos Reid (2006, 14, GPD table 9).

The most common breaches of privacy they have encountered is the selling of personal information by commercial businesses (17%), followed by credit card theft (9%) (Ipsos Reid 2006, 14–15). For most people, privacy breaches are an intellectual concern rather than a real experience. There is, however, another point that requires attention and generates concern: detentions, and resulting searches, at border checkpoints. As shown in table 9.4, this seems to be a security practice that several countries' nationals have faced randomly in the wave of antiterrorism measures taken since the 9/11 attacks.

France and Hungary report a high level of detention at border checkpoints. Reasons for this are not developed in the GPD survey, but arguably one cannot understand this without an examination of the border control regime reinforced after the 9/11 attacks. Basically, there are two predominant border regimes: the international border regime, which controls external (or international) borders of a country; and the EU border control regime, in which internal borders are suppressed and external border controls are tightened (i.e., the Schengen regime). This is not the subject of inquiry in this chapter. However, everything depends on the nature of the border one crosses: there are no checks at internal EU borders, but there are mobile controls inside the member-states and tight checks at external borders. If we consider the GPD survey results according to this framework, we could assume that the figures reported by the French, Hungarian, and Spanish respondents correspond to border checks at the external borders of the EU or abroad at the border of a non-European country. This point is crucial for identifying the nature of the border crossed. However, the high number of French people detained and searched at a border checkpoint is puzzling. To assess these results more fully, we would also need to know the ethnic or religious origin of the people detained. If the people detained are French citizens of North African or Sub-Saharan origin, detentions and searches may be the result of discriminatory police controls based on ethnic profiling.

Americans and Canadians Do Not Object
to Employer Surveillance

Respondents in France and Spain object the most strongly to employers electronically monitoring employees through surveillance cameras and e-mails. Canadians and Americans appear to accept these practices more willingly (see GPD tables 9(f) and 9(g) online).

In France the right to a private life has been extended into the workplace. The French Labour Code, in article L.121–8, prohibits the collection of workers' information without prior identification. If an employer decides to collect personal information through monitoring, he or she must notify the worker prior to installing and using any surveillance and monitoring technology. French respondents accept such monitoring only if the employee has consented.

Attitudes toward the Sharing of Information between
Public and Private Institutions and the Dissemination
of Personal Data Abroad

The dissemination of information is an issue of great concern for citizens, especially when it occurs without their knowledge, which is almost always the case. However, citizens' attitudes depend on the nature of the agencies involved in the information sharing. Citizens appear to accept the sharing of information among government agencies such as the Ministry of the Interior, Customs, and the Ministry of Foreign Affairs as well as among intelligence services: 39% of respondents believe it is acceptable if the citizen is suspected of wrongdoing, and 24% if it is done with the consent of the citizen. Twenty per cent, however, oppose information sharing in any circumstance. There is much less openness when it comes to the government sharing information with private companies: 23% of the respondents believe it is acceptable with consent, but 45% oppose it. Finally, 45% believe it is acceptable to share information with foreign governments if someone is suspected of wrongdoing; 25% are opposed to such exchange (Ipsos Reid 2006, 39).

It would have been interesting to follow up on this last question and to examine it in the context of the transmission of Passenger Name Record (PNR) data of French and European passengers to American authorities before such passengers board an aircraft bound for the United States. PNR content is stored in the database of a computer reservation system that contains passengers' travel information. This information can be about all forms of payment information, meal preferences, special requests like wheel chairs, or any other information that has special protected status in the EU directive on data protection. In 2004 the United States negotiated the PNR transfer agreement[8] with the EU Commission in order to combat terrorism. Even though this agreement was invalidated by the EU Court of Justice in 2006, the United States and the EU Council implemented it. Airline carriers transmit a set of thirty-nine information data fifteen minutes before takeoff. This issue received significant media coverage in France, and human rights organizations raised vehement objections. Nevertheless, the majority of French citizens seem unaware of this transmission of their personal information to the US government. Most of them think – naively – that this agreement does not concern "normal citizens" like them but only wrongdoers.

Trust in Airport and Customs Officials' Respect for Privacy

The French, along with the Spanish, appear to be among the most likely to feel that airport and customs officials respect their privacy. Twenty per cent of the respondents trust officials "completely," 50% "a lot." This confidence is not due to French citizens' belief that security agencies have a great knowledge of privacy protection laws but is understandable in light of the confidence of French citizens in the capacity of their state to protect and respect them (see GPD table 9(h) online).

Indeed, the French look like the descendents of Thomas Hobbes in their delegation of the right of protection to the state and their confidence in the efficiency of state security measures. Even though average French citizens joke that the police are sometimes corrupted or inefficient, they are confident of their security agencies and their efficiency. However, this confidence does not translate into acceptance of all police practices. France is also among the countries where police practices are scrutinized by media and local associations. For instance, 31% of the French respondents claimed it was not at all acceptable for airport officials to conduct extra security checks of visible minorities (Ipsos Reid 2006, 57).

A POLITICAL CULTURE OF A STRONG STATE

A Strong Tradition of a Centralized State

To understand the French attitude toward security technologies and measures, one needs to take a look at some of the basic features of France's political culture, which has been generated around a deep belief in the primacy of the central state. This has always played a dominant role both in shaping economic and social policies and in ushering in progress and modernism.

This state-oriented culture is the product of French absolutism, a form of governance in which a single hereditary ruler exercised complete power (Anderson 1976, Birnbaum 1998). This period, which lasted from the reign of Henri IV (1585–1610) to that of Louis XIV (1643–1715), significantly shaped the French mentality and the structure of French power. The centralization and the bureaucratization of the state were realized under Louis XIV, who centralized power in the hands of the king. The king, in turn, was represented in the provinces by docile yet zealous intendants.

Such a centralized state soon became the champion of social and economic rules and norms via the state bureaucracy, which shaped the norms of social interaction and progress. As James B. Rule notes: "the bureaucratization of the central power operated also through the development of personal information systems – sources of actionable personal data that would enable officials to know the identities of the citizenry." For Rule, with reference to James Scott's famous work, "the aim of that process was to make population 'legible' to the rulers so that they become identified, enumerated and located" (2007, 4).

The state in France is also a product of the philosophical and intellectual developments of the seventeenth and eighteenth centuries. For example, strong beliefs in progress, rationalism, and the social contract are considered fundamental to French republicanism and societal consensus.

According to the French, the ideas of progress and living together can definitely be implemented within a nation that is also the space of the public will. Nation and nationalism constitute the most powerful driving forces of the French political culture (Birnbaum 1998), a culture that holds together despite conflict and disagreements. Nationalism is still deeply rooted in French economic activity despite globalization and Europeanization, and it continues to be the force that supports the promotion of prestigious projects in diverse areas such as international relations, economy, and technology.

Agreement with the ID Card and Some Resistance to Adding Its Biometric Features

As we have seen, 78% of French respondents agree with the existence of a national ID card. The adoption of this card in 1940 during the Third Republic is considered one of the major steps of the state formation process in France. In the view of historian Gérard Noiriel, the ID card was adopted as a consequence of the centralization of diverse paper files identifying individuals after their social integration following criminal activities (1996, 2001). Pierre Piazza considers the advent of the ID card to be a major step in the "administrative colonization" that created in French citizens the belief that they belong to a great community and participate in the development of norms of national behaviour (2004, 17).

The "cardification" of French citizens was realized through two processes. First, people were differentiated into "good guys" and "bad guys" (e.g., "deviants," "wanderers," and "the poor"). Second, a further distinction was made between French citizens and foreigners, who were singled out as being the causes of social, economic, and political troubles. This latter group was put under special scrutiny via specific police files and documents. In sum, the ID card was the symbol of belonging to the nation as a "good guy" (Piazza 2004, 43–61).

However, as Piazza contends, the process of "cardification" did encounter resistance. For instance, in 1921, when police chief Robert Leuiller decided to include fingerprints in the identity cards, his project was strongly opposed as a practice associating "good citizens" with "offenders" (2004, 145–9). After 1968, fingerprints were reintroduced in the ID cards but were again suppressed in 1974 on the same basis.

In 2005 the French government decided to implement Project Identité Nationale Electronique Sécurisée (INES), which was to transform the paper-based ID card into an electronic card with biometric features. As justification, the government cited international obligations, the fight against terrorism, and combating identity theft. This project, however, generated a sort of soft resistance from organizations that defended fundamental freedoms and civil rights by raising concerns about the efficiency of such a card (Piazza 2006). The Forum of Internet Rights (Le Forum des droits sur l'Internet)[9] was established and tasked by the Ministry of the Interior with conducting consultations on this issue. In its final report, submitted in June 2005, the forum raised several questions: about the efficiency of this card for combating terrorism and crime, about its impacts on the social contract, about its technical features, and about the lack of a parliamentary debate on its compulsory nature. Perhaps surprisingly, there was very little emphasis on the privacy issues generated by it. It is also noteworthy that this debate was not accompanied by nationwide public surveys about the attitudes of the French population on this issue.

State and Technology Nexus

The field of technology reveals many of the values of French political culture, especially the primacy given to the state and the public's acceptance that the state is a promoter of progress. Didier Lemeire and Christian Lennerz (1998) list several factors that support this proposition:

1 The technology industry is closely tied to the state, which provides generous subsidies and other forms of economic incentives for the development of leading technologies (e.g., microchips).
2 The state cultivates an image of itself as an advisor and participant in technology programs.
3 Prestigious projects like the high-speed train (TGV) are strongly supported by the whole nation.
4 The government and administration act as French representatives of the high-tech industry abroad. The prime motivation of this sponsorship is prestige thinking.
5 France aspires to be not only a technological nation but also a leader in many fields, such as the European aerospace industry.

All these characteristics were made possible by the strong support of citizens who consider these actions to be normal for enhancing the "grandeur" of their country. This explains the attitudes of French citizens toward security technologies and their trust in the government for protection. Even if many of the security technologies open the way to privacy invasions, most French citizens believe that the state will protect them in the end.

Such a strong and solid relationship between the state and the technology industry, combined with public confidence in the state, may be helpful in keeping up with the pace of technological advances. However, it severely limits the proliferation of public debate and deliberation. In effect, because of the state's promotion of high technology, citizens lack comprehensive information about new products and devices, and they cannot discuss the dangers generated by their usage with the same intensity as citizens of other countries, such as the UK, Canada, and the United States. This raises important concerns about deliberative democracy and privacy protection.

CONCLUSION

French citizens have the reputation of being fairly knowledgeable about their personal information. The preceding analysis reveals, however, that despite their traditional attachment to the concept of "private life," they know very little about the legislation and administrative bodies that protect their privacy in the context of an information society and global surveillance. It also reveals that France has minimal media coverage about the safety of personal information. French respondents also appear to be among the least likely to feel that laws aimed at protecting national security are intrusive upon personal privacy.

The reasons for such a lack of awareness about privacy laws and simultaneous confidence in security laws are to be found in the old tradition of a strong state, which France inherited from Louis XIV, and in a conception of security resembling that seen in Thomas Hobbes's *Leviathan*. Indeed, French citizens have delegated the task of protecting their security to the state, which, to them, is endowed with a strong legitimacy. However, security – long equated with public order – became a hot-button political topic in the 1980s, then extending its scope and focus to new referents. Currently, "security" not only covers protection against physical dangers and risks but is also closely tied to issues of identity and immigration. Thus it became the principal tool of French politicians with which to protect their citizens not only against physical attacks but also against globalization, transnationalization, and economic flexibility. In this context, the state is accepted as the primary actor for fulfilling this task, even though it delegates some security assignments to the private sector. However, the state cannot carry out such a duty without the confidence of its citizens in its capacity to protect the country from the dangers mentioned above.

Based on the data from the GPD survey, the conclusion is that in this context, privacy issues were not ignored – for they did become an increasing concern with the rapid penetration of ICT and security technologies into the daily life of individuals – but they simply were not expressed as political problems. That is, they were not publicized and deliberated upon in the media and the public sphere, and they were not discussed seriously in Parliament. This may be a consequence of the famous trade-off between security and liberty that many observers criticize as limiting fundamental rights. However, it is nevertheless striking to observe such a trend in one of the EU's leading countries, a country for which personal data protection is a topic of real concern and one that, in fact, has adopted legislation capable of enforcing such protection.

NOTES

I am grateful to Elia Zureik, who gave me the opportunity to write this chapter and expertly guided me with his brilliant comments and suggestions. Many thanks to Iza Tigli for her valuable comments and contribution to the data analysis of this chapter.

1 Formerly Thomson, Thales is an electronic and systems group leveraging dual technologies to serve defence, aerospace, and security markets. Among its products are integrated border security systems, aviation safety devices, and identification tools.

2 Oberthur is one of the major players in the high-security industry. It is the third largest privately owned banknote printer worldwide, supplies payment cards with microprocessors, and offers solutions for secure identity documents.

3 Gemalto was formed when Gemplus combined with Axalto in 2006. The company is one of the leaders in software solutions and microchips. It produces secure personal devices such as smart cards, subscriber identity modules (SIMs), e-passports, and so on.

4 Since 2000 several laws related to security have been enacted. Among them, in reverse chronological order, the most notorious are: the law of 23 January 2006 about the fight against terrorism, security, and border controls (this law extends video surveillance to the whole public sphere and adopts measures that enable the control of communications and movements of "risky" people); in 2006 the law on the prevention of delinquency; in 2004 the law on immigration (called Sarkozy law 2); in 2003 the first Sarkozy law on immigration; and in 2002 the Loi pour la sécurité intérieure, setting the basic orientation of the security policy for five years and organizing a judicial counterpart to the repressive system.

5 Carried out by Ipsos Reid between 2004 and 2006 for Queen's University (Ipsos Reid 2006), the GPD survey is an extensive cross-national study encompassing eight countries: Brazil, Canada, China, France, Hungary, Mexico, Spain, and the United States. Its focus includes respondents' knowledge about surveillance technologies and privacy laws; informational, territorial, communicational, and bodily privacy; the use of surveillance technologies in public and private places; and what consumers think of direct profiling and its implications for privacy. The study is also concerned with the intrusiveness of national security laws and airport surveillance and with the collection and sharing of personal information.

6 All GPD tables cited in this chapter are online at http://www.sscqueens.org/book_tables (accessed 7 December 2009).

7 For a discussion, see Martinais and Bétin (2004).

8 Agreement between the European Community and the United States on the process of the transfer of PNR data by air carriers to the US Department of Homeland Security, Bureau of Customs and Border Patrol, Council Directive 2004 OJC (L 183) EC.

9 See http://www.foruminternet.org (accessed 7 December 2009).

PART 3.3

Developing Countries

INTRODUCTION

David Lyon

One major difficulty attending attempts to study surveillance and privacy comparatively is that most research to date has been carried out in the affluent societies of North America and western Europe (often collectively known as the "global North"). In a globalizing world it is imperative to broaden our grasp of these issues, highly consequential as they are for democratic processes and for citizenship. However, when attempts are made to push the envelope, as the Globalization of Personal Data (GPD) survey does by including countries that are less well researched, other problems are encountered. Cultural differences mean that surveillance and privacy are understood differently, political differences mean that there is even less commonality of democratic practice than in the global North, and technological differences mean that levels of development and of public understanding are also at variance with those of at least the most "advanced" countries in the global North.

The reasons why other countries than those of North America and western Europe should be included are manifold, but they relate particularly to the global mobility of persons, goods, and information; to the very rapid economic advances being made in countries such as India and China, which make them both economic and political forces to be reckoned with in new ways; and to the international impacts both of governments, through foreign policies, and of corporations, through aggressive quests for new markets. Each of these plays a role in relation to surveillance and privacy. Rising mobility rates mean more official

scrutiny of goods, information, and persons, particularly as they cross
borders and especially when they may be "suspect" (such as illegal immigrants). Economic growth is linked with technological advances that
inevitably entail enhanced control mechanisms for administration in
all spheres, affecting people in everyday life. And the foreign policies
of richer countries often oblige poorer ones to acquiesce to their demands for items such as identification documents, while corporations,
often headquartered in those richer countries, simultaneously attempt
to press on other countries the "solutions" for population management
or new devices, from cell-phones to laptops, that generate even more
surveillance and privacy questions. By working along similar axes of
technological development and by noting the political-economic implications of the information and communication technologies (ICT)
in quite diverse countries, we may be able to obtain some comparative
understanding of their privacy dynamics. Both the focus groups and the
actual survey proved their worth for understanding surveillance and
privacy issues in these three countries.

In the case of China, whose surveillance and privacy issues are frequently mentioned in the Western press, understanding how ordinary citizens, workers, travellers, and consumers negotiate the world
of new technology surveillance is vital. For example, a fast-growing
company called China Security and Surveillance Technology was listed
during 2007 on the New York Stock Exchange (see Bradsher 2007). It
installs surveillance technologies for police agencies, banks, and jails.
The new technologies are frequently very advanced systems, such as
face-recognition and behaviour-recognition software for closed circuit
television (CCTV) installations. This immediately indicates not only
the high level of technical development in this field – which as the first
chapter in this section shows is predominantly an urban phenomenon
in China – but also the complicity of American companies in supporting the very schemes that are sometimes denounced under the
"human rights" banner in the United States.

The chapter looks at the seven Chinese cities covered by the GPD
survey, commenting first on the astonishingly fast diffusion of ICT
(which is outstripping India, with its rapid ICT growth in a comparable
population of over 1 billion). The first part focuses on Internet usage,
which is subject to widespread disparities along rural-urban, gender,
economic, and education lines. Although this is in some respects little
different from early experiences with ICT in the global North, little
is done in the Chinese case to try to redress these imbalances. This is

explored further within the GPD survey, which does much to confirm the initial analysis, although it leaves open an explanation of the role of public access to Internet and computer services (such as Internet cafés), which has also been important in India and some Caribbean countries, such as Trinidad (Miller and Slater 2000).

The final part of the chapter breaks new ground by analyzing the survey results that discuss familiarity with new technologies and laws that relate to them in public and private spheres. It transpires that respondents in the sample are much more aware of the technologies than of the laws pertaining to them. On the other hand, how they perceive the effectiveness of those laws is related to their knowledge neither of the laws nor of the technologies, a finding consistent with those surveyed in the other countries. It is hard to come to any meaningful conclusions about this, for all the reasons mentioned above and possibly others as well. The Chinese situation is unique in many respects, and the issues are often differently perceived from those in the West. Censorship and political surveillance have generally been seen as more important than "privacy," which has a different history in China (McDougall 2002). Additionally, Western-style data protection regimes are relative newcomers on the Chinese scene (Peerenboom 2002), and such innovations typically take some time to percolate through to the majority of the population. Even with privacy laws dating back more than two decades in Canada, general knowledge of these is relatively thin.

Turning to Mexico and Brazil, the second chapter in this section shows that different histories, conditions, and experiences once again frame issues of surveillance and privacy. In this case, much may be said about the ways that privacy is understood in both countries – which, in this regard, are seen as having more similarities than differences – in relation to the protection of a sphere that relates above all to the family. In a telling argument, the chapter concludes that there is a significant political economy of surveillance and privacy in these two countries that renders privacy a sought-after commodity that is financially out of reach of the majority of the population in both countries. Privacy is seen as being very unevenly distributed, with the regrettable effect that "large sectors of the population are unable to practise or exercise their rights of citizenship."

With regard to both countries, although there are some signs that the social consequences of the diffusion of new technologies such as cell phones, the Internet, and CCTV are considered to be significant, it would be wrong to conclude that this produces any serious concern

about privacy rights or civil liberties, except perhaps among politically conscious minorities. This is related to the complex nexus between
shifting cultural values and political-economic experiences in the two
countries, dominated as they are by extremes of poverty and violence
next to affluence and by what the chapter calls "artificial" democracy.
Although both countries are viewed as having more similarities than
differences, the variations between them are also illustrated in the survey data discussed. For instance, Mexicans seem to have significantly
lower levels of trust than do Brazilians in either governments or corporations to handle their personal data appropriately. Although the
chapter does not elaborate on this particular finding, it would be worth
asking whether it relates to the sheer proportion of relative contact
with the United States. Mexico is in a far closer trading relationship
than is Brazil with its North American partner, even though this is now
being challenged, particularly by China.

Of course, conclusions reached from focus groups and an international survey are always tentative and subject to challenge from
further studies. And the fact that the present volume does not include
material on India to parallel that on China or on countries with more
recent military pasts such as those in Argentina or Peru does not negate
the significance of what is presented here. The GPD survey stands on its
own as a study that attempts to cross cultural and political divides and
especially to include significant actors on the global scene that are all
too frequently overlooked. So-called "developing countries" have their
own trajectory of experiences with surveillance and privacy and will
contribute increasingly to the ways that these will shape citizenship and
democracy in the future.

10

Dimensions of Internet Inequality and Privacy in China: A Case Study of Seven Cities

ELIA ZUREIK

INTRODUCTION

By various accounts, China has the fourth largest economy in the world – after the United States, Japan, and Germany – and before long it is poised to match that of the United States (Hutton 2007).[1] Crucial to China's modernization efforts during the past two decades has been the exponential increase in the adoption of information and communication technologies (ICT), be it in the ownership of telephones, cell phones, and personal computers or in the use of the Internet. In absolute numbers, China ranks first in ownership of mobile and fixed-line phones and second after the United States in the number of Internet users.[2] Notwithstanding these developments, China lags behind industrialized countries on a per capita basis on each of these indicators (table 10.1). Further, as we shall see below, the spread of ICT in China has been uneven in terms of regions and socio-economic indicators.

Although China is pursuing in earnest the path to modernization through technology, the overall progress of its democratization efforts is far from satisfactory by Western standards. Here, technology acts as a double-edged sword. Although on one level ICT facilitates the march toward modernization, on another level it opens up new vistas of access to global information that pose a threat to an authoritarian political system. The role of the Internet is particularly interesting in this regard. The much-touted assumption regarding the role of the Internet in spreading democracy in authoritarian regimes through by-passing state control of the flow of information is being seriously questioned in the case of China and elsewhere where the state censors the Internet (Klein 2008, Bradsher 2007, Tsui 2003).[3]

Table 10.1
GDP and basic ICT indicators for China, Germany, Japan, and the United States
(1999, 2005)

	Population (million)		GDP (billion US$)		GDP per capita (US$)		Fixed-line telephone subscribers (per 100 inhabitants)	
	1999	2005	1999	2005	1999	2005	1999	2005
China	1,264.07	1,315.84	954.3	1,935.7	761	1,480	12.03	56.53
Germany	82.16	82.69	2,150.5	2,724.9	2,6214	3,3029	87.21	162.35
Japan	126.65	128.08	3,940.4	4,585.1	3,1179	3,5877	93.88	120.65
US	279.04	298.21	8,781.5	11,712.5	3,1834	3,9885	98.75	130.23

	Mobile phone subscribers (per 100 inhabitants)		Mobile phone CAGR[a] (%)		Number of PCs (per 100 inhabitants)		Internet users (per 100 inhabitants)	
	1999	2005	1994–99	2000–05	1999	2005	1999	2005
China	3.43	29.90	94.2	35.8	1.23	4.05	0.70	8.44
Germany	28.54	95.78	56.6	10.4	29.70	54.54	20.81	45.35
Japan	44.88	75.33	67.3	7.6	28.66	54.15	21.37	51.54
US	30.84	71.43	28.9	14.2	50.53	76.22	36.55	66.33

a CAGR refers to the compound annual growth rate.
Source: International Telecommunication Union, World Telecommunication Indicators Reports, http://www.itu.int/ITU-D/ict/statistics (accessed 13 November 2009).

This chapter does not deal with the democratization-cum-modernization debate by discussing the impact of the Internet on political life in China. Rather, the purpose is to provide a detailed analysis of a recent public opinion survey conducted in seven Chinese cities[4] and to highlight the correlates of Internet use and the public's attitudes toward various surveillance technologies and privacy issues. As a prelude to discussing the survey data, however, the chapter provides an overview of the scope of Internet use in China as a whole and the background characteristics of the users.

INTERNET IN CHINA

By December 2007, according to the annual survey carried out by the China Internet Network Information Centre (CNNIC 2008), China had 210 million Internet users,[5] nearly a tenfold increase since 2000, when the figure stood at 22.5 million users, and close to 220 times greater than what was recorded in October 1997, the date of the first CNNIC Internet survey. At that time, the number of Internet users was a mere 620,000 (CNNIC 1997). By 2009, the penetration rate was 26.9%, up from 4.6% in 2002. China's penetration rate, with its population of 1.3 billion, is more than three times that of India (7%) with a comparable population of 1.1 billion (Internet World Stats).

These impressive increases in Internet diffusion should not conceal an urban-rural digital divide, as well as a correlation between Internet penetration and level of economic development among China's regions. Internet penetration in cities is 6.5 times higher than in rural regions. Although it is narrowing somewhat, this differential rate has been maintained since 2000 (CNNIC 2006, 66). Put another way, the 2006 survey shows that 83% of all Internet users in China live in urban areas and that only 17% reside in rural regions.

If we examine Internet penetration by region, we notice that the industrialized regions of eastern China – with twice the gross domestic product (GDP) – have a penetration rate of more than twice that of the central and western regions. The eastern region, with 38% of China's population, has a penetration rate of close to 16% for 2006, compared to around 7% for the rest of the country (CNNIC 2006, 67; see Globalization of Personal Data tables 10(a) and 10(b) online).[6]

DEMOGRAPHIC FACTORS

The 2006 CNNIC survey discovered that males account for 58.7% of Internet users and females for 41.3%.[7] Half of the Internet users are below the age of 25; adding the 25 to 30 year olds reveals that 70% of Internet users in China are under 31 years of age (CNNIC 2006, 12). Education is positively correlated with Internet use. Among Internet users, 30.2% have high school education, 24.4% a three- or four-year college diploma, 26.3% a bachelor's degree, and 2.9% a postgraduate degree. Sixteen per cent of the Internet users have education below high school level. The stark influence of education becomes apparent if we partition the data by education background: 84.4% of those with a college diploma and above use the Internet, compared to 20.5% of those with high school education and only 1.8% of those with less than high school education. One-third of Internet users are students, another one-third are professionals, school teachers, and other white-collar workers, and the rest work in government and nongovernmental organizations. Less than one-half of 1% of Internet users are farmers and peasants.

With regard to income, 25% of Internet users have a monthly income below 500 RMB (renminbi is the name of the Chinese currency), 18% between 501 and 1,000 RMB, 53% above 1,000 RMB, and 4% declared no income (CNNIC 2006, 41–55). To put these figures in perspective, according to official data, the disposable per capita annual income in rural China in 2006 was 3,587 RMB (US$450) compared to 11,759 RMB (US$1500) for urban residents.[8] When prorated on a monthly basis, the average disposable income of a rural resident is 300 RMB; for urban residents it is 980 RMB.

We can conclude that the majority of Internet users in China are young, educated, live in industrialized regions, and have a highly disproportionate income relative to the rest of the population.

THE GLOBALIZATION OF PERSONAL DATA SURVEY[9]

Sample Composition

The sample for this study, which is part of the Globalization of Personal Data (GPD) project, is drawn from seven cities located in urban regions. These include China's largest cities and industrial centres such as Shanghai, Beijing, and Guangzhou (referred to as metropolises) as well as provincial capitals (map 10.1). For data on the seven participating cities in terms of population, GDP, and basic ICT indicators, see table 10.2. A total of 17,546 households were randomly selected, of which 11.6% participated in the telephone interview. Respondents were almost evenly distributed between males (51.2%) and females (48.8%). A breakdown of reasons for refusing to participate shows that 58% mentioned lack of time, 22% hung up the phone, and 12% were not interested. Less than 1% mentioned privacy concerns as a reason for refusing to participate in the survey.

DEMOGRAPHIC ANALYSIS

Turning to the findings of the multicountry survey, with special focus on the seven urban centres in China, this chapter carries out four main types of analysis. First, it examines patterns of computer and Internet usage in the home, workplace, and public places such as Internet cafés, public libraries, and community centres. Second, by taking into account age, education, gender, occupation, region, and income, it examines the

Map 10.1
China: Seven participating cities in the GPD survey

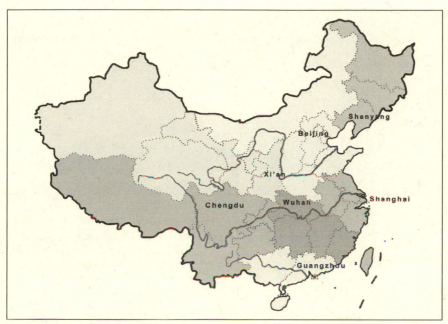

Source: Liang and Huili (2006, 4).

determinants of computer and Internet usage through bivariate and
multivariate analysis. Third, it assesses familiarity with key surveillance
technologies as a function of background variables. Finally, the chapter turns to a discussion of the meaning of privacy in China and the
attitudes to privacy protection in the public and private sectors.

COMPUTER AND INTERNET USAGE

Three-quarters of the Chinese respondents in our sample used the computer from home during the six months preceding the survey, with little
variation across the seven cities in the sample. Slightly more than half
reported using the computer at work. The highest figure was reported by
Guangzhou (59.3%) and the lowest by Shenyang (44.4%). Thirty-nine
per cent reported using computers in public places, with no significant
variations across cities.

Overall, two-thirds indicated that they had used the Internet in the previous six months, with 43% reporting using it at work. This proportion

Table 10.2
GDP and basic ICT indicators for the seven Chinese cities in the sample (2005–06 data)

	Population (million)[a]	GDP (billion RMB)[a]	Annual per capita GDP[b] (RMB)[b]	Per capita ranking	Per capita monthly GDP (RMB)
Beijing	15.36	681.45	44,365	3	3,697.08
Shanghai	17.78	914.395	51,428	2	4,285.67
Guangzhou	9.488	511.575	53,918	1	4,493.17
Chengdu	12.21	237.10	19,419	6	1,618.25
Wuhan	8.58	223.80	26,084	5	2,173.67
Xi'an	8.069	127.0	15,739	7	1,311.58
Shenyang	7.4	224.0	30,270	4	2,522.50
Total	78.9	2,919.32			

	Internet penetration (%)	Internet user accounts (million)	Fixed-line telephone accounts (million)	Fixed-line telephone account penetration[c] (%)	Mobile telephone accounts (million)	Mobile telephone account penetration[c] (%)
Beijing	30.5[d]/28.7[e]	4.66[f]	9.50	61.85	14.70	95.70
Shanghai	34.4[d]/26.6[e]	8.03	9.97	56.07	14.44	81.21
Guangzhou	34.4[d]/20.5[g]	2.49	6.25	65.87	13.55	142.81
Chengdu	23.4[d]	2.09	4.28	35.05	7.90	64.70
Wuhan	16.9[e]	1.32[h]	3.89	45.34	5.45	63.52
Xi'an	25.7[d]	1.19	3.21	39.78	4.20	52.05
Shenyang	21.0[d]	0.76	3.62	48.92	3.48	47.03

a Population and GDP are retrieved from the *Yearbook* of each of these seven cities published in 2006 (originally in Chinese, 2005).

b Per capita GDP here is the result of dividing total GDP by the city's population.

c Data on mobile and fixed-line telephones were obtained by dividing the number of fixed-line telephone accounts and mobile telephone accounts by the city's population, respectively. All the unmarked data are from the *Statistical Gazette of National Economy and Social Development* of the seven cities separately (originally in Chinese).

d These are estimates based on survey data published by the Markle Foundation in 2003, *Surveying Usage and Impact in Twelve Chinese Cities*, directed by Guo Liang, figure 2-2, 16, http://www.markle.org/downloadable_assets/chinainternet_usage.pdf (accessed 12 November 2009).

e These data are from the 2007 annual report of the China Internet Network Information Centre (CNNIC), http://www.cnnic.net.cn/download/2007/cnnic19threport.pdf, (accessed 12 November 2009).

f According to the 2007 annual report of the CNNIC, there were 137.0 million Internet users in China, and Beijing Internet users comprised 3.4% of them, which yields a figure of 4.66 million Internet users in Beijing. See http://www.cnnic.net.cn/download/2007/cnnic19threport.pdf (accessed 12 November 2009).

g The Internet penetration of Guangzhou refers to the data at the end of 2003, obtained from the *Yearbook* of Guangzhou published in 2004 (originally in Chinese, 2003).

h According to the Wuhan government website, the population in Wuhan is 7,811,900, among whom there are 1.32 million Internet users, which yields a penetration rate of about 16.9%. See http://english.wh.gov.cn/html/Introduction/20070926/278.html (accessed 15 August 2008).

reached a high of 46% in Shanghai and Guangzhou and a low of 33% in Shenyang. One-third used the Internet in public places; the highest level in this group was recorded in Xi'an at 44% and the lowest in Beijing at 29.5%.

By using as the basis for calculation the number of usages from the three different places, rather than the number of respondents per se, we discover that there were 3,315 multiple computer usages in a sample of between 1,996 and 1,997 respondents, for an average of 1.6 access points per computer user, and 2,823 Internet usages from the three different access points (home, workplace, and public places), for an average of 1.41 Internet usages per respondent. Whether it is the computer or Internet, urban residents in our sample of seven[10] cities are close to other countries in our national samples of Canada, France, Hungary, and the United States in terms of type of access point. Slightly less than half of the Chinese respondents used the computer and the Internet from home, less than one-third from work, and around one-quarter from public places (see GPD tables 10(c) and 10(d) online).

Since the question regarding access allowed for multiple-choice answers, a breakdown of the various combinations of access points shows that three-quarters used the computer at home only *in addition* to using it in one or two other places, and two-thirds used the Internet at home *or* at home in combination with the two other places. In both cases, the home emerges as the most favoured place for using the computer and the Internet, followed by the workplace and, lastly, by public places (see GPD table 10(e) online).

BIVARIATE ANALYSIS

To draw a more comprehensive picture showing how computer use and Internet use relate to age, education, income, region, gender, and occupation, the correlations with the background variables are considered (see GPD table 10(f) online). Computer use and Internet use at home are highly correlated with income, age, and education. Although the correlations are substantially lower with regard to occupation and region, they remain statistically significant. Older respondents are less likely to use computers and the Internet regardless of their location. Those with high education and income levels consistently use the Internet and computer at home, at work, and in public places to greater degrees than do respondents with lower income and education levels. Region has weak to significant correlations with computer and Internet use for two of the locales – the home and public places. Finally, with regard to gender, more men than women use computers and the Internet at work and in public places.

MULTIVARIATE ANALYSIS

A series of logistic regressions were utilized to provide a more nuanced measure of how the background variables (for both categorical and ordinal variables) relate to computer use and Internet use. A series of regression equations focusing on computer use at home, at work, and in public places as the dependent variable, followed by similar regressions regarding Internet use as the dependent variable (see GPD tables 10(g), 10(h), 10(i), 10(j), 10(k), and 10(l) online), reveals the following results.

For the scaled variables, such as education, income, and age, the analysis shows that for every unit of change in education, the odds of using a computer at home increase by 1.93 times; with every unit of change in income, the odds increase by 1.27 times. However, increase in age has a negative effect on the odds of using a computer at home by a factor of 0.95. In other words, for every unit of change in age, the odds of older respondents using the computer is 0.95 times lower compared to younger ones. The same pattern obtains with regard to use of computers in the workplace: the higher the level of education and income, the greater the likelihood that respondents will use a computer in the workplace. Here, too, increase in age is inversely correlated with computer use. Using the provincial capital of Shenyang as the reference point, we notice that only in Chengdu does the odds ratio compare in a statistically significant manner (.004). The odds that respondents from Chengdu will use computers in the workplace is less than half (.423) of that for respondents from Shenyang. Of the occupational groups, only among the unskilled workers do we see a statistically significant odds ratio (.004) in the use of computers, compared to the professional group acting as the reference point. Relative to the professional and skilled group, the odds that a skilled worker will use a computer in the workplace is less than 1 in 3 (.308).

Increases in education and age contribute to a lesser likelihood of computer use in public places, with an odds ratio of .63 for education and .84 for age. With regard to gender, men are more likely to use computers in public places compared to women, with an odds ratio of 2.15. Of the six cities in the regression model, only Xi'an compares significantly to Shenyang, the reference city, by an odds ratio of 1.6.

The regression models for Internet use as the dependent variable show that when the Internet is used from home (see GPD tables 10(j), 10(k), and 10(l) online), the odds ratio for education is 1.79, and for income it is 1.29. Increase in age is associated with a decrease in Internet use by a factor of .94. The same independent variables appear in GPD table 10(k) (online), regarding the use of Internet in the workplace. For every unit of increase in education, the odds ratio for using the Internet at the workplace is 2.49, and for income it is 1.19. Here, too, older people have lesser odds of using the Internet in the workplace by a factor of .96. Income does not appear as a significant independent variable in the regression model of public places, and the direction of the relationship with education and age is reversed compared to the models (see GPD tables 10(j) and 10(k) online). Increases in education and income levels lower the odds that people will use the Internet in public places by a factor of .65 for education and .82 for income. Gender, on the other hand, emerges as a significant independent variable showing that the odds of men using the computer in public places is more than twice (2.37) that of women. Of the seven cities in our sample, only Xi'an compares in a statistically significant way to Shenyang, the reference city, by an odds ratio of 1.78.

KNOWLEDGE ABOUT SURVEILLANCE TECHNOLOGIES

Included in the GPD survey was an item with six components that probed respondents' knowledge about key ICT technologies that are used in surveillance: the Internet, global positioning systems (GPS), radio frequency identification (RFID), closed circuit television (CCTV), biometrics, and data mining. Using a Likert-scale-type question, the survey asked respondents to indicate whether they are "very knowledgeable," "somewhat knowledgeable," "not very knowledgeable," "not at all knowledgeable," or "do not know."

There are country differences in the level of knowledge about these technologies and also similarities, depending on the type of technology in question (see GPD appendix tables (10.1 to 10.7) online). For example, the majority of respondents either were not very knowledgeable or were not knowledgeable at all regarding data mining, biometrics, and RFID. The size of these majorities differed from one country to another. Between 80% and 90% of respondents in Brazil, Mexico, and China expressed scant knowledge about data mining. In Canada, Spain, and Hungary, from two-thirds to three-quarters of respondents had a low level of knowledge about data mining. At 57%, the United States had the lowest level of unfamiliarity with data mining. A similar pattern obtains with regard to biometrics. Seventy per cent of American and Canadian respondents knew little about biometrics, compared to three-quarters of French and Chinese respondents. Between 80% and 90% of Brazilian, Hungarian, Mexican, and Spanish respondents had little knowledge about biometrics. The level of knowledge about RFID hovered around 40% in Spain and the United States and was one-third in Canada and Hungary. One-fifth of the Chinese and Brazilian respondents, however, said they were knowledgeable about RFID technology. Only 9% of the Mexican sample had any level of knowledge about RFID.

The highest level of familiarity with these technologies was reserved for the Internet. Around 80% of Canadians, Americans, and Spaniards are familiar with the Internet, followed by close to two-thirds of the Chinese and the French respondents and by slightly more than half of the Hungarians. Contrast this to one-third of the respondents in Brazil and Mexico.

It is surprising that, in spite of the mounting diffusion of CCTV, less than half of Canadian, French, Spanish, and American respondents said they were familiar with the technology. Brazil (26%) and Mexico (19%) were least familiar with CCTV. The other surprising finding concerns China: at 60%, China had the highest level of familiarity with CCTV. No doubt this is due to the fact that the campaign to install CCTV in China is rather recent.

The wide use of the GPS in cars accounts for knowledge about the technology in Canada (55%), France (53%), Spain (60%), and the United States (60%). In Hungary and China, one-third said they were familiar with GPS, whereas in Brazil and Mexico the percentages were 13% and 7%, respectively.

MULTIPLE LINEAR REGRESSION

In an attempt to gauge the contribution of background variables to knowledge about the technology in China, we established a technology knowledge index based on summing up the responses to the six items in the question discussed above.[11] The index ranges from 0 (no knowledge at all) to 100 (complete knowledge). Through a stepwise linear regression, we were able to assess the relative contribution of gender, education, income, and age to knowledge about the technology. As predictors, neither region nor occupation yielded statistically significant results in the model. The linear regression equation[12] shows that females are less likely to know about the various technologies by a magnitude of 5.5 compared to males. Every unit of increase in the educational level is accompanied with 1.8 units of increase in knowledge about the technology. Although increase in income is related to an increase in knowledge about the technology (beta = .918), increase in age is inversely related to knowledge about the technology (beta = -.231).

PRIVACY IN THE CHINESE CONTEXT

Family and community continue to form the backbone of Chinese society. As a result, collectivism takes precedence over individualism. This is why publicly divulging certain types of personal information can be seen as detrimental to the well-being of the community as a whole. There is no single word in Chinese that corresponds to "privacy." Traditionally, "privacy" is associated with *Yinsi* (*yin* means hide and *si* personal or private) (Liang and Huili 2006). Unlike in the West, personal privacy in China does not refer to the right of individuals to safeguard against intrusion into one's private domain. *Yinsi* pertains to shameful conduct that, if revealed, could damage the reputation of the individual and community and, indeed, even of the nation. Thus keeping information secret, possibly with the exception of keeping information from family members, is seen as a necessary act and a means to conceal wrongdoing (Lui 2005).

This perception of personal privacy is undergoing change in China, particularly in the area of information privacy. More than a decade ago, a Chinese scholar was able to point out that the debate over privacy in China was evolving beyond the traditional conception that primarily related privacy to personal matters dealing with the intimate affairs of citizens. Thus he summarized the views of legal scholars in China, who argued that "(i) the subject of the right to privacy can only be [a] natural person; (ii) the objects of the right are private activities, personal information and private areas; and (iii) the scope of the right is limited by the public interest" (Zhu 1997, 210).

Although Chinese attitudes to privacy have a long way to go before they equal Western standards, the openness of China to the outside world, particularly as a result of globalization and access to the Internet, and the increase in its economic prowess have spurred discussion over privacy rights in general and over the role of privacy in enhancing electronic commerce in particular. Some argue that China's innovation in the privacy domain will inevitably be greatly influenced by debates in the West over privacy protection (Jingehun 2005). In an overview of changes taking place in the meaning of and attitudes toward privacy in China, Lu Yao-Huai remarked that "people no longer regard individual interests, individual freedom and individual rights as taboo topics of discussion" (2005, 7). For example, a national survey carried out in China in 2003 discovered that 55% of those polled thought that privacy should be respected and protected (8). "Privacy consciousness," according to Yao-Huai, can be discerned along three dimensions: there is recognition of the right to demand privacy in personal communication, particularly among the younger generation; people are now less inclined to interfere with the private affairs of others, including in issues of sexual conduct; and, finally, the concept of privacy has been expanded beyond *Yinsi* to include other spheres of behaviour related to the use of the Internet and to transactions involving personal information.

EMPIRICAL RESEARCH ON PRIVACY

The work of Geert Hofstede has provided the cornerstone for much of the empirical research on and for the debate surrounding the correlations between national cultures and specific values related to work, privacy, and managerial conduct. Most of this empirical research, however, has dealt with case studies focusing on the relationship between national values and managerial culture. Initially, Hofstede developed four indices to compare core values across cultures: Power Distance Index (PDI), Individualism Index (IDV), Masculinity Index (MAS), and Uncertainty Avoidance Index (UAI). Hofstede (1991) later added Long-Term Orientation (LTO) as a specific value differentiating cultures in terms of advocating perseverance, dynamism, and orientation to the future versus short-term orientation characterized by upholding of tradition, stagnation, and stability.

As is pointed out in chapter 1, those who score high on UAI tend to be low risk takers, and those with high IDV scores are more self-reliant and tend to prefer loose communal bonds. High PDI scores indicate authoritarianism and acceptance of inequality in society, high MAS reflects male-centred values and assertiveness in contrast to caring values, and high scores on LTO reflect attachment to tradition. In terms of rankings on the five indices, China scores fairly high on LTO and PDI, with a middle score on MAS, followed by a lower score on UAI and by one of the lowest cross-cultural scores on IDV.[13]

The connection between privacy and Hofstede's values is summarized by Steve Bellman and colleagues (2004) in their discussion of an earlier study by Sandra Millberg and colleagues (1995), which used Hofstede's indices and was based on samples of information systems auditors:

> Although high Power Distance Index (PDI) cultures tolerate greater levels of inequality in power, higher scores are associated with greater mistrust of more powerful groups, such as companies. Low individualism (IND), or collectivist, societies have greater acceptance that groups, including organizations, can intrude on the private life of the individual. High (MAS) cultures place greater emphasis on achievement and material success, and perhaps the economic benefits of using private information, over caring relationships and quality of life. Finally, societies with high Uncertainty Avoidance Index (UAI) tend to reduce uncertainty by embracing clear written rules and regulations, and may be more likely to introduce higher levels of government regulation and privacy. (Bellman et al. 2004, 315)

It is important to underscore that these cultural values are not the only determinants of privacy concerns. In addition to cultural values, Bellman and colleagues isolate two other factors: experience with the Internet and the level of government involvement with regulatory policies. It is hypothesized that the greater the experience with the Internet, the lower the level of concern for violations of information privacy. Further, citizens living in countries with high regulatory government involvement in corporate privacy management tend to endorse strong laws to regulate information privacy.

Bearing in mind that the sample in the Bellman study consisted of 534 valid responses of online consumers from thirty-eight countries (including China) and that the data were collected by e-mail through web advertising, the results are consistent with some (but not all) previous findings, including those of Millberg and colleagues (1995). For example, there is an inverse relationship between privacy concerns and experience with the Internet, a finding that is supported by other studies. Another consistent finding showed that citizens in countries with privacy regulations asked for *more* government privacy regulation. Respondents in the Bellman study were concerned about privacy in specific contexts, such as errors being made in the construction of databases or unauthorized use of personal information by third parties. The concern for privacy issue did not manifest itself in an omnibus, overarching fashion to include privacy in general.

ATTITUDES TO PRIVACY AND INTERNET EXPERIENCE

In the pilot phase of the survey, the GPD project commissioned focus group interviews designed to capture the subjective meaning of "privacy" as an abstract concept in the daily lives of the Chinese. It became clear from the interviews that privacy did not loom large in the minds of the Chinese participants. They became concerned about privacy when it affected their intimate and personal affairs. However, when asked to look into the future, several participants singled out the need to protect personal privacy in light of technological developments. Participants did not consider legislation an effective way of protecting personal privacy, especially when it comes to laws regulating government departments. They would rather, in the words of some participants, use "tricks" to protect their privacy. The workplace emerged as a place in the public domain where privacy was seen as important.

In addition to familiarity with the various surveillance technologies that were discussed earlier in the chapter, the GPD survey inquired into the extent to which respondents were familiar with laws in their countries that are designed to protect personal information in the public and private sectors and about the extent to which these laws are effective in protecting personal information.

It is not surprising to find that across all countries in the study, familiarity with certain technologies exceeded knowledge about the legal system and its effectiveness in protecting privacy of personal information. More than two-thirds – and in some cases as many as 80% – said they were not knowledgeable about laws designed to protect against government surveillance of personal information. Respondents were equally uninformed about laws applicable to the private sector. In the case of China, 65% and 72% said they were not familiar with such laws governing the public and private sectors, respectively.

Only one-third of the respondents indicated they were knowledgeable about public- and private-sector regulations regarding privacy of personal information. They were asked in a follow-up question to indicate the effectiveness of such laws. Excluding those who answered "not sure," the majority in the sample (60%) thought the laws were "very effective" or "somewhat effective" in protecting against government intrusion, while 57% said the laws were effective in the private sector. In China the figures were 63% in both cases. Similar proportions obtain in Mexico, which is surprising bearing in mind that neither Mexico nor China has comprehensive legislation to protect individual privacy similar to what exists for the private sector in Canada (e.g., the Personal Information Protection and Documents Act of January 2004). Thus at one level respondents are not familiar with the privacy laws, yet at another they are willing to entrust the government with privacy legislation. The focus group interviews, however, painted a different picture in which the government as an overseer of privacy did not rank high.

In general, the point is made that individual privacy in China is not a well-developed concept since individual rights occupy a secondary place relative to collective rights.[14] It could also very well be that there are cultural and political factors that impinge on the interpretation of an abstract concept like privacy, which may lead to different standards of what constitutes individual privacy protection.[15]

The idea that there is a relationship between experience with the Internet and privacy issues is a familiar one, as was remarked earlier. Of the 27% who reported using the Internet for online shopping (an indicator of Internet experience), slightly more knew about privacy laws applicable to the private sector compared to those who did not shop online (33% vs 25%), but there was no difference with regard to knowledge about privacy laws applied to the public sector. Roughly 35% of online users and nonusers alike said they were knowledgeable about such laws.

Only 6% used the Internet to contact government officials at various levels, 16% made face-to-face contact, and 78% made no contact at all with any level of government. Of the 6% who contacted officials electronically, 34% indicated that they were knowledgeable about privacy laws governing the private sector. The proportion of knowledgeable respondents who had face-to-face contact with officials was 30%, compared to 27% for those who had no contact. With regard to knowledge about privacy laws in the public sector, 34% of those who used electronic means or had no contact with officials said they knew about privacy laws in the public sector. Close to 40% of those who contacted officials face-to-face said they knew about such laws. In both cases, face-to-face contact is as good an indicator, if not better, of knowledge about privacy laws than is use of the Internet.

There was hardly any difference in the extent of knowledge about privacy laws in the public or private sector when it comes to comparing those who use computers or the Internet from home, work, or public places. One-third of computer and Internet users, regardless of place of usage, reported that they knew about such laws in the public and private sectors.

Experience with technology was also used to assess respondents' perceptions of the effectiveness of privacy laws in protecting individual privacy. There were no significant relationships between using online shopping and assessment of the efficacy of laws in the public and private spheres. Nor was there any relationship between computer use and the efficacy of privacy laws. Thus, overall, the experience factor does not translate into knowledge about privacy regulation or into assessment of the efficacy of such laws. This may be due to the relative newness of the Internet in China. With time, experience with the Internet will bring about a critical mass of users, which in turn will raise the level of awareness of the need for privacy regimes.

In an attempt to assess the relationship between knowledge about the technology, familiarity with privacy protection laws, and the efficacy of these laws, GDP researchers examined the correlations among the three questions. The overall correlations, as well as correlations for individual countries, show that knowledge about the technology is positively correlated with familiarity with privacy laws in a statistically significant manner (see GPD table 10(m) online). However, there are no statistically significant correlations between perception of the efficacy of privacy laws and both knowledge about the technology and familiarity with privacy laws. One can infer from this finding that responses to the efficacy question, which were confined to a fraction of the sample, did not reflect a common understanding of "effectiveness" across the various countries. To ascertain this possibility, extending the use of vignettes to include these questions would have been helpful.

CONCLUSIONS

In presenting the findings on Internet usage in China, this chapter has focused on three aspects. First, it has provided an overview of Internet diffusion, tapping various official and semiofficial sources. These national data present a picture of a phenomenal increase in Internet use in China over the past decade. However, the data also indicate that Internet diffusion reflects existing regional, economic, and gender disparities. People with lower incomes and those in the unskilled and semiskilled occupations are underrepresented among Internet users. The same holds true both for poorer, rural regions and for women compared to men.

Although the history of uneven Internet development in China parallels the trajectory seen in other countries, including Western industrialized countries, China remains fairly behind other industrialized countries in ensuring a wider cross-sectional distribution of Internet use.

Second, the chapter has turned its attention to the findings of the GPD survey, offering a detailed descriptive analysis of frequency of computer and Internet usage according to locale. It is important to keep in mind that the China survey for the GPD project was confined to seven cities, most of which are large, industrial centres, whereas most (but not all) of the other surveys in the GPD project were more representative of the participating countries. With this caveat in mind, one can see that the survey results confirm the national picture regarding correlations among gender, education, occupational background, and age. Overall, region did not act as an important predictor regarding Internet usage – at least in terms of the cities chosen for this study. There must be other factors at play here, such as the spread of Internet cafés and use of the Internet in public places in urban areas.

Third, the chapter has examined the relationship between familiarity with various surveillance technologies, experience with using the Internet, the privacy laws governing the use of these technologies in the private and public sectors, and the efficacy of these laws. The extent of familiarity with privacy laws in both sectors was substantially lower than knowledge about surveillance technologies, although there was a positive correlation between the two. This was not the case with the efficacy of privacy protection laws. Whether in China or in the sample of eight countries, perceptions of efficacy did not correlate in a statistically significant manner with either familiarity with the technology or knowledge about privacy laws.

NOTES

1 A more sombre assessment of China's economic prowess comes from the Organization for Economic Cooperation and Development (2005), which noted inaccurate data reporting and the fact that, on the basis of the per capita gross national income, China ranks 127th out of 208 economies worldwide, taking into account parity purchasing power and currency exchange rates.

2 In 2006 there were 211 million Internet users in the United States, compared to 137 million users in China, 51 million in Germany, and 83 million in Japan (Internet World Stats). With regard to mobile and fixed-line phones,

the International Telecommunications Union (2009, 47–8) estimates that by 2007 China had around 547 million mobile phones and 365 million fixed–line phones.

3 Regarding the general debate about whether the Internet spurs democratization, see Milne (2006). For government monitoring of the Internet in China, see the report by the OpenNet Initiative (2005).

4 See note 8 below for details.

5 The 2007 figure of 210 million Internet users in China includes Internet users in cyber cafés and other public places. Discounting Internet use in public places, the number is estimated at 86.7 million (*Sydney Morning News* 2007).

6 All the GPD tables cited in this chapter, including appendix tables, are online at http://www.sscqueens.org/book_tables (accessed 13 November 2009).

7 Based on gender distribution, the Chinese Academy of the Social Sciences estimates that, in 2009, 53% of Internet users were male, compared to 47% who were female; see http://www.cnnic.cn/uploadfiles/pdf/2009/10/13/94556.pdf (accessed 13 November 2009).

8 See http://english.gov.cn/2007-01/25/content_507348.htm (accessed April 2007). A Gallup national survey carried out in China in October 2006 revealed that the average income of urban residents was 28,748 RMB compared to 11,503 RMB for rural residents (Wu 2007; see also Harwit 2004).

9 The GPD survey was carried out in eight countries (Brazil, Canada, China, France, Hungary, Mexico, Spain, and the United States) between May and September 2006. The same questionnaire was used in all participating countries. Except for in China, the surveys were carried out by Ipsos Reid, a global public opinion firm. In China the survey was carried out by Millenriver Marketing Research in Beijing under the supervision of Guo Laing of the Chinese Academy of the Social Sciences. For more details about the methodology of the survey, see http://www.sscqueens/intl_survey (accessed 12 November 2009).

10 Three of the seven cities (Guangzhou, Shanghai, and Beijing) are metropolises, and four (Chengdu, Wuhan, Xi'an, and Shanyang) are provincial capitals.

11 The original six items in question 1 were coded 1 ("very knowledgeable") through 4 ("not at all knowledgeable"). The scores were added together to create a variable that ranged from 6 (all 1s) to 24 (all 4s). This variable was then scaled and shifted to obtain an index between 0 and 100: $y = 100*(24/18-1/18*x)$, so that now $y = 0$ corresponds to $x = 24$ (all "not knowledgeable"), and $y = 100$ corresponds to $x = 6$ (all "very knowledgeable"). The Cronbach Alpha coefficient of reliability for the sample containing the seven countries is .793. When considered on the basis of individual countries, the Cronbach Alpha ranged from .842 to .639.

12 Technological knowledge = 49.413 − 5.571gender + 1.848education
+ .916monthly income − .231age. With R^2 = .155, the model explained 15.5%
of the variance.
13 See http://www.geert-hofstede.com/hofstede_china.shtml (accessed 12 November
2009).
14 See Arthur Cockfield's chapter in this volume.
15 See Andrey Pavlov's chapter in this volume.

Privacy and Surveillance in Mexico and Brazil: A Cross-National Analysis

NELSON ARTEAGA BOTELLO

INTRODUCTION

In recent years Latin America has seen a significant increase in surveillance devices, particularly electronic ones. Certain control mechanisms have consolidated in the region, thus causing it to conform to a worldwide standard of surveillance. Despite this seeming global standardization, it is still necessary to recognize aspects of diversity in Latin American societies that set them apart. First, there are differences in the types of technology that are used, although this "technological gap" may admittedly be bridged in the future. Second, there are social differences: different surveillance systems in different countries respond to different problems.

Independent of technological developments and the range of problems to which surveillance systems respond in various countries, the proliferation of surveillance implies a change in spatial organization as well as in the legal, economic, and manufacturing sectors. Surveillance thus affects the activities individuals perform daily in both public and private spheres. In fact, the increase in electronic surveillance systems is modifying the border between public and private (Zureik et al. 2006). A certain preoccupation exists: privacy is being violated by the use of surveillance devices since "private" refers, according to Georges Duby (1989), to the limited zone that permits the individual to be protected from exterior demands. It is a place that allows people to relax and let down the defence mechanisms they use in public places. In other words, the private space is one where individuals find freedom from their protective shells.

As David Lyon (1994) points out, the walls of privacy are being digitally dissolved. This does not happen in the same way in all countries: cultural values – such as forms of political and social organization – permeate this dissolution. Such values then uniquely characterize the relationship between privacy and surveillance. This chapter explores how this relationship is defined within two Latin American countries – Mexico and Brazil – that share certain historical, social, and political characteristics (González 1979), which also clearly distinguish them from other countries in Latin America. Indeed, Mexico and Brazil share common political experiences, as authoritarian regimes have been placed in power in both countries for long periods of time; in spite of this, the political systems are allowed to function as artificial democracies that guarantee a system of representation and forms of political participation. This is not true of other dictatorships such as Argentina, Paraguay, Uruguay, Peru, and, of course, Chile. Socially, and having as a context the transition to "real democracy," inequalities, poverty, and violence characterize both countries (Pastor and Wise 1997, Sosa 2004). Finally, the low value placed on individualism, lack of trust among citizens, and a high tolerance for both social inequalities and a concentration of power within the state confirm that they share certain cultural values.[1]

This chapter also considers the backdrop of cultural values, taking into account the historic confidence in the government and strategies for control as well as the actions of individuals concerning personal information (including their experiences of surveillance in public and private places). The hypothesis is that the relationship between privacy and surveillance is triangulated by certain cultural values that serve as examples, counterfoils, or bases upon which the individual may lean in order to construct his or her privacy. In other words – since all metaphors are approximate – cultural values, particularly those with themes related to confidence, governance, authority, and gender relations, create a certain space that allows for the distinguishing of points of tension between privacy and surveillance. These layers and areas are also related to a series of political support systems such as democratic institutions and laws that guarantee the protection of individuals facing state power as well as related to a social structure that tends to question excess social inequalities and power. This chapter aims to determine to what extent layers of cultural values and political support systems complement each other in forming the relationship between privacy and surveillance in Mexico and Brazil.

The Globalization of Personal Data (GPD) survey results (Ipsos Reid 2006) will be used to show that both Mexico and Brazil present a similar, but not identical, set of values, supported by the experiences of and the relationship between surveillance and privacy in these countries. An attempt is also made to show some differences between the countries. To arrive at a deeper understanding, the information from the focus groups is used, specifically where the topics of surveillance and privacy in both Mexico and Brazil were discussed. These focus groups provide valuable information: the dynamic of discussion makes it possible to observe how individuals explore and work with their cultural values in specific circumstances. Their experiences are linked with distinct surveillance devices and with the construction and protection of privacy, resulting in very particular subjective processes around this relationship in each of the countries analyzed.

This chapter is divided into four parts. The first part presents some basic concepts used to understand the relationship between privacy and surveillance. It probes the depths of the characteristics of this relationship, namely the support from political institutions and the foundation of cultural values. After this, a brief account is given of the common and unique characteristics that arise within the political and social contexts of Mexico and Brazil. The objective is to observe "new" areas of government intervention into private life through strategies related to democracy, attention to poverty, and combating delinquency. The third part explores the cultural values of these two countries in order to find the bases that mediate the relationship between privacy and surveillance. Finally, some ideas will be presented to show how privacy and surveillance are fed by the foundation of these cultural values and determined by political support systems.

PRIVACY: POLITICAL SUPPORT SYSTEMS AND CULTURAL VALUES

Privacy is an ambiguous concept; its definition depends upon the particular conditions found in each society. The work that Philippe Ariès and Georges Duby (1990) have done in this sphere demonstrates how private life has been understood throughout history. Variations are tied to the population's own public space, which is why the two terms do not develop independently of each other (Gouldner 1976). More recently, the idea of privacy has come to be based on current liberal thought. This, in turn, is related to people's capacity to resist intrusion into and interference with their individuality and is also related to their ability to control what is revealed in front of others (Introna 1997). Control facilitates a certain amount of autonomy, particularity, and self-possession, which allows us to understand privacy as the individual's personal space and to a great extent as a personal belonging. For Lyon (1994), however, this concept is not helpful in understanding how privacy is constructed upon the new stage of technological information. People's personal information is circulated via databases or they are observed by video cameras, thus precluding the existence of full autonomy and individuality: people cannot themselves guard the information that is revealed to others.

The discussion about privacy has been carried out within the context of developed nations, where certain organizational structures – political institutions and social conditions – have defined the model of privacy. In contrast to its characterization by countries that have displayed important economic development since the Second World War,[2] privacy clearly adheres to distinct connotations in societies where one can observe dynamic differences from developed countries in the social and economic order. This is the case in Latin American countries, where privacy exists in a given place that connects individuals with their closest family and community circles. In a way, this substitutes for the protective social systems that can not be provided by the state, but it also implies that individuals' words and actions are constantly controlled by these family and community circles.

This suggests that an analysis of the model of privacy in underdeveloped countries such as Mexico and Brazil can be understood by distinguishing their characteristics from those of developed countries. According to Robert Castel (2003), for individualism and privacy to develop, support is necessary from political institutions and social conditions. Individuals establish intersubjective relationships and create spaces for privacy; nevertheless, they need pre-existing conditions to establish conceptions of this type. To enter into the adventure of analyzing individuality, autonomy, and privacy, it is first necessary to explore what political support society may provide in this sense. Once these bases have been established, it is necessary to explore the particularities of the privacy model based on the cultural values of each society – understanding these as certain beliefs that guide our attitudes and behaviours (Bellman et al. 2003).

The level of cultural values is not subject to a closed structure in which the individual has little opportunity to act (Giddens 1991). As Michel Wieviorka (2004) has claimed, the majority of cultural approximations do not intervene but rather are on the margins of the processes of subjectivity. This is why it is necessary to observe how in certain experiences

individuals explore and work with values, which are "ideological resources, ways of control and integration, which at the same time appeal
to a 'non social' subjectivity, although socially defined" (Dubet 1994,
254). In this manner, each individual can be considered an actor capable
of "consciously" organizing his or her relationship with his or her world.
Therefore, crystallization of values in experience are also interesting – in
the multiple logic of an individual's actions.

In the case of the countries analyzed here, the relationship between
privacy and surveillance takes on congruent forms, reminiscent of similar scopes of experiences (see table 11.1). For example, the GPD survey
results (Ipsos Reid 2006) show that more than 80% of citizens in Brazil
and Mexico believe that the use of closed circuit television (CCTV) in the
community and in commercial centres reduces criminal incidents.

Similarly, less than 25% of the population in both countries approve
of the government and private businesses exchanging information about
people with the objective of providing a certain level of security. A sample of these surveillance strategies could probably be observed in the fact
that 50% of Mexicans are quite or somewhat worried about providing
personal data online through a website, whereas 70% of Brazilians are
very or somewhat worried about providing personal data online through
a website.

In spite of this contrast, 79% of Brazilians and 69% of Mexicans are
in favour of identity cards, although the laws linked to safeguarding
national safety are considered violations, in many cases, of private life.
The relationship between surveillance and privacy is found to be, in this
sense, closely tied to the more widespread use of surveillance technologies on a global scale. These technologies – among them CCTV, identity
cards, and national digital fingerprint systems – are less pervasive than
in more developed countries; there is even less familiarity with new technologies such as global positioning systems (GPS), biometric systems,
and facial recognition programs. Indeed, the presence of improved forms
of surveillance, both in Mexico and in Brazil, shows the existence of an
important acceptance of CCTV surveillance of employees' activities in
their work environments.

If these results permit an approximation of the relationship between
privacy and surveillance, this should not be understood as localized in the
multiple logics of individuals' actions. Rather, it is the result of the articulation of the foundation of cultural values in the context of the space determined by the support from political institutions and social conditions.

Table 11.1
Surveillance and privacy relation (%)

	Brazil	Mexico	Hungary	Spain	France	US	Canada
Effectiveness of CCTV in public spaces in order to minimize violence	80	81	87	75	65	71	66
Confidence in the government's ability to protect personal data	20	35	51	34	30	39	48
Confidence in the private sector's ability to protect personal data	23	36	53	45	40	47	47
National security laws and private-life intervention	51	48	40	54	41	57	48
Acceptance of CCTV for monitoring employees	27	17	34	49	48	47	45
GPS and familiarity with the implementation of new surveillance technologies	14	6	37	61	54	60	55
Biometrics and familiarity with facial and other bodily recognition	11	4	13	18	23	29	28

Source: Ipsos Reid (2006).

DEMOCRACY, POVERTY, AND VIOLENCE: NEW INTERVENTIONS INTO PRIVACY

Mexico and Brazil have lived through an intense political transformation, as well as a change in social structure, in the past twenty-five years (Castells 1998). It is, above all, interesting to present the links between democratic transition and increases in poverty, inequality, and crime (Arteaga 2005, Caldeira 2000). These three subjects, aside from inaugurating new forms of coexistence, allow for the emergence of control mechanisms with the aim of reinforcing projects to be dealt with. All this takes place on a stage where it is not possible to observe a generalized transformation of authoritarian institutions into democracy (Ward 1993) but rather their coexistence. That is why citizens seem not to be able to find legitimate effective means to regulate social relations and conflicts, above all between individuals and institutions.

The democratization process, marked by increases in poverty and criminal violence, has facilitated the creation of personal data collection systems. Based upon the principle that information is essential in order to establish convenient and adequate democratic policies, as well as to fight poverty and crime, both governments manifest a constant demand for personal data. In the case of poverty, for example, political and social programs demand a series of data about potential beneficiaries. This information allows the government to determine whether people qualify for a program (de Araujo and de Lima 2005, Arteaga 2005). As for how this relates to violence, the collection of information about social conditions in so-called "dangerous" neighbourhoods is growing in the hope that it will help to establish crime prevention policies (Arraigada and Godoy 1999, de Mesquita and Loche 2005).

It seems strange that increased collection of personal data should be accompanied by arguably mediocre laws in the area of privacy protection. Mexico obviously lags behind Brazil, Chile, and Argentina (Ipsos-Bimsa 2004a). In effect, in Mexico privacy is a concept of legal order, an abstract right far removed from daily life. The violation of privacy is a recurring phenomenon in a Mexican's life: telephone tapping without a judicial order; illegal video-recordings aimed at identifying "inappropriate" behaviour; the exchange of database information among banks, department stores, and public and private organizations; and the sale of databases such as the electoral registry.[3]

Brazil, on the other hand, provides constitutional protection for both privacy and personal data.[4] Invasion of privacy in the home is prohibited, as is surveillance of private electronic communications without a legal warrant. Access to information, confidentiality, and the right to correct false data about people are all guaranteed in the Constitution. However, there is no office directly in charge of supervising the protection of privacy and personal data. Further, 64% of Brazilians are not knowledgeable about the laws that protect personal information in government departments, and 71% do not know about the laws that protect personal information used by private companies (Ipsos Reid 2006).

The contrast between the legislative frameworks of Mexico and Brazil lies, it seems, in the fact that both share an authoritarian past with artificial democratic systems. In the case of Mexico, the path to real democracy has followed a series of modifications to the electoral laws without touching the general Constitution. This starkly contrasts with what has happened in Brazil, where a military dictatorship held power for more than twenty-nine years. This experience made Brazilian society – like other Latin American societies that experienced military rule – more sensitive to the necessity of incorporating a "habeas data" provision into their constitutions in order to protect individuality and the personal data of its citizens. In Mexico, once a real democracy was installed, preoccupation centred on the construction of a transparent electoral structure. Currently, privacy and protection of personal data do not seem to be priorities, as measured by the fact that the bases of democracy have not been sufficiently consolidated.

THE LAYER OF CULTURAL VALUES

The presence of authoritarian political regimes in the history of Mexico and Brazil is accompanied by an intangible sphere of cultural values, which is understood as the beliefs that guide attitudes and behaviour (Bellman et al. 2003). Certainly, in acquiring democratic regimes, these countries have permitted certain changes in these cultural values, but the persistence of nondemocratic practices in large sections of social and political life in both countries suggests that changes have not been rapid or profound. This is perhaps clearer if one observes that both countries show a resistance to change within their cultural values (Hofstede 1980).

According to the World Values Survey (2006), in both Mexico and Brazil one may see in values such as confidence, ability to govern, and authority some points of convergence and divergence that allow for the observation of certain nondemocratic cultural values. A lack of interpersonal trust demonstrates the lack of success in establishing social networks that permit the consolidation of a civil society that is both strong and autonomous compared to state power, but it also demands better social control in order to guarantee governability – even if this means some liberty is lost.

In the GPD survey, when Mexicans and Brazilians are asked to identify whether the state's principal governance objective is order or liberty, the data are too close to obtain a definitive answer. When they are asked the same question with regard to respondents' level of confidence in private businesses' ability to protect client personal information, the same tendency emerges. Clearly, there is a lack of confidence in Mexican and Brazilian society in the way government and private companies handle and use personal information. This distrust increases with the high level of misunderstanding that exists in both societies with respect to the laws that protect personal information in governmental departments and in private companies.

Such distrust seems to have crystallized with the implementation of national security policies that have affected both countries since 11 September 2001. Both Mexico and Brazil have changed their national security policies, even though many of these changes were in response to other issues, such as drug trafficking in Mexico and border control in Brazil. The GPD survey found that most of the citizens from both countries regard these national security laws as highly intrusive on personal privacy. Perhaps surprisingly, this distrust exists simultaneously with citizens demanding greater governmental control over society.

The data presented up to this point show that Mexico, like Brazil, has a tendency to exhibit a society with a low resistance to state power and a diminished predilection to question authority. There is also a lack of trust among the people of Mexico and Brazil that precludes the establishment of strong and autonomous social networks vis-à-vis state power, social networks that would still accept some loss of liberty in exchange for greater social control. It is with respect to these various layers of cultural values that it is necessary to form a sense of privacy and, with this, to establish a perspective on surveillance devices.

PRIVACY AND SURVEILLANCE IN MEXICO AND BRAZIL

The political support systems and the layer of cultural values are put into sharp focus through the analysis of specific experiences related to privacy and surveillance. Next, the results are examined from four focus groups carried out in 2004 by Ipsos Reid on behalf of the GPD project on the topic of privacy in Mexico and Brazil. Two groups were polled in Mexico City and two in São Paolo. In each city, one group was made up of workers and travellers, the other of consumers and the general public. Eighteen people participated in Mexico (Ipsos-Bimsa 2004b, 2004c, 2004d) and twenty people in Brazil (Ipsos Opinion do Brasil 2003a, 2004b, 2004c). The groups corresponded to a very specific sector of both societies and thus reflect the opinions only of that sector. Although the two groups are not statistically representative of the sectors, they provide us with the attitudes and experiences of a limited number of urban residents who belong to the middle and professional class.[5]

Putting up Walls: Surveillance as a Privacy Device

Mexicans generally link privacy with personal security. To a large extent, the insecurity that characterizes the country, particularly Mexico City, is an unavoidable backdrop. It is perhaps not surprising that the word "security" can be immediately associated with certain control devices (e.g., alarms, electric fences, closed residential zones, and clear streets) and with the uses of very specific public spaces (e.g., not walking in areas considered dangerous or ignoring strangers begging in the street).

The priority that Mexican society has long given to security has made possible the connotations acquired by the ideas of privacy and surveillance. Primarily, it is believed that enjoying privacy requires surveillance mechanisms to protect the physical space where individuals and their families carry out their daily activities. This safeguards their integrity and protects them from dangerous environments. For that, the protection of privacy is not considered a universal right within a framework of legal norms but a property right acquired by those who can afford it.[6] This is associated with privileged lives characterized by comfort and well-being, a lifestyle that clearly excludes many members of society. The idea of exclusivity permits the understanding that privacy is one more factor that justifies hierarchical relationships. This is natural within a Mexican society that tends to be extremely tolerant of inequality in the concentration of power and money. Gated communities protected by CCTV systems, private police, and other surveillance devices that safeguard the people are considered a triumph of privacy: they permit individuals to distance themselves from others. As privacy is understood as a form of property, from its curtailment is derived a feeling of loss and of diminished control over certain physical spaces. Those who mentioned a loss of privacy observed that in offices people are watched constantly, not only by their bosses but also by their co-workers. One focus group participant commented, "now you don't have much privacy in the workplace, because you are in a cubicle, and you are right next to other person, and they could hear everything you say, everything you do and that is less privacy."

Other examples are shown with the use of cellular phones – any person can be reached in any place and at any time – as well as with the expansion of video surveillance systems in public places and private spaces. A focus group respondent said, "All the cameras that the restaurants have, sometimes you feel that they are watching you when you are in the bathroom, you don't know if they are watching you or not."

Loss of privacy is also associated with a certain feeling of intrusion into personal data. For example, the majority of participants approved of the implementation of the personal ID card (Clave Unica de Registro de la Población, or CURP)[7] as well as of companies' insistence that their employees give a huge amount of personal data for "reasons of security." The necessity of giving personal data to qualify for mortgage loans and credit cards and the increase in telemarketing reinforce a sense of lost privacy.

However, when investigating how this loss of privacy has been experienced, one sees that there remains again the sensation of loss of the individual-family duality, value, or property – for example, through robberies in public places and at home as well as through debit and credit card fraud. This distinct fear motivates the perception that more surveillance systems are required, even if this implies the loss of certain freedoms. It is believed that in the future privacy will be reduced because of new technologies that will permit an account of what each person does and who each person sees. There is a sense of resignation to this scenario, in which it seems clear that no legal framework can regulate either the different surveillance mechanisms or the handling of personal information. It is true that there are occasional explicit references to privacy as an established right somewhere in the Constitution; however, privacy is considered more of a legal good intention than a reality.

Generally speaking, Mexicans apparently cannot be thought of without their first set of relationships. If other options are even considered, such as whether the state should guarantee security and privacy, certain factors militate against the emergence of important social pressure that could effect change. For example, a low propensity to question authority and a weak civil society make widespread social change unlikely. In addition, the lack of confidence between citizens normally precludes the consolidation of spontaneous complaints into true civil rights or social movements. Privacy and surveillance, therefore, work hand in hand in Mexico to build protective "walls" that permit security for and tranquility in the person-family duality. A parallel trend emerges in Mexicans' expectations regarding the protection of personal data. People are careful not to give too much information in order to avoid the risk that this information may be wrongly used. A focus group participant stated, "right now, all information that you give now you have distrust as how people are going to use it, maybe against you."

The Sacred Space: Privacy and Family Security in Brazil

In Brazil the idea of privacy is also closely linked to the idea of security, likely due to the context of violence caused by crime and delinquent behaviour in the country. Privacy is associated with isolation and tranquility, something that fundamentally refers to intimacy, freedom, the capacity for movement, and respect for the person and his or her individuality. These aspects are considered inherent to the dynamics of the family environment and home. Privacy is not thoroughly understood by

Brazilians if it is not accompanied by economic prosperity. It is for this reason that reference to a physical space is always required in order to establish the idea of privacy.

Privacy is understood as something connected to the person and his or her world of closest relationships – that is, to the localized space of these activities. In this sense, privacy can be understood as a property or value and thus associated, for example, with living in a residential zone where there is tranquility and where neighbours are least bothersome. In another sense, privacy is referred to as interpersonal intimacy, freedom, and capacity to move without restriction (such as to enter any place without being discriminated against because of skin colour). In this sense, it takes on the characteristics of a right. The greater the privacy in terms of value or property, the greater Brazilians consider the level of security and protection of individuality. There is such a close link between the concepts of privacy and security that these two terms seem to dissolve into each other. As one focus group respondent commented, "our privacy is invaded due the lack of security, one thing leads to another" (Ipsos Opinion do Brasil 2004a).

This latter idea refers both to protection from everyday risks – for example, a robbery or a kidnapping – and to the encouragement that close relationships provide in terms of emotional support for the individual. Images of comfort, well-being, tranquility, and economic success are also included. This situation can perhaps be explained by the fact that the country lived through a profound economic and social crisis between the mid-1980s and early 1990s. Instability and violence defined the social life of Brazilians; strong group and community relationships provided a way to confront the precarious conditions of those years.

However, this appears to be changing little by little. For instance, younger people consider family to represent a protective space that fosters privacy and security; they also propose that leaving the family unit implies creating a private space that is more intimate and personal. In this sense, the concept of privacy that young people share begins to have a close link with ideas of independence and freedom: the loss of privacy is also associated with the acquisition and loss of the physical spaces where everyday activities are carried out.

The majority of participants agreed that there is a generalized sense of loss of privacy. The principal reason for this is the widespread use of technology (e.g., television, Internet, or cellular phones). That television appears as a primary factor responsible for the loss of privacy supports the idea that Brazilians feel that this technology creates a loss of intimacy and isolation that home previously guaranteed. A focus group respondent mentioned, "Politicians invading our privacy with politics on TV, we can't change channels and watch whatever we want. No option of watching something else on television." A similar assessment was made about the impact of computers, especially as an Internet connection node. Cellular phones also reduce opportunities for physical seclusion, as another respondent stated: "Especially with cell phones. People find you anywhere, at anytime. It wasn't like that ... Internet too, you get a message, e-mail, without knowing ... Each time more your privacy is taken away. I saw some chips that are arriving now, monitor, then your privacy is gone, they'll find you everywhere."

For Brazilians, technology represents a threat that, unfortunately, is expanding and consolidating. At the same time, the majority of people realize that the rapid proliferation of CCTV systems in public and private spaces allows security and police units to observe people's behaviour; as one focus group participant stated, this is considered a threat to privacy: "Today we are being watched everywhere ... you cannot make a movement that they're not filming, there's just cameras missing inside the bathrooms, because they are everywhere else."

It is thought that the expansion of these systems is an answer to violent behaviour in the country, which jeopardizes the security of individuals and their property. Control devices in public and private places are considered a necessary evil, with the acknowledgment, in general, that sacrificing a certain amount of privacy to obtain a little more security is inevitable, even desirable, and certainly something that the state should do. Moreover, Brazilians believe that the problem of surveillance and control lies not merely in the fact that it is ubiquitous but also in the fact that the population is not always informed that they are being observed. Secrecy exacerbates invasions of privacy.

In this sense, the future of privacy does not look at all promising. Technology will make personal information more readily available from ever larger sectors of the population. A certain resignation is becoming evident. On the one hand, Brazil's Constitution contemplates the protection of personal data. On the other hand, certain legal mechanisms permit regulatory actions of the government or companies, particularly in the use and exchange of personal information. The majority of the people who formed the focus groups – lawyers among them – were unaware of this: they could mention only the laws linked to copyrights and patents. In this sense, it is possible to observe an air of dissatisfaction with the government's capacity to protect the use of personal data and to guarantee privacy protections. The reaction can be seen in the proliferation of personal surveillance initiatives aimed at protecting oneself from the eventual misuse of one's personal information.

Mexico and Brazil: Convergent and Divergent Experiences

The construction of privacy in Mexico and Brazil is found to be linked to people's own experiences with family and the home. In the context of these close relationships, greater comfort, well-being, and security must be sought. To achieve these outcomes, significant economic investments are considered necessary. This is why privacy is seen as a value and not so much as a right – although the focus group interviews illustrate that this may gradually be changing in Brazil. In both countries, the spaces furthest from the home are considered potentially more risky for privacy, and it is believed that extreme precautions must be taken. The layers of cultural values that give low consideration to individuality in Mexico and Brazil appear consistent with the fact that privacy cannot be understood apart from family and group networks. This situation, however, is not experienced with the same intensity in both countries: Brazilians champion bodily privacy, whereas Mexicans put priority on communication privacy.

However, that in both countries threats to privacy are found outside the "bubble of protection" of people and their families does not mean that people in both countries share the same fears. Comparing perceived degrees of threats to the types of privacy most valued shows that Mexicans think that the biggest threat to privacy is the misuse of their personal information; Brazilians see it in surveillance of the body. The topic of surveillance in Mexico and Brazil appears to encompass many experiences that are increasingly assimilated as common and acceptable, such as the monitoring of workplace activities. Such measures are justified as guaranteeing the security of both the company and the work environment.

The expansion of CCTV systems in public spaces is also considered necessary in order to control traffic and prevent acts of vandalism and crime. The majority of Mexican and Brazilian focus group participants approved of these devices, considering them necessary in order to secure the spaces where they are installed, even though they acknowledged that criminals are adapting by developing strategies to sabotage the effectiveness of these devices (such as covering their faces). However, these devices can be used for purposes other than security. In the case of Mexico, the police can hide crimes or even coordinate them in collusion with organized crime groups. In Brazil it was also mentioned that criminal groups in various neighbourhoods of the country's major cities use the devices to track the arrival of police in those areas. In other areas, such as airports, the increase in surveillance is not questioned. It is believed to be beneficial in providing security and necessary for the national security of each country.

PRIVACY AND SURVEILLANCE: TRADITIONAL VALUES AND VALUES OF SELF-EXPRESSION

In the case of the two countries studied here, it can be observed that the construction of privacy is made up of three levels: (1) it refers to a person in relation to his or her family; (2) it is associated with the defining of a space where close social links between people and the community are established; and (3) it pertains to information about people. Each level refers to certain aspects of privacy, such as a space, a property, a personality, or a certain autonomous individual. This privacy is developed in the Mexican and Brazilian contexts at the place where values of self-expression and traditional values cross. In other words, the experiences of privacy in both societies are influenced by the advancement of spiritual individuality. This individuality develops contrary to a collective spirituality but with a strong reference to group relationships. Further, this individuality operates as a supposed rescuer of what is considered traditional: the closed community that craves distance from those expressions of modern life that are considered harmful. Thus privacy centred on collectivity is achieved as more than an adjusted individuality or a dependence on groups.

To talk about privacy in the context of the family – and not about the family as the centre of privacy – implies that private life originally existed within the family but that a private individual life was subsequently built in which individuals had autonomy; in this sense, the family was involved in a process of deinstitutionalization (Prost 1989). In addition, the functions of the family are quite different from those shown in authoritarian societies in the mid-1980s. Privacy in Mexico and Brazil acquires a connotation where the family collective does not disappear, yet it still manages to inform the constitution of individuality, autonomy, and freedom.

By this logic, the relationship of surveillance is presented in two ways: (1) it is observed as a form of keeping the individual and his or her sphere of relationships far from external risks; and (2) surveillance represents a threat when it is carried out from outside the sphere of one's relationships. The problem comes back, then, to each person's strategies and capacities – both economic and political – for eluding surveillance. These strategies and capacities are unleashed to make the protection of privacy more likely than its violation. This enables us to see that privacy is understood as a property or a value that only a select few can access. This supports the idea that people can achieve greater degrees of privacy if they have greater economic resources. Privacy, then, is yet another factor contributing to inequality in the social structures of Brazil and Mexico. The authoritarianism that still survives in the new age of democracy in both countries appears not to favour a change in this scenario.

The government continually demands more personal information for various reasons. This can be seen as one more form of intrusion on privacy, and the government does not adequately explain how it uses the information obtained from its citizens. This invites the inference that privacy is continually being eroded. Without doubt, this trend will lead more people in Mexico and Brazil to think of themselves only in relation to their closest associates, and it will discourage trust between citizens.

The presence of cultural values that discourage questioning authority figures and, in reality, encourage simply accepting their decisions leads to a civil society incapable of confronting the demand for information emanating from both public and private entities. In this sense, this chapter observes how tensions between privacy and surveillance are, to a certain extent, the reflection of both the sources of political support systems and the layers of cultural values. Mexico and Brazil are presented as societies where the consolidation of surveillance technologies will intensify existing social fragmentation, constructing privacy based on the idea of group mediation, which is perceived as going against the flow of society. The consequence of this is disturbing: leaving behind the discussion of privacy in the context of the surveillance society, we can see that Mexican and Brazilian societies, and indeed the greater part of Latin America, regard privacy as an architecture that depends on personal resources. This legitimates the unequal access to privacy, which creates a barrier – in addition to the many that already exist – built upon poverty and violence. The result is that large sectors of the population are unable to practise or exercise their rights of citizenship.

NOTES

1 In fact, the watershed of values could be denominated under the same Iberian culture, as well as the same religious foundation of Catholicism. It would nevertheless be a mistake to think that they are similar societies.

2 This economic development was itself accompanied by a system of social protection made up of democratic regimes that guaranteed the change of power and political representation.

3 The Federal Law of Transparency and Access to Public Government Information (FLTAIPG), approved in June 2003, guarantees citizens' right to information about government actions. Certainly, it is possible to find in this law some principles aimed at protecting personal data. For example, the third article states that personal data is confidential and cannot be revealed except for legal purposes if this data includes information about ethnic or racial origin, moral or emotional attributes, telephone, properties, or political ideology or includes information that reveals physical and mental conditions, sexual preference, or any other information that affects people's privacy. The Federal Access to Information Institute (IFAI) is the public organization in charge of implementing, within the framework of the aforementioned law about access to information, the mechanisms needed to safeguard the privacy of personal data. It was for this reason that the Main Directorate of Personal Data was created in 2003, although it closed its doors one year later due to financial problems (Smith 2005).

4 The Mexican Constitution – which dates from 1917 – seems to be fundamentally oriented toward establishing protections needed to tie privacy to the rights of freedom of expression so that citizens will not be bothered in their person, family, home, personal documents, and communications (this latter point was added in the constitutional reform of 1966). The Protection for Consumers Law, created in 1992, is a secondary law that, in the same manner, protects the privacy of personal data.

5 It is important to point out that Mexico and Brazil have more or less the same technological infrastructure, telephone service, and cellular services. Likewise, similar percentages of their populations use the Internet, and they share similar percentages for growth in their numbers of Internet users. Nevertheless, in the worldwide ranking in this respect, Mexico is ranked fifteenth and Brazil tenth (Yurke 2005).

6 When at any given time privacy is linked to rights, it is done in the sense of moral themes more than in a strict legal sense. From there, it may be associated with issues such as the right to solitude or inner peace and with other types of feelings related to solitude.

7 CURP is an instrument of data recording that is assigned to all people who live in Mexico as well as to Mexicans who live abroad. It has eighteen elements represented by letters and numbers that are generated from the information contained in the proof of identity documents of the person (i.e., birth

certificate, naturalization card, or migratory document) and that refer to (1) first and last names, as well as the middle name, (2) date of birth, (3) sex, and (4) place of birth. These latter two elements of the CURP avoid a duplication of the code between individuals.

PART 4

Actors

Citizens and Identity

INTRODUCTION

L. Lynda Harling Stalker

Citizenship and nationality can be seen as key to our identities. They encompass a sense of where we belong and the values we hold to be important. What happens when our governments attempt to formalize and digitize our identities through means such as national ID cards, smart cards, and readable passports? What happens when not only printed on the card are the proverbial "name, rank, and serial number" but also embedded is biometric information – anything from fingerprints to iris scans to DNA profiles? Over the past few years, and some would say particularly since the terrorist events of 11 September 2001, governments have increasingly augmented the amount of personal data they collect and store on their citizenry. The national ID card and pseudo-national ID cards have become the physical culmination of these data. This has prompted debate about privacy protection guaranteed by governments (if such a guarantee is possible), the social sorting of citizens based on their biometric profiles, and the monitoring and tracking of people's movements (both within borders and at border crossings). The chapters in this section contribute to the debates by discussing and analyzing public opinion on the use of national ID cards.

This section starts with David Lyon's discussion on national ID cards' evolution from a paper-based system to one that potentially includes biometrics, radio frequency identification (RFID) tags, and machine-readable capability. By examining the responses to the Globalization of Personal Data (GPD) survey, Lyon points out that acceptance, in theory, of a national ID card does not necessarily mean acceptance of the latest "smart card" rendition of identification. Through his analysis, he shows that one needs to query connections between acceptance and variables such as trust in government's ability to safely store databases of information, trust in governments not to infringe too greatly on civil liberties in the name of national security, and acquiescence to data flows within government, between governments, and between governments and the private sector. Lyon takes to task previous surveys conducted by manufacturers of biometric and RFID technologies for "manufacturing consent" on the issue without delving deeper into people's opinions on the various levels needed to administer an electronic national ID card system. He advocates that policymakers consider the findings of this research when making decisions regarding the implementation of identification systems. Lyon also provides readers with an appendix summarizing the national ID card situation in each country.

Emily Smith takes on the task of contextualizing the GPD survey in relation to previous public opinion polls done in Canada over the past decade on the issue of national ID cards. Throughout her chapter, she highlights the questions asked, the findings, and the perceived implications for government and private businesses. Smith argues that polling on national ID cards is done either because businesses are trying to establish a rationale for their products or because the government is trying to develop a platform on the issue. During her analysis, she found that the agenda of the poll commissioning agent was noticeable through biased wording in questions. In some cases, questions bordered on fear-mongering. Smith's chapter demonstrates the importance of surveys such as the one carried out by the GPD project. An academic survey designed primarily for research purposes can move us from an agenda-laden task to one that attempts to be impartial.

In his chapter, Jeffrey Roy takes a slightly different look at the connection between our identities as citizens and the role of government. He does not look specifically at national ID cards per se but at what he calls "the nexus between privacy, identity, and the digital policies and electronic governance initiatives." To assess this nexus, Roy sets out initially to examine the cases of the United States and Spain, two countries that represent very different political models. The US model involves a neoliberal approach, where less government is better and individualism is a guiding political principle. Spain, on the other hand, is more like its European counterparts, favouring a governance model that is more socially oriented and parliamentarian. In light of advancements in technology and the push for e-government mechanisms, Roy asks what implications digitizing our identities has for democracy when accessing government services? Using the GPD survey data, Roy looks at questions related to perceptions of trust (in both government and the private sector), data flows, national ID cards, and control over information. He finds that, for the most part, the results reflect the political structures in place. For example, Americans are most leery of government, and Spaniards have lower levels of trust in private companies. He then applies the results of his analysis to a third country – Canada. Canada, as a nation whose political structure is a hybrid of American federalism and European parliamentary rule, can, according to Roy, learn from the experiences of the United States and Spain to develop best-government procedures. He argues that this is necessary in order not to succumb to complacency.

These three chapters come together to provide thorough discussion of the intersection between our identities and political structures. Technological advances and political will have veered toward more digitized forms of identity as manifested both in the physical card and in the virtual realm of e-government services. How does this shift affect notions of democracy and citizenship? The GPD survey highlights some valuable insights into how people perceive governments and their relationships with them. The chapters in this section take the next step by contextualizing and theorizing what happens at the intersection between individual privacy and governmental surveillance practices.

12

National ID Card Systems and Social Sorting: International Public Opinion

DAVID LYON

National ID card systems are being developed in many countries. These build upon but also transcend some of the limitations of earlier systems. They are electronically enabled, such that national registries are created in searchable database form, they are based on biometrics as well as prerecorded data such as birth certificates, and they feature machine-readable plastic cards for citizens, which in some cases use radio frequency identification (RFID) scanners. Such "smart" ID card systems are thus different in several respects from earlier manual and paper file systems. Among others things, they facilitate social sorting, the profiling and categorizing of populations in ways that were not previously possible and with consequences that are at present largely unknown (Lyon 2004, 2009). They thus have consequences for citizenship as conventionally conceived, for they promise to alter in significant ways the relation between the "state" and the "citizen."

These innovations do not simply make existing systems more efficient but actually introduce new dimensions to national identification. The technologies are one aspect of this, allowing, for example, for cross-system checks and data-mining, not only within but in some circumstances between nation-states. Another is the outsourcing of services in an increasingly deregulated environment, such that corporations become crucially significant players in the game of ID provision. And a third is the appearance of "emergency rules" and national security laws that have become routine since the terrorist events 11 September 2001 (Agamben 2005, Bigo 2006). That these changes are occurring in several countries at once underscores the need for some comparative understanding, especially at a relatively early stage in the development of these new systems.

One aspect of such fresh understanding is to consider what the "end-users" themselves – the citizens in question – see as the issues at an early stage of their development. The Globalization of Personal Data (GPD) project addresses this not only by asking about the perceived need for ID schemes but also by soliciting opinion on how well governments might protect personal information in the national registry database. These views may also be cross-checked against responses to other questions. Another part of the GPD survey (question 5) asks about how far governments strike a balance between national security and individual rights in their handling of personal data, and elsewhere (questions 17 and 18) the survey taps into the perceived privacy intrusiveness of national security law and the appropriateness of governments sharing personal data with third parties.[1] The survey was designed to take account of the fact that today it is not so much ID *cards* that are socially and politically significant but the technological *systems* that make them work in new ways. Carrying plastic machine-readable and embedded-chip cards is merely the visible dimension of an invisible data network based on the searchable registry database.

Having answers to these questions is very important for research and policy purposes. Many important questions are raised by ID card systems, among which is how ordinary citizens respond to their development. Given the huge costs of rolling out contemporary "smart" ID systems, it is incumbent on government authorities to ensure that sufficient public support exists for their smooth introduction and for the various costs that will fall on those citizens. The new technologies in use do make a difference (and this is not to minimize the ways that they themselves are socially shaped), corporate competition for procurements is strong, and governments often believe themselves to be acting in "unusual" or emergency circumstances with regard to the "war on terror." In the present climate, it is doubly important to have independent research that is funded sufficiently to allow for adequate sampling and that bears the broader context in mind. Otherwise, the survey research is likely either to bear too strongly the marks of its provenance or to contain questions that are simply skewed, or both. Let me give an example of each.

Public opinion surveys are one valid tool for discovering the extent of popular support for ID systems, but these – including the GPD survey – have limitations. In June 2007, for example, it was reported that "Half of Europeans support ID cards."[2] But the sample was only 500 people across all of Europe, and the study was sponsored by a company that provides software and hardware for such systems. Respondents said they would join a biometric national identity scheme, with 83% saying they would provide fingerprints and 66% expressing their willingness to give a digital photograph of their eyes. Concerns about loss of personal privacy and fears about information being used for secondary purposes were behind the reticence of those undecided or against such schemes. The company concerned concluded that "outreach" should occur targeting dubious citizens and that a strong case should be made for cards. In the survey report, this was placed alongside statements such as that of the UK Home Office minister, Liam Byrne, who said that "Unless we invest in identity systems we leave our borders and our economy open to abuse, we leave individuals defenceless against fraud and we risk leaving the benefits and safety nets we've worked so hard for, vulnerable to attack."[3]

Governments clearly have a lot at stake here and sometimes produce flawed instruments for gauging public opinion. A case in point is the survey conducted about national ID cards during the short-lived and abortive Canadian "debate" on this topic in 2003. An EKOS survey for Citizenship and Immigration Canada (CIC) made an implicit association in its questions between immigrants and terrorists before asking about biometrics, ID cards, and whether the Canadian government should be given extraordinary powers to deal with possible "terrorism-related offences." Who knows whether the majority who thought that ID cards and biometrics are a good idea (despite there being only 15% who knew even in 2006 what biometrics is) and the two-thirds who felt that extraordinary powers are acceptable responded thus because of the strongly implicit "terrorism-immigrant" association in the first question (see Zureik et al. 2006, 6).[4]

This is clearly an area fraught with potential political pitfalls. Pollsters may offer highly questionable data based on inadequate or leading questions, but politicians may well make dubious use of survey statistics as well. After Privacy International labelled the UK an "endemic surveillance society" (along with China and Russia, for instance) and rated the UK well down their list of privacy-friendly societies, Genewatch UK warned of the dangers of the British DNA database, which is one of the largest in the world, and the Information Commissioner launched a detailed report on the "Surveillance Society" (Surveillance Studies Network 2006). In response, then UK prime minister Tony Blair reassured his citizens in November 2006 that the ID card scheme is just what Britain needs.[5] "Buried in the body of the reports," he claimed, "was the voice of real people." However, the only "statistic" he quoted was that "less

than 50% of consumers feel their identity is safe." Apart from this figure, Blair assured hearers that "unsurprisingly the public do not have a
problem with being protected from thugs, or having CCTV [closed circuit
television] cameras that catch murderers, or DNA that solves horrendous
crimes that left victims and families without justice for 20 years." In the
press briefing that followed, however, he stressed that "modernity" – by
which he meant being technologically up to date – was the key factor
propelling the introduction of ID cards.

More generally, the value of public opinion polling in the area of
surveillance and privacy is that it helps to show that these things matter to people. As Colin Bennett and Charles Raab (2003, 57) say, "In
broad-brush terms, the most common finding in survey after survey
is that privacy is regarded as a very important personal value, and is
thought to be threatened by new information and communication technologies used in commerce and government." More than thirty years
ago, Stephen Margulis (1977) observed that such studies show that
people aspire to greater control over the collection, use, and disclosure
of personal information.

Two things must be noted here. First, the studies of public perceptions
refer primarily to North American and European situations. Surveillance
practices are in many respects transnational today, which demands an
understanding of broader, global contexts. Second, very important shifts
have occurred over the past two decades that have prompted more
attention to surveillance than to privacy and that have framed the issues
somewhat differently. The personal information economy has grown
rapidly in a context of global market deregulation and thus raises issues
of dignity and control as much as issues of convenience and justice (Perri
6 2005, 36). Apart from in the United States, "privacy" is unlikely to
remain the fault-line it was once thought to be. Equally, the priority
given to "national security" is skewing older surveillance-and-privacy
concerns in new ways, this time contextualizing them in a political realm
of civil liberties and human rights (Lyon 2003).

This means that specific issues need to be explored – such as public
opinion on forms of identification – in order to indicate the particular,
local, and contemporary force of these findings. Undoubtedly, both government departments and business corporations attempt to use polls for
their own ends, both initiating and interpreting them for their respective
audiences of citizens and consumers. For example, Alan Westin (2003)
has suggested that in the post-9/11 world public acceptance of intelligence gathering on ordinary citizens depends on perceived threat levels

and on the extent of actual civil liberties abuses, even though within contemporary fear cultures the desire for protection rises. And Oscar Gandy (2003) notes that business corporations act as interest groups trying to influence public policy, using opinion polls on privacy to do so.

Of the countries surveyed in the GPD survey, Japan[6] already has a smart, biometrics-based ID system in place; the United States, Spain, and China have such systems currently under development (although the US system envisions "Real ID," not "national ID"); Hungary, Brazil, France, and Spain have nonbiometric IDs with no national database (although France is planning to upgrade); a smart national ID card was rejected by Canada in 2003 (although US pressure may yet prevail for some national ID measure in Canada); and Mexico has no electronic system in place at all (although the United States is pressing for an upgraded Border Crossing Card, or a *matricula consular*, in Mexico). These situations are in flux, however, and thus marked by volatility (see appendix 12.1 below for further details).

NATIONAL ID CARDS: THE KEY SURVEY QUESTIONS

As noted above, contemporary national ID card systems involve not merely citizens carrying cards that they may be required to produce on demand but also an electronic registry database (or linked databases) containing personal data. The former is common to ID card systems, whereas the latter is a new, technologically enabled phenomenon with potentially momentous consequences. Thus two key questions in the GPD survey are 9 and 10: "To what extent do you agree or disagree with having a government-issued national ID card that everyone must carry on them at all times and present it when asked by the police or other security forces?";[7] and "In order to put national ID cards into use, the government would need to have a national database containing personal information on all citizens. This information could include address, gender, race, and tax information. How effective do you feel efforts to protect this type of information from disclosure would be?"

These two questions provide a sense of how amenable these citizens are to having a produce-on-demand ID card *and* of how safe they believe their personal information would be in the database. Interestingly, as we shall see, those survey respondents who seem to think nothing of having a national ID card system (such as the citizens of Brazil, Hungary, France, and Spain, each of which in fact has a system of sorts) also believe that they can trust their governments with the database. In Canada and the United States citizens are dubious on both counts, although this is the case in the United States even more so than in Canada. This is interesting, not least because even those countries (included in our survey) that have national ID systems do not yet have experience with systems that use electronic databases.

The point of having the two questions adjacent in the survey is to go beyond the mere acceptance levels for ID cards in order to connect these levels with a little more detail about the systems involved. "Race," gender, and tax information are included as examples of the sorts of data that might be found in a national registry database, facts that might elude those who think merely of the end-user aspect of the ID card (which has often been promoted, as in the UK case, in terms of convenience and efficiency, in addition to efficacy in combating terrorism, fraud, and illegal immigration). It was thought that the additional information about the nature of ID card systems might temper the responses, thus giving a clearer sense of acceptance from more knowledgeable respondents.

To make more sense of this, however, the responses to other questions have to be examined. More specificity is introduced, such that respondents were asked not only about the existence of a national database but also about how well the government of the country attends to privacy, civil liberties, and human rights issues. Question 5 asks, "When it comes to the privacy of personal information, what level of trust do you have that the government is striking the right balance between national security and individual rights?" This question explores the level of confidence that citizens have in their government's ability to maintain appropriate standards of "individual rights" even when "national security" may appear to be at a premium.

Finer-grained approaches to this matter can be gleaned by comparing the results obtained thus far with question 17, which asks, "To what extent do you believe laws aimed at protecting national security are intrusive upon personal privacy?" Whatever the general views, then, on whether or not governments care about individual rights when national security is seen to be paramount, we can also discover whether citizens think that such national security laws are privacy-intrusive. Add to this an external factor, namely how far data collected by government should be shared with third parties, and further nuance is obtained. Question 18 asks, "To what extent do you think it is appropriate for a government agency to share a citizen's personal information with third parties, such as other government agencies, foreign governments and the private sector?"

These further questions give a broader context for the answers. They help us to understand whether citizens believe that governments set on a national security agenda "go too far" in prying into personal life or in sharing personal data with other agencies. Even if they believe that ID cards are a good idea and that they can trust governments to keep their registry data secure, might they have doubts at a broader level?

THE ID CARD AND THE NATIONAL REGISTRY: WHAT DO THEY THINK?

One might surmise that contemporary public opinion would fall back on prior experience or a knowledge of history to form views on the desirability of carrying an ID card but that understanding the significance of having personal details stored in a national registry database – an unprecedented situation – may present more of a challenge. What happens if a question about the national registry database is placed after one on carrying ID cards? Does knowledge of the database modify attitudes to carrying cards? This is the distinctive feature of new ID card systems, and it enables forms of surveillance hitherto unattainable.

The experience of the British is instructive here because the UK ID card system was steered through Parliament in 2005–06 with much media attention, and public debates over the merits of the system were still strong in 2007. In February 2006, for instance, before the GPD poll was taken, a UK survey with a sample of 2,000 people showed that despite government claims that 80% support ID cards, only 52% actually do. Two-thirds of those sampled believe that "health tourism" and benefit fraud will be reduced, and a slightly lower proportion think ID cards will reduce bogus asylum seekers. Only 21% thought ID cards would reduce terrorist threats. Interestingly, more than 70% thought the data might be misused, and 61% feared that data might be passed to foreign governments without proper authorization.[8]

As further details of the database emerged during 2006, however, concerns grew among the population, such that by December 2006 a similar poll carried out by the same group showed that 39% opposed the identity register and that 21% (or 4.8 million, extrapolated to the whole population) said they would resist it to the point of risking a fine. In the survey 52% were unhappy with their details being kept in the database, due above all to concerns that unauthorized persons may obtain access to them. Within this group more than three-quarters believed their data would fall into the wrong hands, while almost as many said the system could contain harmful errors about them.[9]

Interestingly enough, when Japan launched a database containing the eleven-digit identifying number, the Juki-Net system, in 2002 *before* the ID cards began to appear, protests were immediate, widespread, and unprecedented. Objections included that it would make an easy target for identity theft, that Juki-Net has links with private-sector transactions despite the lack of a comprehensive privacy law in the commercial sector, and that the new system further erodes personal autonomy (Schwartz 2003). Public opinion polls at this time recorded that 3 out of 4 Japanese people opposed Juki-Net. Major cities such as Yokohama (3.4 million) allowed citizens to choose whether to allow their data to be entered. Other cities simply refused to participate. The court cases that followed have been in process ever since, although only 2 out of 13 cases have been won by plaintiffs. In the case of Japan, unlike in some other countries, one thing is clear: the registry database is the key issue.

Question 9 of the GPD survey asked, "To what extent do you agree or disagree with having a government-issued national ID card that everyone must carry on them at all times and present it when asked by the police or other security forces?" Seventy-eight per cent of French respondents agreed that everyone should have a government-issued ID card that they must carry at all times. In China 77% agreed. In Canada 53% thought this way, with 62% of Quebeckers agreeing. In the United States only 42% were in agreement. For countries that already have ID cards, such as Hungary and Brazil – although this is also true of France – the overwhelming majority supported the idea. In China, too, the idea of carrying some form of citizenship document is commonplace. It should be noted that at the request of Ipsos Reid, the wording of question 9 was changed for Hungary and Brazil, which of course influenced the responses.

When viewed proportionally, of all the countries in the category of "strongly agree," France made up 26.3% of the responses, Spain 24.6%, Mexico 23.9%, the United States 11.5%, and Canada 13.6%. France, Spain, and Mexico were in strongest favour of the implementation of a national ID card. France had 43.7% strongly agreeing with the idea of a national ID card and 34.3% somewhat agreeing. Spain had 41.0% strongly agreeing and 27.4% somewhat agreeing. Mexico had 36.9% strongly agreeing and 32.9% somewhat agreeing.

The United States and Canada were least in favour. In the United States only 19.2% strongly and 24.8% somewhat agreed with national

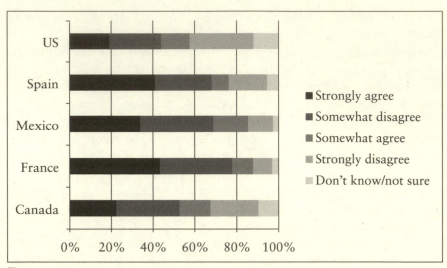

Figure 12.1
Responses to question 9 of the GPD survey

ID card implementation. However, the United States also had the largest number strongly disagreeing with this idea (30.4%). In Canada, while 22.7% strongly agreed and 30.2% somewhat agreed, 14.6% somewhat disagreed and 23.2% strongly disagreed. The amount of "don't know/ not sure" responses in the United States and Canada (11.6% and 9.3% respectively) was higher than in other countries. Spain, after the United States and Canada, ranked highest in the "strongly disagree" category, with 18.1% of overall respondents being from Spain. Mexico and France ranked least in the "strongly disagree" category, with 11.9% and 9.1% respectively. Mexico had the highest responses of "somewhat disagree," at 16%.

The "special" cases of Hungary and Brazil, countries that have already adopted national ID cards and are thus unable to answer question 9 like the other countries, when asked an adjusted question, had much higher responses in agreement than even France, Spain, and Mexico. Brazil had 56.3% strongly agreeing and 23.0% somewhat agreeing. Hungary had 76.5% strongly agreeing and 16.9% somewhat agreeing, compared to 9.6% strongly disagreeing in Brazil and 2.1% strongly disagreeing in Hungary. The amount of "don't know/not sure" responses was 3.0% and 1.0% respectively. Thus those respondents whose country had already implemented a national ID card were far more in favour of its existence than were respondents in the countries that had not.

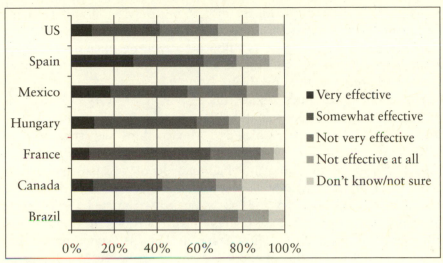

Figure 12.2
Responses to question 10 of the GPD survey

What difference, then, does knowledge of a national registry database make? Question 10 of the GPD survey asks, "In order to put national ID cards into use, the government would need to have a national database containing personal information on all citizens. This information could include address, gender, race, and tax information. How effective do you feel efforts to protect this type of information from disclosure would be?" The responses to this question show a markedly different trend from extreme responses of "strongly agree" to "somewhat agree." This is a very interesting change. It would appear that inclusion of the question about the processing of personal information in a database prompts the more cautious responses. Would the responses differ even more, one might ask, if these respondents better understood the methods of data extraction and linkage required for the national registry database to function or if they considered the role of biometric enrollment or RFID in the card systems?

This is the most significant finding in terms of qualifying other surveys about the desirability to citizens of ID cards; enthusiasm drops dramatically as soon as details about national databases are discussed. In Hungary, for example, with an almost universal acceptance of cards (77% strongly agree and 17% somewhat), the strong agreement that government will protect data in the registry shrinks to 11%, with 48% somewhat agreeing. In this respect, Canadian and American attitudes are more consistent. Respondents are dubious both about having cards

(Americans 44% and Canadians 53%,[10] but only 23% and 19% respectively strongly agree with having cards) and even more so about the likelihood that governments will protect their personal data in a national registry (only 10% in Canada and 9% in the United States believe that protection would be effective).

For Spain, Brazil, and Mexico, the responses of "very effective" to the national registry question all hovered near 30%. Spain was highest at 29.2%, Brazil next at 25.0%, and Mexico third highest at 20.9%. Interestingly, France here had the lowest number of respondents answering "very effective" (6.0%), which may denote less trust in government and more trust in another sector (this is a predictor of the results found when questions 10 and 18 were cross-tabulated for France). Hungary had higher response figures in this category, at 10.7%, than Canada at 10.1% and the United States at 8.6%. As stated previously, France ranked last in this category (for the context, see Ayse Ceyhan's chapter in this volume).

For "somewhat effective," Hungary ranked first at 48.4%, followed by France at 41.5%, Mexico at 35.2%, and Brazil at 34.9%. Of these four, two have national ID systems already in place (Hungary and Brazil). Spain, Canada, and the United States were the lowest in this response at 33.1%, 32.8%, and 28.7% respectively. This clear shift toward the middle range of possible responses to the question is stark when examining all countries surveyed. Not only is there clustering further away from extreme responses of agreement, but there is a clear increase in the amount of "don't know/not sure" responses. Thus we can only imagine what other forms this trend might take if biometric or related questions were asked.

Generally, experience of having or using a national ID card – even if it is a paper document without an accompanying electronic registry – correlates positively with the belief that they are a good idea. Five countries – Brazil, France, Hungary, Mexico, and Spain – already have ID cards, and between 34% (Mexico) and 77% (Hungary) strongly agree with having them. But it is not at all clear that the respondents in these countries are really in a good position to comment on the kinds of cards that in fact their countries are adopting or at least debating, namely biometric and RFID-enabled electronic cards.

Yet the experience of paper cards displaying limited data and storing none is very different from that of carrying cards that have multiple functions and purposes and that depend on remote machine-readability and a biometric authentication device. Even the experience of carrying ID cards with stored personal data in embedded chips is not yet widespread anywhere, with the partial exception of Malaysia, which arguably has the most advanced national ID system anywhere. Concerns have been expressed both about stored data becoming available to third parties, including commercial interests (Chance 2004), and about the risks of including religious markers in the data (Fussell 2001). Thus to understand the likely responses, some wider triangulation is needed.

This is why the GPD survey looks at the specific ID questions in relation to others about levels of trust that people have that governments are striking a right balance between national security and individual rights in their handling of personal information (Q5), about whether laws aimed at protecting national security are privacy-invasive (Q17), and about how far it is appropriate for government departments to share personal information with other departments, foreign governments, or private-sector organizations (Q18). Although none of these refer directly to the national ID issue, understanding responses in relation to these questions reveals something about the levels of trust and confidence necessary for an ID system to work successfully and safely and for people to feel that their cards are indeed contributing to their security and general social and political well-being and not otherwise.

ID CARD SYSTEMS: TRUST, PRIVACY, DATA SHARING, AND DEMOGRAPHICS

As mentioned earlier, several questions in the GPD survey that do not refer to ID card systems are nevertheless relevant as a means of checking responses about carrying cards and about national registries. They have to do with trust in government to protect personal data in a time of threats to national security (Q5), the privacy intrusiveness of laws aiming to protect national security (Q17), and the sharing of personal information with third parties, corporations, other government departments, and foreign governments (Q18). The responses to these questions may usefully be compared with responses to questions about carrying cards and about national registries.

Trust

Low levels of trust that governments will protect personal data when national security is a high priority relate to strong disagreement with ID cards. There is also a strong relationship between high levels of trust and reasonably high levels of trust and agreement with ID cards. This relationship is seen throughout the responses of the countries surveyed. However, in Brazil doubts creep in when respondents are asked about the effectiveness of government in protecting personal data. This seems to indicate that although many have a high level of trust, they are not sure how effective the government would be in securing their personal information. In Hungary people with high levels of trust that the government strikes the right balance between security and rights think the government is only somewhat effective (55% to 60%) in protecting personal data in a national registry. In Spain no less than 80% of those with high levels of trust strongly agree with ID cards. The United States gives clear evidence of the correlation between trust in government and the use of national ID cards (40% with high levels of trust strongly agree and 40% with low levels of trust strongly disagree). The protests against the Juki-Net system in Japan also suggest low levels of trust in government to handle personal data with care.

Privacy

Question 17 of the GPD survey states, "The government has enacted laws aimed at protecting national security. To what extent do you believe laws aimed at protecting national security are highly intrusive upon personal privacy?" In Brazil over 60% of those who responded "highly intrusive" to this question strongly agreed with ID cards. This trend is not seen in any other countries. For instance, 45% of the Chinese sample who said government measures are not intrusive agreed strongly with having ID cards. This is a very interesting extreme factor. In the United States just over 30% of those who see laws as not very intrusive strongly agreed with ID cards, but around 50% of those who see these laws as highly intrusive strongly disagreed with ID cards.

For question 10 cross-tabulated with question 17, again, even though national security laws are seen as highly intrusive in Brazil, data protection is also seen as highly effective (just over 30% of those who see security laws as highly intrusive responded that data protection would also be very effective). For France, over 50% of those who say laws are not intrusive strongly agreed with ID cards. In Hungary 60% of respondents who say laws are highly intrusive still believed that they are "somewhat effective." In Spain nearly 50% of those who do not think national security laws are intrusive strongly agreed with ID cards. Spaniards who see national security laws as intrusive seem to think, with respondents of other countries, that efforts to protect data are not very effective. In the United States much ambivalence is in evidence. For instance, 35% to 40% of those who see national security laws as highly intrusive also believed that government data-protection efforts are largely ineffective.

Data Sharing

Question 18 of the GPD survey asks, "To what extent do you think it is appropriate for a government agency to share citizen's personal information with third parties, such as other government agencies, foreign governments and the private sector?" For cross-tabulations of question 9 with question 18, there were high refusal rates in Brazil for the category of strong agreement with ID cards. Very interestingly, in France over 60% agree with data sharing with private third parties, to a greater extent than when asked about government agencies and foreign governments. In Hungary this is also the case: more are content with third-party than with government data sharing. In Mexico, on the other hand, respondents are more likely to agree with foreign government (50%) than with private-sector (40%) data sharing. In Spain there appears to be more concern about government agencies than about private ones, yet respondents appeared sanguine about data sharing with foreign governments. But in the United States the lowest level of confidence is reserved for private companies. In Brazil between 35% and 40% of those who think it is the government's right to share data in any circumstance maintain that the government would be very effective in securing information. There are more responses in the "don't know/not sure" category than with question 9. In China 60% of those who think data should be shared in any circumstance believe that the government would secure personal information.

The least that can be said about these findings is that they further modify the conclusions regarding national registries and ID cards. If assent to ID cards declines as details emerge of a national registry database, the issues are complicated further – and, one could argue from these data, willing compliance with ID card systems would also shrink – when questions are raised about trust in government, privacy intrusiveness, and the extent of data sharing with other departments, governments, and corporations. Although no clear trends emerge when these categories are cross-tabulated with the main two ID card system questions, they should all give pause to any who wish to claim that their system is "supported by the polls."

CONCLUSIONS

In general, there is a strong relationship between a nation already having a national ID card system – albeit a nonadvanced one – and its citizens approving the idea. Put the other way round, those who hold old-style ID cards feel there is no particular problem with them. Those with no experience of national ID cards, notably Canadians and Americans, are much more dubious. Of course, this begs the question of why certain countries have not adopted ID card systems. However, any acceptance of the idea of ID cards is immediately muted when respondents are asked about the effectiveness of efforts to protect personal data in the national registry. Even in France, which shows a relatively high acceptance of ID cards (78%, with 44% strongly agreeing), there is considerable doubt about the effectiveness of government data protection. And with regard to the level of trust in government to strike the right balance between individual rights and national security in protecting personal information, across all countries those who have low levels of trust are uneasy about ID cards. Brazil and Hungary are interesting cases here, as they both indicate high acceptance levels for ID cards but low levels of trust in government.

Because the GPD questions did not ask about biometrics or RFID (although the GPD data indicate that universally there is a relatively low level of understanding of these crucially important technologies) or even about record linkage (such as already occurs in the most advanced system, Malaysia's MyKad), we do not know how much further support for ID cards would dwindle if respondents had greater knowledge of these factors. Nevertheless, this general finding alone at least suggests the limitations of asking unqualified questions about the acceptance of ID cards. It also suggests, in terms of policy development in this area, that many citizens are being offered new national ID systems in relative ignorance of their surveillance capacities and with insufficient information to make judgments about the acceptability of such systems within their political and democratic traditions.

It is impossible to generalize about public attitudes to national ID cards, but it is evident that in several settings issues of trust in government, how well privacy may be protected, and degrees of acceptance of data sharing with third parties are important matters. By and large, it seems to be the case that countries with common-law traditions (such as Australia, Canada, the United States, the UK, and New Zealand) tend – or have tended – to be less favourably disposed toward ID card systems in general, but after 9/11 especially, this has to be seen in relation to perceived terrorism threat levels. The reason for this is that ID card systems have been widely touted, by both governments and corporations, as means of reducing the opportunities for terrorist activity, an idea that is hotly disputed by civil liberty and privacy advocates.[11] They are, moreover, being promoted in contexts where the rule of law is weakening in the face of derogation and "emergency measures."

The question of national ID card systems lies at an increasingly crucial intersection between the lives of ordinary citizens and the future of nation-states in a rapidly globalizing world. The GPD findings illustrate some of this complexity, in which conventional notions of citizenship are overlaid with new challenges to what might be thought of as "rights to mobility" and "rights to transaction" (Isin and Turner 2007) that arise both within and outside of national borders. Although democratic traditions within common-law countries may have somewhat curtailed the development of national ID card systems in the past, globalizing conditions that push countries such as the United States to seek measures to "free trade" and "foil terror" at their borders have a logic that points toward the development of identification systems. Under such conditions, knowing what citizens think is significant, even if the main lesson learned is how some purported democratic governments can obtain what amounts to "uninformed consent" for far-reaching measures with major surveillance implications and potentially undemocratic consequences.

National ID cards are being planned or put into production in a number of countries simultaneously. The GPD survey shows that some of the basic issues surrounding the introduction of new ID cards are far from popularly understood, let alone resolved. Trust in governments to protect personal data and to maintain a "balance" between seeking security and ensuring liberty is not strong, generally, yet these cards are directly implicated in the kinds of entitlements that citizens may expect from their governments. The public opinion findings suggest a further estrangement of citizens (and citizenship) from their governments at the very intersection point – markers of citizenship – where a high level of trust and mutual dependence might be expected and deemed appropriate.

APPENDIX 12.1: THE STATUS OF ID SYSTEMS
AND SURVEY RESULTS BY COUNTRY

Brazil

Brazilian citizens have used ID cards since the start of the twentieth century. Each state in Brazil prints its own ID card, but the layout and data are the same for all of them. Since 2000 the ID cards printed in Rio de

Janeiro have been fully digitized and have used a bar code that encodes a colour photograph, a signature, two fingerprints, and other citizen data.

In Brazil 60% strongly agree that national security laws are intrusive, and only 20% trust their government with personal data despite their equanimity about ID cards (79% agree and 56% strongly agree). Brazilians are also suspicious of government agencies sharing their data with others.

Canada

In 2003 the Department of Citizenship and Immigration tried, through Minister Denis Coderre, to initiate debate on national ID cards. The main reasons cited were increased security demands by the United States, especially after the terrorist attacks of 11 September 2001. Most privacy commissioners in Canada, federal and provincial, are against a national ID card system because of the increased surveillance potential and privacy and liberties risks.

China

Reportedly planning the largest ID card experiment in the world, China hopes to replace its paper cards, which have been carried since the 1980s by 960 million Chinese citizens. The old card is used by all who are over sixteen years old, although only migrant workers in cities take care to have it on them in case it is requested by authorities. Some citizens are asked (illegally) to produce them for security purposes when accessing buildings, a request with which they generally comply. The new card is contactless, being machine-readable with an embedded chip, and is issued by the Ministry of Public Security. A biometric may be added later, and 61% of citizens in three major cities would approve of this (Lui 2005).

China's ID card law has no provisions controlling how government or companies gather information, although it does restrict the kinds of data on the card – including name, address, birth date, gender, photograph, and eighteen-digit number. Citizens have no right to see or correct data (Batson 2003). Students have begun to use the new cards to identify themselves for exams in Beijing (McLeod 2006).

China, curiously, reports that most of its citizens are content with how governments treat personal data, do not believe national security laws are intrusive, and are even confident about foreign governments obtaining their personal data. That 77% agree – especially younger people – that ID cards are neutral and needful suggests something about the cultural differences between China, where holding an electronic card may be seen as cool (Lui 2005), and, say, Canada.

France

The *carte d'identité de français* was originally issued in 1921 (Piazza 2004) and reissued as the *carte d'identité* in 1940, to be replaced again by a *carte nationale d'identité*, without central records, in 1955. It was laminated and renamed the *carte nationale d'identité securisée* in 1988 and made machine-readable in 1995. They are used to access health, education, voting, banks, and the post office. Police can ask for identification but not necessarily for the ID card itself. Everyday life would be difficult without it. Since 2001 proposals have been made for a biometric-based electronic card called the *carte d'identité électronique sécurisée* (INES), which would be similar to the UK scheme. When the government-funded Forum des droits sur l'internet (FDI) was asked to poll citizens in 2005, 74% were in favour of new ID cards, 75% approved of the fingerprint database, and 63% were in agreement with their compulsory use.

France has had paper ID cards for decades and introduced electronic ones more recently – hence, one assumes, the solid agreement (78%) with having a card – but there is growing discussion of a biometric INES and some awareness of the new issues this raises.

Hungary

National ID cards have been compulsory in Hungary since the post-Second World War communist regime was in power. They have a name, signature, date of birth, photograph, and number but no address, database, or biometrics and are fairly easy to forge. The cards are required for access to government services but are seldom demanded by retail outlets or police.

Among the countries in our sample, Hungary is the most supportive (93%, including 77% who strongly agree) of ID cards. This takes some explaining, although perhaps the communist past may help our understanding. Interestingly, 60% of those who believe national security laws are highly intrusive also think that the government is somewhat effective in protecting data in the national registry. This suggests, perhaps, that intrusiveness is not directly associated with weak data protection.

Mexico

In Mexcio the General Population Act regulates the National Registry of Population and Personal Identification. The registry's purpose is to register all persons making up the country's population using data that enable their identity to be certified reliably. The aim is ultimately to issue a citizen's identity card, which will be the official document of identification, fully endorsing the data contained in it concerning the holder. The federal government is discussing a plan for a national ID card system that will use face and finger biometrics and contactless RFID and that will adhere to the standards of the International Civil Aviation Organization (ICAO). The central registry database will be linked with social security, taxation, passports, and criminal justice departments.

Mexicans are moderately supportive of ID cards (69%, only 34% strongly) and only moderately sure of the effectiveness of protection of data (55%, only 18% strongly). However, even those who agree with ID cards disapprove of governments sharing their data, although they are more open to sharing with other governments than with corporations.

Spain

Spain has used ID cards since 1944, and they are compulsory for citizens over the age of fourteen. ID cards must be produced for police on request, and they contain a name, photograph, place of birth, nationality, gender, and signature. Fingerprints are stored on a database. For those under thirty, it is valid for five years and thereafter for ten years until age seventy. Spain's new ID card system rollout began in February 2006, and it is expected that half a million cards will be in use by the end of the year, 2 million in 2007, and a further 6 million in 2008. Eventually, more than 30 million Spaniards should have the card (see STMicroelectronics 2006).

Spain appears to be trusting of government and positive about ID cards (68%, 41% strongly), although there is uncertainty over the effectiveness of data protection (62%, only 29% regarding it as very effective). Curiously, Spain's citizens are more content to share data with other governments than with their own. Similar to in other countries, the more national security law is seen as intrusive, the less effective the government is thought to be in protecting data. ID cards in Spain seem to be regarded as a sign of high-tech superiority.

United States

The US House of Representatives approved the Real ID Act in February 2005 with the aim of frustrating terrorists and illegal immigrants. Since 2009 all who live or work in the United States have required a federally approved ID card to travel on an airplane, open a bank account, collect Social Security payments, or take advantage of nearly any government service. The driver's licence has been reissued to meet federal standards. The cards are machine-readable and will establish what amounts to a national identity card.

US results show that the more people trust government, the more they will accept ID cards (although the United States is the lowest in the sample at 44% support for ID cards, down to 19% who strongly support them). However, 50% of those who see national security law as intrusive also disagree strongly with ID cards. There is also some ambivalence in that, for example, 20% of those who think national security laws are not intrusive also say that government efforts to protect personal data are ineffective.

NOTES

My thanks to Kylie Hamilton for research assistance in the preparation of this chapter.

1 See the appendix to this volume for the wording of the questions.
2 See http://www.itpro.co.uk/news/116027/half-of-europeans-show-support-for-id-cards.html (accessed 24 July 2007).
3 See http://www.itpro.co.uk/news/115979/id-cards-a-public-good-says-government.html (accessed 24 July 2007).
4 For more discussion of public opinion polling on national ID cards in Canada, see Emily Smith's chapter in this volume.
5 See http://www.pm.gov.uk/output/Page10368.asp (accessed 24 July 2007).
6 Survey results for Japan were not available at the time of writing, although the focus group results obtained in 2004 indicate relatively low levels of personal concern about "privacy" in that country. Even at that time, however, some indicated unease with the Juki-Net national identification registry system as an example of privacy concerns. See also Murakami Wood, Lyon, and Abe (2007).
7 For Brazil and Hungary, pretesting showed that the question meant little, as a form of national ID card is already in existence. Apparently, this was not a problem in, say, France or Spain, so there is a small anomaly here.

8 Reported in the *Daily Telegraph* (London), 27 February 2006, http://
  www.telegraph.co.uk/news/main.jhtml?hml=/news/2006/02/27/nid27.
  xml&sSheet=/news/2006/02/27/ixhome.html (accessed 24 November
  2009).

9 Reported in *The Daily Telegraph* (London), 5 December 2006, http://www.
  telegraph.co.uk/news/main.jhtml?xml=/news/2006/12/04/ndata04.xml (accessed 24 November 2009).

10 However, see François Fournier's chapter in this volume for details of differences between Quebec and the rest of Canada.

11 See, for example, http://www.aclu.org/privacy/gen/14898res20030908.html
  (accessed 24 November 2009).

13

A National ID Card in Canada: Public Perceptions and an Inevitable Future?

EMILY SMITH

INTRODUCTION

Canadian citizens do not currently have a single national identity card. Several ID documents are used in Canada, such as birth certificates, driver's licences, passports, and citizenship cards. These are all considered foundation documents that can be used to secure other identity cards, with the birth certificate being the most important. The Department of Citizenship and Immigration currently has three existing identification systems to recognize Canadian citizens: the passport, permanent resident card (sometimes called the maple leaf card), and citizenship card. Creating one national ID card is a politically charged topic that has come in and out of national discussion at various times in Canadian Parliament.

The idea of a national ID card was initially proposed in Canada to replace social insurance number (SIN) cards, which are used for administering government programs and are a requirement to work in Canada or to receive government benefits. This was proposed as a means to prevent the abuse of SIN cards, which were originally meant for federal government use only, but government control was lost and other uses evolved (such as verifying cheques). The idea of national identity cards received the greatest attention in the months following the terrorist attacks in the United States on 11 September 2001. After this dramatic event, finding a means to ensure the secure identification of citizens became a renewed issue in the United States and ultimately in Canada as well. This dialogue and the possible development of national ID cards in Canada are largely tied to US policies and pressure.

PUBLIC OPINION POLLS ON
NATIONAL ID CARDS IN CANADA

Public opinion polling on the introduction of national ID cards in Canada has also occurred throughout this process. As Oscar Gandy (2003) points out, government and business often sponsor public opinion polling as a means to assess public will and to influence policies and laws in the country on a range of issues. Similarly, Solveig Singleton and Jim Harper (2001) claim that when public opinion polls are used in policymaking, especially in the area of personal privacy, they need to be taken "with a grain of salt" because the survey design and questions are often used to manipulate the results. With an awareness of these concerns, results from various surveys on the topic of national ID cards are highlighted in the next section, keeping in mind where possible the context of the debates around the issues addressed, the influence of the survey sponsors, methodology, question types and wording, intentions, and the character of results. The polls discussed are not meant to be exhaustive but are a cross-section of the types of surveys that have taken place on national ID card issues in Canada from 2001 to the present.[1] In general, most findings presented in public opinion polls on national identity cards indicate that the majority of Canadians support their implementation. However, when one examines the design and order of questions, as well as how the results were reported, it becomes very clear that these results have been strongly influenced by the interests supporting these surveys.

Public opinion polls conducted immediately following the terrorist attacks of 9/11 revealed extreme differences in opinion across the board. It is a well-documented effect that a serious event can sway opinions for a short time. For example, EKOS Research Associates conducted a survey on *Security, Sovereignty and Continentalism: Canadian Perspectives on September 11* on 27 September 2001. The survey found that 77% of Canadian respondents agreed with the statement "I think that our lives will be deeply and permanently changed by these terrorist attacks" (EKOS 2001).[2] This study also found that 59% of respondents would not mind giving up some of their national sovereignty to increase the overall security of North America. Likewise, in October 2001 an Ipsos Reid/*Globe and Mail*/CTV poll[3] showed that the majority of respondents (58%) believed that "terrorism threats to individual Canadians currently outweigh the protection of their individual rights and freedom and due process of law – and that everything should be done to provide the police and intelligence officials with the tools they say they need to protect collective safety of Canadians against terrorism" (Ipsos Reid/*Globe and Mail*/CTV 2001; see also GPD figure 13(a) online).[4] Thirty-eight per cent of Canadians did not agree with these statements. This poll also found that although half of respondents thought it would be necessary to give up some of their civil liberties (46% did not believe it would be necessary), they would not agree to officials intercepting their mail (74%) or monitoring their telephone calls and e-mail (71%) or their credit card and financial transactions (61%) without being told. Thus it is clear that immediately following 11 September 2001 respondents appeared more than ready to give up their longstanding rights for a hyped but vague notion of national security.

In 2001, during this time of heightened security concerns, public support for national identity cards in Canada was found to be extremely high. When asked whether they supported or opposed various initiatives being applied to all Canadians, not just newly arrived immigrants or those awaiting to obtain their citizenship, 80% of respondents supported the statement "You would submit yourself to providing fingerprints for a national identity card that would be carried on your person at all times to show to police or security officials on request"; only 19% opposed this statement (Ipsos Reid/*Globe and Mail*/CTV 2001). This is the highest level of support reported within the polls examined. Breakdowns by region, gender, and age were provided for these responses. The most support for this provision was from the Atlantic region (87%), Quebec (82%), and Ontario (81%), with Saskatchewan/Manitoba (77%), British Columbia (76%), and Alberta (76%) not far behind. Older respondents were more likely to support these provisions (84%), followed by middle-aged (82%) and younger people (75%). More women (85%) than men (76%) indicated they would submit fingerprints for ID cards.

During the height of the 2003 discussions in Canada over introducing a national identity card, the federal government department of Citizenship and Immigration Canada (CIC) commissioned EKOS to conduct a national public opinion poll on document integrity and biometrics (see House of Commons, Canada 2003, 6–8; EKOS 2003a).[5] This poll was designed to test how receptive the public was to adopting ID cards despite privacy concerns. The findings of this survey were presented at a high-profile conference on the topic "Biometrics: Implications and Applications for Citizenship and Immigration," held in Ottawa and sponsored by CIC in October 2003. This survey found that the majority of respondents supported the idea of the federal government issuing ID cards to Canadians.[6] Sixty per cent supported the idea of voluntary ID cards, while 59% supported issuing mandatory cards. This support was higher for cards that contained biometrics, such as fingerprints or eye scans, with 71% support for voluntary cards and 66% for mandatory cards. However, this increase in support can be explained by the leading wording of the question "What if a new national ID card contained a copy of the cardholder's fingerprint or eye scan *to ensure that the card could not be used by anyone else?*" (EKOS 2003a, emphasis added). The italicized part of the question inherently implies the success of using biometric technology within national identity cards; this section of the question should have been eliminated to obtain a less biased response.

When the two questions mentioned above were asked at the end of the survey, rather than at the beginning, they elicited 10% to 15% higher support for ID cards and for ID cards with biometrics, which clearly indicates the influence of other questions asked throughout the survey (House of Commons, Canada 2003, 7; see also GPD figure 13(b) online). Participants at the CIC conference raised methodological concerns about this survey (see Zureik 2004, 2). Interestingly, in 2004 the Government of Canada's Privy Council Office presented a review of survey findings on *Public Opinion on Privacy Issues* to the Assistant Deputy Minister (ADM) Privacy Committee. It reported the finding of this EKOS 2003 study that Canadians appear to strongly support national ID cards but claimed that further analysis revealed that this seemed to be the case when the card was not actually used, as respondents did not see the card as being "for them." The Privy Council Office found that concern over privacy issues increased as Canadians saw themselves as personally affected (Government of Canada 2004).

Ipsos Reid also conducted a survey on national ID cards in Canada and the United States later in 2003 and reported Canadian support for national identity cards.[7] Ipsos Reid reported that 47% of Canadians strongly (22%) or somewhat (25%) agreed with the following statement, compared to 40% of Americans who strongly (19%) or somewhat (21%) agreed: "Due to increased concerns about terrorism, everyone living in [Canada/the United States] should have a government-issued national identification card that they must carry on them at all times and present when asked to by police or members of other Canadian security forces. Do you strongly agree, somewhat agree, somewhat disagree or strongly disagree?" However, 42% of Canadian respondents strongly (37%) or somewhat (15%) disagreed, and 59% of American respondents also strongly (45%) or somewhat (14%) disagreed (Ipsos Reid 2003; see also GPD figure 13(c) online). Thus, despite the reporting of the findings, there were almost as many respondents in disagreement as there were in agreement with issuing national identity cards, and the greatest response of Canadians came from those who strongly disagreed, at 37%.

EDS Canada conducted a *Privacy and Identity Management Survey* over the Internet in partnership with Ipsos Reid in 2005.[8] EDS Canada is a company that provides a wide range of information-technology solutions for businesses and government, including identity management and the use of biometric technologies.[9] Its survey focused on Canadian consumers' expectations for the security of information they provide to businesses over the phone or Internet. EDS Canada indicates in a white paper on its findings that "As the need for privacy, security and strong identification management is stressed in virtually every aspect of our lives, it becomes increasingly important for organizations to shoulder the responsibility of addressing customers' requirements in those areas" (EDS Canada 2005, 1). With these goals in mind, it carried out its consumer survey and reported that the results showed that the public strongly supported a private and secure credential with biometrics to provide a high degree of identification/authentication. EDS Canada also found that consumers have a strong expectation for the security of information that they provide to businesses over the phone and Internet and are willing to provide more personal information to businesses they trust than to ones that are unfamiliar or with which they have no prior relationship (EDS Canada 2005, 4).

Not surprisingly, the EDS Canada survey has the most biased question wording and findings. One of its main findings was that Canadians appear to strongly support the use of a private and secure credential. The question was worded in a leading fashion: "A private and secure credential *is an effective way to protect your information*. Would you prefer to have one private and secure verification credential that will be accepted by all organizations to verify who you are before providing access to your records or systems?" (EDS Canada 2005, 8, emphasis added). Sixty-two per cent of survey respondents answered "yes," only 17% responded no, and 22%, a high proportion, were unsure (see GPD figure 13(d) online).

Similarly, EDS Canada found that Canadians strongly support biometrics to deliver both security and convenience. Sixty-five per cent of survey respondents indicated an acceptance of the use of biometrics, 16% found them unacceptable, and 19% were unsure (EDS Canada 2005). Fingerprints and iris scanning had the greatest acceptance, at 40% and 34%. Of those who accepted biometrics, when asked for the reasons to use biometrics, the majority (89%) cited increased security, 54% chose convenience, and 39% wanted to speed up their transactions. Of the 12% who opposed the use of biometrics, 43% were fearful of the information being accessed by criminals, 32% were suspicious about how biometrics work, and 28% did not believe in their accuracy. The interests of EDS Canada are further emphasized when it suggests that these concerns "are likely to be alleviated by the increasing use of bio- metrics in various national security programs" (EDS Canada 2005, 8). From these results, EDS Canada claims that customers strongly support a single identification credential and that biometrics would be a highly acceptable means to provide authentication. Clearly, the business mo- tivations of EDS Canada strongly influenced the question design and re- porting of results. It concluded its report with tips for consumers and chief privacy officers about how to protect the information of clients and about how EDS Canada can satisfy these requirements.

Another business-oriented survey was conducted by TNS, a custom market-information company,[10] and by TRUSTe, an online privacy pro- vider, in March and May 2006 on the topic of national identity cards.[11] This study also reported strong public support for national ID cards with biometrics. This survey found that 7 out of 10 Canadians would support a new national identity card issued to every citizen (69%), that 2 out of 10 (22%) would oppose it, and that 1 out of 10 are undecided (Kapica 2005). When Americans were asked the same question, the re- sults showed that only half of the respondents would support a new national ID card, that one-third would be against it, and that 17% are undecided. The companies conducting this survey claim that Canadians expressed slightly more support for including biometric information on government-issued documents and less support for private-sector uses of biometric data. However, although Canadians were seen as more in favour of biometric ID in government-issued documents, the survey re- sults showed they are worried that the costs might be prohibitive and that governments could abuse the system (Kapica 2005).

This survey uncovered strong support for biometrics in identity docu- ments because the questions linked the use of biometrics with the im- portance of identity documents. For example, the poll found that 85% of Canadians and 79% of Americans support the idea that "the pass- port is the most important identifying document and therefore the most appropriate for adding biometric identifiers" (Kapica 2005). Besides passports, other identity documents that received strong support for including biometric data were driver's licences, social insurance cards (social security cards in the United States), and provincial health insurance cards. Reports on the study claim that the public perceives biometric data, such as fingerprints and retinal scans, as a way to help prevent fraud and ID theft, but the questions' wording was not available. This survey was conducted while governments in both countries were planning to introduce biometrics into ID cards.

A more recent poll that addresses biometric identification was carried out by Ipsos Reid on behalf of Citizenship and Immigration Canada. This poll is part of annual tracking to assess public opinion on immigration policy.[12] The poll found that, overall, support for immigration levels is steady, although in recent years there has been increased concern (by several percentage points) over the use of fraudulent identity documents. Importantly, the poll findings indicate that Canadians show a limited understanding of biometrics, with 38% of respondents claiming they know "nothing" about biometrics and only 2% being able to define fingerprint analysis and eye scans as biometrics. However, respondents supported government use of biometrics for national security – either to prevent prospective immigrants from using fraudulent identity to enter the country or for convenience when travelling. The majority of respondents in this poll said that protecting national interest is more important than protecting privacy (Workpermit.com 2006). However, the poll questions were not available for review.

It becomes very apparent that the wording and placement of questions, the type of survey (publicly or privately funded), reporting, and world events strongly impacted the outcome of results for the above questions about national identity cards. The majority of these polls were used by various organizations and governments that have a stake in the outcome of the national identity card debates and thus a motive to provide evidence of public support for issuing national identity cards. Although almost all of these surveys attempted to obtain respondent samples that were representative of the demographic variables of the Canadian population, very few breakdowns in results based on these factors were analyzed.

THE GPD SURVEY RESULTS

The international survey on privacy and surveillance conducted under the umbrella of the Globalization of Personal Data (GPD) project is a unique source for polling data on national ID cards. The GPD project involved a network of researchers who investigated the flows of personal information in various contexts and the social, political, and economic consequences of these flows. One of the main aims of the GPD project was to investigate the responses of ordinary citizens to the increased travels of their personal information in all aspects of their lives – as employees, consumers, citizens, and travellers. The international survey was designed to reveal complex cross-cultural attitudes to issues of privacy and surveillance. Construction of the survey instrument was an intensive process that included focus group interviews in the nine countries of the survey: Canada, the United States, Mexico, Brazil, China, France, Hungary, Spain, and Japan. The focus group results were summarized and analyzed, and extensive background reports were prepared in each of the nine countries. Cross-cultural comparative works on values and attitudes were examined. Using all of this background information, Elia Zureik, the lead researcher for the international survey, oversaw the design of the questionnaire in consultation with numerous other researchers in the field. This is the first survey of this magnitude to be conducted on the topic, and it is a unique survey in that it originated in an academic setting, apart from business or government influence.

In constructing the questionnaire, the GPD researchers identified national identity cards as one of the issues to be addressed. This was due to the increasing political salience of national ID cards discussed in current surveillance and security studies.[13] In the end, it was decided that not only would there be a question about whether respondents would support the introduction of a national identity card, but there would also be one about how their opinions would change if they were aware that this meant a database of information would be stored about them. The advantage of this survey is that results from these questions can be examined alongside responses to numerous other relevant questions within the survey, including ones on trust, information sharing by government, and demographic variables. The section below examines some of these findings.

QUESTION 9: GOVERNMENT-ISSUED NATIONAL ID CARDS

Question 9, regarding the acceptance of a national identity card, asked: "Some have suggested that everyone should have a government-issued national ID card that they must carry on them at all times and present it when asked by police or other security forces. To what extent would you agree or disagree with this idea?" Just over half of respondents

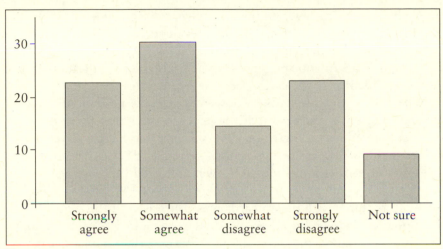

Figure 13.1
Canadian results for question 9 of the GPD survey (%)

in Canada (52.9%) agreed with this statement, with 22.6% choosing "strongly agree," and 30.3% – the largest number of respondents – choosing "somewhat agree." Just over one-third (37.8%) disagreed with this statement, more of whom strongly disagreed (23.2%) than somewhat disagreed (14.6%). Almost 10% (9.3%) selected "don't know/ not sure." Thus a slim majority of Canadian respondents agreed with the idea of a government-issued national ID card, with most of those in agreement only somewhat agreeing, while those who disagreed were more likely to strongly disagree (see figure 13.1).

Demographic variables also reveal some variations in results. When broken down regionally, the responses to question 9 show some interesting trends.[14] The strongest support for identity cards came from Quebec and Manitoba/Saskatchewan. Just over 60% of Quebec respondents agreed with the idea of national ID cards (61.8%), almost equally divided among those who strongly (28.2%) or somewhat (33.6%) agreed. This was followed closely by Manitoba/Saskatchewan (with 59.4% in support of ID cards), who had fewer strongly agreeing (24.6%) than somewhat agreeing (34.8%). The Atlantic provinces were the next greatest supporters of ID cards, at 56.3%, with 26.3% strongly agreeing and 30% somewhat agreeing. Ontario followed at 50.8%, of whom 19.2% strongly agreed and 31.6% somewhat agreed. The strongest opposition to identity cards came from Alberta and British Columbia. Just over half (54.5%) of Albertan respondents disagreed with question 9, with more strongly disagreeing (31.7%) than somewhat disagreeing (16.8%). Less than half (44.7%) of British Columbia residents opposed the card, with 28.5% strongly disagreeing and 16.2% somewhat disagreeing. Ontario (40.6%) and the Atlantic provinces (37.6%) also had significant numbers in disagreement with the cards (see GPD figure 13(e) online).

When responses are broken down by age, very slight differences emerge. The strongest age predictor in response is that those over age 65 were most likely to agree that everyone should have a government-issued national ID card; 64% either strongly (28.3%) or somewhat (36.5%) agreed with this idea. This was followed by those aged 18 to 24 (53.5%), 45 to 54 (53.1%), and 35 to 44 (51.7%). The group most likely to disagree with the ID cards was comprised of those aged 55 to 64 (46.2%), followed by those aged 25 to 34 (41.7%) and 35 to 44 (39.9%). Therefore, the oldest (especially) and the youngest (slightly) age categories were most in agreement with the idea of a national ID card (see GPD figure 13(f) online).

In terms of gender, there were almost negligible differences in responses. Somewhat more men than women strongly (men 25.3%, women 20.3%) or somewhat (men 32.2%, women 28.5%) agreed with the idea of ID cards, while slightly more women than men somewhat (women 15.1%, men 14%) or strongly (women 23.9%, men 22.4%) disagreed with the idea (see GPD figure 13(g) online).

There were also no significant findings in relation to ethnicity in the responses to question 9. Those who identified themselves as of mixed ethnic background and as Asian/Pacific Islanders were most in agreement with a government-issued national ID card, at approximately 60%. This was followed by respondents who identified themselves as Caucasian/white (53%), as belonging to another population group (52.3%), and as black/African (50%). The strongest disagreement with the cards came from those in another population group (41.7%), from those identifying as Caucasian/white (37.8%), and from those of black and mixed ethnic backgrounds (33.3% each). The highest nonresponse rates were from those who identified as North American Indian/Inuit (21.4%) and as black/African (16.7%) (see GPD figure 13(h) online).

Results from question 9 were cross-tabulated with results from question 5, which asked: "When it comes to the privacy of personal information, what level of trust do you have that the Canadian government is striking the right balance between national security and individual rights?" This comparison was made in order to determine how the level of trust in government protection of individual rights influenced responses to the question of whether the government should issue a national identity card. A strong pattern emerged when these results were cross-tabulated. Those who had very high or reasonably high levels of trust that the government is striking the right balance between national security and individual rights also strongly or somewhat agreed with the idea that the government should issue a national identity card. Similarly, those who had fairly low and very low levels of trust in the government striking the right balance also disagreed somewhat or strongly that there should be a government-issued ID card (see GPD figure 13(i) online).

Even stronger relationships were found between results when comparing questions 9 and 17. Question 17 asked: "The government of Canada has enacted laws aimed at protecting national security. To what extent do you believe laws aimed at protecting national security are intrusive upon personal privacy?" Those who believed laws aimed at protecting national security are highly intrusive upon personal privacy also strongly disagreed with the idea that everyone should have a government-issued national ID card, at 44.1%. The opposite cross-tabulation was also true: those who strongly agreed with the idea of a government-issued ID card also believed national security laws are not intrusive at all on personal privacy, at 49.1%. This clearly shows that individuals who were concerned about laws to protect national security intruding on personal privacy were opposed to issuing a national ID card and that those who were not concerned at all about laws protecting national security intruding on personal privacy agreed with the idea of a national ID card (see GPD figure 13(j) online).

Comparing the results of question 9 with those of question 18 shows similar trends. Question 18 asked: "To what extent do you think it is appropriate for a government agency to share citizen's personal information with third parties, such as other government agencies, foreign governments and the private sector?" Those who believed it is the government's right under all circumstances, or if the citizen is suspected of wrongdoing, to share citizens' personal information with other government agencies, foreign governments, and the private sector also strongly or somewhat agreed with government-issued national ID cards. Respondents who strongly disagreed with government-issued ID cards were also more likely to say that it is not appropriate for a government to share citizens' personal information with other government departments, foreign governments, and the private sector in any circumstance unless the government has the express consent of the citizen (see GPD figures 13(k), 13(l), and 13(m) online).

QUESTION 10: EFFECTIVENESS OF
PROTECTING PERSONAL INFORMATION
IN A NATIONAL ID CARD DATABASE

Question 10 in the GPD survey dealt with the effectiveness of government at protecting citizens' national identity information held within a database. The question was asked as follows: "In order to put national ID cards into use, the government would need to have a national database containing personal information on all citizens. This information could include address, gender, race, and tax information. How effective do you feel efforts to protect this type of information from disclosure would be?" Just over 40% (42.9%) of all Canadian respondents believed this would be effective. Of this number, there were far fewer respondents who felt strongly that efforts to protect this information from disclosure would be very effective (10%) and more who felt that they would be somewhat effective (32.8%). Just under 40% (37.4%) said it would not be very effective (25%) or not effective at all (12.4%). A high percentage (19.7%) – almost 1 out of 5 – answered "don't know/not sure." Therefore, respondents were more clustered around the middle range answers to this question, indicating that they were not as confident that personal information held in national ID card government databases would be protected from disclosure (see figure 13.2).

In terms of regional differences, almost half of respondents in the Atlantic provinces were most likely to agree that efforts would be very (8.8%) or somewhat (40%) effective at protecting this type of information from disclosure. This was closely trailed by Manitoba/Saskatchewan (44.9%) and Quebec (44.6%). Interestingly, Ontario, Alberta, and British Columbia respondents were equally split between agreement and disagreement with this statement: 41.8% for Ontario, 40.6% for Alberta, and 40% for British Columbia (see GPD figure 13(n) online).

Only minimal variations in response to question 10 emerged for age breakdowns. Those aged 25 to 34 were most likely to believe that efforts to protect information from disclosure would be very or somewhat effective (67.8%), followed by those aged 18 to 24 (62.6%) and 45 to 54 (59.3%). Those most likely to believe these efforts were not very effective or not effective at all were aged 35 to 44 (36.7%), 18 to 24 (34.8%), and 45 to 54 (33.7%). The most notable age predictor was that those aged 18 to 24 believed the efforts to protect databases would be somewhat effective, at 43.6% (see GPD figure 13(o) online).

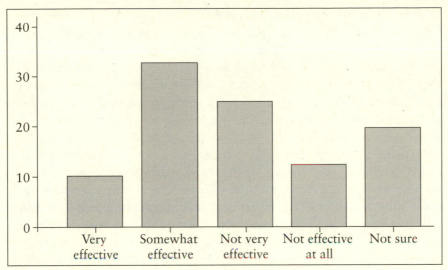

Figure 13.2
Canadian results for question 10 of the GPD survey (%)

Again, there were minimal differences by gender in response to question 10. Yet the same pattern emerged, with slightly more men than women choosing "very effective" (men 24.5%, women 25.5%) and "somewhat effective" (men 38.3%, women 31.8%) and with more women than men believing these efforts would not be very effective (women 15.9%, men 13.4%). More women (8.4%) than men (5.6%) responded "don't know/not sure" (see GPD figure 13(p) online).

Those who identified themselves as black/African were most in agreement that efforts to protect databases from disclosure would be very or somewhat effective (50%), followed by 48.5% of those in another population group and by 42.9% of those who identified as Caucasian/white. The black/African group was also most in disagreement (41.6%), followed by those of mixed ethnic backgrounds (40.6%) and by those in another population group (39.4%). The most significant discovery in examining the ethnicity of respondents for question 10 is the high non-response rates from those who identified themselves as North American Indian/Inuit (35.7%), as Asian/Pacific Islander (30%), and as having mixed ethnic backgrounds (21.9%) (see GPD figure 13(q) online).

Again, strong connections in responses were made when cross-tabulating results from question 10 with those from question 5. Very high and reasonably high levels of trust that the Canadian government is striking the right balance between national security and individual rights corresponds with beliefs that efforts to protect personal information in a national government databases from disclosure would be very or somewhat effective. At the same time, fairly low and very low levels of trust correlate with beliefs that efforts to protect information from disclosure would not be very effective or not effective at all. The strongest connections were seen between very high and reasonably high levels of trust (40.7%) and belief that efforts would be somewhat effective (38.4%) (see GPD figure 13(r) online).

Cross-tabulating the responses to questions 10 and 17 does not result in a strong relationship between results, as was seen when cross-tabulating the responses to questions 9 and 17. Those who felt that laws aimed at protecting national security were intrusive on privacy also believed that efforts to protect national government ID card databases would be effective. The strongest cross-tabulation occurred between those who believed laws were somewhat intrusive and those who believed databases would be somewhat effective (45.6%). However, those who claimed that laws are not intrusive also felt that efforts to protect databases would be effective. There was also a relationship between those who agreed database protection would not be effective and those who agreed laws are not intrusive. The strongest cross-tabulation in this group was made between those who responded "not very effective" and those who chose "not very intrusive" (27.7%). This demonstrates that these individuals were not as sure of their responses to both questions (see GPD figure 13(s) online).

A relationship is also shown between question 18 and 10. Respondents who believed it is the government's right in all circumstances, regardless of whether the citizen is suspected of wrongdoing, to share citizens' personal information with other government agencies, foreign governments, and the private sector also believed that efforts to protect information in databases from disclosure would be very or somewhat effective. Those who believed databases are not very effective or not effective at all at protecting personal information from disclosure were also more likely to say that it is not appropriate for a government to share citizens' personal information with other government departments, foreign governments, and the private sector under any circumstance unless the government has the express consent of the citizen (see GPD figures 13(t), 13(u), and 13(v) online).

CONCLUSION

Examining the GPD survey results in relation to various demographic variables and questions related to government trust and information sharing produces a more nuanced picture of public attitudes in Canada toward national ID cards than was hitherto available. Although a slim majority of citizens support the introduction of a government-issued national identity card, a significant number also oppose it. When respondents are asked about storing national ID card information in a government database, their belief in the effectiveness of protecting personal information is not as strong. The Canadian public become much less sure of their responses to ID cards when databases are involved. This shows that the public need more information on what national identity cards would entail in order to better understand the risks involved in storing their information.

Demographic variables reveal considerable differences in results, especially by region, with the Quebec and Manitoba/Saskatchewan regions supporting government-issued ID documents most clearly and British Columbia and Alberta most strongly objecting. There were some findings for age, with the oldest and youngest age groups being in support of ID cards, and for ethnicity, with high nonresponse rates from North American Indian/Inuit, Asian/Pacific Islander, and those of mixed ethnic backgrounds. Very minimal effects were found for gender, with men faintly more in support of ID cards and women more opposed.

An interesting finding of the GPD survey is that citizens' trust in government can be used as a predictor of whether Canadians will support the introduction of a government-issued national ID card and whether they believe efforts to protect the database containing their personal information will be effective. In addition, those who believe laws aimed at national security are intrusive upon personal privacy are also less accepting of national ID cards. Insofar as these survey results reveal how other political viewpoints influence responses, they provide a more complex picture of Canadian public opinions on national ID cards. Further quantitative analysis is needed on the strength of these predictors.[15]

Previous polling on the topic by various groups demonstrates how survey sponsors, question wording, and reporting of findings are used to influence the outcome of polls in the sponsors' favour, bringing their effectiveness into question. The GPD survey findings highlight the need for more public education on what national ID cards would entail so that a more accurate reading of public opinion can be obtained based on respondents' awareness of what would actually be involved in the process. Regardless of these survey findings, politicians have made it apparent that the Canadian federal government's decision on whether to implement a national ID card is likely to be shaped more by US policies and pressure, not to mention financial constraints, than by public opinion.

NOTES

1 It is difficult to obtain the original questionnaires and raw data for these surveys, so in most instances the published summaries of findings must be relied
upon. Where available, the methodology of these surveys can be found in the
notes below.

2 This was a Canadian national random sample involving a telephone survey of
1,228 members of the general public. Results were considered valid within +/-
2.8 percentage points 19 times out of 20. Data were statistically weighted to
ensure that regional, gender, and age composition would reflect the Canadian
population according to census data.

3 This poll was conducted from 2 to 4 October 2001 with a randomly selected
sample of 1,000 Canadian adults. The results are considered accurate within
+/-3.1 percentage points 19 times out of 20. The data were statistically weighted to reflect the regional, age, and gender composition of the Canadian population according to 1996 census data.

4 All the GPD figures cited in this chapter are online at http://www.
sscqueens.org/book_tables (accessed 20 November 2009).

5 This EKOS poll was conducted in February 2003 with a random sample of
3,000 Canadians.

6 Respondents were asked, "Would you support or oppose the idea of the federal government issuing [voluntary/mandatory] ID Cards to Canadians?"

7 This Ipsos Reid poll was conducted from 7 to 9 October 2003. It is based on a
randomly selected sample of 1,039 Canadians and 1,001 Americans. It is considered accurate within +/-3.1 percentage points 19 times out of 20 if the entire
adult Canadian and American populations had been polled.

8 This study involved the same survey being administered to two separate consumer groups over the Internet from 13 to 17 January 2005, and it targeted
a broad demographic distribution of the Canadian population. Group A was
asked to respond to questions as though the organization in question was one
with which they had a pre-existing trusting relationship. Group B was asked to
respond as though the organization in question was one with which they had
no pre-existing trusting relationship. This was to determine whether consumers
provide different amounts and types of information to these organizations. The
number of valid consumer survey responses was 1,735, with 887 in Group A
and 848 in Group B. This study also provided the demographic distributions
of respondents by region, income group, age, Internet experience, gender, and
household composition. Results are accurate within +/-2.4 percentage points
19 times out of 20.

9 EDS Canada has now become HP Enterprise Services; see http://www.hp.com/hpinfo/newsroom/press/2009/090923xa.html (accessed 20 November 2009).

10 See http://www.tnsglobal.com (accessed 20 November 2009).

11 This was a survey of 1,157 Canadian and 1,003 American Internet users. The survey was conducted from 17 to 25 March 2006 in the United States and from 26 to 30 May 2006 in Canada. Survey results are representative of the online US and Canadian adult populations and are considered accurate within +/-3 percentage points (3.1 in the United States and 2.9 in Canada) 19 times out of 20.

12 There was a margin of error of +/-2.8%.

13 At one point, the GPD survey contained more than two questions on the topic of national identity cards. Due to space limitations and the great spectrum of topics that were to be addressed, these two questions were almost cut. However, several researchers fought for their inclusion in the final version of the survey.

14 When one views demographic breakdowns in results, it must be kept in mind that demographic variables were weighted to Canadian census data, meaning there is not equal representation within each category.

15 It would be interesting to see whether responses to the national ID questions elicited the same results cross-culturally, as this would show whether citizen trust is always the best predictor of agreement with government-issued national identity cards. Additional study would also be valuable on how public responses to the prospect of national ID cards would change if biometric information was to be stored on the cards.

14

Privacy, Identity, and Digital Policy: A Comparative Assessment of the United States, Spain, and Canada

JEFFREY ROY

INTRODUCTION

The purpose of this chapter is to examine the nexus between privacy, identity, and the digital policies and electronic governance initiatives of governments in three different national jurisdictions included in the Globalization of Personal Data (GPD) survey on surveillance and privacy: Spain, the United States, and Canada. Undertaking a comparison of Spain and the United States is useful on two fronts beyond this direct two-country comparison: first, it allows for a broader comparative consideration of North American and European dimensions of privacy and identity issues; and second, it enables Canada to be situated within both national and continental perspectives.

The guiding premises underpinning this investigation are twofold: first, that the terrorist attacks both in the United States on 11 September 2001 and in Spain on 11 March 2004 have bolstered public-sector action aimed at stronger security measures that make use of new digital technologies in order to augment capacities for identity authentication and management; and second, that resulting privacy concerns, even if trumped by security, remain important political considerations in the two countries in shaping government action.

IDENTITY, INTEROPERABILITY, AND PRIVACY

With respect to public-sector action and democratic accountability, identity and privacy tradeoffs may be viewed through administrative and political lenses, both of which are intertwined with the emergence of electronic government, or e-government, during this past decade. E-government may be defined as "the continuous innovation in the delivery of services, citizen participation, and governance through the transformation of external and internal relationships by the use of information technology, especially the Internet."[1] Building on this definition, one can point to four significant dimensions of public-sector change in a digital era: service, security, transparency, and trust (Roy 2006). All of these dimensions are interrelated in some manner with the widening presence and rapidly expanding importance of a digital infrastructure encompassing information and communication technologies and online connectivity.

Across the four dimensions of e-government, perhaps no issue has received more attention than that of privacy – tied to ongoing concerns about the handling of personal information. At a basic level, many individuals continue to shun online shopping for fear that releasing confidential details, such as credit card information, into a virtual gateway could result in a host of potential unintended consequences arising from how such data is shared and used.[2]

At the same time, however, significant growth rates of both Internet use and online services would suggest that although some segments of the population may continue to shy away from online channels (or face barriers associated with the digital divide), clients and citizens in all sectors will be proportionally more likely to move in such directions over time.[3] Banking online offers some support for this view: in 2003 online banking transactions in Canada rose 30.7% to 192.1 million transactions (in comparison to 26.6 million in 1999), whereas telephone banking transactions fell by just under 5% to 87.7 million (the transaction volumes for both of these banking channels trail behind the volume at electronic banking machines, which nonetheless fell 6.2% in 2003 to 1.131 billion transactions).

Perhaps concerns about privacy and personal information weigh even more heavily on government efforts to deliver services online than do fears about malicious acts. This characterization reflects the interaction of the technical, organizational, and socio-political variables that shape debates about information management and security. Moreover, government services often differ qualitatively from those of the commercial sphere, with more obligatory relationships resulting in the collection of highly sensitive information across a wide range of entities and functions that collectively comprise "the public sector."

There may well be sound reasons, many of them security-related, for governments to take a more cautious and gradual approach in terms of privacy than their private-sector counterparts. The political risks of security breaches in the state settings are often perceived to be far more serious than similar risks in the private sector, a comparison most often attributed to the public sector's significantly greater holdings of personal and sensitive information (Joshi et al. 2002, Holden 2004). This relationship is complex and dependent to a significant degree on the level of trust accorded to the public sector by the citizenry. In jurisdictions where trust is high, technical solutions are more readily supported and the organizational changes required for more innovative and integrated forms of service are more feasible. The converse is true as well: lower levels of confidence and trust translate into more organizational resistance and technical cautiousness. Indeed, it is impossible to separate out service-delivery capacities of e-government given the broader institutional reforms that shape the setting of democratic governance within which such processes occur.[4]

Nonetheless, even within a standardized set of social and political conditions, all governments must address the perceptions and realities of privacy within the broader spectrum of information and identity management that is at the core of both better client-centric responsiveness externally and the corresponding need for new forms of coordination internally. Doing so would involve two interrelated components: first, putting in place an infrastructure of reliable interoperability; and second, ensuring mechanisms for accurate identity authentication (Lips et al. 2006).

Some observers worry that a willingness to relax privacy in the name of public safety ignores the wider implications of an information architecture that is based less on individualized human behaviour and more on patterns and profiles emerging from electronic data flows:

> A classic error is repeated endlessly in numerous contexts, and it reveals the depth of the misunderstanding that surrounds surveillance today. The claim is frequently made that if we have done nothing wrong, we have nothing to hide and thus nothing to fear ... The problem is that this is not how things work, especially in the context of surveillance as social sorting, as an aspect of complex assemblage of governance practises. Against the personal claims of individual innocence, surveillance practises are profoundly social, in the sense that persons are clustered into categories, whether as potential consumer

groups or potential lawbreakers. It is one's often unwitting membership of or association with certain groups that makes all the difference.
(Lyon 2004, 140)

Prior to 11 September 2001, such concerns were but a small and limited outgrowth of the widening interest in "customer relationship management" and in personal marketing techniques that often depend on
this type of individual clustering and response. More recently, such issues
have garnered increased interest and attention in light of the expanded
security imperative now pursued by governments, nowhere more so than
in the United States.

COMPARING THE UNITED STATES AND SPAIN

Since autumn 2001, the mindset of governments in most countries
– notably the United States – has been dramatically reframed. The
American fixation on homeland security denotes an important new face
of e-government in terms of resources and priorities.[5] The United States
is not alone: around the world, many governments have been quick to
establish new antiterrorism and homeland security measures that are
premised on new or expanded capacities for coordinated information
sharing, planning, and responding on a government-wide scale (Henrich
and Link 2003; Kim and Lee 2004).

A sophisticated and reliable digital infrastructure is a necessary pre-
cursor to such government-wide action – and as a result, interoperability
has become a guiding principle in such efforts. Moreover, in fostering a
systemic view of security within a jurisdiction such as a country, interoperability across sectors (notably, the private sector) also becomes an important element (Dutta and McCrohan 2002). Strategies for cyber-security
rely heavily on cooperation between the public and private sectors (Lane
and Roy 2006).[6]

A key issue in such an environment is an absence of sufficient openness
on the part of public authorities (Reid 2004). US government watchers
claim that during the first decade of the twenty-first century the culture
of secrecy has been significantly reinforced at the expense of transparency and public accountability.[7] Another, related dimension of such concern is that secrecy is becoming the norm in security matters – due in
part to covert activity but also to the extraordinary level of complexities
that permeate an increasingly ubiquitous and invisible infrastructure extending across the realms of both government and commercial activities:

Law enforcement and intelligence services don't need to design their own surveillance systems from scratch. They only have to reach out to the companies that already track us so well, while promising better service, security, efficiency, and perhaps most of all, convenience. It takes less and less effort each year to know what each of us is about ... More than ever before, the details of our lives are no longer our own. They belong to the companies that collect them and the government agencies that buy or demand them in the name of keeping us safe. (O'Harrow 2005, 300)[8]

The existence and reliability of such identifiers thus become critical enablers of the functioning of the system as a whole. With respect to individual privacy, one cause for concern is the efforts of the federal government to systemically interlink unique identifiers and virtual information flows. Priscilla Regan's detailed analysis of the provisions of the USA Patriot Act (2001) demonstrates the critical extensions of information gathering capacities on the part of law enforcement authorities, accompanied by a weakening of political and judicial oversight mechanisms that has led to what she regards as a total absence of accountability. More specifically, Regan formulates three fundamental implications from her analysis: "[F]irst, the capstone of the creation of a domestic surveillance system; second, the government's ill-conceived assemblage of unmanageable amounts of information; and third, the possibility of the creation of a national identification system in the United States" (Regan 2004, 490).

Indeed, the latter implication is supported empirically by three simultaneous initiatives led by US federal government authorities: (1) within the federal government, the creation of new smart cards envisioned for all federal employees, the first of which were administered in October 2006; (2) federal legislation requiring states to meet national specifications for technologically bolstered and interoperable driver's licences; and (3) the proposed development of a national ID card for Americans travelling abroad as a low-cost alternative to a passport (and somewhat related new ID requirements for foreigners entering the country, with the US leading international efforts to develop biometrically enabled, electronic passports recognizable across jurisdictions).

Such developments have clearly recast the internal, administrative architecture of digital networks, moving them away from a pre-9/11 emphasis on new service models and toward a security fixation. Driven by the views of the US public, key questions are apparent in terms of

transparency and trust. Before turning to an analysis of US survey results, I will first review the main contours of Spain's political environment in terms of e-government and the relative balance between service
and security.

The Spanish Case

In terms of both aspirations for and the adoption of e-government over
the past decade, Spain occupies something of a middle ground between
those countries typically thought of as technological leaders and developing nations. Clearly more wealthy and democratic than the latter
group, and firmly implanted as a core member of the European Union,
Spain nonetheless lags behind many of its northern European cousins
in Internet accessibility and usage. In 2005, 21% of Spanish households
(most of them concentrated in Spain's largest cities) possessed a broad-
band Internet connection, while just 3% of Spanish enterprises received
orders online for their products or services (just 8% of Spanish individuals
reported an online purchase) (European Communities 2005).

For such reasons, the Spanish national government (quasi-federal, with
seventeen autonomous regions, each with its own parliament and control
over its own system of local governments) has viewed e-government as
prompting two interrelated reform objectives: first, to improve the performance of the public sector in terms of new service delivery channels presented by the Internet and new information technologies (while
refurbishing the internal administration to do so); and second, to foster stronger socio-economic and political development throughout the
country as a whole by encouraging the usage of digital infrastructure.

Within this context, the emergence of smart cards as a basis for electronic and more integrated services is a cornerstone of efforts to promote both digital government and a digital society more broadly. The
new electronic ID card (e-ID) envisions not only faster and more accurate (and paperless) ID authentication processes but also the usage
of electronic signatures and contracts as a basis of virtual engagements
between citizens and companies, on the one hand, and between citizens
and public-sector authorities, on the other.

Following initial and ongoing pilot initiatives in various Spanish communities, the current objective is to enable countrywide usage of these
new cards by the end of 2009 – even though a more gradual and flexible
timetable is envisioned for issuing the cards to all citizens in light of the
aforementioned figures on varying Internet access and usage across the

country. Although these new cards will be embedded with a microchip to facilitate secure online transactions and real-time access to photographs and digitalized handwritten signatures, there are no immediate plans for the incorporation of biometric devices (despite ongoing discussions at the European level).

It bears noting that despite the service improvement connotation of such cards, the lead public-sector authority in development and implementation has been the national police, acting within the mandate of the Ministry of Internal Affairs. No stranger to domestic terrorist activities (primarily rooted in the Basque region), Spain was itself jarred by international terrorism on 11 March 2004 when subway bombings in Madrid killed 191 people and wounded nearly 2,000 more. Some observers contend that the political fallout from the event greatly shaped the outcome of the next day's national election – bringing a new government to power.[9] Nonetheless, even though the new government would quickly take distance from the United States (announcing a military withdrawal from Iraq), security and terrorism remain key priorities of Spain's federal government and may not differ greatly from efforts of the US federal government with respect to ID mechanisms and the balancing of security and privacy.

Similarities and Differences

Before I compare Spain and the United States in terms of public attitudes, it is worth underscoring this institutional contrast between the United States and the European Union (as well as most EU member-states and most parliamentary jurisdictions, including Canada). In the United States the absence of an independent privacy authority (criticized by some) is offset in some manner by Congressional oversight – whereas in parliamentary jurisdictions the absence of sufficient political oversight (as with other domains, such as financial management and spending) has been compensated for through the appointment of new and specific bodies. By contrast, the European model is arguably a more complex hybrid (for more discussion of private-sector privacy laws, see Arthur Cockfield's chapter in this volume).

Prior to 9/11 it was common to assert that privacy differed greatly across Europe and the United States in terms of both public sentiment and legal regimes. This somewhat generalist claim (which, despite shifts discussed below, remains relevant today) held that in terms of the possession and management of personal information, European distrust was directed primarily at the private sector, whereas in the United States most citizens were overtly suspicious of government. Accordingly, stricter European privacy laws covering corporate behaviour have been a particular point of distinction and often contention between the two continents (Prins 2001, Archick 2006).

Such overtones seem to be reflected in the results from the GPD survey, which show that Spaniards are more distrusting of the private sector on most matters than are North Americans (Canadian and US results are quite similar). It is notable, for instance, that of the three countries, Spain is the only one where more than one-half of the population reject the notion of their government sharing personal information with the private sector. Similarly, just over 70% of Spanish respondents support (with over 40% in strong agreement) the notion of a government-sponsored national ID card, while fewer than one-half of US citizens concur. A similar result is apparent in the implicit Spanish support for the creation of a national database to underpin ID cards, expressed as a high degree of confidence in "having a say" in how such information is handled: nearly 80% of Spaniards feel they would have at least some say, with one-half of this portion confident that they would have "complete say" (by contrast, less than 20% of US and Canadian citizens feel they would have "complete say," with just over one-half of respondents in both countries stating that they would have at least "some say").

This general predisposition toward a greater level of confidence in such an undertaking helps to explain why identity management and interoperable mechanisms as a basis of more integrated service delivery have been somewhat less politically sensitive in many European jurisdictions. The added layer of terrorism and security merely reinforced this level of comfort with more assertive state strategies. Such is the case for Spain – which is seemingly inclined, on the one hand, to deploy new technologies, notably a smart card, in order to improve service and transcend traditional bureaucratic processes while, on the other hand, embracing the need for stricter security measures in the aftermath of Spain's own internationally rooted terrorist attacks in 2004.

The United States, by contrast, has embarked upon a path of identity management and interoperability that would have been unthinkable prior to 2001, even with the advent of e-government and its service emphasis. Indeed, the United States would appear to be undergoing two simultaneous shifts in terms of the public mood pertaining to privacy and information flows across the public and private sectors: first, most dramatically, in the public's general support for federal government initiatives tied to security; and second, more subtly, in the public's widening unease about company breaches and in the growing calls for stricter legislative and regulatory enforcement of misconduct (Holmes 2005).

In terms of governmental action, the GPD survey results suggest, however, that the US president does not garner unqualified support for security initiatives such as a national ID card – with nearly one-third of Americans strongly disagreeing (and another 15% also disagreeing). Aside from Congressional oversight and alternative proposals in areas such as border controls and a new ID card for international travel, US states can also act as powerful correctives, as can critical media and an underlying current of suspicion toward government, which has long been a defining characteristic of the US political culture.

Partly derived from the preceding discussion, a case can be made that such a viewpoint may be a somewhat extreme characterization of both continents. In the United States, for example, it is not clear that the "vast" majority are concerned about industry. Moreover, it is the efforts of European governments and European parliamentarians that have prodded the European Union to challenge the United States on several fronts – including secret CIA prisons and the transfer of air passenger information between European and US authorities. Finally, on the matter of radio frequency identification (RFID) usage, the European Union has shown itself to be consultative and prepared to draft new laws to reassure public opinion that seems uneasy with the potential usages of this new technological instrument (although in line with the European market-state dichotomy of trust and suspicion, the unease would seem directed more at industry than at governments).[10]

As an EU member-state (predisposed toward high degrees of government intervention) strongly influenced by terrorism for both domestic and international reasons, and with a parliamentary model not known for its formal checks and balances politically, Spain would seem to run the risk of its citizens being overly deferential to the trustworthiness of their government in terms of both political motives and administrative competencies. Such a characterization is partially tempered by Spain's increasingly entrenched democratic culture and by the added layer of (at times questioned) European oversight (itself influenced by northern European countries that are strong proponents of open and transparent government),[11] but it is one that should be safeguarded both for its potential consequences in that country and for its relevance to the Canadian case.

Where Spain and the United States would seem to converge, by contrast, is in the growing activism and visibility of central (i.e., federal) governments in leading the charge on pursuing the nexus between e-government, service, and security (a convergence that is at the heart of privacy matters). Although the international survey on privacy did not examine intergovernmental dynamics, a related investigation of the nexus between e-government and federalism confirmed the centralizing tendencies of national efforts, calling into question the relevance and sustainability of traditional models of political federalism (Gasco and Roy 2006). This theme, enjoining the Canadian case examined below, is quite relevant indirectly for matters of privacy and security insofar as centralization shapes patterns of administrative organization and democratic engagement, which are central determinants in government priorities, actions, and outcomes.

CANADIAN COMPLACENCY

Canadian governance and politics have often been characterized as reflecting a middle ground between the traditions of a larger and more activist state found in much of Europe, on the one hand, and the market-leaning, antimonopolistic culture, both economically and politically, found in the United States, on the other. The most obvious example of this middle ground is the political structures found in Canada, which consist of a hybrid between Westminster, parliamentary democracy and English and French historical influences and which incorporate more contemporary constitutional additions such as the Charter of Rights, viewed as more American in its emphasis on individuality protections and judicial intervention and oversight.

On matters of privacy and flows of personal information across the private and public sectors, an argument can be made that this middle ground seems to be serving Canadians reasonably well. As with other parliamentary jurisdictions, privacy commissioners in this country (federally and provincially) have been influential stakeholders in challenging governments. A case in point is the controversy that erupted in British Columbia when the privacy commissioner found that outsourcing arrangements involving American firms and BC government organizations (especially those in the realm of healthcare) may have been placing at risk the personal information of BC citizens due to provisions of the Patriot Act (Roy 2005a).

In this case, it was the privacy commissioner who became the catalyst for media attention and legal inquiry, resulting in corrective government action that has largely quelled the controversy. Similarly, on a variety of other matters that have engulfed the US federal administration in controversy (including allegedly illegal wiretapping as well as information sharing between telecommunications companies and governments), the Canadian polity has been relatively peaceful and silent. Finally, recent efforts by the Royal Canadian Mounted Police (RCMP) in the spring of 2006 to foil what appeared to be advanced planning and preparation by a terrorist ring based in Toronto reassures Canadians that the post-9/11 realities require strong domestic vigilance (with the overriding importance of security trumping privacy concerns in the eyes of many).

Conversely, the case can be made that there is a level of complacency in Canada that resembles that of Europe – particularly with respect to government. Such complacency has been challenged by echoes of US debates over telecommunications companies transferring customer records to federal authorities, a practice that is now ongoing in both countries (Geist 2005). Yet the prospect of new federal legislation that will greatly augment government wiretapping and surveillance capacities (while also placing new requirements on companies to take part in such processes by providing the relevant information to do so) has met with little public outcry.

Any such complacency may well have been jarred by those findings of the Arar Commission (2006) that – quite in addition to documenting the injustice inflicted upon one Canadian citizen – exposed mismanagement and a worrying absence of oversight and accountability both within and over Canada's federal police service, which also leads domestic antiterrorism efforts. Yet, here again, little public outcry ensued.

This complacency would seem to be supported by findings from the GPD survey, with Canadians on par with Americans and Spaniards in feeling that they have some, a lot, or complete say in what happens to their personal information. Moreover, Canadians are the most optimistic in feeling that their domestic laws are working well, with over 60% feeling the laws on government information holdings are somewhat (50.7%) or very (12.9%) effective and just over 50% feeling the laws on private industry are effective. Similarly harmonized results are evident in terms of the willingness of Canadians to allow governments to share their personal information (either unconditionally, when wrongdoing is suspected, or with public consent, presumably for service convenience): among the three countries, Canada has the lowest rate of individuals who flatly prefer that no such sharing occur (with just 15.8% reporting this option).

Canada's middle-ground perspective vis-à-vis Europe and the United States seems to find additional resonance with respect to proposals for a national ID card – a de facto reality in Spain that may explain why over 40% of Spaniards strongly agree with this notion. By contrast, over one-third of Americans strongly disagree. Canadians are in the middle of both camps, with 22% in strong agreement with the cards and 23% in strong disagreement. Opinion is similarly divided on the workability and efficacy of a national database, with only the Spaniards showing a majority confident that such a system is likely to be successful.

CONCLUSIONS

A plausible case can be made from the preceding analysis that in terms of the erosion of privacy and the overall efficacy of information management within a jurisdiction as a whole, Canadians more than Europeans should be worried about complacency (despite the contradictory logic in such a claim since a public is unlikely to be worried about matters on which it is complacent).

The US political system and its inherent checks and balances are important variables in shaping governmental action – especially at the federal level. Although Spain's parliamentary model features a more concentrated set of authority structures, there is a strong dosage of European realism aimed at challenging American perspectives and regulating information flows and privacy both pan-regionally and domestically (with an important degree of cross-fertilization at both levels). Still, it should also be noted here from the discussion in this chapter that there is room for concern in terms of Spanish complacency – in light of inherently supportive European tendencies toward government action generally and a growing degree of convergence between European and American measures (as well as intercontinental collaboration).[12]

What is difficult to explain is why echoes of US-based controversies in Canada as well as domestic episodes such as the Arar affair have failed to generate more public awareness and political scrutiny and dialogue. Although privacy commissioners deserve credit for drawing attention to key issues and mobilizing awareness, their inherently adversarial role as a watchdog of government limits their voice as a stakeholder in proactively formulating policy and administrative change. What is most disconcerting about security and privacy matters at present is the complete absence of political oversight on the part of elected officials. Since 9/11 and the subsequent creation of the federal Department of Public Safety and Security (fashioned after the American Department of Homeland Security), proposals to create a new parliamentary committee to oversee the federal government's security apparatus have continuously languished. The second and final report by Justice Dennis O'Connor, the head of the Arar Commission (2006), addressed the question of public-political oversight of the RCMP, although it remains to be seen the degree to which any such recommendations will yield reform (Roy 2007).

One conclusion resulting from the analysis and argumentation of this chapter is that the current Canadian complacency is contributing to a form of political paralysis with respect to the refurbishment (and especially the technological refurbishment) of the federal government's security and service apparatuses – which are interwoven with matters of information management and privacy. Although the obvious exception to this claim is the breakneck speed at which antiterrorism legislation was formed and adopted in the days and weeks following 9/11, since that time there has been little proactive effort on the part of successive federal governments to foster public dialogue. The aforementioned absence of action with respect to a national ID mechanism is a case in point. So too are compounding difficulties plaguing the federal government's efforts to deliver services online, with problems pertaining to online identity management being a central issue.

This conclusion is intimately tied to the transparency and trust variables of the e-government equation – and to their consequences for identity and privacy. On the one hand, the implied notion of deferential trust toward government that characterizes much of Europe as well as Canada is increasingly challenged both by current events (with identity theft, privacy breaches, and cyber-insecurities growing in scope and regularity) and by a broader societal shift in terms of information sharing, openness, and education that is personified by the Internet itself. On the other hand, however, across both Europe and North America, national governments since 9/11 have done much to reinforce and increase the scope of secrecy both explicitly (in terms of security matters) and implicitly in terms of online, customer-centric processes that downplay the citizenship aspects of governance in favour of real-time service simplicity, efficiency, and interoperability.

This widening imposition of a syndrome of executive branch secrecy is perhaps the greatest threat to democratic accountability generally and personal privacy specifically. The risk lies in technocracy – driven by the virtualization of service and security apparatuses with a lessening of traditional political oversight and a failure to create new mechanisms of public engagement and review. Such conditions may support complacency in the short term, but at some point systemic breaches (of the sort that entrapped Maher Arar), coupled with compounding questions about both competency and trustworthiness, will take their toll. At such time, privacy and identity will be catalysts for a much needed and more holistic rethinking of the organizational and institutional architectures that are required for this new century.

A derivative matter (admittedly one not directly supported by the survey evidence invoked in this chapter but nonetheless related) is the potential for an erosion of federalism in federalist jurisdictions (such as the three examined here) in favour of larger, more administratively and technologically centralized administrations at the national level. The growing assertiveness of federal-national governments on matters of service and security threatens to erode the proximity-based arguments in favour of more localized and decentralized forums for public engagement (Gibbons 2004, Roy 2006). Although any precise findings about the Spanish case are beyond the scope of this chapter, it seems clear that federal government actions in the United States are further augmenting the visibility, spending, and political relevance of Washington, DC (presumably at the expense of state legislatures and local governments). Such is one ironic aspect of the unfolding legacy of President George W. Bush, who came to power in 2000 (importantly prior to 9/11) on a Republican-inspired agenda of less government generally and less federal government (reduced in scope and more respectful of state jurisdiction) specifically.

In Canada the US-inspired expansion of the secure state federally (which has built upon federal government efforts to lead in the realm of online service delivery) and the Conservative Party's hopes for a more devolved and less acrimonious form of federalism (especially in Quebec) do not make for an easy mix. Yet it must be underlined that the risks of technocracy are greatest at the national (and transnational) level, whereas the most responsive and innovative forms of governance tend to be nurtured through proximity and participation (Evans 2002, Woodward 2003, Roy 2006). This disconnect is perhaps the greatest challenge to progressive and open governance renewal in a digital age.

NOTES

1 Among others, this definition was deployed by the Government of Mexico in recent years, although its precise origins are unknown. I adopted it as the basis

for an article that develops the framework of the four dimensions discussed in this section (Roy 2005b).

2 Although technical risks are real, perceptions also matter, as many proponents of online channels have observed that security risks are also present in many daily credit card transactions, such as when giving a credit card to a server in a restaurant or when ordering a purchase by telephone. This mix of technological capacities and social adaptation/acceptance forms the context within which multichannel service strategies must exist for different groups of customers and citizens.

3 Although marginal, as discussed in the previous section, the threats to individuals and individual organizations can nonetheless prove to be real and consequential.

4 Of relevance to security-related matters is the bolstered public support for stronger governmental action and the relatively higher levels of trust accorded by the citizenry to law enforcement authorities versus other governmental actors. For instance, a 2003 Statistics Canada survey of 25,000 individuals revealed that 82.1% had confidence (either "a great deal" or "quite a lot") in the police, in comparison to other groups such as banks (68.1%), major corporations (45.8%), and Parliament (42.8%); see *Globe and Mail*, 7 July 2004.

5 The US federal government had adopted an e-government agenda based largely on improved service delivery prior to September 2001. However, service transformation projects managed by the Office of Management and Budget (OMB) have had trouble securing even modest funding levels for pilot initiatives over the past several years, whereas the president's proposed 2006 budget calls for $41.1 billion for the Department of Homeland Security, within which the usage and deployment of information and communication technologies (ICT) feature prominently. For budgetary details, see http://www.dhs.gov/xabout/budget/editorial_0807.shtm (accessed 3 December 2009).

6 Prior to 9/11 the federal government focus on cyber-security was indirect and fragmented across various e-government and e-commerce initiatives. In February 2003 the US president tabled the country's first ever "national strategy to secure cyberspace," elevating the issue within the executive branch in both the White House and the Department of Homeland Security.

7 In 1999, for example, 126,809,769 pages of government information were declassified. By 2004 this number had dropped to 28,413,690. See "Secrecy Report Card – An Update," April 2005, http://www.openthegovernment. org/otg/SRC2005.pdf (accessed 3 December 2009).

8 In March 2005 Canada's *Globe and Mail* newspaper reported that at a technology convention in Seattle, security experts had held a contest inviting hackers to manipulate the search engines Google and Yahoo in order to find confidential information on citizens and organizations. They did just that: using Google for about one hour, contestants gathered information on nearly 25 million people (of potential use for fraudulent activities). In its corporate response, reported by the *Globe and Mail*, Google said that its service is "a reflection of the Web. Although we aggregate and organize information published on the Web, we do not control the information itself nor do we control access to it." Yahoo responded in a similar manner: "we continually optimize our Web search to provide users with a comprehensive and relevant experience by indexing content that is part of the public domain." Indeed, there is no evidence suggesting that either company is somehow directly at fault, but the nature of the incident as well as the corporate responses will, for many, reinforce the suspicions of Robert O'Harrow (2005) and others.

9 Campaigning for re-election (with a new leader), the Conservatives initially blamed Basque separatists for the Madrid subway bombings. When it became evident that al-Qaeda had carried out the attacks, this proved a huge problem for the government (and a boost for the opposition, which had been behind in polls but would subsequently win the election) in light of Spain's support for the US-led Iraq War.

10 "Only 15% of the 2,190 organizations and individuals who contributed to a survey the EU ran during the consultation exercise thought that industry would do a good job of (self-) regulating how firms used RFID tags"; see BBC Online News, 27 October 2006.

11 Finland's turn at the rotating presidency of the European Union in 2006 featured pledges to instil greater openness in European institutions, transparency being an engrained aspect of the Scandinavian political culture.

12 In October 2006 US and EU authorities signed a new deal for the sharing of airline passenger information, as the previous one had been struck down by European courts. Since 9/11 more generally, "the EU has made improving law enforcement cooperation with the US a top priority" (Archick 2006, 2).

Consumers and Workers

INTRODUCTION

Yolande E. Chan

Organizations increasingly collect, store, and share personal information in the global marketplace and have to manage the privacy and security of their clients and workers. The first two chapters in this section explore consumer willingness to disclose personal information. Consumer purchasing behaviours are examined in North America and Europe. Jason Pridmore focuses on consumers in Canada and the United States, while Ola Svenonius focuses on consumer behaviours in Hungary, France, and Spain. Pridmore studies loyalty programs, and Svenonius examines electronic commerce. Finally, in the third chapter in this section, Avner Levin uses conceptual legal perspectives to attempt to uncover whether there is a global approach to workplace privacy. To answer this question, he examines how employers, employees, legislators, and courts have dealt with issues of workplace privacy.

The loyalty programs discussed by Pridmore permit companies to track consumer buying behaviours and "mine" consumer data. In return, customers receive discounts, free items, and other loyalty benefits. This exchange results in consumer data becoming a commodity that the corporation can use to increase profitability while also improving the products and services offered to customer segments. Detailed customer profiles are used to improve marketing effectiveness (e.g., via targeting segments of the market that are likely to purchase the organization's products and services) or as sources of direct income (e.g., when customer information is sold to other organizations). What is not discussed

often in the corporate literature on loyalty programs is that nontar-
geted customers are less likely to receive promotions and other buying
incentives. In effect, some customers are privileged, whereas others are
disadvantaged.

Pridmore uses the Globalization of Personal Data (GDP) survey data
to examine consumers' knowledge of loyalty profiling, their awareness
of possible consumer responses to company attempts to create customer
profiles, and their concerns. In the GDP survey, two-fifths of Americans
and two-thirds of Canadians surveyed say they carry at least one loyalty
card. Unexpectedly, participation in loyalty programs do not correlate
with consumers' acceptance of customer profiling. Consumers appear to
be largely indifferent to this usage of their data.

Data from focus groups completed prior to the survey suggested a
wide range of consumer knowledge on profiling – from buyers who regarded loyalty programs simply as purchasing incentives to those who
viewed these programs as mechanisms to track and exploit customers.
Pridmore examines loyalty ambivalence in terms of customer desire
for privacy *despite* customer desire for purchasing conveniences and
discounts. Overall, Pridmore demonstrates that the GDP survey reveals
a complex relationship between participation in loyalty programs and
willingness to provide consumer data.

In his study, Svenonius focuses on consumer data made available
through Internet purchasing, as contrasted with data obtained as a result of the use of loyalty cards. When consumers purchase goods over
the Internet, they must provide companies with more information than
when they participate in conventional over-the-counter or cash-based
trade. Internet retailers therefore attempt to establish credible trust
relationships with potential customers. Svenonius argues insightfully
that Internet retailers stand to gain by improving consumer protection
and consumer rights regimes in traditional "brick and mortar" retail
settings. He argues that Internet consumer behaviours are influenced
by consumers' past experiences in other conventional settings. Where
institutional settings and regulations have promoted strong consumer
protection positions, consumers are more likely to feel empowered
and to be relaxed about Internet purchases. Svenonius introduces the
concept of trust, arguing that this trust can be based on earlier Internet
experiences and other information disclosure experiences.

Svenonius explores the relationship between political cultures and
attitudes to data privacy in Europe. France, Hungary, and Spain have
very different political histories and were selected for study. French

consumers are known for their strong civic engagement and political activism. By comparison, Hungary is a young capitalist economy that has only recently been restructured. It is reputed that Hungarian companies are relatively unconcerned about consumer protection and that Hungarian consumers have relatively low levels of knowledge about consumer legislation. Spanish consumers are very different. Spain endured a fascist dictatorship that ended in 1975. So Spanish customers are among the most skeptical in Europe regarding consumer rights regimes.

The countries also differ in terms of their exposure to e-commerce. The citizens in France, Hungary, and Spain have Internet penetrations of approximately 43%, 30%, and 39% respectively. Using data from the GDP survey, Svenonius explores consumers' sense of control over personal information and their trust in companies that provide products and services via the Internet. He demonstrates that, in the three countries studied, Spanish consumers are most worried about providing personal data on websites. Hungarian respondents are least worried, but they are also less knowledgeable about Internet issues in general. French consumers are positioned in the middle of the three populations. Fifty per cent were worried about providing personal data, whereas 40% are not.

As Svenonius predicted, purchasing disinhibition effects are seen in the GDP data. Positive prior experiences with Internet trade and conventional trade seemed to encourage Internet buying. In two of the three countries, where Internet penetration and the standard of living were both high, the GDP survey data upheld Svenonius's proposed model well. However, the behaviours of Hungarian respondents are not fully explained. Svenonius concludes that the model may be better suited for western European countries and that data protection regimes may need to be taken into account when predicting consumer behaviours. He encourages Internet sellers to work to promote effective privacy and protection for consumers. In the long run, their sales and profits are likely to increase if customers feel secure. Perhaps consumer protection can do more for Internet-based companies' sales than can loyalty programs.

In the final chapter, Avner Levin looks at two definitions of privacy: (1) the property approach, which emphasizes employers owning the workplace and its resources and thus maintaining control over how these spaces are used; and (2) the rights approach, which puts primacy on a minimum standard of dignity and on ensuring every human being's right to a private life, including while at work. Levin draws on comparative qualitative examples of workplace privacy from case law, statutes, and labour arbitration decisions, as well as on quantitative work from the GDP survey results in eight countries, to determine whether and to what extent the concept of dignity as a social value is evident in workplace privacy legislation. Global perspectives reveal significant connections between the GDP survey results and qualitative information within each country.

Levin uses the social value of dignity as the conceptual basis for his analysis of workplace privacy, which differs cross-culturally. For example, the US approach to protecting privacy tends to be oriented toward liberty, whereas in the European Union protection focuses on dignity as more important. Using dignity rather than privacy as a concept to protect workplace privacy enforces the protection of social norms as a fundamental human right over government intrusions. These differences become apparent in the case law and legislative examples: dignity is well entrenched in EU legislation but is absent from US statutes, which protect only the reasonable expectation of privacy; Canada tends to fall somewhere between the US and EU approaches, whereas China does not have any information protection legislation. The cross-cultural differences are further reinforced by the GDP survey data: EU respondents feel a stronger connection to the rights approach to privacy; US respondents align with the property approach; Canadian respondents support both approaches; and respondents from China support the rights approach. Despite the fact that the concept of dignity as a foundation for workplace privacy has different meanings in different jurisdictions, it could be used as a more encompassing cross-cultural legal approach to privacy within the workplace in order to withstand changes in technology.

Loyalty Ambivalence in the United States and Canada: The GPD Survey, the Focus Groups, and the Context of Those Wonderfully Intrusive Loyalty Cards

JASON PRIDMORE

INTRODUCTION

Globally, although most notably in Canada, Australia, and many European and Southeast Asian countries, an increasing number of retailers maintain loyalty programs with customer-specific identifiers. These identifiers may come in the form of key-ring tags or radio frequency identification (RFID) devices, among others, but are most commonly barcode or magstripe cards designed to keep tabs on a consumer's buying behaviour. Cards range from those used in proprietary programs to coalition/multistore cards to co-branded credit cards and more. These often fill some wallets to overflowing as consumers seek the benefits of membership and loyal shopping practices. Alternatively, some reject these cards as a nuisance or gimmick or as a form of privacy infringement. Yet in some form or another, as best as can be discerned from the projections of corporate literature on the subject, customer-specific loyalty programs are here to stay. John Deighton, a professor of business at Harvard's Business School, writes that these "identity programs" are indicative of a future of "pervasive portable digital identities" in which "some version of our reputation travels with us wherever we go, whether we like it or not" (Deighton 2005, 249). This type of prospect should and could be something that provokes sincere concerns about privacy and surveillance among many in society. However, as the Globalization of Personal Data (GPD) survey indicates, there is not a clear relationship between participation in these programs and concerns about the corporate tracking of data produced in the use of loyalty cards.

A number of factors contribute to this ambiguous relationship, and the GPD survey responses, specifically in the United States and Canada, actually indicate an ambivalence already present both in similar loyalty research and in the English-speaking focus groups that were part of the GPD survey's development. This chapter sets out to make clear the connections between membership in programs in the United States and Canada and surveillance and privacy concerns, contextualizing both against a backdrop of differentially savvy consumers and relatively sophisticated marketing practices. Rather than seeing consumers as simply naive about their own consumptive practices being surveilled by loyalty programs, this survey reiterates that there remains a very complex and diverse relationship with loyality cards, which are seen as simultaneously beneficial and intrusive.

THE IMPORTANCE AND PREVALENCE OF LOYALTY CARDS

The global proliferation of loyalty programs has occurred largely in the past twenty years. In its essence, loyalty marketing is about rewarding those customers who frequently make purchases at a particular establishment. Historically, myriad methods have been employed to bestow particular benefits upon frequent shoppers. These include discount punch or stamp cards that require customers to obtain a prerequisite number of punches or stamps through previous purchases in order to receive a free item or a purchase discount. Other examples, such as in the Canadian context, include the distribution of proprietary forms of "money" that can be used for future purchases, as exemplified by the Canadian Tire Corporation's use of Canadian Tire "money." The currency is awarded in small increments based on dollars spent for each purchase and can be applied directly against the cost of any purchase. Although both proprietary currencies and discount cards remain relatively pervasive, they are increasingly less attractive as corporate marketing tools because they do not provide specific details about their customers. In the "personal information economy," gathering customer-specific information using unique identifiers has gained an unparalleled primacy and has increasingly become the point of engaging in loyalty marketing (Perri 6 2005).

Several factors have contributed to corporations' desire for and ability to gather and use customer information for marketing purposes. First, the cost of information and communication technologies (ICTs) has dramatically decreased. Whereas consumer information may have been seen as requiring too much of a company's resources that may have been better spent on internal ICT infrastructure, the minimal cost of consumer data gathering is now seen as providing a potentially large return on investment. Likewise, the decreasing costs of data storage and retrieval, the use of new forms of data analytics such as data mining and knowledge data discovery (KDD), and the application of these data within the predominant business strategy of customer relationship management (CRM) have greatly expanded the desire for personal information about consumers (CIPPIC 2006). This desire likewise comes in tandem with an increased availability of consumer data, provided by numerous third-party corporations that sell this information as a commodity and by public distributors of relevant population data – specifically government statistics bureaucracies, such as the US Census Bureau, Statistics Canada, and the UK Home Office, among others (Burrows and Gane 2006; CIPPIC 2006). Loyalty programs have become one means by which corporations are able to tie transactional data directly to each customer. These programs glean relatively specific sets of lifestyle data in the application process, attach these to specific patterns of historical consumption, and often add externally obtained third-party data in order to form a total, or "360 degree," view of consumers (Danna and Gandy 2002).

Within Canada and the United States, the use of loyalty cards is relatively pervasive. According to the GPD survey, 40.6% of people in the United States (approximately 88 million adults) and 66.2% of people in Canada (approximately 18 million adults) carry at least one loyalty card (see figure 15.1). These percentages are lower for both countries than the figures indicated by other surveys, although some of these surveys do not purport to canvas for demographic representation.[1] In the United States a number of factors contribute to a lower level of loyalty program memberships as compared to Canada, including distinctive market regions, no viable nationwide coalition programs, and the widespread use of credit cards that maintain their own loyalty reward systems. In Canada there is a much higher penetration of loyalty cards for certain companies. The largest coalition program, Air Miles, boasts 69% of Canadian households as members. The loyalty program of the largest nationwide pharmacy chain, Shoppers Optimum, claims to have 50% of Canadian women as members. Although the other major coalition program, Aeroplan, has only 29% of Canadians as members, it claims to have 92% of Canadian business travellers.

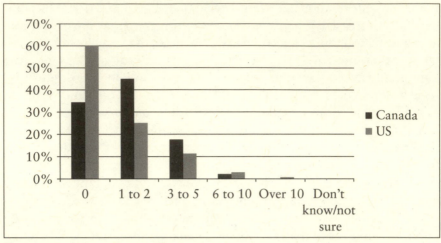

Figure 15.1
GDP question 27: Number of programs from which survey respondents collect rewards or points

A large number of consumers tend to be in a number of these programs, which range from frequent flyer programs and supermarket discount cards to retail points cards. Like the Canadian examples of Air Miles and Aeroplan, there are also coalition (multiple partner) cards. Both coalition and proprietary cards may themselves be co-branded with credit cards, such as Visa or American Express, through particular financial institutions. Likewise, increasing numbers of financial institutions offer rewards programs in conjunction with the use of their own type of credit card (specifically a Visa or Mastercard connected with a reward program like CIBC's Aventura in Canada or CitiBank's Citi Rewards program in the United States). Competition between these programs, from frequent flyer and shopper cards to credit card rewards programs, is relatively fierce given the value that such programs represent to consumers. The term "loyalty" has often been seen as a misnomer because many consumers are members of several of these programs. However, large investments have been made to ensure that members are in fact at least somewhat loyal to the companies in whose loyalty programs they are enrolled and that these programs are profitable. For the most part, this profitability is accomplished by using the consumer information gathered in the programs to create relatively detailed profiles of each consumer that can be sold (in some cases) or used to market goods or services to specific categories of consumers. These consumers seem largely unaware or indifferent to the data analysis and processing that stem from their use of loyalty cards, and this ambivalence and/or apathy is something evident in the GPD survey responses. These responses are best contextualized against the backdrop both of other surveys that focus on consumer profiling and of the focus groups that were convened prior to the survey data being collected.

CONTEXTUALIZING CONSUMER PROFILING AMBIVALENCE

In the GPD survey, immediately following question 27, on rewards pro-grams,[2] is a question that is not specifically about loyalty. Question 28 reads, "Many businesses create profiles about their customers that include information about purchasing habits, personal characteristics and credit history. How acceptable to you would it be for a business to use information from your customer profile to inform you of prod-ucts or services that they think would be of interest to you?" Although this question does not specifically mention rewards programs, the order of the questions seems likely to have forced a connection between the two. However, a statistical analysis of responses specifying membership (or not) in these programs indicates no clear affinity with the responses given in regards to customer profiling in any of the countries surveyed, including the United States and Canada. Members of loyalty programs responded in mixed ways concerning the acceptability of consumer pro-filing, as did those who were not members. In the GPD survey results, participation in customer-specific loyalty programs did not, as might have been expected, correlate with an acceptance of profiling, nor did nonmembership indicate that profiling was seen as less than acceptable. What can be inferred from these data is only that people either don't know or don't care about the connections between the two. What is clear is that the responses to the question on profiling indicate ambiva-lence toward this practice, something that is even more Canada. On the acceptability of profiling, respondents are evenly split between those who see it is acceptable (45% in both Canada and the US) and those who see it as unacceptable (45% in Canada and 42% in the US). The remaining respondents (10% to 13%) were perhaps ambivalent them-selves, indicating that they either did not know or were unsure about the acceptability of profiling (see figure 15.2).

Although the GPD survey suggests ambivalence on the part of re-spondents regarding the acceptability of profiling, a question remains as to whether people are fully aware of or concerned about consumer

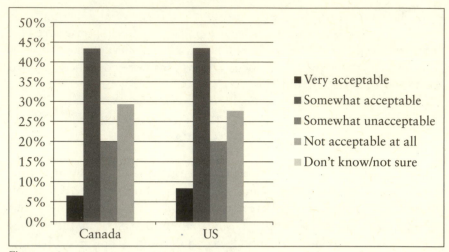

Figure 15.2
GPD question 28: Acceptability of consumer profiling

profiling. Are they simply resigned to this inevitable practice? Are they even aware that businesses create profiles through loyalty programs? Are they concerned about this or are they just apathetic? Several further questions can be asked to contextualize the ambivalence or potential apathy found in the responses to the GPD survey on these questions:

- What can we gather from other consumer-oriented questions in the survey?
- What is the relationship between this survey's responses and the outcomes of similar surveys?
- What can be understood from other sets of literature about these GPD data?
- What information can be drawn from the analysis of GPD focus group data?

These questions are focused on the degree to which consumers are knowledgeable about profiling practices and on how concerned they are about these practices.

CONSUMERS' KNOWLEDGE OF LOYALTY PROFILING

Are consumers aware that loyalty programs provide an important means for consumer profiling? In many cases, the answer is "no." Loyalty programs, although their very name suggests an incentive for customer retention, have increasingly become central means for collecting personal information for use in relationship marketing. Timothy Graeff and Susan Harmon (2002) indicate that in an open-ended survey of 480 US participants about the collection and use of personal data, 49.8% of consumers believed loyalty cards to be primarily about loyalty and competitiveness, with another 15.5% suggesting they have to do with individualized promotions and price discounts. Only 16.5% mentioned or associated it with database marketing and the collection and use of data on customer buying habits. This limited knowledge was also born out in the focus groups convened prior to the GPD survey,[3] as is clear in these discussions led by a moderator in different Canadian and US focus groups:

> MODERATOR: Well, why do they exist?
> STEVE: Because there is no company ... they exist, they're just waiting on market share, that's what it's all about, they want to see how much of a market share can they get out of you.
>
> MODERATOR: What are the purposes of these programs?
> TAMAYA: To make you spend money.
> MODERATOR: Make you spend money.
> KEITH: To make you spend money wisely.
> TAMAYA: Wisely?
> LISA: To make you loyal to the company.

As is apparent, these participants are in line with the majority of US respondents in Graeff and Harmon's survey. But likewise, there are also participants who know that these programs entail more than just the loyalty aspect, although they are often not sure how much information these companies may know:

> MODERATOR: Well, what type of personal information do these programs collect?
> SONIA: They know exactly where you shop and how you spend your money.
> MODERATOR: Anything else?
> SONIA: They probably know more, but I'm not aware of it.
>
> MODERATOR: What's the purpose of these programs?
> JAY: ... They are to make you buy more, sort of like an incentive. Also, I think it's tracking your movements, what you buy, and how.

Although there is a predominant lack of knowledge about how these programs are connected to the collection of personal information, Graeff and Harmon's survey does indicate that some consumers are particularly knowledgeable when it comes to understanding this relationship. On occasion, such knowledge was also evidenced in the GPD focus groups:

> CAMPBELL: I think it's the cost of doing business. If you know who your customer is, then you'll be more financially savvy in developing your business toward that customer ... They want to know distinctly who their customer is, what they're buying and what they want, so that they can see a six-month projection based on the past six months, that our majority of customers are in this age bracket, they're buying this and that, they can be better prepared for it.

CONSUMERS' KNOWLEDGE OF PROFILING AND USE OF EVASIVE RESPONSES

Again, as Campbell's focus group response indicates, some consumers are actually very cognizant of their consumptive habits being surveilled and their preferences profiled. In cases where consumers are highly knowledgeable about these practices, they may engage in what Tiffany Barnett White describes as "disclosure management" (2004, 49). For her, this includes a reluctance or refusal to disclose information; indeed, she shows that consumers are not always willing participants in their own surveillance. This point is likewise made explicit in the responses to question 7 of the GPD survey. In Canada and the United States 77% of respondents in both countries (the highest proportion among all eight countries in the survey) say they have refused to give information to a business when they found it unnecessary. According to a survey of US consumers conducted by Alessandro Acquisti and Jens Grossklags (2005), the decision to engage in disclosure management is based on multiple factors, including what consumers know, how much they care, and how costly or effective their actions are perceived to be. Given this, their survey further indicates that consumers often lack enough information regarding privacy-sensitive decisions and are likely to trade off long-term privacy for short-term benefits.

What is clear is that when consumers are informed about privacy protection mechanisms, they are likely to use them. Several well-known and highly publicized examples of information control are evident, for instance, in the GPD survey, where respondents indicated a relatively high use of these privacy control mechanisms. In response to question 7, 71% of Canadian participants and 77% of those in the United States indicated they have asked to be removed from a company's marketing list. Likewise, 66% of respondents in Canada and 73% in the United States have requested that their name and address not be sold to another company. These strategies have become a bit more well known in both countries likely due to the changes made in accordance with and the media coverage of the Do Not Call Registry, run by the Federal Trade Commission in the United States (see Dommeyer and Gross 2003). These strategies require minimal effort and are largely a socially accepted means of protecting one's privacy. However, consumers rarely use pro-active privacy protection strategies, which are either less well known or less socially acceptable. For instance, according to the GPD survey, only 28% of Canadians and 37% of Americans have asked a business about policies on the collection of consumer information, something that could be a rather time-consuming venture. Likewise, rarely have respondents asked about what other personal information a company has in its consumer records (18% in Canada, 24% in the US). Although taking these protective actions may require more time than consumers are interested in spending, consumers also do not tend to lie or give incorrect information when talking to a marketer. Only 20% of GPD survey respondents in Canada and 22% in the United States have used dissimulation as a means to protect privacy. This strategy is seen as a creative but less socially acceptable form of privacy protection, as evidenced by the female participant's comment, by the laughter, and by the change in Keith's response in the following GPD focus group interaction:

MODERATOR: What other things? What other things does anybody do to protect their privacy?
KEITH: Lie.
MODERATOR: Lie.
Female participant: That's not good.
[Laughter.]
KEITH: Selectively I give information.

When it comes to consumers' knowledge of surveillance practices and privacy protection strategies, the GPD survey results mirror those of an earlier survey of US consumers indicating that most consumers have relatively little knowledge of marketing practices and regulations (Dommeyer and Gross 2003). Although the earlier survey indicates that consumers may be somewhat well informed about some privacy protection strategies, mainly those that have gained a high degree of recognition (e.g., the Do Not Call Registry and technology like caller ID), their use of other strategies remains rather minimal. When it comes to the specifics of connecting loyalty programs to profiling, a number of respondents to the Canadian and US portions of the GPD survey likely did not make a connection between the two, as Graeff and Harmon suggest, observing that "very few consumers associated such discount cards with collecting and using personal information" (2002, 309). Those respondents who are more knowledgeable either see consumer profiling as inevitable and therefore somewhat acceptable or regard this practice as beneficial (as discussed below). It is important to note that no matter the respondent's knowledge, very few see consumer profiling practices as very acceptable (6% in Canada, 7% in the US).

CONSUMERS' CONCERNS ABOUT LOYALTY PROFILING

So is it the case that consumers do not care about consumer profiling? Many do not, particularly when it comes to receiving some means of compensation. Although surveys, including the GPD survey, indicate that consumer privacy is a fairly high concern (yet to differing degrees), this concern tends not to be a very powerful disincentive for joining loyalty programs (Smith and Sparks 2004). In fact, as mentioned, consumers are "willing to trade privacy for convenience or bargain the release of personal information for relatively small rewards" (Acquisti and Grossklags 2005, 26). For example, even though the moderator in the following GPD focus group encounter raises the potential for omniscient tracking by a corporation, June remains unfazed:

> MODERATOR: So that doesn't bother you, in terms of being able to track everything that you buy? Any issues there? June?
> JUNE: Not really, no. It doesn't really bother me.

Of course, June's response is not exactly enthusiastic one way or the other; she simply indicates that this tracking (and perhaps profiling) does not concern her. Others simply appreciate the incentives they receive:

> MODERATOR: ... you said reluctantly. You're not forced to. Why?
> SONIA: I got it at work as an incentive for us, and that's how I started. And I just carried it on, but I know ...

MODERATOR: But why don't you stop?

SONIA: Because I'm greedy, I want my points.

[Laughter.]

MODERATOR: Okay. Lena? Why do you participate?

LENA: I want my points. I get free movie passes, I give them away at Christmas time. You get gifts, you know, whatever you are looking for.

Still others are not only unconcerned about consumer profiling but also rather enthusiastic about it. These consumers see profiling as incredibly beneficial, particularly as it increases the convenience of their shopping and service experiences:

VANESSA: I think it's how they market it. I mean, I look at Amazon. com. They are the most successful online bookstore because as soon as you log in, "Welcome back, Vanessa! Today we have ..." Here's ten towels that you might love. It's customer relationship management, and it works. Absolutely!

FEMALE PARTICIPANT: I don't see a problem with that.

VANESSA: I mean, they're basing it on your interests, right?

VALENTINE: And then you still have to decide if you want to buy it.

Despite these examples, there are a number of people who have genuine privacy concerns. In fact, even those like June, Sonia, Lena, and Vanessa are likely to have more serious concerns when it comes to disclosing particularly sensitive information. General buying habits are one thing, especially for those with middle-class or higher incomes, but one's socio-economic status, financial data, personal identifiers, and items that lead to more junk mail tend to be areas of strong concern. North American consumers in general, it appears, are less concerned about lifestyle disclosures, demographics, or shopping habits (Phelps et al. 2000; Paul 2001). This is clear from the responses to question 19 of the GPD survey, which show strong objection to and qualified acceptance of companies being able to sell personal information to other companies. In Canada 49% of respondents object to this practice, and 31% find it acceptable with the consumer's consent. The numbers for the United States are similar, with 48% objecting to the practice and 28% allowing for it with consent. Graeff and Harmon's (2002) survey of US consumers returned a similar number, with 84% disagreeing or strongly disagreeing with the practice of companies selling personal information.

In some sense, consumer concerns centre on issues of trust and personal vulnerability. Shopping habits and basic demographics are seen as less of a concern, but the prospect of personally sensitive data ending up in the wrong hands remains an often vocalized fear:

> JAY: ... I don't want my information to be spread around or like people using my information, so I try to hide the information that I can. Because I think that the privacy is my responsibility and is how they keep out.
> MODERATOR: So you just mean your personal information or what?
> JAY: No, no I'm saying that my personal information can be used. I know it can be used and I don't trust systems that I don't know.

> ELLEN: ... there are specific types of information that I don't mind people knowing what I do, but there's other types of information that I really want to be mine, and not to have anybody aware of. But I think the fact that there is more data in many different banks now than there ever was makes us much more vulnerable to some degree.

Jay and Ellen are at the opposite end of the spectrum from those respondents mentioned above who are less concerned about their personal information becoming available through consumer surveillance. Both sets of reactions seem to vary on the basis of one's knowledge of this practice and the level of trust consumers have in the corporations with which they do business. Although the GPD survey does not get us into the specifics of what drives or does not drive these concerns, it does reiterate what is evident in GPD focus groups and other surveys on consumer privacy and surveillance. Some consumers are concerned and others are not. Some consumers are knowledgeable about being profiled, but most are not, especially when it comes to the role that loyalty programs play in this practice. Yet as suggested below, the concerns regarding consumer surveillance and the role of loyalty programs in helping to create consumer profiles are legitimate, and it is worth evaluating whether the short-term gains in consumer discounts and rewards are greater than the potential long-term privacy losses.

THE ISSUES WITH CONSUMER PROFILING AND LOYALTY DATA

What long-term privacy concerns does consumer surveillance raise, particularly in regards to the use of loyalty programs? Why should consumers care about this? What should they know? Although most consumers consider information about their shopping habits to be relatively mundane and innocuous, loyalty programs do in fact provide a lot of detailed personal information. In large measure, as Andrew Smith and Leigh Sparks state, "consumers appear to be highly unaware of the level and volume of data held on them" (2003, 372). Loyalty programs serve to create what may be called *biographies of consumption* that are representative of the lives of millions of consumers (Evans 1998). In fact, Smith and Sparks (2004) reveal that an anonymous woman they call "Eve":

- is overweight but very concerned about her appearance, especially her poor complexion;
- has long hair, occasionally wears contacts and glasses, and has numerous problems with her feet;
- has hay fever and struggles to overcome a common cold several times a year;
- has a boyfriend or partner she occasionally buys items for;
- is someone who plans holiday gifts and cards well in advance.

All of this information was surmised from two years of loyalty card data, prompting the authors to state, "The products she buys say a lot about her. They provide an 'archaeological' record of who she is. Retailers are party to sensitive information" (Smith and Sparks 2004, 379). The data that the authors are privy to in this example are relatively limited, whereas retailers can make connections between shoppers with similar spending behaviours as well as add on layers of other variables – from geo-demographics to financial indexes – that would indicate even more crucial and illuminating details about this particular consumer.

Essentially, the data gathered from loyalty programs serves several purposes. It is used to inform corporate decision making, define a customer's experience of marketing communication, and define experiences in the service process (Rowley 2005). As some consumers recognize, these uses of consumer data can provide great benefits, but they also lead to categories of preferred and nonpreferred consumers, the latter of whom "are less likely to be offered incentives to continue to engage" (Rowley 2005, 107). The integration of loyalty data with other forms of data leads to reiteration of Oscar Gandy's "panoptic sort": a "cybernetic triage" that separates consumers based on their presumed economic and political value rather than on their initiative and self-determination (1993, 1). In the end, consumers with a higher perceived value get the best of corporate treatment, whereas those with poorer transaction records that perhaps are coupled with other factors like social class and location receive far less attractive offers, if they receive any at all (Rowley 2005). Although there are certain ethical concerns about this sorting of consumers into categories, it does remain a benefit to some consumers eager to gain whatever advantages they can. Yet the distinctions between categories are never transparent, and they may lead corporations to take actions, whether marketing or service-related, that do not always match the consumer's expectations of treatment.

CONCLUSION

The responses to the GPD survey question on the use of loyalty cards have a number of connections to the responses to the survey's subsequent question on consumer profiling. The quantitative data in the survey add to a contextualized understanding of the ambivalence evident in the answers to the two questions. Some consumers are knowledgeable about the role that loyalty cards play in consumer profiling and others are not. Some consumers care deeply about this issue and others do not. Yet in the end, the sentiment of Smith and Sparks regarding their anonymous "Eve" is important: "we know more than she would be comfortable with" (2004, 382). Yet it is not just comfort that remains the concern. The categories created through consumer data profiling have real effects on consumers' life chances and opportunities. As Jennifer Rowley states, consumers need to "enhance their awareness not only of the data that organisations hold about them, but also of the knowledge-based processes that businesses use to create value from that data" (2005, 109).

It is interesting to note that the survey process itself may have created some of this awareness. Although one of the GPD focus group participants had regularly used a loyalty card in the past, the questions raised by the moderator led her to rethink her use a bit:

> ANGIE: I use it. But the theory bothers me. It's hard to explain. The idea of it bothers me because I know that I'm never going to get more than you're supposed to, or ... I'm not really getting a big benefit out of it, but it's just kind of like it's an incentive ... probably before this conversation I only thought of it as maybe I will get a benefit somehow, but you're making us kind of think.

Angie may weigh the opportunities against the concerns of loyalty card use and still decide to continue to participate, yet at some level her use of the card may be far more informed than it was prior to this discussion. Although the categories and processes of consumer surveillance remain far from transparent, the tools for protecting one's privacy may be illuminated through the distribution of these survey results. Nonetheless, Angie's dilemma, expressed at the end of the above quotation, is indicative of what the gpd survey tells us: there remains a complex relationship between loyalty program participation and concerns over consumer surveillance and profiling.

NOTES

1 ACNielsen indicates that 81% of the US population and 97% of the Canadian population participate in loyalty programs. However, those surveyed in each country are already members of ACNielsen's HomeScan program. See http://us.acnielsen.com/pubs/2004_11_fff_loyalty.shtml (accessed 26 October 2006) and http://www2.acnielsen.com/pubs/documents/2004_q1_ci_frequent.pdf (accessed 16 October 2006).

2 Question 27 states, "Some companies offer customer rewards programmes where you can earn points or rewards based on how often you buy something from them or use their services. How many of these types of programmes do you collect points or rewards from?"

3 Examined here are the results from focus groups carried out in 2004 by EKOS Research Associates on behalf of the GPD project in Canada and the United States. Four groups were conducted in Toronto in English and four in Montreal in French in May 2004 with a total of fifty-nine participants, and two followed in Chicago in July 2004 with a total of twenty participants. Participants were divided into four types: workers, travellers, consumers, and citizens. The findings are available at http://www.sscqueens.org/intl_survey_background (accessed 23 November 2009).

Exploring Consumer Rights Regimes and Internet Consumption in Europe

OLA SVENONIUS

A major question in the field of surveillance studies has been the potential for corporations to collect information from individuals and the potential to utilize these data for their respective purposes. Consumers provide sellers with more information when consuming over the Internet than in conventional cash-based trade, which makes the issue of information retention, usage, and communication most important. Internet retailers[1] have had difficulties in establishing credible trust relationships with their potential customers.[2] They try to solve consumers' lack of trust by using different strategies, such as branding and applying different trust certificates.[3] Issues of consumer trust and privacy are the subjects of a vast body of research. However, this research has failed to acknowledge the importance of prior experience with conventional cash-based trade and with regulatory regimes in consumer protection.

Based on experiences from earlier research projects concerning consumer issues in other areas, I argue here that efforts by Internet retailers to promote trust might be in vain because the behaviour of consumers on the Internet is influenced by views and experiences of consumer protection in quite different circumstances, namely in conventional trade. The point of departure is thus that differences in Internet consumption can be traced back to the type of consumer rights regime.

EXPLORING CONSUMER BEHAVIOUR

This chapter is an exploratory study of the impact of regulatory regimes on consumer behaviour on the Internet, which is operationalized as the percentage of survey respondents who have engaged in Internet consumption (Blaikie 2000, 73–4). I aim to establish a link between consumer protection and Internet consumption and to explore the causal mechanisms behind this behaviour by using findings from the Globalization of Personal Data (GPD) survey. Three countries have been included in the current analysis: France, Spain, and Hungary. The selection was made due to differences in political history based on the assumption that each country's recent political experiences (with communist, fascist, or long-standing liberal regimes, respectively) would influence the current state of consumer protection and culture. Within the population of European Union member-states, these countries represent a maximum in variation regarding general political history.[4] This roughly corresponds to a diverse-case method, as discussed by John Gerring (2007, 97ff). In this case, the more immediate focus is on differences in legislation, consumer organizations, mediation boards, and consumer culture.

A theoretical discussion follows below. In the subsequent analysis, I first establish the value on the independent variable (i.e., the consumer rights regimes) and then present the data on the dependant variable (i.e., Internet consumption) before analyzing the trust and privacy concerns that mediate this relationship.

TOWARD A MODEL FOR CONSUMER BEHAVIOUR

This section provides an outline of the theoretical model that will be applied to the GPD survey data later on. The model combines privacy concerns in terms of information disclosure and institutionalized consumer protection, which I call the *consumer rights regime*.[5] This is a basic causal model where the consumer rights regime guarantees the feeling of trust among the consumers that leads them to engage in Internet consumption. Trust, in turn, is influenced by privacy concerns.[6] Consumer policies influence both trust in the regulatory framework and privacy concerns insofar as they affect consumers' earlier experiences with conventional trade.

Information Disclosure, Trust, and Consumer Power

The Internet requires consumers to be very aware of what type of disclosure they are willing to accept and who receives the information; this is nearly impossible to trace for most people. Thus consumers have to rely on other factors when purchasing over the Internet, such as a legislative framework granting them efficient means to punish deviant behaviour.

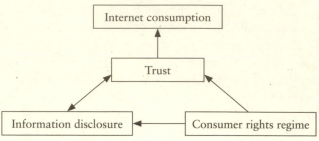

Figure 16.1
Basic theoretical model of consumer trust

Consumers' trust in online retailers can be analyzed by who is trusted, on the one hand (i.e., the brand itself or the Internet site) (see Metzger 2006), and by different types of trust, on the other. The focus here is on the latter. Daryl Koehn argues that trust can be achieved through transparency, openness, and mutual respect (2003, 5). However, as Miriam Metzger (2006) has shown, knowledge strategies and transparency might have little to do with consumers' purchasing behaviour. In Metzger's study, trust in a website or vendor did not have a strong relation with information disclosure (and thus with Internet consumption) (2006, 167). Instead, the most influential factor was earlier experience of e-commerce. Metzger states, "It may be that past experience with ecommerce is a powerful determinant of future online ecommerce behavior. Research on social exchange theory finds that when risk-taking results in a successful outcome, people's perceptions of the risk of engaging in future similar actions is lowered. Applied to the Internet, people may feel emboldened by prior positive experiences with ecommerce and/or online disclosure, creating a type of 'disinhibition effect'" (2006, 168).

I propose a similar argument, with the small but significant difference that I do not see this as a question that applies only to e-commerce. I argue that strategies to promote trust may be beneficial, but if a society cannot provide a sound basis for the more intimate types of trust through sufficiently effective consumer protection, such as reliable voice and exit options (see Hirschman 1970), these strategies will be much less effective.

Behrang Rezabakhsh and colleagues (2006) underscore the importance of the consumers' sanctioning power in relation to Internet retailers. If sanctions are not delivered or prove ineffective, consumers will be far more careful with their money in the future (Rezabakhsh et al. 2006, 10). A quick look at existing investigations shows that different types of fraud or misconduct are very common on the Internet, which makes the power to sanction misbehaviour essential.[7] Therefore, the system that provides consumers with these powers should be important for Internet consumption.

Institutionalism and Consumer Rights Regimes

The entities that make up a system of consumer protection can be divided into legislation, consumer organizations and protection agencies, and mediation boards. These parts aggregate into a policy regime, here called a consumer rights regime, which is an institution in itself. The theoretical assumption is that the design of a consumer rights regime provides the foundation for consumers' privacy concerns and thus significantly affects consumer behaviour in the Internet economy. The question is a methodological one: although the objects of analysis are typically the Internet retailers or international policy regimes,[8] I suggest that in order to understand the basic mechanisms for consumer behaviour – and the shaping of trust relationships over new platforms for information communication technologies (ICTs) – it is essential to go back to the consumers' views and experiences. Depending on the organization and effectiveness of arbitration and mediation practices in each country, different experiences are made and shaped into the normative dimension of the consumer rights regime in a kind of consumer socialization process.

The consumer rights regime manifests itself in formal regulations and social norms, such as morality and fairness, on behalf of both consumers and private companies. The regime is assumed to influence consumers' behaviour on the Internet, such as the way they disclose their personal information and their consumption habits. Trust in terms of willingness to submit personal information and in terms of reliance on the consumer rights regime is a prerequisite for the Internet to be a vital part of the marketplace. If consumers view it as effective, they should be confident in their interaction with Internet retailers and companies in general.

Thus, if one wants to analyze how the consumer rights regime affects consumers' trust in Internet retailers, the issues of transparency, control over information, and general trust in private corporations (as discussed above) seem central. The GPD survey included several questions that probed these factors. The argument is that if the consumer rights regime is experienced as effective in a country, then the matter of trust and privacy will be less important than if consumers had to protect themselves completely.

CONSUMER RIGHTS REGIMES
IN CONTINENTAL EUROPE[9]

In this section, the consumer rights regimes of each country are described and discussed in order to establish the value on the independent variable. The focus is on the institutional setting and the consumer culture in each country, beginning with France.

France

The French consumer rights regime is typical for Continental Europe. High reliance is placed on the numerous consumer organizations, which are central to the system. Responsibility for consumer protection is shared between the consumer protection agency Direction générale de la consommation, de la concurrence et de la répression des fraudes (DGCCRF) and the Mouvement consumériste. The latter consists of eighteen organizations that are officially recognized by the DGCCRF. Apart from these organizations, which receive state funding, a large number of other purely autonomous organizations exist.[10]

The organizations, as opposed to the state, enjoy a high degree of support from the public. In a Eurobarometer survey in 2006, the French consumer organizations were outranked only by the Dutch in public confidence (81%), whereas the state agencies received an EU-average verdict of about 55% (Eurobaromenter 2006, 93, 95).

Consumers in France do not have easy access to arbitration. Arbitration in France is potentially costly and difficult to access because the special arbitration courts charge fees and because considerable paperwork is connected with the procedure (Sculze and Schulte-Nölke 2003, 20). The regular arbitration bodies are the responsibility of the regional administrations, which are free but not obliged to set up arbitration boards (European Commission, Consumer Affairs 2007). This results in underdeveloped contact between French consumers and the arbitration boards. However, this might be irrelevant. According to a representative of the French branch of the European Consumer Centre, French consumers are socialized to believe in their rights as consumers. This might be enough to construct something one might call "virtual trust." The consumer rights regime is thought to be more developed than it actually is, which presumably makes it a major factor in French consumers' behaviour on the Internet market.[11]

The prediction is that French consumers will be rather active on the Internet. Even though they might not trust the companies, they feel secure enough to share their information with them in a commercial relationship. If it is indeed the case that the trust lies with the consumer rights regime instead of with the companies themselves, French consumers will tend to be wary and to make high efforts to strengthen their privacy.

Hungary

Even though Hungary has renowned privacy protection, it is still the country that has experienced the most privacy infringements, as compared to the other two in this analysis (Privacy International 2003; Ipsos Szonda Hungary 2004, 5–6). As for consumer protection, Hungarian companies are characterized as unconcerned or uninterested. This is especially true for companies in monopolistic positions that have little to risk by not being consumer friendly.[12] The disinterest of Hungarian companies is mirrored in the population's low level of knowledge and awareness about consumer legislation. Only a small group of people are well informed and active, and these tend to be young or middle-aged academics (European Commission, Working Party 1999).

Consumer arbitration is carried out by branch organizations or regional chambers of commerce in a system that was introduced in 1999. The system is near perfect on paper but problematic in practice. For example, administrative costs are paid by the complaining party (Act CLV, section 33, § 2; Consumers International 2000a, 49). Katalin Cseres points toward problems regarding partiality and insufficient experience in the arbitration system as well (2004, 52). Consumers thus seem to be left out of the consumer protection regime, which could produce low levels of trust among the Hungarian population. Many of these issues can be traced back to the understandable lack of experience when dealing with consumer issues, a legacy of the socialist period.[13]

To conclude, the high costs of consumer arbitration, the many high-profile cases of misuse of personal information, and domestic companies' lack of interest in consumer issues may seriously impair the chances for effective consumer protection in general and Internet consumption in particular. Thus one can anticipate a low level of Internet consumption and low trust in private companies. It remains to be seen to which extent the socialist period still affects Hungarian consumers. An antipathy toward state institutions and state companies may very well influence both trust and consumption levels.

Spain

Spanish consumers have a special relationship with privacy, the state, and activism, which can be traced back to the fascist dictatorship that ended in 1975. The organization Consumers International describes the cultural atmosphere as a "detachment from 'everything that is public'" (2000b, 23). This very tense relationship tends to lessen among younger generations but is still present and will certainly be important in the analysis of the GPD survey data.

A special feature in Spain is its system of local courts that have effective jurisdiction over participating companies. A large number of companies have volunteered to participate in the program, which was initiated in the early 1980s.[14] The problem is that participation is voluntary and that companies not in the system are unaffected by its verdicts. The Spanish system functions a bit like a "white list" of consumer-friendly companies. In addition, Spanish municipalities employ consumer advisors who have the power to perform inspections and to engage in legal actions. These two factors are atypical in a Continental European context (Consumers International 2000b, 23–30, 38–9; OECD 2002, 2).[15]

The rather extensive system for arbitration and mediation is, however, not reflected by a corresponding ease in resolving conflicts with retailers. In a recent survey by Eurobarometer, Spanish consumers shared the bottom position with the Slovaks, with only 17% stating that conflict resolution through an arbitration, mediation, or conciliation body was easy. Spanish consumers are among the most skeptical in the entire EU when it comes to reliance on the consumer rights regime. Consumer protection in general, consumer organizations, arbitration and mediation boards, and companies all get very low satisfaction scores (around 46%) and are beaten in the race to the bottom only by Lithuania, Slovakia, and in some cases, Portugal (Eurobarometer 2006, 98). In 2000, Consumers International reported that 64% of Spanish consumers have had a reason to present a consumer complaint but have not done so because of a lack of trust in the system (2000b, 23).

In terms of the theoretical model sketched above, Spanish consumers do have the formal prerequisites to act in an international market with confidence, but it seems that their collective experiences of a weak consumer rights regime (in practice) reduce their propensity to accept the risk of commercial transactions on the Internet. According to the model,

I expect Spanish consumers not to rely on the Internet as a marketplace and to be rather restrictive with disclosure of personal information.

Summary

This section has provided brief profiles for the three countries studied here. It has been shown that each country has both weaknesses and strengths in its consumer rights regime. Domestic mediation and arbitration systems and informal norms vary immensely between the EU member-states. They depend on earlier experiences with consumer rights regimes and on cultural and historical factors.

Consumer protection in France enjoys the most support among the three, although the Spanish system of arbitration courts and municipal consumer advisors provides an institutional framework that might actually be more effective if the Spanish consumers make use of it. In Hungary consumer protection is rather new in its present form, and Hungarian consumers must seemingly navigate through many obstacles to make their voices heard against any private or public company. In the next section, the GPD survey data are evaluated in light of these results.

CONSUMER RIGHTS REGIMES IN THE GPD SURVEY DATA

The GPD survey provides the values for the dependant variable (see table 16.1 below). French consumers are most active in Internet purchasing: 45% had purchased a product or service over the Internet during the year prior to the survey. The Spanish consumers were not as active: only 31% indicated Internet purchases. Hungarians are the least active consumers on the Internet, with 17% of the interviewees having bought something on the Internet during the same period. Of the Internet users, the share of consumers who use the Internet for shopping is 64% in France, 42% in Spain, and 35% in Hungary. This shows that even though Hungary has a much lower rate of Internet usage, the share of consumers who use it for consumption is not much lower than in Spain. Thus the predictions from the previous section are fairly accurate. Now I turn to investigating whether the predictions on causal mechanisms are equally correct.

Control over Personal Information[16]

The analysis begins by examining the answers given to question 2 of the GPD survey, which covers control over personal information.[17] What

Table 16.1
Purchased a product or service over the Internet, by country and Internet use*

| | Yes | | No | | Don't know/Not sure | |
	Count	%	Count	%	Count	%
France	443	64.3	246	35.7	0	0.0
Spain	303	41.7	422	58.0	2	0.3
Hungary	165	34.6	311	65.2	1	0.2

* Internet users are defined as people who have given a positive answer to one of the alternatives (i.e., "at home," "at work," or "at a public place") for question 39c: "Have you used the Internet in the past 6 months?"

attracts most attention is the high proportion of Hungarian respondents who claim to have no say over what happens to their personal information. Thirty per cent gave this answer, which is twice as many as in Spain and three times as many as in France. Around 70% of the Hungarian population claim to have little or no say over these issues.

Spanish consumers are somewhat more confident regarding information disclosure. About one-third of the respondents consider themselves to have "complete say" or "a lot of say" in the matter. Fifty per cent answered "some say" (which is interpreted negatively as "little" here). Thus the number of respondents who claim to have little or no say over what happens to their personal information almost reaches the Hungarian level, but with a considerably lower degree of respondents claiming to have "no say."

In contrast, French consumers are almost overly positive regarding their degree of control, especially when taking their degree of knowledge about regulation into consideration: 75% of the French respondents claim little or no knowledge about applicable regulations. Over 60% of French respondents claim to have a lot or full control over their personal data, which seems surprising given that 50% of the French respondents express worries about giving out their personal information on websites (discussed further below). This matches the picture of the French consumer well: high confidence and high awareness about privacy as a normative value but low awareness about concrete matters such as data mining and regulations.

Only 5.8% of French Internet users selected the alternative "no say," which is about one-fifth of the total for their Hungarian counterparts. One interpretation is that French consumers might be unwilling to yield personal information in general and thus feel that they have a high degree of control over it. Another is, of course, that the respondents provided their reactions to actual facts, meaning that French consumers experience less privacy infringements and/or that French Internet retailers comply with legislation more fully.

Trust in Private Companies

In this section, questions 6 and 11 in the GPD survey are analyzed. Question 6 concerns trust in private companies' efforts to protect personal information, and question 11 relates to how worried respondents are about yielding their personal information to Internet retailers. The latter is discussed first so that worries regarding privacy on the Internet can be contrasted with the level of trust in private companies in general.[18]

Spanish consumers are most worried about yielding basic personal data on websites, with 62% of all respondents claiming to be "very" or "somewhat" worried.

Hungarian respondents, being the least knowledgeable about Internet-related issues, are more likely not to know whether to be worried about their personal information.[19] Surprisingly, Hungary also has the lowest proportion of respondents stating that they are "very" or "somewhat" worried about their personal data (45%). It would seem logical that the population that is most unsure would also be most worried – due, for example, to unfamiliarity with the technology. Thirty-nine per cent of Hungarian respondents claim to be "not very worried" or "not worried at all."

French consumers are split when it comes to worries about privacy infringements. Fifty per cent are "somewhat" or "very" worried, whereas some 40% are not. The majority of the worried (38%) answered "somewhat worried," which means that the proportion of those who are very concerned in France is significantly small. There seems to be no real mainstream on this issue, perhaps because the actual experience of privacy infringements is rather low. French non-Internet users tend to be much more worried about privacy, with 56% stating they are either "very" or "somewhat" worried, and they have a much higher uncertainty frequency (19%). According to the model presented in this chapter, this reaction would be based on prior experiences in conventional trade. The actions of private companies and the effectiveness of consumer protection influence the general trust that consumers have in the consumer rights regime. Luckily, the GPD survey data from question 6 provide a measurement of trust in private companies.[20]

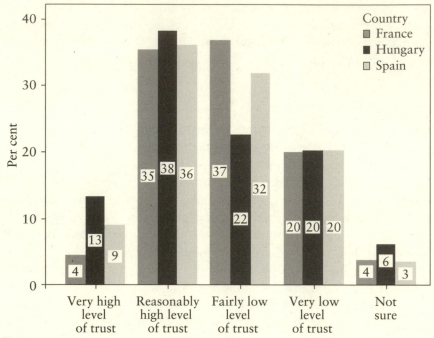

Figure 16.2
Responses to question 6 of the GPD survey

The responses to question 6 show that Hungary is the country where trust in private companies is highest. Over 50% of Hungarian respondents have a "very" or "reasonably high" level of trust in private companies. These response frequencies are surprising in light of the characteristics of the Hungarian consumer, described above. Of all three countries, Hungary has experienced the most privacy infringements, and its consumer rights regime is rather weak, especially since many companies are not very consumer-friendly. Nonetheless, Hungarian respondents are more likely to trust private companies than are those from Spain or France. This might be an indication that the socialist period still plays a major role in Hungarian society.[21]

France is, again, the other extreme. Fifty-seven per cent of the French population have a "rather" or "very" low level of trust in private companies.[22] The low trust in private companies is somewhat surprising given that French respondents have the highest Internet shopping rate *and* high confidence in French legislation. French respondents might have negative attitudes to private companies but high faith in the consumer rights regime. Thus they are less reluctant to disclose information than are their Spanish counterparts.

As in some of the other cases, the Spanish are split and positioned between the two extremes represented by France and Hungary. Fifty-two per cent of the Spanish claim to have a "rather low" or "very low" level of trust in private companies, and 45% claim the contrary.

The question of worries about privacy raises the issue of actions to promote it, such as withholding personal information, reading privacy policies, and asking private companies not to sell the information they retrieve. Question 7 of the GPD survey probes for activity to promote one's privacy. It contains ten alternatives of proactive action, of which seven are directed toward private companies.[23] In the next section, figure 16.3 shows an index that was created out of the responses to these alternatives.[24] It serves to illustrate the propensity of consumers to take action to protect their privacy in the three countries.

ACTIVITY INDEX

The majority of Hungarian respondents fall into the "low" category, in contrast to the French and Spanish respondents, who are more evenly distributed over the "low" and "middle" categories. Again, the Spanish respondents fall between France and Hungary, with 50% in the "low" category and 41% in the "middle."

Now, what does this figure have to say? Is it relevant that Hungary has a 5% lower score for high-level activity? Actually, not many strong conclusions can be drawn from this finding because the alternatives are not weighted against each other. In addition, the crude division into three groups is somewhat arbitrary. However, what this figure does show is that Hungarians claim to have low activity for the different ways of protecting one's privacy that were included in the survey and that this share of Hungarians is higher than in the two western European populations. The differences between France and Spain are not strong enough for one to make a valid statement. Nonetheless, this figure for Hungary summarizes the results of the current analysis rather well, despite its obvious fallacies. In the following section, the results of the entire analysis will be discussed and put into the context of the theoretical model.

DISCUSSION

I want to recall the basics of the theoretical discussion presented at the outset of this chapter. It focused on the importance of national consumer rights regimes with regard to Internet consumption and disclosure of personal information. The basic statement is that peoples' views of

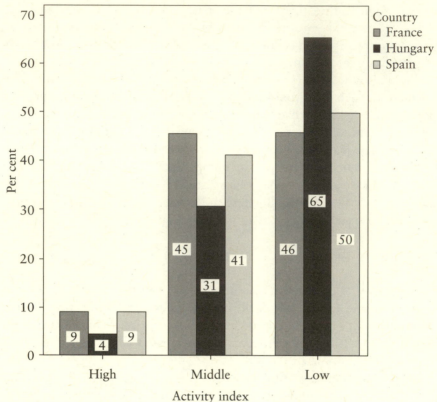

Figure 16.3
Consumers' propensity to actively promote privacy

the consumer rights regime will affect their judgment about how and when to submit personal data to Internet retailers. Strategies to promote business-to-consumer trust will not be sufficient, according to the model.

Table 16.2 shows a simplified picture of the results from the analysis of the GPD survey data. It has been demonstrated above that the results are far more diversified, and this small table can hardly do them justice. However, it points out the general trend. The analysis shows that French consumers are most reliant on the national consumer rights regime. They also act accordingly, and thus we see the highest Internet consumption rates in France. The French claim to have more say about what happens to their personal information than do the Spanish and Hungarian respondents, and they trust the effectiveness of the national legislation more than do the other two populations. However, these characteristics are not combined with higher subjective knowledge levels about the legislation itself.

Table 16.2
Summary of empirical findings in the GDP survey data

	France	Hungary	Spain
Internet consumption (% of total pop.)	45	17	31
Internet consumption (% of Internet users)	64	35	42
Say about ones information	60% – a lot or complete say	70% – little or no say	65% – little or no say
Effectiveness of applicable laws	Medium	Skeptical	Medium
Worries about information disclosure	Average	Not very worried	Very worried
Trust in private companies	45% – medium	31% – medium	41% – medium
Activity	46% – low	65% – low	50% – low

In terms of worries about information disclosure, Spanish respondents are most likely to be worried. In terms of trust in private companies, French respondents are most worried, whereas Hungarian respondents are more likely not to be worried at all. The Spanish answer frequencies are closer to the French than to the Hungarian but are again regarded as positioned somewhere in the middle. The last issue concerned how active the survey respondents claim to be. A crude activity index makes the positions of the three countries fairly clear. Hungarians have most respondents in the "low" category, whereas French and Spanish respondents are more equally divided between "low" and "medium." The French "win" in terms of activity since Spanish respondents have a higher share of low-activity respondents.

It is obvious that the consumers in France have strong and high beliefs in the degree of protection they enjoy. French consumers are worried about privacy, but they seem to feel empowered by "the system," which allows them to act with more confidence in relation to retailers generally, not only on the Internet. The "disinhibition effect" that Miriam Metzger (2006) mentions (discussed above) seems to explain French consumers' behaviour. France is the country where this is displayed most clearly.

In Spain and Hungary the mechanisms are more difficult to discern. Neither country displays a clear direction that can be associated with the theoretical model, although both show tendencies that can be interpreted accordingly. In Spain confidence in the consumer rights regime is low, and so is the degree of international consumption over the Internet. Spanish consumers are rather likely to distrust private companies and are very likely to be worried about sharing personal information with them. The Spanish consumers also have a constrained relationship with the public domain, and they seldom file complaints, although many of them would have a reason to do so. The public sector and the consumer mediation boards are seen as slow and bureaucratic. Just as French consumers seem to have created "virtual trust," the Spanish seem to have created "virtual *dis*trust." What does this tell us? The Spanish population has had negative experiences with parts of the consumer rights regime (i.e., private companies), and they have a very negative image of Spanish consumer protection systems.

The solution the respondents seem to have chosen is not to rely on the help that is potentially there but to be very wary of the way that they interact with private companies. It seems credible that the insufficiency of the consumer rights regime influences Internet consumption in Spain as an "inhibition effect" (see the theoretical discussion above).

Internet consumption, the dependant variable, is around 20% lower in Spain than in France, even though consumers in both countries are protected by similar data protection legislation. Over 60% of Spanish respondents claim to have little or no say over what happens to their personal information after it is submitted to an Internet retailer. These figures say a lot, especially since Spanish respondents claim to be more knowledgeable about the Internet than both French and Hungarian respondents. Recalling the predictions from the country descriptions, we can now see that the GPD survey data support these assumptions. There is support for the model in the Spanish case, although there are fallacies, about which one has to be aware.

Hungary is different from the two other countries because of a number of factors. It is an eastern European country, with a political culture that distinguishes it from both Spain and France. The experience of consumer protection institutions and the mentality of the private sector are quite different from what is seen in Spain and France. Possibilities for arbitrations are fewer and potentially costly for the consumer. Attitudes toward privacy are very different from those in western Europe. A vast majority of Hungarians claim to have either little or no say about submitted personal information. They are generally skeptical of the effectiveness of the Hungarian privacy legislation, although they do not know very much about it. It seems almost contradictory that the Hungarian responses for question 11 (on worries about privacy on the Internet) show the lowest frequencies of all three countries for the alternatives "very" and "somewhat" worried.

Equally surprising is that the majority of Hungarians claim to have a "reasonably high" or "very high" level of trust in private companies. The important question that follows is: what explanatory value does the consumer rights regime have in this context? The assumption is that consumers' views of the consumer rights regime shape their future behaviour on the Internet. Katalin Cseres (2004) describes the Hungarian consumer rights regime as theoretically positive but practically problematic. Thus one can assume that, to the extent that consumers in Hungary have experienced problems, these have been difficult to solve through conventional consumer protection measures. One would assume that Hungarian respondents would be reluctant to submit personal information, that they would not trust private companies, and that they would be more active in trying to protect their privacy. Since this is not the case according to the data from the GPD survey, one must conclude that something is missing from the theoretical model. Material values may be more influential than the will to defend one's privacy, or the experiences of a communist system may have produced a tendency to appreciate private organizations. In any case, other variables should be considered.

CONCLUSION

The assumption in this chapter is that differences in concerns about information privacy and Internet consumption can be traced back to the type of consumer rights regime that exists. In two of the three cases analyzed here, this assumption found support in the GPD survey data. The hypothesis presented in this chapter does not explain the behaviour of Hungarian respondents to the GPD survey. In the French and Spanish cases, the model is adequate; however, it is by no means perfect. A number of other variables may have been brought in, such as national variance in privacy legislation. One task is thus to develop the model further and/or to apply it to other countries. Is it, for example, correct that the model suits western European countries better? Is there a "Western bias"?

This chapter presents an important argument that the "disinhibition effect" is relevant, not only for experiences of Internet trade but also for experiences of conventional trade. This is a major point that has far-reaching consequences. For example, developing privacy certificates is important, yet countries must ensure that all consumers in need have ready access to assistance. This is important not only in conventional trade but also for Internet retailers, despite the perceived international marketplace within which they operate.

NOTES

I would like to thank Elia Zureik, L. Lynda Harling Stalker, and Emily Smith at Queen's University and Robert Lewis at McGill-Queen's University Press for their great help in commenting on and editing this chapter.

1 The term "Internet retailer" or "online retailer," used throughout the chapter, is here associated with any type of company (Internet-based or not) that offers products to consumers over the Internet.

2 See Cheung and Lee (2006) for a discussion of this problem.

3 One such certificate is TRUSTe®; see http://www.truste.org (accessed 5 March 2007).

4 Among members of the European Union, it is possible to control for a number of important factors due to the common legislation on data protection and contract law.

5 The term "consumer rights regime" is broader than the more common phrase "consumer protection," which refers only to legislation. "Consumer rights regime" also includes extralegal mechanisms, such as voluntary dispute settlement.

6 Compare Hoffman et al. (1999). See also Cheung and Lee (2006) and Metzger (2006) for an overview of other factors.

7 See, for example, the European Consumer Centre (ECC) Internet purchase trial (ECC 2003b).

8 Such international policy regimes typically focus on privacy statements, certificates of various kinds, trust and its generation, EU legislation, and recommendations of the Organization for Economic Cooperation and Development (OECD).

9 Due to space requirements, the analysis of the consumer rights regimes will be limited. Even though this is unfortunate, the exploratory character of this study does not require lengthy analysis of this kind. For a discussion of consumer privacy laws in each of the countries in the survey, see Arthur Cockfield's chapter in this volume.

10 E-mail interview with Bianca Schultz, legal adviser at the French European Consumer Centre in Kehl, Germany, November 2006.

11 Ibid.

12 E-mail interview with István Garai, president of the National Association for Consumer Protection, Hungary, November 2006.

13 The latter statement is qualified by the fact that to some extent consumer protection has existed in Hungary since the 1970s. See Cseres (2004, 47, 55ff) for a detailed description of consumer protection in Hungary before 1990.

14 The number of participating companies was 72,362 in 2002 and is considered to be very high, especially since many major companies have joined the program.

15 Interview with Regina Fernandez at the European Consumer Centre (ECC) Madrid, 8 November 2006.

16 The full questions and graphic display of the answers in frequencies are available in the appendix that concludes this volume.

17 The wording of question 2 is: "To what extent do you have a say in what happens to your personal information?"

18 The wording of question 11 is: "When it comes to privacy, how worried are you about providing personal information on websites, such as your name, address, date of birth, and gender?"

19 There is a slight bias here due to the relatively large share of non-Internet users in Hungary. Hungarian Internet users were less knowledgeable than were their French and Spanish counterparts but not as much less knowledgeable as the data appear to claim. Non-Internet users were structurally less knowledgeable than were Internet users in all three countries.

20 The wording of question 6 is: "What level of trust do you have that private companies, such as banks, credit card companies and places where you shop, will protect your personal information?"

21 See Iván Székely's chapter in this volume for more discussion of results in Hungary.

22 Nonetheless, over 60% claim to have "a lot" or "complete" say about what happens to their personal information. Compare this figure to the French responses for question 2 as described above.

23 One such proactive action is: "Refused to give information to a business because you thought it was not needed." See the appendix to this volume for the full wording of the questions.

24 The alternatives are listed in a multiple-choice question in the GPD survey as items 7.1, 7.3 to 7.7, and 7.9. The index was created by categorizing responders into three groups: high activity (6–7 positive responses), mid-level activity (3–5 positive responses), and low activity (0–2 positive responses). There was no weighting of the different alternatives. The "unsure" alternative was included in the "low activity" category of the index.

17

Is There a Global Approach to Workplace Privacy?

AVNER LEVIN

INTRODUCTION

Workplace surveillance both produces and reproduces the power relationship between employer and employees and, as Elia Zureik (2002) points out, has significant, broader political and economic implications for society at large. The advent of new technology has not only added to the arsenal of monitoring tools at the employer's disposal but has also significantly changed the nature of monitoring, in turn creating a new form of monitoring referred to as "dataveillance" (Lyon 2001, 143–5). With the introduction of new telephone technology, such as Voice over Internet Protocol (VoIP), forms of monitoring for all workers will be easily and readily available (Swire 2004, 911–12), and it is now technologically possible to survey all employees all the time, in an imperceptible manner (Jeffery 2002). Workplace privacy is likely to erode as a result, and a conceptual legal basis for workplace privacy that will withstand technological changes is required. This chapter raises the following question: Is there a legal concept of privacy for employees, and if so, what is its conceptual basis?

It has long been argued in North American jurisprudence that such an adequate basis is to be found in the idea of reasonable expectations. Worker privacy is based on the reasonable expectation of privacy that workers have in the workplace. Where no reasonable expectation exists, no privacy exists; and where some reasonable expectation of privacy exists, some measure of privacy should be protected by the law. The idea that employees have, or should reasonably have, no expectation of privacy at work is ubiquitous and obviously a useful tool in the hands of employers. It also resonates well with the US tort of Intrusion of Seclusion and with Fourth Amendment jurisprudence, which constructed the test of reasonableness with respect to the activities of the US government against its subjects (e.g., *Katz v. US*, 389 US 347).[1] The test has been logically extended to the workplace of public employees (e.g., *O'Connor v. Ortega*, 480 US 709) and seems to equally apply to the private-sector workplace as well. Significantly, the test of whether workers, and individuals in general, enjoy a reasonable expectation of privacy is decided not only by examining the expectations of society in general in a particular situation (e.g., do members of society expect video surveillance inside washrooms?), sometimes termed the "objective expectations," but also by examining the specific expectations of the individual in the particular situation in question (e.g., would workers, if notified by the employer of new cameras installed in their washroom, expect privacy in that location?), sometimes termed "subjective expectations." As regards privacy as a legal concept, no reasonable expectations of privacy can exist where no subjective expectations of privacy have originally existed.

At the basis of the reasonable expectations approach to workplace privacy is the assumption that employers, since they own the workplace and its resources, are free to act in the workplace as they please. This *property-approach* to workplace privacy allows employers to freely dictate to employees the manner in which resources such as computers and telephones will be used. In turn, employees have only privacy rights or, more accurately, expectations of privacy – to the extent that employer policies allow. However, the idea of employees enjoying only reasonable expectations of privacy, coupled with the elasticity of the notion of reasonable expectations as subject to easy change as a result of technological advancements and subsequent employer notifications, raises the question of whether the *property-approach* is appropriate for governing the analysis of privacy in the workplace or whether other approaches and conceptual bases might be equally or more useful.

This chapter examines one such approach, the *rights-approach*, and one such concept, the notion of dignity, as a basis for privacy in the workplace (Isajiw 2001, Rothstein 2000). The *rights-approach* focuses on the dignity and right to private life that is afforded every human being. Such rights can be balanced against other interests in the workplace but can never be fully ignored. Employees are therefore entitled to some minimal standard of dignity, privacy, and a private life even while working and using workplace resources, similar to their entitlement to other minimal standards, such as minimum wages and health and safety standards.

I open with a discussion of dignity and its implications for the idea of privacy, followed by a discussion of the dignity of workers in the second section of this chapter. In the third and main section, I draw on the excellent comparative qualitative research already completed on workplace privacy as well as on the excellent comparative quantitative work done on worldwide privacy protection by the Globalization of Personal Data (GPD) project. The GPD survey provides cross-jurisdictional data that can be analyzed to determine whether dignity as a conceptual basis for workplace privacy is prevalent within each of the jurisdictions included within the project and whether there exists a global approach to privacy in the workplace. These results can then be compared with qualitative information – in the form of case law, statutes, and labour arbitration decisions – that exists with respect to the countries surveyed. The jurisdictions included in this chapter, for which both qualitative and quantitative information is available, are Canada, the United States, Brazil, Mexico, France, Spain, Hungary, and China. Finally, the chapter considers whether, on the basis of the comparative work done, dignity is a concept that illuminates workplace privacy and, if so, to what extent.

PRIVACY AS THE PROTECTION OF DIGNITY

An analysis of such a conceptual basis for privacy attempts to determine what societal values are upheld by means of the protection of privacy. Few doubt that privacy, as important a value as it may be, ultimately serves other, more important values. As the subsequent discussion demonstrates, one such value is dignity, yet there are of course others, such as liberty and autonomy.[2] For example, American privacy protection seems to focus on protecting liberty, whereas European privacy protection seems to focus on protecting dignity (Levin and Nicholson 2005, Whitman 2004). As a fundamental value, dignity is susceptible to harms by means other than privacy, which is why some (e.g., Rothstein 2000) prefer to distinguish between privacy and dignity.

The origins of the idea that privacy protection is the protection of dignity can be traced back to a seminal article by Louis Brandeis and Samuel Warren, "The Right to Privacy" (1890). Their justification for privacy protection is the protection of an individual's dignity, sense of self-worth, social standing, reputation, desire to avoid scrutiny, desire to avoid unnecessary humiliation, and identity. Understood and defined in such a manner, dignity is first and foremost a social value, conceptually distinct from other values that privacy may protect, such as an individual's liberty. The protection of dignity is the protection of a certain social status and subsequently of certain relevant social norms, although this status and these norms may vary from one society to another. Therefore, an individual's dignity does not necessarily suffer from government actions as much as it potentially suffers from the thoughts and perceptions of other members of society, and if the goal of privacy protection is ultimately the protection of dignity, it is clear that privacy must be protected within society first and from government later. To some degree, of course, an erosion of liberties will result ultimately in the erosion of dignity, and to this extent government intrusions will be worrisome even for those concerned primarily with the protection of dignity. For example, the current draft of the European Constitution states that the European Union is founded on the value of human dignity (EU Draft Constitution, § 1–2) and that the EU Charter of Rights is founded on the value of human dignity (EU Draft Constitution, Preamble to part 2). The Constitution devotes an entire title within that charter to dignity (EU Draft Constitution, part 2, title 1, § 2–67 and § 2–68). Last but not least, the EU Charter of Rights devotes a title to solidarity, and within that title the right of workers to dignity is enshrined as well (EU Draft Constitution, § 2–91[1]).

THE DIGNITY OF WORKERS

To understand privacy as the protection of dignity in the workplace, it is first important to understand the meaning of dignity in the workplace. All the jurisdictions discussed below recognize in some form that there can be a distinction for legal purposes between, on the one hand, a person who performs some work for pay for another person and, on the other, a person who is in the employment of another person. There are legal obligations that arise only when an employment relationship exists, such as (in certain jurisdictions) a minimum wage; others, such as health and safety obligations, exist at all times. All of these arguably contribute to the dignity of employees, and when such standards do not exist or when they exist in a diminished form (e.g., when workers and employers can largely "contract out" of these standards), the dignity of employees is diminished as well. Viewing workplace privacy as a potential addition to current employment standards raises several important questions. For example, should a privacy standard be one that employer and workers are able to contract out of (Gomez-Arostegui 2005, Oliver 2002), or does it exist at all times, similar to health and safety obligations?

I argue that the obligation of one person to respect another's dignity is based on a premise that dignity is a value respected between members of society regardless of either their social status or the contractual or employment relations they have with each other. For this reason, I shall refer to the dignity of *workers*, a term broad enough to capture all of employment law's nuances. All workers are owed some measure of dignity while performing their tasks, which emanates not necessarily from their work but from their status as members of a society that respects them as individuals. Indeed, it seems that in the context of employment, employees often struggle to maintain the dignity that is inherently theirs as human beings.

Dignity entitles workers, first and foremost, to the recognition that their persona as a worker is to be kept distinct from other aspects of their lives and that other aspects of their lives are to be kept distinct from their work and unknown to their employer (Fisk 2006). However, the concession that workers "have a life" outside of work is one that is often difficult for employers to make. Indeed, many of the measures introduced into the workplace thanks to technological advancement and employer initiative are indeed privacy-invasive since they blur the distinction between work persona and private life and in so doing harm dignity. What is entailed, therefore, by the notion of dignity in the workplace, protected by privacy, is the understanding that such measures are to be used in a way that will limit the intrusion of employers into the lives of their workers. This conclusion, arrived at from a legal perspective, is supported by management control theory as well (Zweig et al. 2006). The golden mean, according to David Zweig and colleagues, is a level of monitoring and surveillance that allows employees and employer to maintain a level of trust and respect (2006, 10). Indeed, research has shown that employers who are leaders in terms of workplace privacy measures identify trust as a crucial component of their relationship with their employees (Levin et al. 2006).

It is important to verify next whether the notion of dignity is helpful in illuminating the different ways that workers enjoy privacy, to a greater or lesser degree, across several jurisdictions. The following section discusses workplace privacy protection in several jurisdictions for which GPD data exist, as well as some qualitative information, including leading case law on this topic.[3]

WORKPLACE PRIVACY PROTECTION

Each section below dedicated to a distinct jurisdiction focuses on the two forms of surveillance addressed in the GPD survey: monitoring of e-mails and video surveillance (GPD 2006). The relevant questions from the GPD survey are questions 21 and 22 (see the appendix to this volume). The four possible responses to question 21 were:

1 Yes, it is the right of the employer under any circumstance.
2 Yes, but only for the purpose of evaluating employee's performance.
3 Yes, but only if the employee gives informed consent to be monitored.
4 No, under no circumstances should an employer monitor their employees.

The four (similar to the above) responses to question 22 were:

1 Yes, it is the employers' right under any circumstance.
2 Yes, if the employee is suspected of wrong-doing.
3 Yes, as long as the employer has the expressed consent of the employees.
4 No, under no circumstances should an employer share information about employees.

For both sets of answers, based on the discussion of the notion of dignity above, answers 3 and 4 reflect the *rights-approach*, or a perception that workplace privacy is based on dignity, whereas answers 1 and 2 reflect the *property-approach*, or a perception that workplace privacy is based on the "reasonable expectations" of employees. The responses of participants who refused to answer or did not know the answer were discarded for the purposes of this chapter.

The European Union

As mentioned, excellent qualitative work has already been done reviewing workplace privacy protection in the EU and comparing it to other jurisdictions (*Comparative Labor Law and Policy Journal* 23 2002, Alvim and Filho 2002, Nouwt et al. 2005). Within the EU, the status of dignity as a right to which workers are entitled is well entrenched in EU legislation, member-state legislation, and the resulting case law and labour tribunal decisions. Some member-states already have a constitutional right to personal information protection (Cannataci and Mifsud-Bonnic 2005, 7–8). The EU Privacy Directive and the corresponding member-state legislation do not presently apply to the actions of surveillance directly. Rather, they apply indirectly, because of the processing of the information produced by the different forms of surveillance (Article 29 2001). It is this processing that falls under the jurisdiction of the directive, not the act of surveillance itself.

France

France is a bastion of workplace privacy. The right to a private life is protected in France through article 8 of the EU Convention on Human Rights and through article 9 of the French Civil Code. This right has been implemented into strong workplace privacy protection through the French Labour Code (Vigneau 2002a). Article L.121–8 of the Labour Code prohibits the collection of worker information without prior notification. Article L.120–2 further establishes that surveillance and monitoring must be proportional to, and justified by, their purpose. Additional Labour Code articles require that all actions taken by the employer are to be taken in good faith and in consultation with the workers' representative (e.g., a trade union) (Aranda 2002b; French Labour Code, articles L.122–35 and L.432–2–1). These articles establish that surveillance must be transparent, proportional, and justified (or relevant), and many jurisdictions have attempted to implement these three principles within their system of privacy protection (Eltis 2004).

The leading workplace privacy case is the Supreme Court's "Nikon Case" (Arrêt 4164 2001), according to which employers are not allowed to read employees' private e-mail (or other correspondence) even if the e-mail is sent using employer resources and even if the act of using employer resources for private purposes is in violation of an employer's policy. This decision, despite awarding employees with strong protection, has left employers somewhat at a loss since employers are allowed to discipline employees for forbidden use of employer resources provided that the discipline is proportional to the harm caused by the unauthorized use. The Supreme Court stated that workers have a right to a private life even in the workplace (although there is no such explicit right in the French Labour Code).

Surveillance is therefore justified in the workplace when it serves the employment relationship (i.e., when it is conducted for the purposes of assessing and evaluating employees). Workers must of course be notified and consent to the surveillance, in line with the principle of transparency, but it is clear that even the requirement that surveillance be justified prohibits surveillance in areas of the workplace that are unrelated to employee evaluation, such as lockers and washrooms. Further, due to the implementation of France's information protection legislation in line with the EU Privacy Directive, workers' personal information is subject to additional restrictions even if the employer collects it in a transparent and proportional manner and for a justifiable purpose. For example, information can be kept only for a period of time that is appropriate to the purpose for which it has been collected.

The Social Chamber of the French Supreme Court has ruled that unless workers are notified and consent to the use of surveillance equipment for the purpose of their evaluation, which could lead to their termination, the information collected by such means cannot serve as the basis for their dismissal (Vigneau 2002a, 372–3). As a result, employers have been put in the position where their surveillance activities are secondary to the protection of worker rights, although even French law recognizes both the legitimate purposes that surveillance in the workplace can serve and that employers do have property rights in the resources and systems used by their employees.[4]

GPD survey results for France (GPD 2006) are presented in table 17.1, together with the total support per question for either the *rights-approach* or the *property-approach*. The quantitative results of the GPD survey overwhelmingly support the qualitative conclusion that workplace privacy in France is based on the dignity of workers rather than on their reasonable expectations of privacy.

Spain

The Spanish Workers' Statute was passed before the forms of surveillance discussed in this chapter became prevalent. As a result, it does not explicitly address (or forbid) new forms of monitoring (Aranda 2002a, 440). Similarly, Spain's Information Protection Agency has ruled that Spain's information protection legislation does not completely prohibit surveillance and monitoring but allows it within limits (Flint 2004). It has been left up to Spain's courts and tribunals to find these limits and to strike a balance between employers and workers, surveillance and dignity.

Generally, Catalonian courts have adopted a North American tack (Reinhard 2002, 528). Most notably, in what is known in Spain as the Deutsche Bank case, the Catalonian court upheld the dismissal of an

Table 17.1
GPD survey results for questions 21 and 22 (%)

Question	Response	Jurisdiction							
		France	Spain	Hungary	Brazil	Mexico	Canada	US	China
21a (closed circuit television)	1	3.6	7.5	12.0	21.1	13.8	16.7	26.9	3.7
	2	5.5	20.0	14.7	24.0	39.8	16.7	17.3	14.5
	Property	9.1	27.5	26.7	45.1	53.6	33.4	44.2	18.2
	3	31.7	23.2	37.5	24.3	23.5	36.8	29.5	31.0
	4	56.2	47.5	30.8	27.3	20.6	22.0	15.9	49.9
	Rights	87.9	70.7	68.3	51.6	44.1	58.8	45.4	80.9
21b (e-mails)	1	4.5	5.9	7.3	11.3	5.6	19.6	27.0	3.1
	2	5.0	10.7	9.5	9.9	12.3	11.8	14.6	6.2
	Property	9.5	16.6	16.8	21.2	17.9	31.4	41.6	9.3
	3	30.1	22.3	34.4	24.4	30.6	30.9	27.4	25.6
	4	57.2	58.3	43.7	47.6	48.2	30.8	21.9	63.6
	Rights	87.3	80.6	78.1	72.0	78.8	61.7	49.3	89.2
22a (government)	1	2.9	7.3	16.1	11.7	7.3	6.3	6.3	2.7
	2	36.2	29.6	34.7	27.1	33.5	35.8	39.7	19.3
	Property	39.1	36.9	50.8	38.8	40.8	42.1	46.0	22.0
	3	23.5	22.3	28.0	27.0	28.8	33.4	25.1	46.3
	4	32.5	36.1	16.3	29.6	26.9	18.2	20.7	30.7
	Rights	56.0	58.4	44.3	56.6	55.7	51.6	45.8	77.0
22b (private sector)	1	0.8	3.7	1.1	9.9	4.0	1.7	1.7	3.3
	2	19.1	12.5	13.7	20.8	19.6	17.7	20.4	11.0
	Property	19.9	16.2	14.8	30.7	23.6	19.4	22.1	14.3
	3	24.2	21.3	35.3	26.8	35.6	34.4	28.6	47.7
	4	51.5	59.8	46.4	37.7	36.9	39.9	42.1	36.8
	Rights	75.7	81.1	81.7	64.5	72.5	74.3	70.7	84.5

employee who sent hundreds of personal e-mails from work (Flint 2004, 316). On the other hand, the Barcelona Employment Tribunal set aside the dismissal of an employee who inadvertently infected the employer's system with viruses due to personal e-mail and Internet use (Flint 2004, 318). Given that so far only one Spanish Supreme Court decision related to workplace privacy has confirmed that employers have propriety rights in information systems (Aranda 2002a; Flint 2004, 319), it remains to be seen where Spain will find the balance between workers and employers.[5] GPD survey results for Spain are presented in table 17.1. The quantitative results reflect the perception that Spain incorporates to a greater extent than other EU member-states the *property-approach*. Generally, the distinctions between member-states are insignificant compared with an overall adoption of dignity as a basis for workplace privacy throughout the EU.

Hungary

Hungary has been one of the first countries in the former Eastern Europe to embrace the ideals of freedom of information and personal information protection. Workplace privacy has been shaped in Hungary by these ideals, with a focus on the rights of government employees to be protected from requests for their personal information by the public.

Article 59 of the Hungarian Constitution states that Hungarians have the right to the protection of their reputation (i.e., dignity) and of their privacy (Székely and Szabo 2005, 253). Currently, however, no legislation or provisions within labour-related legislation exist with respect to workplace privacy; as a result, there is presently no case-law with respect to workplace privacy (255). Rather, employers and employees are guided by findings issued by Hungary's privacy commissioner, many of which focus on the presence of employee consent, whether explicitly or implicitly, as the test for whether workplace surveillance is lawful (263–5). Currently, it appears the commissioner is moving away from enforcement of the Data Protection and Freedom of Information Act and toward applying a standard of "reasonableness" to the conduct of employers (282).[6]

GPD survey results for Hungary are presented in table 17.1. The Hungarian results reflect strong support for, or perhaps acceptance of, the disclosure of personal information to government, which may be a product of Hungary's relatively recent democratic history.

Table 17.2 demonstrates the overall close affinity within Europe regarding the *rights-approach*. As the table demonstrates and as is demonstrated in graphic form by GPD figure 17(a) (online),[7] there is more support within Hungary and Spain for the notion that the employer is free to use workplace resources for surveillance than there is within France. Overall, however, there is hardly any doubt that Europeans view workplace privacy as based on the dignity of employees.

Asia – China

China does not currently have information protection legislation, although such legislation is currently being drafted by China's new Ministry of Industry and Information (Greenleaf 2008). China does offer constitutional protection for the dignity of Chinese citizens (Chinese Constitution, article 38). Caution must be taken, however, so as not to analyze privacy protection in China through a narrow, legalistic, and perhaps misleading perspective. A thorough analysis of the status of privacy protection in China, and in the Chinese workplace in particular, is well beyond the scope of this chapter. It is not at all clear whether the *property-approach* and *rights-approach*, both of which rely on a common bedrock of a liberal-democratic political and economic system, are relevant to the Chinese workplace. It is interesting to note, however, that the GPD project was able to conduct a survey of privacy within China.

GPD survey results for China are presented in table 17.1. The results portray China as a bastion of workplace privacy and of the *rights-approach* in particular, on par with, if not surpassing, some of the EU member-states surveyed. However, it is clear that the Chinese results require much more of a careful and nuanced analysis before any conclusions with respect to the existence, let alone the strength, of the *rights-approach* versus the *property-approach* are formed.[8]

South America – Brazil

Comparisons of Canadian or American jurisprudence often tend to focus on the European Union or on other common-law jurisdictions. It is therefore quite helpful to be able to incorporate the research done within Brazil on workplace privacy, particularly in terms of establishing the degree to which dignity can indeed be viewed as a universal human right in the context of the employment relationship.

An encouraging starting point in the search for dignity as a universal value is the Brazilian Constitution. The Constitution states that Brazil is founded on "the dignity of the human person" (title 1) and goes on to expound on the obligations of the state to ensure the dignity of its citizens (title 7–1, § 170; title 8–7, § 227). The Constitution further establishes individual rights to privacy, private life, honour, and image (title 2, chapter 1, § 5–10) and declares the secrecy of correspondence of data and telephone communications (among others) "inviolable" (title 2, chapter 1, § 5–12). Finally, the Constitution creates both an individual right to *habeas data*, which allows individuals access to information, and a right to correct information about themselves that is held by government or other public bodies (title 2, chapter 1, § 5–72). Interestingly, although the Constitution includes a long list of social rights in the workplace, neither the right to privacy nor the right to dignity is included (title 2, chapter 2, § 7). The Brazilian Constitution is more similar to the Mexican Constitution than to the American or Canadian constitutions. From the perspective of Brazilian privacy advocates, these additional constitutional terms are invaluable since Brazil has, up until now, not passed information protection legislation.

Brazilian case law reflects both the contextual interpretation of key values such as dignity and the paramountcy of Brazil's Constitution. Even in instances where employees are notified of and/or consent to surveillance and where the employer monitors employees in accordance with the measures to which they have consented, courts have attempted to find a balance between the constitutional right to privacy and the practical consent to surveillance (Alvim and Filho 2002, 290). In other words, workers cannot contract out of their constitutional right to privacy.

As to the ultimate protection awarded to workers on the basis of such values as dignity (deemed constitutional values in Brazil), it is perhaps a sobering realization for North American advocates of dignity in the workplace that Brazilian workers in many industries have to undergo physical searches on a daily basis as they leave work (although such searches are known in some industries in North America). Brazilian case law has evolved to accommodate both the reality of physical searches and the constitutional right to dignity (Alvim and Filho 2002, 290–1).

GPD survey results for Brazil are presented in table 17.1. One immediate conclusion from these results is the clear distinction within Brazil between the use of video cameras in the workplace and the monitoring of e-mails. Use of surveillance cameras is viewed far more as the employer's prerogative than is the monitoring of e-mails. This distinction could be based perhaps on the ubiquity of video cameras in Brazil due to personal safety and security concerns. Coupled with the different cultural context that the value of dignity takes on in Brazil, the GPD survey results indicate that a representation of the European value of dignity as the foundation of workplace privacy worldwide is perhaps an oversimplification.

North America

The development of workplace privacy in both Canada and Mexico has been influenced by US conceptions and by the North American Free Trade Agreement. Canada has resisted US influence somewhat more so than Mexico and is attempting to forge a conceptual middle ground between the US and the EU perceptions of workplace privacy. Mexico is devoid of any meaningful privacy protection, as can be discerned from the following short overview.

Mexico

In the Mexican Constitution, there is no mention of an explicit right either to privacy or to dignity, nor is there protection from privacy invasive measures in the workplace, despite an extensive section in the Constitution dedicated to labour (title 6). The personal information of Mexican citizens and workers is not protected by Mexican law. Workers are prohibited by article 135 of the Federal Labor Act from using the employer's resources for any purpose other than those intended by the employer, and employers have inserted explicit terms into their contracts of employment in which workers consent to whatever measures of monitoring and surveillance the employer intends to use (Vargas 2004, 119). This situation can be attributed to the availability of workers and the lack of government regulation.[9]

GPD survey results for Mexico are presented in table 17.1. The Mexican results indicate the similarity between Mexico and Brazil in the conceptualization of workplace privacy, which appears to be based on cultural similarities rather than on legislative or judicial similarities, as Brazil has some personal information protection built into its Constitution, whereas Mexico does not (both countries lack personal information protection legislation). As with the Brazilian results, although there is overall support for the *rights-approach*, the Mexican results appear to strengthen the conclusion that the European value of dignity is not a universal one.

Canada

Canada occupies a middle ground between the two poles of the US and the EU approaches to privacy (Levin and Nicholson 2005). Canadian federal information protection legislation in the form of the Personal Information Protection and Electronic Documents Act (PIPEDA) applies only to those workers who fall under federal jurisdiction. Canada, therefore, is unlike the European Union in this respect since the EU Privacy Directive has been found to apply to the workplace and has been implemented by the various member-states. Canada is also unlike the European Union since its Constitution does not include an explicit right to dignity or to a private life.

The Canadian provinces have been largely left to their own devices with respect to regulation of workplace privacy. Quebec, British Columbia, and Alberta all have in place such legislation. The legislation of the western provinces permits employers to collect, use, and disclose personal information on workers as long as the collection, use, and disclosure are reasonable (Personal Information Protection Act [PIPA], §§ 15, 18, 21 [AB], §§ 13, 16, 19 [BC]). In other words, the legislation does not base the protection of workplace privacy on dignity. Quebec's legislation, however, at all its levels, is based on the protection of a person's private life.[10] It is therefore difficult to establish a common ground among all provinces: some tend to follow the US approach, but Quebec quite naturally draws upon the EU (French) approach to workplace privacy.[11]

Canadian privacy commissioners (federal and provincial) have issued few findings on workplace privacy specifically. The most significant case was about the installation of video surveillance cameras in the workplace. The case established a four-part test to determine whether surveillance was reasonable: "Is the measure demonstrably necessary to meet a specific need? Is it likely to be effective in meeting that need? Is the loss of privacy proportional to the benefit gained? Is there a less privacy-invasive way of achieving the same end?" (*Eastmond v. Canadian Pacific Railway* 2004). The privacy commissioner has issued other findings since this ruling, which are significant since they specifically address the need to balance employer concerns with worker dignity (Office of the Privacy Commissioner of Canada 2006).[12]

GPD survey results for Canada are presented in table 17.1. There is support in Canada for both the *rights-approach* and the *property-approach*, although overall the majority of Canadians perceive the dignity of workers, rather than reasonable expectations, to be the foundation for their privacy in the workplace. Levels of support for the *rights-approach*, however, are lower than they are in any of the EU member-states surveyed.

The United States

In the US Constitution, there is no mention of an explicit right to dignity, privacy, or a private life (but see California Constitution, § 1[1];

Reinhard 2002). Workers in the public sector enjoy some protection through the Fourth, Fourteenth, and at times First Amendments, yet it is worth recalling that these constitutional protections boil down to a test of whether the workers had reasonable expectations of privacy. For example, a court in Ohio decided that school janitors had no reasonable expectation of privacy in their break room (*Brannen v. Kings* 2001; Mawdsley 2004). The United States also does not have comprehensive federal workplace privacy legislation. Several states, among them Connecticut, Delaware, Indiana, and Illinois, have legislation on particular workplace privacy issues, such as disclosure of personnel records or the requirement to notify workers of monitoring and surveillance. West Virginia, for example, either restricts electronic surveillance, particularly video surveillance, or forbids it outright, regardless of its stated purpose, if it is carried out "in areas designed for the health or personal comfort of the employees or for safeguarding of their possessions, such as rest rooms, shower rooms, locker rooms, dressing rooms and employee lounges" (West Virginia Code, § 21–3–20).

This remarkable piece of legislation appears to do away with the US common-law requirement of reasonable expectations of privacy and appears to provide privacy to workers based on their right as individuals to dignity. West Virginia, however, is the exception to the rule. On the whole, there is no workplace privacy legislation at the state level in the United States (Faleri 2002), which contributes to widespread surveillance and monitoring in US workplaces (American Management Association 2005).

Little reported case law exists with respect to workplace privacy in the United States. The most significant case to date to offer direction to US employers has been *Smyth v. Pillsbury*, and it is significant since the court found that a worker had no reasonable expectation of privacy even though the employer had a policy in force stating that workers would not be terminated on the basis of their e-mails. Although ten years have passed since the trial court decision, it has not been appealed, nor has it been overturned or its scope narrowed in the few subsequent cases (see, e.g., *Garrity v. John Hancock* 2002; *Thygeson v. US Bancorp* 2004).

GPD survey results for the United States are presented in table 17.1. The United States is the jurisdiction with the strongest support for the *property-approach*. GPD table 17(a) (online) demonstrates the distinctions within the Americas. As shown in table 17.2 and in GPD figure 17(b) (online), Canada and the United States do not demonstrate the same distinction between video surveillance and e-mail monitoring that is

Table 17.2
Comparison of privacy approaches of the European Union, the Americas, and China (%)

	Video surveillance		E-mail monitoring		Disclosure to government		Disclosure to private sector	
	Property	Rights	Property	Rights	Property	Rights	Property	Rights
Americas	44.3	49.5	28	65.5	41.9	52.4	24	70.6
Americas without US	44.4	50.8	23.5	70.8	40.5	54.6	24.5	70.4
European Union	21.1	75.6	14.3	82	42.3	52.9	17	79.5
China	18.2	80.9	9.3	89.2	22.0	77.0	14.3	84.5

evident in Mexico and Brazil. Overall, support levels for the *rights-approach* over the *property-approach* are lower within the Americas than they are within the European Union, as table 17.2 demonstrates.

CONCLUSION

A remarkable fit exists between the results of the GPD survey and the qualitative information available with respect to each of the surveyed jurisdictions, with the exception of China. The survey results consistently support the tentative conclusions made based on the qualitative information with respect to the existence and the strength of the *rights-approach* and the *property-approach* within each of the other jurisdictions. Nevertheless, the survey results do not support several assumptions about comparisons between jurisdictions, notably about the strength and universality of the *rights-approach* to workplace privacy and about the uniformity with which the various methods of surveillance and monitoring are treated by case law and legislation within jurisdictions. A more accurate conclusion based on the empirical survey results as well as on case law and legislation would be that the European Union is a relative bastion of the *rights-approach* and of dignity as the foundation of workplace privacy (Reinhard 2002). Although the *rights-approach* may end up as the foundation of workplace privacy in other jurisdictions, it is probably premature to conclude that it is fulfilling that role presently and certainly premature to conclude that the *rights-approach* and the notions of dignity and a private life have consistent meaning beyond the jurisdiction of the European Union.

Basing workplace privacy on dignity provides for personal information protection that is much more robust than the alternative of reasonable expectations. Workplace privacy could be protected – in a manner similar, for example, to that seen with health and safety – via a joint committee. Alternatively, organized labour could advocate for the introduction of new legislative minimal employment standards that would prohibit certain forms of intrusion as excessive, similar to that of West Virginia, mentioned above (West Virginia Code, § 21-3-20). However, due to the fractured nature of the labour movement in the United States, it is unclear whether the US labour movement will have the bargaining power to play any substantive role in workplace privacy protection.[13]

Another suggestion, and perhaps a more promising one, is for the independent privacy overseeing bodies (the various commissions) to take a more active role in the protection of workplace privacy on the basis of their mandate to govern information privacy, as they appear to have done in the European Union (Bignami 2005). Although this suggestion would not go far in the United States, where there is currently no such body, and only a remote chance that such a body would be created in the future, it might be more appealing to those jurisdictions that already have a Privacy Commission in place. A privacy commissioner could afford to take an objective, consistent, and principled approach to workplace privacy, balancing the employer's purposes that justify surveillance and monitoring with the worker's right to a private life by examining whether the proposed surveillance is both relevant and proportional to the purposes it is purported to achieve (Vigneau 2002b). The Canadian federal privacy commissioner, and subsequently the Canadian Federal Court, adopted exactly this approach in the *Eastmond* case and in subsequent findings discussed above, and it has been advocated for England as well (Oliver 2002, 350–2).

This chapter enquires whether the notion of dignity is at the foundation of workplace privacy protection worldwide. The answer, based on the results of the GPD survey, is that it is not. At the same time, dignity maintains a strong empirical foothold in all jurisdictions, cultural and social distinctions notwithstanding, and it has been advocated as a strong and coherent basis for the protection of workers and their privacy. The historical development of employment and labour law has increasingly moved away from a contractual basis and toward recognition of individual rights such as dignity. The time has come for dignity to manifest itself in the area of workplace privacy as well.

NOTES

1 For a critique of Peter Swire's (2004) opinion that *Katz* should best be understood as establishing a "reasonable expectations" test and that perhaps better privacy protection could be achieved by legislative means, as well as a critique of Swire's ensuing discussion, see Colb (2004) and Kerr (2004a, 2004b).

2 For a detailed list of values, see Koops and Leenes (2005).

3 Many complaints never evolve into formal legal disputes or are resolved through labour arbitration (Reinhard 2002, 529).

4 For more discussion of privacy in France, see Ayse Ceyhan's chapter in this volume.

5 For more discussion of survey results in Spain, see Jeffrey Roy's chapter in this volume.

6 For more discussion of survey results in Hungary, see Iván Székely's chapter in this volume.

7 All GPD tables and figures cited in this chapter are online at http://www.sscqueens.org/book_tables (accessed 23 November 2009).

8 For analysis of results in China, see Elia Zureik's chapter in this volume.

9 For more discussion of survey results in Mexico, see Nelson Arteaga Botello's chapter in this volume.

10 The Quebec Charter of Rights and Freedoms applies to the private sector and includes a right to a private life (§ 5). Furthermore, under the Quebec Civil Code, not only does every person have a right to privacy (established in "Chapter III: Respect of Reputation and Privacy"), but employers must also respect the health, safety, and dignity of employees (§ 2087).

11 For an analysis of survey findings in Quebec, see François Fournier's chapter in this volume.

12 For a comparison of Canada's PIPEDA legislation to private-sector privacy laws in other countries in the survey, see Arthur Cockfield's chapter in this volume.

13 Another suggestion is that employers (acting as principals) and workers (acting as agents) may reach an agreement to the benefit of both parties regarding workplace privacy (Kesan 2002, 322–30); however, it is difficult to determine how exactly individual workers would obtain the necessary bargaining power.

PART 5

Conclusions

18

Cross-Cultural Study of Surveillance and Privacy: Theoretical and Empirical Observations

ELIA ZUREIK

The chapters in this volume confirm certain known findings about privacy and surveillance research, highlight differences from other findings, and present fresh insights for the comparative study of privacy and surveillance. Theoretical and methodological concerns are key in cross-cultural research, particularly when investigating an abstract notion such as privacy. With regard to the countries covered in the Globalization of Personal Data (GPD) study, research on surveillance and privacy received more attention in the industrialized countries (i.e., the United States and Canada), less in other western European countries (i.e., France and Spain), and substantially less in countries whose entry into the world of information and communication technologies generally – and of privacy specifically – is rather recent (i.e., Hungary, Mexico, Brazil, and China).

Cross-cultural differences presented challenges on several fronts. These included the design of a common research instrument for use in the eight countries of the GPD study, capturing the meaning and significance of privacy in different national settings, and the actual interpretation of the data. Since we did not have a frame of reference to fall back on when interpreting the data collected from nearly 9,000 respondents, we had to chart virgin territory and try to capture the significance and meaning of privacy in each country. We did this by contextualizing the data and noting important cultural and historic experiences that characterize the eight countries. At the outset of our research, we were mindful of the fact that issues pertaining to personal data are not exhausted by referring to privacy issues alone. The uses of personal data carry implications that we have hardly begun to understand, and ours is the first survey that even attempts to investigate them. Much of our special methodology, discussed in several chapters, was geared to "going beyond" privacy.

A leading aim of the survey was to "go beyond" privacy discourses in order to really start exploring both the social meanings of proliferating personal data, as understood through public opinion polling, and the implications for surveillance and loss of privacy.

I begin my discussion of the conclusions by highlighting the importance of privacy in the context of differing cultural and political experiences. I then consider the efforts to use the GPD findings for theory testing, the privacy of consumers and workers, and the debate over ID cards. The chapter ends with observations regarding the comparative study of privacy and surveillance.

HOW IMPORTANT IS PRIVACY?

It must be said that, as an individual concern, privacy is not an issue that dominates people's lives – not in the sense that academics, theorists, and even privacy advocates talk about it. It is only when privacy is brought to the level of daily experience in cases involving credit and identity fraud and violation of individual rights through surveillance that people become aware of the importance of privacy and express the need for its protection.

Several dimensions characterize attitudes to privacy among the respondents in the GPD study. First, there is the cultural factor, which reflects collectivist orientations in some countries and individualist ones in others. For example, respondents' attitudes to privacy in China, Brazil, Mexico, and to some extent Spain have been shaped by traditional societal orientations, with the effect that protection of individual privacy does not loom large in the minds of respondents. In Spain, as in other collectivist societies, privacy is generally regarded as a concern for outgroups as opposed to an issue affecting individual intimate relations, and it is closely tied to values such as honour and control over one's image.

In spite of cultural similarities, local conditions play an important role in shaping the practice of surveillance, as the cases of Mexico and Brazil demonstrate. In his chapter, Nelson Arteaga Botello shows, for example, that the presence of "habeas data" in Brazil's Constitution does not impact the daily lives of Brazilians in a meaningful fashion to ensure privacy protection. In both countries, corruption, authoritarianism, crime, and poverty are accompanied by privacy violations through illegal telephone tapping, video recordings, and identification of certain public behaviour deemed inappropriate. Personal safety is paramount in both countries, which lies behind the contradiction in the data. For example, Arteaga Botello points out that although the GPD survey found that the majority of citizens in both countries consider national security laws to be intrusive, this distrust is overshadowed by citizen demand for greater government control to ensure the protection of property and bodily security. In fact, personal security is regarded as a precondition for privacy, leading to support for surveillance devices such as closed circuit television (CCTV) to safeguard the private sphere. As a result of this prerequisite, security-based privacy is treated as a kind of privilege from which a significant part of the population is excluded. In terms of the four types delineated in the GPD study, it is bodily and spatial privacy rather than informational or communicational privacy that concerns people most. Even when there is formal protection of privacy (as in Brazil), the public lack the means to engage in proactive measures to safeguard their privacy.

An interesting observation made by Arteaga Botello concerns the use of CCTV for reasons other than, if not opposed to, those for which it was originally intended. For example, the police are known to cooperate with criminal gangs by programming the cameras to conceal their crimes. By extension, criminal groups use CCTV to track the movement of police so that they can alert their groups to police actions.

To varying degrees, most of the countries in the GPD study welcome government protection of information privacy, with China putting the greatest amount of trust in the government. The lowest level of trust is seen in the United States, where respondents place a high level of trust in the private sector's capacity to protect privacy – although this attitude may now be undergoing significant change in light of recent revelations about the private sector's excesses and its failure to safeguard the trust of consumers.

Second, if we think of privacy protection on a continuum from high to low government regulation, Canada occupies a middle ground between the US's minimalist position and Europe's position, which tilts in favour of government involvement in regulating privacy protection.

In the United States privacy measures encourage "opt out" clauses, whereas the Canadian legislation stresses "opting in." Opting out puts the responsibility on consumers to declare their desire not to be included in the database; opting in leaves it up to the companies to obtain consumers' consent before sharing their personal information. To a very large extent, this is mirrored in the GPD survey findings. The majority of respondents would approve of the sharing of personal information if they were consulted in advance or if a person was suspected of wrongdoing.

Nearly one-half of the respondents reject outright the sharing of information with third parties, particularly with foreign third parties such as governments and foreign businesses. Overall, the American attitude to privacy is driven more by criteria of market efficiency and less by the desire to protect personal information.

Within Canada there are no significant differences between anglophones and francophones in terms of perceptions of the security of personal information. However, Quebecers are more inclined to report that they experience less privacy now than they did ten years ago. This loss of privacy is tied to factors such as technology and aggressive marketing strategies. Overall, Canadians are reluctant to allow invasions of privacy in their workplace and private lives.

Third, historical factors play a decisive role in shaping attitudes to privacy. In Hungary privacy was not regarded as possible during an oppressive period of communist rule, when the lack of privacy reflected the notion of the transparent citizen and the self-determining state, as opposed to a self-determining citizen and a transparent state.

Finally, historically, France has managed to enshrine the protection of "private life" in its Constitution. Rather than see a causal connection between the events of 11 September 2001 and the need to protect national security at the expense of privacy, French respondents link concerns for security to events taking place in France, such as youth riots near Paris that took place at the time of the survey.

THEORY TESTING

Irrespective of cultural variations, and even though culture plays a determining role in shaping attitudes in general, it is possible to focus on certain cognitive and experiential processes and to test their relevance to understanding privacy orientations. This part of the chapter discusses several attempts made in the volume to test cross-culturally the methods and findings of the GPD survey. In his chapter on surveillance and resistance, Andrew Grenville sets up a model that enables him to partition the multicountry data into three groups: those who are satisfied with current surveillance practices, those who are skeptical about and alienated from the technology altogether, and those who are informed enough to use their knowledge to resist surveillance technologies. These groups are similar, but not identical, to those developed by Alan Westin, whose pioneering work on the United States provides the basis for the chapter by Stephen Margulis and colleagues.

In Grenville's chapter, the mediating factors that give rise to the three segmented groups are: (1) knowledge of the technology, (2) awareness of being monitored, (3) level of trust that the government and private sectors respect people's privacy, and (4) one's control over personal information. These factors behave sequentially, with knowledge affecting experience, which in turn impacts trust and, finally, control of personal information. Resistance, the dependent variable in the model, is measured by assessing whether respondents provide information, refuse to provide information, or intentionally provide false information to private- or public-sector organizations. Regardless of the country, these predictive factors correlate with each other, with the exception of the control factor (i.e., the extent to which people feel they have control over their personal information).

One can argue that this exception is due to the varied meanings that people across cultures give to "control." For example, the chapter by Andrey Pavlov demonstrates that there is an element of cultural relativity in the definition of abstract concepts such as one's control over personal information. The meaning of "complete" or "a lot of" control over personal information varies by country, depending on its culture and political experience. Thus it is possible to weigh the cultural factor by comparing self-assessment in the responses to the survey questions against a hypothetical individual in vignettes designed for the GPD study. In response to the self-assessment questions, three-quarters of the Chinese participants indicate they have "a lot of" or "complete" say over personal information relative to other countries, significantly higher than in Canada and the United States. Can one conclude from these self-assessments that people in China actually have considerably more control over their personal information than do respondents from other countries? The vignettes used in Pavlov's chapter show that Chinese respondents' answers remain fairly high on all the vignettes, including those that clearly present people as having little control over information. The implication is that standards for what constitutes control in China are different, and thus the issue needs to be explored in further research. In his chapter, Pavlov uses a novel technique of model building to correct for the gap between self-assessment and assessment of others in the vignettes.

Although the GPD survey did not include items identical to the four items used in the Harris-Westin Index, there were eleven items in the GPD survey that allowed for "conceptual replication" and thus for assessment of their correlation with the Harris-Westin privacy concern index. Of the five factors that eventually emerged from the analysis of the GPD data, one factor – common to both the United States and Canada – came close to the Harris-Westin Index; the other four did not. This led Margulis and colleagues to remark that "privacy concerns are culturally specific." Equally important, the analysis of the GPD survey found that privacy concerns among the public in the United States and Canada, the two countries for which comparable data are available, are more comprehensive and go beyond the sorts of concerns covered by the four Harris-Westin items. Regarding the role of government in protecting privacy rights, the US respondents put more weight on individuals to secure such protection, whereas Canadian respondents saw a role for the government in this regard. In both countries, low levels of knowledge about privacy laws were found to correlate with perceived low levels of control over personal information.

In his chapter's examination of the Hungarian data, Iván Székely contrasts privacy attitudes in 1989, based on a survey in which Székely was involved, with the 2006 GPD survey. Although the questions used in 1989 were not identical to those used in the 2006 GPD survey, Székely was able to draw useful contrasts that highlight the evolution of privacy in Hungary. The levels of disobedience and resistance to privacy invasions were similar in the surveys of 1989 and 2006, with 8% in both surveys refusing to provide personal information to officials. Between one-third and one-half of the respondents in both surveys were willing to sacrifice information privacy for law and order and for security.

The centrepiece of Székely's analysis is to explain why Hungary presented results in both 1989 and 2006 that reflect "extreme values" compared to other countries. By extreme values, he means the tendency for Hungarians to be in the forefront of either accepting privacy invasion measures (e.g., surveillance in the workplace, data sharing, CCTV, national ID cards, and consumer profiling) or showing the lowest score for knowledge about privacy issues (e.g., laws and the Internet) and for activity to protect personal information. The explanation he offers for this tendency relates to the "new capitalism" that has swept Hungary since the collapse of the Soviet Union. This change has ushered in (1) concern for personal career and power and disregard for others, (2) lack of familiarity with data processing technologies, (3) the spread of multinational companies that use surveillance technologies in the workplace, and (4) a political culture that pays lip service to individual rights for its own political ends.

Another seeming contradiction with which Székely grapples concerns the differing results offered by the qualitative and quantitative data collected by the GPD survey. The quantitative data present a docile image of Hungarians with regard to privacy rights, as discussed above. However, the focus group interviews present more nuanced data showing informed attitudes, awareness of existing privacy regimes in Hungary, and ways to assert personal privacy rights. Here, he introduces the notion of the "sensitizing context" in reconciling the so-called contradiction. The sensitizing context occurs when the interviewer hones in on the interviewee's personal experience by removing the "threshold of abstraction" and asks the interviewee to react to specific events involving the person in question. He offers the example of a policeman stopping people to inspect their ID cards, to which citizens would object. However, he says, if such screening was carried out through the use of sophisticated "invisible" technologies, such as mobile terminals, there would be less tendency to object to privacy infringements. Thus, he concludes, "if a sensitizing factor makes an 'abstract' violation of privacy visible and understandable, people easily perceive it and react quickly." At the policy level, he calls on civil society to play a role in educating the public about privacy through "the social necessity of mediation." At the level of research, he correctly calls on privacy researchers to turn their attention to studying information technology professionals and data controllers, a focus that is underrepresented in privacy and surveillance research.

CONSUMERS, WORKERS, AND CITIZENS

Although e-commerce has become a central feature of globalization, the implications of the flow and gathering of personal information for privacy are not transparent to the average consumer. Loyalty programs go beyond their declared purpose of drawing customers to buy companies' products. Unknown to most credit card holders, loyalty programs build extensive databases of consumer profiles that are in turn sold for profit. This is done in spite of the fact that most consumers, as shown in this volume, oppose the sharing of personal information with third parties without prior consent. As Jason Pridmore remarks in his chapter, "consumers rarely use proactive privacy protection strategies."

Trust and the existence of pivotal privacy regulatory policies in three Europen Union member-states seem to be crucial factors in enhancing the appeal of online consumption, as demonstrated by Ola Svenonius in his chapter dealing with France, Spain, and Hungary. He shows how, in a country like France where nongovernmental consumer protection organizations exist, online consumers tend to be proactive in protecting their privacy rights. Spain, where municipal and regional arbitration bodies are available to consumers, comes next. Hungary has the weakest consumer protection regime of the three countries.

The workplace is an arena in which surveillance occurs, yet the law is not clear about its legality. In most cases, particularly with regard to e-mail and the use of CCTV, the law sides with employers. The argument is that workers' time and the space in which work occurs are the property of employers, who have the prerogative in deciding how and where workers use their time. Research has shown, however, that workers are not opposed to being monitored in the workplace as long as they are told about it in advance and the evidence is discussed with them. In his chapter on workplace surveillance, Avner Levin distinguishes between employers' attitudes to workplace surveillance in terms of two approaches: the *property-approach* and the *rights-approach*. The former gives employers the right to control the pace of work even if doing so requires surveillance. Workers' privacy is governed by the so-called "reasonable expectation" principle, according to which worker privacy is contingent on employer consent. The *rights-approach*, on the other hand, "focuses on the dignity and right to private life that is afforded every human being." The latter is very close to the EU position, which enshrines the dignity of workers in the EU Charter of Rights. Considering dignity to be a social value and cornerstone of the *rights-approach*, Levin argues that privacy protection is perceived differently in different countries depending on political and cultural factors.

Trust, transparency, quality of service, and information security are the main factors in configuring privacy regimes and determining the success or failure of various e-governance initiatives. The chapter by Jeffrey Roy, which deals with Canada, the United States, and Spain, shows this to be the case. As with e-commerce, high trust contributes to a greater use of e-governance. In Europe the public are more suspicious of the private than the public sector when it comes to privacy guarantees, but in the United States this is reversed. Canada occupies a middle ground between Spain and the United States. The GPD data show that there is greater support for national ID cards in Spain than in Canada and the United States. Using the Maher Arar case as an example, Roy singles out Canada as a complacent society for failing to protest the conduct of the Canadian security agencies in collecting and sharing personal information about Canadian citizens. The lack of oversight and the fact of complacency contribute to "political paralysis" in the innovation of electronic technologies and the management of security services.

In his chapter on the United States, Stephen Marmura highlights the role played by the media in popularizing the view that greater national security comes with less privacy. Surveillance seems not to privilege privacy, let alone to allow for a discussion of the social and political implications of more government intervention in the daily affairs of citizens. The US public have seen the media devote substantially more attention to issues of terrorism than to privacy rights, albeit largely not attention to the root causes of terrorism. Although since 2001 there has been a decline in public support of intrusive surveillance measures by the state, Marmura argues that there remains substantial public tolerance of privacy violations by the government due to media influence.

The attitudinal study of surveillance is usually dominated by a focus on privacy. Methodologically, the GPD survey makes an original contribution to surveillance studies by going beyond the privacy discourse to enquire about peoples' reactions to various surveillance measures encountered at borders and airports and to the way governments and the private sector handle personal information. This volume, in turn, uses these data to examine the sources of respondents' information about privacy and surveillance issues, with particular reference to the role of the media.

Citizen reactions to governments' attempts to introduce national ID cards are examined in two complementary chapters by David Lyon and Emily Smith. Whereas Smith is concerned with Canada, Lyon analyzes the GPD data comparatively, covering the eight countries in the survey. Both chapters single out for scrutiny the pitfalls in the design of survey instruments dealing with a sensitive topic that has government and corporate interests at stake. Governments are interested in national ID cards for political ends, such as managing their populations and keeping track of the movement of people within and across borders; the private sector is interested mainly in the commercial aspects, such as the production and use of the cards. In both instances, issues of privacy and surveillance loom large, particularly in the aftermath of 9/11.

As Lyon points out, with the introduction of "smart cards," embedded with advanced technologies such as biometrics and radio-frequency identification chips, it will be possible to cross-reference personal data with other existing databases in order to carry out profiling of individuals. Privacy considerations would thus be jeopardized, and the national ID card could become a tool of surveillance. Indeed, he argues, it changes "in significant ways the relation between the 'state' and the 'citizen.'"

As stated in several of the book's chapters, and stressed in this conclusion, one of the shortcomings of quantitative large-scale surveys is that the questions asked are not contextualized. The GPD survey attempted to overcome this problem by linking attitudes to national ID cards to other relevant issues. In addition to the central question of whether people agree with the introduction of national ID cards in their country, the GPD survey probed into three other areas revolving around (1) the government's ability to protect information stored in its databases, (2) the government's ability to strike a balance between privacy and enacting laws designed to protect national security, and (3) whether governments should be allowed to share information collected from citizens with third parties, be they foreign governments, other government departments, or the private sector. These three areas centre on citizens' trust in government. Smith and Lyon show that when willingness to endorse the introduction of national ID cards is cross-tabulated with answers to other questions in the survey, those respondents who have low trust in the government's ability to protect against privacy invasion are reluctant to accept the introduction of electronic national ID cards. In the words of Smith, "an interesting finding of the GPD survey is that citizen trust in government can be used as a predictor of whether Canadians will support the introduction of a government-issued national ID card."

When compared to the "rest of Canada," Quebecers endorse the use of national ID cards in greater numbers, for which François Fournier's chapter offers historically and politically informed explanations. He argues that Quebecers have historically viewed ID cards as a means of affirming their collective identity. French Canadians appear to be less informed about privacy laws, even though Quebec is acknowledged to be an early pioneer in privacy legislation. He attributes this lag in awareness to the poor role played by civil society and privacy advocacy groups in educating the public about privacy protection.

IMPLICATIONS FOR THE STUDY
OF PRIVACY AND SURVEILLANCE

Empirical study of privacy in an international context has highlighted the complex nature of privacy not only in terms of its meaning but also in terms of drawing meaningful comparisons across countries and cultures. Context, history, and culture are all intertwined, making problematic any universal claims about the importance of privacy. Although a quantitative study such as that undertaken by the GPD project is indispensable for theorizing about the nature of privacy, it is well to keep in mind that small-scale qualitative research is essential to safeguarding against what C. Wright Mills called "abstracted empiricism."

The ability of cross-cultural research to test for theory and to address methodological considerations is clearly demonstrated in this volume. The authors capture similarities and differences across countries in a field of research that so far has not extended to privacy in an international context. Hopefully, the findings reported here will open new vistas for researchers and policy makers who are engaged in studying and advocating privacy.

At a time when the globalization of information and communication technologies is so widespread, it behoves researchers to recommend ways and policies to safeguard privacy, even though privacy does not rank high on people's list of priorities. The events of 9/11 and the issue of terrorism have given added weight to the need to educate the public about the ramifications of surveillance technologies for personal privacy and freedom. Although this volume demonstrates that people are wary about the invasive nature of technology and its surveillance potential, the public exhibit limited familiarity with legal and technical means to protect their privacy. The disconnect between awareness and action on the part of the public can exact a high toll during times of political crisis, when governments have not hesitated to introduce legislation to curtail individual privacy in the name of national security. As this volume demonstrates, although immediately after 9/11 people were willing to sacrifice personal privacy for the sake of national security, a few years later this was no longer the case. People have become more critical of the public and private sectors' inability to protect the flow of personal information and to strike the right balance between security and the need to protect privacy. Overall, however, the contribution of the media has been to strengthen the case for state surveillance by presenting the issue in a binary fashion, with surveillance pitted against the weakening of security.

Finally, the data collected for this volume contain a wealth of information that has not been thoroughly excavated. For example, we know that countries are not homogenous entities in terms of their social structure. There are regional, social, and class differences and other demographic factors such as age, gender, and education that shape attitudes to privacy and surveillance. The chapters on China and Quebec highlight some of these within-country regional variations. Further analysis of the GPD data will shed light on these issues.

NOTE

The author extends his thanks to Dan Trottier for his assistance in the preparation of this chapter.

Appendix

INTERNATIONAL SURVEY
MAY 2006
60-1003-10
BY L. LYNDA HARLING STALKER

RESPONDENT ID: __ __ __ __ __

INTERVIEWER ID: __ __ __ __ __

Date of Interview: __ __ / __ __ / __ __ __ __ (Month/Day/Year)

Country of Respondent: __ __

Location of Respondent (region/city): __ __ __

Hello, my name is [INTERVIEWER'S NAME] and I'm calling from Ipsos-Reid, a professional public opinion research company. Please let me assure you we are not selling anything. We are conducting a confidential risk-free random survey about attitudes toward privacy issues on behalf of a University. Please be assured that your participation is voluntary and your responses will remain confidential and anonymous. This survey is for academic purposes only.

[Note to interviewer: if respondent asks what university, please say "queen's university"] [If respondent asks where queen's university is, please tell them "it is located in canada"]

[Note to interviewer: if respondent asks where IPSOS is, please tell them "it is a company with offices in [Insert country of interview] and around the world"]

[Note to interviewer: if respondent asks duration of survey, please read the following] The survey will take approximately 20 minutes to complete depending on your answers.

A: Is now a convenient time to participate in the survey?
Yes [Continue to QC]
No [continue to QB]

B: Would it be possible for me to speak with another adult member of your household who might be interested in completing the survey?
Yes [repeat intro for new respondent and ask QA, then ask QC if yes to QA. If new respondent says no to QA, ask QD]
No [ask qd for 25% of respondents. For remaining 75% thank and terminate interview]

C: First of all are you 18 years of age or older?
Yes [Continue to "Read to all" section (after QD)]
No [ask QB]

D: It would be helpful for us if you could briefly explain why you are not interested in participating in this interview. [Record all that apply. Do not read list]
  1. Don't have the time
  2. I am not interested
  3. Unfamiliar with the topic
  4. Privacy concerns
  5. Other (specify)
  6. [Do not read]: dk/unsure

[Once completed QD. Thank and terminate interview. All others continue]

[Please read to all who qualify]
Before we start, if there are any questions that you do not wish to answer please feel free to point these out to me and we will go on to the next question. This survey is not connected with a political or media organization. Our interview may be recorded for quality assurance purposes. If you have any questions or concerns about this survey, please let me know at the end of the survey and I will provide you with the contact information for the person you can direct your comments to. [If the respondent asks for contact information, please provide the following name and email address to the respondent at the end of the interview. Contact name: Elia Zureik Contact email: privpoll@queensu.ca

E. Record sex of respondent [Do not ask question. Record only]: watch quotas
   Male   ☐₁
   Female   ☐₂

F. Which of the following categories best describes your age? You may stop me when I read the correct category. (Read list. Record only one response.) (Watch quotas)

Under 18 ☐ terminate
18–24 ☐₁
25–34 ☐₂
35–44 ☐₃
45–54 ☐₄
55–64 ☐₅
65+ ☐₆
DK/unsure ☐₉ [Do not read]

[If DK/unsure or refuse at qf, do not terminate. Continue to Q1. Try
To get completes for qf that are close to the established quotas (within +/– 5%)]

[Ask all]

1. In general, how knowledgeable are you about each of the following? Would you say you are very knowledgeable, somewhat knowledgeable, not very knowledgeable or not at all knowledgeable? First is [Read first item. Record response. repeat scale as necessary] Next is [Read next item. Record response. check one box for each row]

[randomize list]	Very knowled-geable	Somewhat knowled-geable	Not very knowled-geable	Not at all knowled-geable	[do not read] DK/not sure
a) Internet	☐₁	☐₂	☐₃	☐₄	☐₉
b) Global Positioning System (GPS) used in automobiles	☐₁	☐₂	☐₃	☐₄	☐₉
c) Radio Frequency Identification (RFID) Tags on consumer products	☐₁	☐₂	☐₃	☐₄	☐₉
d) Closed Circuit Television (CCTV) in public spaces	☐₁	☐₂	☐₃	☐₄	☐₉
e) Biometrics for facial and other bodily recognition	☐₁	☐₂	☐₃	☐₄	☐₉
f) Data mining of personal information	☐₁	☐₂	☐₃	☐₄	☐₉

2. To what extent do you have a say in what happens to your personal information? Would you say you have [Read list. Record one response]

Complete say ☐₁
A lot of say ☐₂
Some say ☐₃
No say ☐₄
[Do not read] Don't know/not sure ☐₉

[Note to interviewer for Q2: if respondent says "don't know/unsure at Q2, please probe twice to try and get a response from the response list (codes 1–4) before accepting a don't know/unsure response] possible probe: Is there anything in the list of response options that I read to you that reflects your opinion? [Interviewer: re-read response list if necessary]

Mexico only: please read the following to all respondents before you read Q3. Throughout the survey, we will be referencing "government" and "government departments". When we refer to government, we are referring to the federal government in general, and not just the president.

3. How knowledgeable are you about the laws in [Insert name of country where interview is conducted] that deal with the protection of personal information in government departments and private companies? First, let's start with [Insert one of gov't dept or private companies. randomize]. Would you say you are [Read list. Record one response]. And how about [Insert gov't dept or private companies – whichever wasn't asked first] [Read response list if necessary. Record one response]

	Government departments	Private companies
a) Very knowledgeable	☐₁	☐₁
b) Somewhat knowledgeable	☐₂	☐₂
c) Not very knowledgeable	☐₃	☐₃
d) Not at all knowledgeable	☐₄	☐₄
[do not read] Don't know/unsure	☐₉	☐₉

[Mexico only: for Q4, if necessary repeat following instruction: Please recall that when we refer to government, we are referring to the federal government in general, and not just the president.]

[Ask Q4 for each item (gov't dept, private companies) that respondent is very/somewhat knowledgeable of in Q3. Do not ask if "not very/not at all knowledgeable" or "dk" in Q3]

4. To what extent do you believe laws are effective at protecting your personal information that is held by government departments and private companies? First, let's start with [Insert item very/somewhat knowledgeable in Q3. Insert in same order as Q3]. Do you believe the laws are [Insert scale. record one response]. And how about [Insert next item very/somewhat knowledgeable in Q3.] Do you believe the laws are [Read scale. Record one response only]

	Government departments	Private companies
Very effective	☐1	☐1
Somewhat effective	☐2	☐2
Not very effective	☐3	☐3
Not effective at all	☐4	☐4
Not sure	☐9	☐9

[Mexico only: for Q5, if necessary repeat following instruction: Please recall that when we refer to government, we are referring to the federal government in general, and not just the president.]

[Ask all]

5. When it comes to the privacy of personal information, what level of trust do you have that the [Insert country of interview] government is striking the right balance between national security and individual rights? Do you have a [Read list. Record one response]

    Very high level of trust ☐1
    Reasonably high level of trust ☐2
    Fairly low level of trust ☐3
    Very low level of trust ☐4
    Not sure ☐9

6. What level of trust do you have that private companies, such as banks, credit card companies and places where you shop, will protect your personal information? Do you have a [Read list. Record one response]

    Very high level of trust ☐1
    Reasonably high level of trust ☐2
    Fairly low level of trust ☐3
    Very low level of trust ☐4
    Not sure ☐9

[Mexico only: for Q7 & Q8, 9: <u>if necessary</u> repeat following instruction: Please recall that when we refer to government, we are referring to the federal government in general, and not just the president.]

7. Have you ever done the following for the purpose of protecting your personal information? [Read list. Record yes or no for each] [Randomize list]

	Yes	No	[Do not read] Dk/not sure
a) Refused to give information to a business because you thought it was not needed?	☐1	☐2	☐9
b) Refused to give information to a government agency because you thought it was not needed?	☐1	☐2	☐9
c) Asked a company to remove you from any lists they use for marketing purposes?	☐1	☐2	☐9
d) Asked a company not to sell your name and address to another company?	☐1	☐2	☐9
e) Asked a business you were thinking of dealing with about policies on the collection of consumer information?	☐1	☐2	☐9
f) Asked a company to see what personal information besides billing information they had about you in their consumer records?	☐1	☐2	☐9
g) Purposefully gave incorrect information about yourself to a marketer?	☐1	☐2	☐9
h) Purposefully gave incorrect information about yourself to a government agency?	☐1	☐2	☐9
i) Read the on-line privacy policies at websites when making a purchase from a private company?	☐1	☐2	☐9
j) Read the on-line privacy policies at government websites when sending them information electronically?	☐1	☐2	☐9

8. Have you personally, to the best of your knowledge, ever experienced any of the following? For each item, please indicate yes, no or not sure. If you have never experienced a particular situation, or if a situation does not apply to you, please say "no". [Read list. Record one response for each] [randomize list].

	Yes	No	Not sure/ DK
a) Detention at a border checkpoint resulting in a search	☐1	☐2	☐9
d) Detention by airport officials resulting in not being able to board the airplane	☐1	☐2	☐9
e) Detention by airport officials resulting in being denied entry into a country	☐1	☐2	☐9
f) Victim of identity theft (e.g. someone uses your name)	☐1	☐2	☐9
g) Victim of credit card fraud	☐1	☐2	☐9
h) Your personal information monitored by a government agency	☐1	☐2	☐9
i) Your personal information monitored by an employer	☐1	☐2	☐9
j) Your personal information sold by a commercial business	☐1	☐2	☐9

[Ask Q9 for all countries except Hungary and Brazil]

9. Some have suggested that everyone should have a government-issued national ID card that they must carry on them at all times and present it when asked by police or other security forces. To what extent would you agree or disagree with this idea? Do you [Read list. Record one response]

    Strongly agree ☐1
    Somewhat agree ☐2
    Somewhat disagree ☐3
    Strongly disagree ☐4
    Not sure ☐9

[Ask Q9b for Hungary and Brazil only]

9b) To what extent do you agree or disagree with having a government-issued national ID card that everyone must carry on them at all times and present it when asked by the police or other security forces? Do you... [Read list. Record one response]

    Strongly agree ☐1
    Somewhat agree ☐2
    Somewhat disagree ☐3
    Strongly disagree ☐4
    Not sure ☐9

[mexico only: for Q10, Q12, <u>if necessary</u> repeat following instruction: Please recall that when we refer to government, we are referring to the federal government in general, and not just the president.]

10. In order to put national ID cards into use, the government would need to have a national database containing personal information on all citizens. This information could include address, gender, race, and tax information. How effective do you feel efforts to protect this type of information from disclosure would be? Would you say they would be [Read list. Record one response]

    Very effective ☐₁
    Somewhat effective ☐₂
    Not very effective ☐₃
    Not effective at all ☐₄
    Not sure ☐₉

11. When it comes to privacy, how worried are you about providing personal information on websites, such as your name, address, date of birth, and gender? Are you [Read list. Record one response]

    Very worried ☐₁
    Somewhat worried ☐₂
    Not very worried ☐₃
    Not worried at all ☐₄
    Not sure ☐₉

12. Who do you think should have the most say over how companies use their websites to track people's activities and personal information online? Should it be [Read list. Record one response] [Randomize list, but always ask "not sure" last]

    Government ☐₁
    Companies that run the websites ☐₂
    People who use the websites ☐₃
    Not sure ☐₉

13. How much coverage have you seen or heard through the media (TV, radio, newspapers, magazines, online information, advertisements) regarding concerns about the safety of your personal information? Do they provide [Read list. Record one response]

    A lot of coverage ☐₁
    Some coverage ☐₂
    Not much coverage ☐₃
    No coverage at all ☐₄
    Not sure ☐₉

[Mexico only: for Q14, if necessary repeat following instruction: Please recall that when we refer to government, we are referring to the federal government in general, and not just the president.]

14. In your opinion, would you say the media pays: [Read list. Record one response]
    [Randomize order of first and second items]
    More attention to stories about terrorism ☐1
    More attention to stories about government violation
        of personal privacy of citizens ☐2
    Pays equal attention to both ☐3
    Not sure ☐9

15. Would you say the media pays: [Read list. Record one response]
    [Randomize order of first and second items]
    More attention to stories about terrorism ☐1
    More attention to stories about private sector
        violation of personal privacy of consumers ☐2
    Pays equal attention to both ☐3
    Not sure ☐9

[Mexico only: for Q16 & 17: if necessary repeat following instruction: Please recall that when we refer to government, we are referring to the federal government in general, and not just the president.]

16. When it comes to media coverage of privacy of personal information, in your opinion, how much attention does each of the following groups receive by the media? Please use a scale from 1 to 4 where 1 represents low amounts of attention and 4 represents high amounts of attention? If you are unsure, please say "don't know". First is [Read first item. Repeat scale if necessary]. Next is [Insert second item. Repeat scale if necessary].

[Randomize list]	1	2	3	4	DK/Not sure
a) Low-income persons	☐1	☐2	☐3	☐4	☐9
b) Visible minorities	☐1	☐2	☐3	☐4	☐9
c) Middle class people	☐1	☐2	☐3	☐4	☐9
d) Celebrities	☐1	☐2	☐3	☐4	☐9
e) Government officials	☐1	☐2	☐3	☐4	☐9
f) People like you	☐1	☐2	☐3	☐4	☐9
g) Immigrants	☐1	☐2	☐3	☐4	☐9
h) Homeless	☐1	☐2	☐3	☐4	☐9
i) High-income people	☐1	☐2	☐3	☐4	☐9

17. The government of [Insert country of interview] has enacted laws aimed at protecting national security. To what extent do you believe laws aimed at protecting national security are intrusive upon personal privacy? Are they [Read list. Record one mention]

      Highly intrusive   ☐₁

      Somewhat intrusive   ☐₂

      Not very intrusive   ☐₃

      Not intrusive at all   ☐₄

      Not sure   ☐₉

[Mexico only: for Q18 & Q19, if necessary repeat following instruction: Please recall that when we refer to government, we are referring to the federal government in general, and not just the president.]

18. To what extent do you think it is appropriate for a government agency to share citizen's personal information with third parties, such as other government agencies, foreign governments and the private sector? First, let's start with sharing [Insert first item]. Which of the following best describes your beliefs [Read response list. Record one response]? How about sharing [Insert next item. Read response list if necessary]?

[Randomise order of asking government agencies, foreign governments, and private sector]

[Randomize order of asking government agencies, foreign governments and private sector]	Yes, it is the government's right under all circumstances	Yes, if the citizen is suspected of wrong-doing	Yes, as long as the government has the expressed consent of the citizen.	No, under no circumstances should government share information about citizens	Not sure
	(1)	(2)	(3)	(4)	(9)
a) With other government agencies					
b) With foreign governments					
c) With the private sector					

19. To what extent do you think it is appropriate for a private sector organisation to share or sell its customers' personal information with third parties, such as the national government, foreign governments and other private

sector organisations? First, let's start with sharing [Insert first item]. Which of the following best describes your beliefs [Read response list. Record one response]? How about sharing [Insert next item. Read response list if necessary]?

[Randomise order of asking national government, foreign governments, and other private sector organisations]

[Randomize order of asking national government, foreign governments and other private sector organisations]	Yes, it is the organisation's right under all circumstances	Yes, if the customer is suspected of wrong-doing	Yes, as long as the organization has the expressed consent of the customer	No, under no circumstances should organisations share information about their customers	Not sure
	(1)	(2)	(3)	(4)	(9)
a) With the national government					
b) With foreign governments					
c) With other private sector organisations					

20. Some communities and private companies in [Insert country] are using surveillance cameras, also known as Closed Circuit Television or CCTVs, to monitor public places in order to deter crime and assist in the prosecution of offenders. In your opinion, how effective are [Insert first item from list] in reducing crime? Are they [Read response list, include not sure]? How about [Insert next item. Read response list if necessary] [Record one response per item]

Randomize list	Very Effective	Somewhat Effective	Not Very Effective	Not Effective At All	Not sure
a) Community CCTVs (such as outdoor cameras in public places)	☐1	☐2	☐3	☐4	☐9
b) In-store CCTVs	☐1	☐2	☐3	☐4	☐9

21. To what extent do you think employers should be allowed to monitor their employees electronically with surveillance cameras and to read the e-mails their employees send or receive on the employer's computers. First, let's start with [Insert first item]. Which of the following best describes your beliefs [Read response list. Record one response]. How about [Insert next item. Read response list if necessary]

[Randomize order of asking cameras and email]	Yes, it is the right of the employer under any circumstance (1)	Yes, but only for the purpose of evaluating employee's performance (2)	Yes, but only if the employee gives informed consent to be monitored (3)	No, under no circumstances should an employer monitor their employees (4)	Not sure (9)
a) Electronically monitor with surveillance cameras					
b) Read E-mails					

[Mexico only: for Q22, if necessary repeat following instruction: Please recall that when we refer to government, we are referring to the federal government in general, and not just the president.]

22. To what extent do you think it is appropriate for an EMPLOYER to share their employees' personal information with third parties, such as the government or the private sector? First, let's start with sharing with [Insert first item]. Which of the following best describes your beliefs [Read response list. Record one response]. How about sharing with [Insert next item. Read response list if necessary]

[Randomize order of asking government and private sector]

[Randomize order of asking government and private sector]	Yes, it is the employers' right under any circumstance (1)	Yes, if the employee is suspected of wrong-doing (2)	Yes, as long as the employer has the expressed consent of the employees. (3)	No, under no circumstances should an employer share information about employees (4)	Not sure (9)
a) Government					
b) Private Sector					

23. To what extent is your privacy respected by airport and customs officials when traveling by airplane? Is it [Read list. Record one response]
    Completely respected □₁
    A lot of respect □₂
    Somewhat respected □₃
    Not respected at all □₄
    [Do not read] don't know/not sure □₉

[Do not read] not applicable (never travels by airplane)

[Note to interviewer for Q23: if respondent says "don't know/unsure at Q23, please probe twice to try and get a response from the response list (codes 1–4) before accepting a don't know/unsure response] possible probe: is there anything in the list of response options that i read to you that reflects your opinion? [Interviewer: re-read response list if necessary]

[Mexico only: for Q24,Q25, if necessary repeat following instruction: Please recall that when we refer to government, we are referring to the federal government in general, and not just the president.]

24. Do you think [Insert country] government should have the right to collect personal information about travellers? Would you say [Read list. Record one response]
    Yes, under any circumstances □₁
    Yes, only if there is expressed consent by the affected traveller □₂
    No, unless there is suspected wrong-doing by the traveler □₃
    No, under no circumstances □₄
    Not sure □₉

25. Do you think the [Insert country] government should be able to share travelers' personal information with foreign governments? Would you say [Read list. Record one response]
    Yes, under any circumstance □₁
    Yes, only if there is expressed consent by the affected traveler □₂
    No, unless there is suspected wrong-doing by the traveler □₃
    No, under no circumstances □₄
    Not sure □₉

26. How acceptable do you feel it would be for airport officials to give extra security checks to visible minorities? Would it be [Read list. Record one response]
    Very acceptable □₁
    Somewhat acceptable □₂

Not really acceptable   □₃
Not acceptable at all   □₄
Not sure   □₉

27. Some companies offer customer rewards programmes where you can earn points or rewards based on how often you buy something from them or use their services (for example frequent flyer programmes or [local examples like Air Miles]). How many of these types of programmes do you collect points or rewards from? If you don't belong to any, just say "none". [Do not read list. Record response]

[Q27 range: 0–999]
    [Record number] _____
    [Do not read] none   □₀
    [Do not read] not sure   □₉₉₉

28. Many businesses create profiles about their customers that include information about purchasing habits, personal characteristics and credit history. How acceptable to you would it be for a business to use information from your customer profile to inform you of products or services that they think would be of interest to you? Do you feel it is [Read list. Record one response]
    Very acceptable   □₁
    Somewhat acceptable   □₂
    Somewhat unacceptable   □₃
    Not acceptable at all   □₄
    Not sure   □₉

Note to scripting/interviewer: for Q29–36 the questions are split into two groups: group a and group b. Group a questions will be asked of a random selection of 50% of the respondents. Group b questions will be asked of a random selection of 50% of respondents. Do not ask one respondent questions from group a and b. If respondent is randomized to group a, then they must be asked all group a questions. They cannot be asked any group b questions. If respondent is randomized to group b, they must be asked all group b questions, they cannot be asked any group a questions.

Note to interviewer for Q29–Q36: if respondent says "don't know/unsure for any question in this section, please probe twice to try and get a response from the response list (codes 1–4) before accepting a don't know/unsure response] possible probe: is there anything in the list of response options that i read to you that reflects your opinion? [Interviewer: re-read response list if necessary]

We are now nearing the end of the survey. Once we have completed this group of questions I will just have a few final questions for statistical purposes.

The following questions reflect a series of situations that we would like to get your opinions on, based on the information I provide you for each scenario. Please understand there are no right or wrong answers, we are interested in your opinion.

[Names in Q29–Q36 will change to reflect country of interview]

Group a: (Q29–Q32)
Randomly ask group a questions of 50% of respondents. Randomize the order of the questions within group a. Respondent must be asked all questions in group a.

29. [Mike] goes to the drug store to buy film, which was advertised to be on sale. He finds out at the store that in order to receive the discount, he must apply for a customer loyalty card, which involves filling out an application form. It requires [Mike] to fill out his home address, occupation, and marital status. He fills the form out to get the special pricing. To what extent does [Mike] have a say in what happens to his personal information? Is it [Read list. Record one response]

Complete say	☐1
A lot of say	☐2
Some say	☐3
No say	☐4
[Do not read] Don't know/unsure	☐9

[Mexico only: for Q30, Q32: if necessary repeat following instruction: please recall that when we refer to government, we are referring to the federal government in general, and not just the president.]

30. As part of the concern for national security, assume that the government creates a database to search for terrorist activity. All government records are merged with any available commercial data such as bank records, credit statements, and travel manifests. Citizens, such as [James] are required to provide fingerprints, photographs, and iris scans. [James] does this. To what extent does James have a say in what happens to his personal information? Is it [Read list. Record one response]

Complete say	☐1
A lot of say	☐2
Some say	☐3
No say at all	☐4
[Do not read] Don't know/unsure	☐9

31. [Mary] pays cash at a large, crowded department store and provides no information about herself to the cashier. The cashier asks for [Mary's] postal code/zip code; [Mary] refuses and still makes her purchase. To what extent does [Mary] have a say in what happens to her personal information? Is it [Read list. Record one response]

   Complete say   ☐₁
   A lot of say   ☐₂
   Some say   ☐₃
   No say at all   ☐₄
   [Do not read] Don't know/unsure   ☐₉

32. Assume that as part of the concern for national security, the government creates a database to search for terrorist activity. The government requires everyone, including [Rita], to submit an annual form containing detailed information about themselves. The form asks for employment information, criminal activity, and any travel abroad by the individual or any family members in the last five years. [Rita] complies, but decides not complete the section on travel. To what extent does [Rita] have a say in what happens to her personal information? Is it [Read list. Record one response]

   Complete say   ☐₁
   A lot of say   ☐₂
   Some say   ☐₃
   No say at all   ☐₄
   [Do not read] Don't know/unsure   ☐₉

Group B (Q33–Q36)
Randomly ask group b questions of 50% of respondents. Randomize the order of the questions within group B. Respondent must be asked all questions in group B.

33. [Magda] is traveling out of the country. She is selected to have all her baggage opened and checked. She cannot board the plane until this is done. To what extent is [Magda's] privacy respected by airport and customs officials when traveling by airplane? Is it [Read list. Record one response]

   Completely respected   ☐₁
   A lot of respect   ☐₂
   Somewhat respected   ☐₃
   Not respected at all   ☐₄
   [Do not read] Don't know/unsure   ☐₉

34. [Shekeel] is travelling out of the country. He has to have a metal detecting wand passed over him before he can board the plane, while other passengers do not. To what extent is [Shekeel's] privacy respected by airport and customs officials when travelling by airplane? Is it [Read list. Record one response]

Completely respected   ☐₁
A lot of respect   ☐₂
Somewhat respected   ☐₃
Not respected at all   ☐₄
[Do not read] Don't know/unsure   ☐₉

35. [Mohammad] is travelling out of the country. Because of the racial profiling, he is separated from the other travellers. He is asked very detailed questions about his marital status, his family situation, his employment, the purpose of his trip, past political affiliations, and his associates. Airport and customs officials then do a physical search of his baggage and person. After finding nothing, he is free to travel. To what extent is [Mohammad's] privacy respected by airport and customs officials when travelling by airplane? Is it [Read list. Record one response]

Completely respected   ☐₁
A lot of respect   ☐₂
Somewhat respected   ☐₃
Not respected at all   ☐₄
[Do not read] Don't know/unsure   ☐₉

36. [Hanna] is traveling out of the country. She shows her passport and is permitted to board the plane. To what extent is [Hanna's] privacy respected by airport and customs officials when traveling by airplane? Is it [Read list. Record one response]

Completely respected   ☐₁
A lot of respect   ☐₂
Somewhat respected   ☐₃
Not respected at all   ☐₄
[Do not read] Don't know/unsure   ☐₉

Demographics (ask all respondents)

Now we have a few final questions that we will be using for statistical purposes only. Remember, all your responses will be kept strictly confidential, as the findings will only be reported in aggregate format.

[Ask all respondents]

37. How many times in the last year have you traveled by air? Please include all flights both within and outside your country.

[Q37 range: 0–999]
    [Record number] _____
        [Do not read] Don't know/unsure   ☐₉₉₉

38. Have you purchased a product or service over the internet in the past year?
    Yes   ☐₁
    No   ☐₂
    [Do not read] Don't know/unsure   ☐₉

[Mexico only: for Q39, if necessary repeat following instruction: please re-call that when we refer to government, we are referring to the federal gov-ernment in general, and not just the president.]

39. In the past year have you contacted the local, state or national government for any reason? [Read list. Accept multiple responses. Check each that applies]
    By email/internet or other electronic means   ☐₁
    Face-to-face, over the telephone or by mail   ☐₂
    No contact   ☐₃
    [Do not read] Don't know/unsure   ☐₉

[For Q39. If code 1 and/or code 2 are selected, do not select code 3 (no contact) or code 9 (don't know/unsure). Multiple responses are allowed for code 1 and code 2]

39b) For each of the following scenarios, please indicate yes or no for each. Have you used a computer in the past 6 months
     [Note to interviewer: if respondent indicates they currently are not em-ployed/do not work, please select the "no" option]

[Randomize List]	Yes	No	[Do not read] Don't know/Not sure
a) At home	☐₁	☐₂	☐₉
b) At work	☐₁	☐₂	☐₉
c) At a public place (e.g. library, internet café, etc)	☐₁	☐₂	☐₉

39c) For each of the following scenarios, please indicate yes or no for each. Have you used the Internet in the past 6 months
     [Note to interviewer: if respondent indicates they currently are not em-ployed/do not work, please select the "no" option]

[Randomize List]	Yes	No	[Do not read] Don't know/Not sure
a) At home	☐₁	☐₂	☐₉
b) At work	☐₁	☐₂	☐₉
c) At a public place (e.g. library, internet café, etc)	☐₁	☐₂	☐₉

40. What year were you born in?

| 1900–1988 | — — — — |
| 9999 | Do not read (Don't Know/Not Stated) |

41. Canada: What is the highest level of formal education that you have completed? [Read list]
[Customize according to country of interview]

	Education Categories
01	Grade school or some high school
02	Complete high school
03	Complete technical or trade school/Community college
04	Some community college or university, but did not finish
05	Complete university degree, such as a Bachelor's
06	Graduate degree, such as a Master's or Ph.D.
99	Do not read (Don't Know/Not Stated) (Don't Know/Not Stated)

United States: What is the last year of school you completed? [Read list. Enter single response.]

	Education Categories
01	Grade school or some high school
02	Completed high school
03	Some college but did not finish
04	Completed a two year college degree
05	Completed a four year college degree
06	Completed a post-graduate degree such as a Master's or Ph.D.
99	(Don't know/not stated)

[Ask all]

42. What is your current employment status? [Read list. One response only]
[Customize according to country of interview]

Working full time	☐1
Working part time	☐2
Not employed	☐3
Student	☐4
Homemaker	☐5
Retired	☐6
Self-employed	☐7
[Do not read] Don't know/Not stated	☐9

(If "working full-time, part-time or self-employed" in Q.42, Then ask Q.43 Otherwise skip to Q.44)

43. Which of the following best describes your current occupation? Is it best described as....? (Read list. One response only)
[Customize according to country of interview]

Professional/Managerial □₁
Sales/Clerical □₂
Technical/Skilled □₃
Unskilled/Laborer □₄
Other occupations [do not specify] □₅
[Do not read] Not sure □₉

(Ask all respondents)

44. And which of the following categories best describes your annual household income? That is, the total income before taxes – or gross income – of all persons in your household combined? Just stop me when I reach your category. Read list.
[Insert appropriate categories for each country]
[Customize according to country of interview]

	Income Categories
01	Under $10,000
02	$10,000 to just under $20,000
03	$20,000 to just under $30,000
04	$30,000 to just under $40,000
05	$40,000 to just under $50,000
06	$50,000 to just under $60,000
07	$60,000 to just under $70,000
08	$70,000 to just under $80,000
09	$80,000 to just under $100,000
10	$100,000 and over
99	[Do not read]: Don't know/Not stated
999	[Do not read] Refused

[Supplier to record following data as appropriate:]
[Ask all respondents]

45. What language do you speak at home? [Do not read list. select all that apply. Record response]

Afrikaans □₁
Arabic □₂
Mandarin □₃

Cantonese ☐4
Danish ☐5
Dutch ☐6
English ☐7
Farsi ☐8
French ☐9
German ☐10
Greek ☐11
Hebrew ☐12
Hindi (or other Indian language) ☐13
Hungarian ☐14
Italian ☐15
Japanese ☐16
Portuguese ☐17
Polish ☐18
Punjabi ☐19
Russian ☐20
Spanish ☐21
Tagalog(or other Philippines language) ☐22
Tamil ☐23
Thai ☐24
Turkish ☐25
Urdu ☐26
Vietnamese ☐27
Custom ☐28
Custom ☐29
Custom ☐30
Custom ☐31
Custom ☐32
Other language (Please specify) ☐33

46. [Ask in us only] Are you of Hispanic ethnicity?
Yes [Skip to Q47] ☐1
No [Skip to Q47] ☐2
[Do not read] Not sure/refused [Skip to Q47] ☐99

47. [Ask all]
Are you [Read list. randomize]
[Customize according to country of interview]
Asian/Pacific Islander ☐1
Black/African [Insert country of interivew] ☐2
Caucasian/White ☐3

North American Indian/Inuit   ☐4
Mixed ethnic background   ☐5
Another population group (specify)   ☐6
[Do not read] Don't know/refused   ☐99

48. [Do not read] record language of interview:
      English   ☐1
      French   ☐2
      Hungarian   ☐3
      Portuguese   ☐4
      Spanish   ☐5

Thank you for your time.

Contributors

NELSON ARTEAGA BOTELLO is a professor and researcher of sociology in the Faculty of Political and Social Science at the Universidad Autónoma del Estado de México. He received his doctorate at the University of Alicante, Spain. He is a member of the National System of Investigators (SNI) in Mexico. His main research interests are problematization fields and "dispositifs" through violence, public security, and surveillance. His publications include *En busca de la legitimidad: Violencia y populismo punitivo en México, 1990–2000* (2006), *Violencia y estado en la globalización* (2004), *Pobres y delincuentes: Estudio de sociología y genealogía* (2006), and *Sociedad de la vigilancia en el Sur-Global: Mirando América Latina* (2009).

AYSE CEYHAN is a political scientist. She teaches at Sciences Po-Paris. Specializing in issues of security, identity, and technology, she leads the Security and Technology Research and Expertise Group at Maison des Sciences de l'Homme (http://www.geest.msh-paris.fr). Among her publications are *Identification Biométrique* (2010, co-editor) and "Technologization of Security: Management of Uncertainty and Risk in the Age of Biometrics," *Surveillance and Society* 5, no. 2 (2008): 102–23.

YOLANDE E. CHAN is a professor and E. Marie Shantz Research Fellow in Management Information Systems (MIS) at Queen's University. She holds a doctorate from the University of Western Ontario, a master of philosophy degree in management studies from Oxford University, and bachelor of science and master of science degrees in electrical engineering and computer science from the Massachusetts Institute of Technology. Prior to joining the School of Business at Queen's University, she worked with Andersen Consulting (now Accenture). Currently, she serves as director of The Monieson Centre. Dr Chan conducts research on information privacy, knowledge management, strategic alignment, and information systems performance. She has published her findings in journals such as *Information Systems Research*, MIS *Quarterly Executive*, *Journal of Management Information Systems*, *Journal of Strategic Information Systems*, *Information and Management*, IEEE *Transactions on Engineering Management*, *Communications of the* AIS, and *Academy of Management Executive*. Dr Chan is a member of several journal editorial boards.

ARTHUR J. COCKFIELD, BA (University of Western Ontario), LLB (Queen's University), JSM and JSD (Stanford University), is an associate professor in the Faculty of Law at Queen's University, where he has been appointed a Queen's National Scholar. Prior to joining Queen's University, he worked as a lawyer in Toronto and as a law professor in San Diego. Professor Cockfield has authored, co-authored, or edited eight books and over forty academic articles and book chapters focusing on tax, privacy and law, and technology theory. He is the recipient of a number of fellowships and grants for this research.

FRANÇOIS FOURNIER's academic background is in political science (MA) and sociology (PhD). He is a consultant on socio-political issues. For the past fifteen years, he has been working and publishing in a variety of research environments and fields, developing considerable methodological expertise in qualitative approaches. From 2002 to 2007, he worked at the Centre for Bioethics of the Institut de recherches cliniques de Montréal (IRCM) on the ethics of biomedical research and personal health information privacy. Since 2007 Mr Fournier has been conducting research in the field of cultural diversity, immigration, and integration.

ANDREW GRENVILLE is the chief research officer of Angus Reid Strategies/Vision Critical. He supervised the fielding and basic analysis of the Globalization of Personal Data (GPD) survey in seven of the countries while employed at Ipsos Reid. Mr Grenville has twenty-five years experience in survey research and has conducted hundreds of studies in over forty countries around the globe. He has a special interest in segmentation, having identified different schools of thought on everything from urinary difficulties to experiences of the supernatural. Mr Grenville had the privilege of collaborating with David Lyon on a study entitled "God and Society in North America" in 1996, a survey of religion, politics, and social involvement in Canada and the United States.

L. LYNDA HARLING STALKER received her doctorate from Carleton University and was a postdoctoral fellow with the Globalization of Personal Data (GPD) project at Queen's University. She has written on the many concerns that affect self-employed workers in peripheral regions. She now holds a position in the Department of Sociology at St Francis Xavier University in Nova Scotia.

AVNER LEVIN, BSC, LLB, LLM, SJD, is the chair of the Law and Business Department and the director of the Privacy and Cyber Crime Institute at Ryerson University's Ted Rogers School of Management. Professor Levin researches the legal regulation and protection of privacy and personal information in various sectors across jurisdictions, both within Canada and internationally. His research into online social network privacy and workplace privacy has been funded by the Office of the Privacy Commissioner of Canada's Contributions Program. Professor Levin is a frequent media commentator on issues of privacy, surveillance, and the law.

AARON LOWEN received his doctorate in economics from the University of Iowa in 2003 and is an associate professor in the Economics Department in the Seidman College of Business at Grand Valley State University. His research covers a wide variety of topics, including nonprofits, privacy, international joint ventures, the gender wage gap, recycling and waste disposal policy, anticorruption policy, and the effects of testosterone on market-related behaviour.

DAVID LYON is the director of the Surveillance Studies Centre (http://www.sscqueens.org/davidlyon) and a professor of sociology at Queen's University. His most recent books are *Identifying Citizens: ID Cards as Surveillance* (2009) and *Surveillance Studies: An Overview* (2007).

STEPHEN T. MARGULIS is currently a professor of management in the Seidman College of Business at Grand Valley State University (GVSU). Before this appointment, he was the Eugene Eppinger Professor of Facilities Management at GVSU. He has been publishing on behavioural aspects of privacy for some thirty years. His most recent privacy publication is a collection entitled "Contemporary Perspectives on Privacy: Social, Psychological, Political," *Journal of Social Issues* 59 (2003),

which he developed and edited and to which he contributed two articles. His favourite privacy publication is the collection "Privacy as a
Behavioral Phenomenon," *Journal of Social Issues* 33 (1977), which he
also developed and edited and to which he contributed. In addition to
university teaching and research, he worked for ten years for the US federal government at a premier federal research laboratory, the National
Institute of Standards and Technology, followed by work in the private
sector as director of research at BOSTI, an environmental design research
and consulting firm in Buffalo, New York.

STEPHEN MARMURA received his doctorate in sociology from Queen's
University in 2004. He specializes in the area of communication and
information technology (CIT), and is the author of *Hegemony in the
Dgitial Age: The Arab/Israeli Conflict Online* (2008). As a postdoctoral fellow with the Surveillance Project, he was involved in the location
technologies research cluster and also investigated surveillance issues in
the mass media. He now holds the position of assistant professor in the
Faculty of Sociology at St Francis Xavier University in Nova Scotia.

ANDREY PAVLOV is a doctoral candidate in the Department of
Mathematics and Statistics at Queen's University, where he received his
master of science degree in 2005. He holds a degree in probability and
statistics from St Petersburg State University. Mr Pavlov was a statistical
consultant with the Globalization of Personal Data (GPD) project.

JENNIFER A. POPE is currently an associate professor of marketing at
Grand Valley State University. She recieved a doctorate in marketing and
international business from the University of Texas-PanAm in 2003. She
has done research primarily in nonprofit marketing, privacy and marketing, and international business relationships. She has published in *The
International Journal of Business Disciplines, Journal of Transportation
Management, Journal of International Business and Entrepreneurship
Development*, and *Journal of Business and Economic Studies*, among
others. She has lived in England, Germany, and Taiwan and regularly
teaches marketing classes in Germany.

JASON PRIDMORE is the senior researcher with the DigIDeas project,
a European Research-funded project on the social and ethical impacts
of digital identification systems. Dr Pridmore received his doctorate in
2008 from the Department of Sociology at Queen's University, where

he was a postdoctoral fellow with the New Transparency Project, under the auspices of the Surveillance Project. His doctoral work focused on the role of retail loyalty and rewards cards as forms of consumer surveillance, drawing on empirical research involving marketing executives and loyalty card consumers. He is the author of an expert report on the surveillance of consumers and consumption, part of *The Report on the Surveillance Society* commissioned by the Office of the British Information Commissioner in 2006.

JEFFREY ROY, PhD (Carleton), MBA (Ottawa), BA (Waterloo), is an associate professor in the School of Public Administration at Dalhousie University. He specializes in multi- stakeholder governance, service transformation, and electronic government. Prior to joining Dalhousie in 2006, Mr Roy was a faculty member of the University of Ottawa's School of Management and Centre on Governance. In October 2005 he served as chair of an international research conference on e-government held in Ottawa, and in 2007 he helped to organize a conference on public-sector service delivery in concert with Service Canada and Service Nova Scotia and Municipal Relations. Mr Roy is also an associate editor of the *International Journal of E-Government Research*, a featured columnist in *Canadian Government Executive*, and the author of two books on digital governance, *E-Government in Canada: Transformation for the Digital Age* (2006) and *Business and Government in Canada* (2007). He is a contributor to the United Nation's 2008 and 2010 *Global E-Government Reviews*, and his research is presently funded by the Social Sciences and Humanities Research Council of Canada.

EMILY SMITH is a research associate with the Surveillance Studies Centre at Queen's University. She holds a master's degree in sociology from Queen's University, where she concentrated on workplace surveillance. In preparation for the Globalization of Personal Data (GPD) international survey, she wrote background research reports on privacy in Hungary, Mexico, and the United States as well as reports on trends in public opinion polling and on comparison of the GPD survey with Alan Westin's "privacy dynamic." She is also an editorial assistant for the online journal *Surveillance and Society*.

OLA SVENONIUS is a doctoral candidate at Södertörn University in Stockholm. He holds a master's degree in political science from Södertörn University. He has studied political science, economics, German, and

philosophy in Stockholm, Bonn, Östersund, and Berlin. He has participated in several research projects focusing on surveillance and social
control, public transport, and consumer issues. Since 2007 he has been
doing doctoral research in political science at Södertörn University that
analyzes surveillance and security in local transport systems in the Baltic
Sea Region.

IVÁN SZÉKELY, social informatist, is an internationally known expert in
the multidisciplinary fields of data protection and freedom of information. A long-time independent researcher, consultant, and university lec-
turer, as well as former chief counsellor for the Office of the Hungarian
Parliamentary Commissioner for Data Protection and Freedom of
Information, Mr Székely is at present counsellor of the Open Society
Archives at Central European University and an associate professor at
the Budapest University of Technology and Economics. Mr Székely was
a leader of the first privacy and data protection research in Hungary and
in the region (1989–90), and he is a founder of Hungary's newly democratic informational-legal system and the introducer of data protection
auditing in Hungary.

ELIA ZUREIK is an emeritus professor of sociology at Queen's University.
His published work in communication and information technology
(CIT) includes journal articles dealing with consumer behaviour (2005),
biometrics and governance (2003), computer crime (1990), and trade
union response to CIT deregulation in the telephone industry (1988).
He is a co-editor of *Global Surveillance and Policing: Borders, Security
and Identity* (2005), *Computers, Surveillance and Privacy* (1996), and
*The Social Context of Information and Communication Technology: A
Bibliography* (1987). He recently completed a study on nation build-
ing and the use of the Internet in Palestine, funded by the Canadian
International Development Research Centre.

References

INTRODUCTION

Bauman, Zygmunt. 2000. *Liquid Modernity*. Cambridge, UK: Polity Press.

Bennett, Colin, and David Lyon, eds. 2008. *Playing the Identity Card: Surveillance and Identification in Global Perspective*. London and New York: Routledge.

Boyne, Roy. 2000. "Post-Panopticism." *Economy and Society* 29, no. 2: 285–307.

Gandy, Oscar. 1993. *The Panoptic Sort: A Political Economy of Personal Information*. Boulder, CO: Westview Press.

Goold, Benjamin J. 2009. *Surveillance*. London and New York: Routledge.

– and Daniel Neyland, eds. 2009. *New Directions in Surveillance and Privacy*. Cullompton, UK: Willan.

Hier, Sean, and Josh Greenberg, eds. 2007. *The Surveillance Studies Reader*. Oxford, UK: Open University Press.

– and Josh Greenberg, eds. 2009. *Shades of Surveillance: Moralism, Inequality, Politics and Resistance*. Vancouver: University of British Columbia Press.

Lessig, Lawrence. 1999. *Code and Other Laws of Cyberspace*. New York: Basic Books.

Lyon, David. 2002. "Surveillance Studies: Understanding Visibility, Mobility and the Phenetic Fix." *Surveillance and Society* 1, no. 1: 1–7. http://www.surveillance-and-society.org/journalv1i1.htm (accessed 5 November 2009).

– 2007. *Surveillance Studies: An Overview*. Cambridge, UK: Polity Press.

– Stephen Marmura, and Pasha Peroff. 2005. *Location Technologies: Mobility, Surveillance and Privacy*. Ottawa: Office of the Privacy Commissioner. http://www.sscqueens.org/files/loctech.pdf (accessed 5 November 2009).

– ed. 2003. *Surveillance as Social Sorting: Privacy, Risk and Digital Discrimination*. London and New York: Routledge.

– ed. 2006. *Theorizing Surveillance: The Panopticon and Beyond*. Cullompton, UK: Willan.

Marx, Gary. 1988. *Undercover: Police Surveillance in America*. Berkeley: University of California Press.

Orwell, George. 2008. *Nineteen Eighty-Four*. 1949. Reprint, London: Penguin.

Regan, Priscilla. 1995. *Legislating Privacy*. Chapel Hill: University of North Carolina Press.

Rule, James. 1974. *Private Lives and Public Surveillance: Social Control in the Computer Age*. New York: Schocken Books.

Salter, Mark. 2008. *Politics of the Airport*. Minneapolis: University of Minnesota Press.

Surveillance and Society. http://www.surveillance-and-society.org.

Surveillance Studies Network. 2006. *A Report on the Surveillance Society*. Prepared for the Information Commissioner of the UK. http://www.ico.gov.uk/upload/documents/library/data_protection/practical_application/surveillance_society_full_report_2006.pdf (accessed 5 November 2009).

Weber, Max. 1958. *The Protestant Ethic and the Spirit of Capitalism*. New York: Scribners.

Zureik, Elia, and Mark Salter, eds. 2005. *Global Surveillance and Policing: Borders, Security, Identity*. Cullompton UK: Willan.

PART I

INTRODUCTION

Goffman, Erving. 1959. *The Presentation of Self in Everyday Life*. New York: Doubleday.

Harper, Jim, and Solveig Singleton. 2001. "With a Grain of Salt: What Consumer Privacy Surveys Don't Tell Us." http://cei.org/PDFs/with_a_grain_of_salt.pdf (accessed 9 November 2009).

King, Gary, Christopher J.L. Murray, Joshua A. Salomon, and Ajay Tandon. 2004. *"Enhancing the Validity and Cross-Cultural Comparability of Survey Research."* *American Political Science Review* 98, no. 1: 191–207.

CHAPTER ONE

Aiseu, Ana, Andrew Clement, and Jane Aspinall. 2004. "Situating Privacy Online: Complex Perceptions and Everyday Practices." *Information, Communications and Society* 7, no. 1: 92–114.

Amoore, Louise, and Marieke De Goede. 2005. "Governance, Risk and Dataveillance in the War on Terror." *Crime, Law and Social Change* 43 (Spring): 149–73.

Bellman, Steven, Eric J. Johnson, Stephen Kobrin, and Gerald L. Lohse. 2004. "International Differences in Information Privacy Concerns: A Global Survey of Consumers." *Information Society* 20: 313–24.

Bennett, Colin J. 1996. "Frequently Asked Questions about Privacy: A Comparative Analysis of Privacy Surveys." Unpublished manuscript, University of British Columbia.

– and Charles D. Raab. 2003. *The Governance of Privacy: Policy Instruments in Global Perspective*. Cornwall, UK: Ashgate.

Davis, Darren, and Brian S. Silver. 2004. "Civil Liberties vs. Security: Public Opinion in the Context of Terrorist Attacks on America." *American Journal of Political Science* 48, no. 1: 28–46.

Davison, Robert M., Roger Clarke, H. Jeff Smith, Duncan Langford, and Feng-Yang Kuo. 2003. "Information Privacy in a Globally Networked Society: Implications for Information Systems Research." *Communications of the Association for Information Systems* 12: 341–65.

Etzioni, Amitai. 1999. *The Limits of Privacy*. New York: Basic Books.

Gandy, Oscar H. 2003. "Public Opinion Surveys and the Formation of Privacy Policy." *Journal of Social Issues* 59, no. 2: 293–9.

Giddens, Anthony. 1991. *Modernity and Self-Identity*. Cambridge, UK: Polity Press.

Goffman, Erving. 1959. *The Presentation of Self in Everyday Life*. New York: Doubleday.

Haggerty, Kevin D., and Amber Gazso. 2005. "Seeing beyond the Ruins: Surveillance as a Response to Terrorist Threats." *Canadian Journal of Sociology* 30, no. 2: 169–87.

Harling Stalker, L. Lynda. 2007. "Every Word Counts: Writing the International Survey on Privacy and Surveillance." Background paper commissioned by the Globalization of Personal Data (GPD) project, Queen's University, Kingston, ON. http://www.sscqueens.org//book_tables (accessed 9 November 2009).

Harris, Louis, and Alan F. Westin. 1991. *Harris-Equifax Consumer Privacy Survey 1991*. Atlanta: Equifax.

Hofstede, Geert. 2001. *Culture's Consequences: Comparing Values, Behaviors, Institutions, and Organizations across Nations*. Thousand Oaks, CA: Sage.

Inglehart, Ronald, and Christian Welzel. 2004. "What Insights Can Multi-Country Surveys Provide about People and Societies." Paper presented at the American Political Science Association Meetings, Chicago. *APSA-Comparative Politics Newsletter* 15, no. 2: 14–18.

Introna, Lucas D. 1997. "Privacy and the Computer: Why We Need Privacy in the Information Society." *Metaphilosophy* 28, no. 3: 259–75.

Ireland, Oliver, and Rachel Howell. 2004. "The Fear Factor: Privacy, Fear, and the Changing Hegemony of the American People and the Right to Privacy."

North Carolina Journal of International Law and Commercial Regulation 29, no. 4: 672–89.

Katz, James E., and Annette R. Tassone. 1990. "Public Opinion Trends: Privacy and Information Technology." *Public Opinion Quarterly* 54, no. 1: 125–43.

LaRose, Robert, and Nora Rifon. 2003. "Your Privacy Is Assured – of Being Invaded: Web Sites with and without Privacy Seal." Paper presented at the International Association for the Development of the Information Society (IADIS) International Conference e-Society, Lisbon, Portugal. http://www.iadis.net/dl/final_uploads/200301L009.pdf (accessed 9 November 2009).

Lippmann, Walter. 1945. *Public Opinion.* 1922. Reprint, New York: Macmillan.

Maden, Caryn. 2003. "Privacy in Canada." In *International Report on Privacy for Electronic Government,* 253–314. Report funded by the Ministry of Public Management, Home Affairs, Posts and Telecommunications of Japan. http://joi.ito.com/privacyreport/Contents_Distilled/EnglishSection/Canada_E_p252-314.pdf (accessed 9 November 2009).

Margulis, Stephen T. 2003a. "On the Status and Contribution of Westin's and Altman's Theories of Privacy." *Journal of Social Issues* 59, no. 2: 411–30.

– 2003b. "Privacy as a Social Issue and Behavioural Concept." *Journal of Social Issues* 59, no. 2: 243–62.

Market and Opinion Research International (MORI). 2003. *Is It Safe to Combine Methodologies in Survey Research?* London: MORI Research Methods Unit.

Marx, Gary. 2001. "Murky Conceptual Waters: The Public and the Private." *Ethics and Information Technology* 3, no. 3: 152–69.

– 2008. "Surveys and Surveillance." In Frederick Conrad and Michael Schrober, eds, *Envisioning the Survey Interview of the Future,* 254–66. New York: John Wiley and Sons. http://web.mit.edu/gtmarx/www/surveysurveil.html (accesed 5 October 2009).

Milberg, Sandra, Sandra J. Burke, H. Jeff Smith, and Ernest A. Kallman. 1995. "Values, Personal Information Privacy, and Regulatory Approaches." *Communications of the ACM* 38, no. 12: 65–74.

Mills, C. Wright. 1959. *The Sociological Imagination.* New York: Oxford University Press.

Osborne, Thomas and Nikolas Rose. 1999. "Do Social Science Create Phenomena? The Example of Public Opinion Research." *British Journal of Sociology* 50, no. 3: 367–96.

Pivacy International and the Electronic Privacy Information Center (EPIC). 2003. "Privacy and Human Rights 2003: An International Survey of Privacy Laws and Developments." http://www.privacyinternational.org/survey/phr2003/overview.htm#The Right to Privacy (accessed 9 November 2009).

Raab, Charles D. 1999. "From Balancing to Steering: New Directions for Data Protection." In Colin Bennett and Rebecca Grant, eds, *Visions of Privacy:*

Policy Choices for the Digital Age, 68–93. Toronto, Buffalo, and London: University of Toronto Press.

Regan, Priscilla. 1995. *Legislating Privacy: Technology, Social Values and Public Policy*. Chapel Hill: University of North Carolina Press.

Schwartz, Barry. 1968. "The Social Psychology of Privacy." *American Journal of Sociology* 73: 741–52.

Telhami, Shibley. 2003. "Arab Public Opinion on the United States and Iraq." *Brookings Review* 21, no. 3: 24–7.

Westin, Alan F. 1967. *Privacy and Freedom*. New York: Atheneum.

– 2003. "Social and Political Dimensions of Privacy." *Journal of Social Issues* 59, no. 2: 431–53.

Worcester, Robert, Marta Lagos, and Miguel Basanez. 2000. "Problems and Progress in Cross-National Studies: Lessons Learned the Hard Way." Paper presented at the World Association for Public Opinion Research(WAPOR)/ American Association for Public Opinion Research (AAPOR) annual conference, Portland, OR.

Zureik, Elia. 2004. "Overview of Public Opinion Research Regarding Privacy (Appendix A)." http://www.sscqueens.org/sites/default/files/Overview_Appendix_A.pdf (accessed 9 November 2009).

CHAPTER TWO

Alexander, Cheryl R., and Henry J. Becker. 1978. "The Use of Vignettes in Survey Research." *Public Opinion Quarterly*, no. 42: 93–104.

King, Gary, Christopher J.L. Murray, Joshua A. Salomon, and Ajay Tandon. 2004. "Enhancing the Validity and Cross-Cultural Comparability of Survey Research." *American Political Science Review* 98, no. 1: 191–207.

SOFTWARE

Jonathan Wand, Gary King, and Olivia Lau. 2005. *Anchors statistical package for R, v. 2.0.*

CHAPTER THREE

APEC Data Privacy Subgroup. 2004. "APEC Symposium on Data Privacy Implementation Mechanisms: Developing the APEC Privacy Framework." Santiago, Chile, March.

Cable Communications Policy Act of 1984. Pub. L. No. 98–549, 98 Stat. 2794 (19 June 1984), codified at 45 USC 551.

Children's Online Privacy Protection Act. USC, title 15, chapter 91, §6502.

Cockfield, Arthur J. 2001. "Transforming the Internet into a Taxable Forum: A Case Study in E-commerce Taxation." *Minnesota Law Review* 85: 1171–1217.

Council of Europe Convention No. 108 of 18 September 1980. Strasbourg. http://conventions.coe.int/treaty/EN/cadreprincipal.htm (accessed 15 January 2008).

Criminal Law of China. 1 October 1997. http://www.humanrights-china.org/405c2001927164838.htm (accessed 15 January 2008).

Englander v. Telus Communications Inc. 12 November 2004. FCA 387.

European Commision. 1995. Commission Directive 95/46/EC of the European Parliament and of the Council of 24 October 1995 on the protection of individuals with regard to the processing of personal data and on the free movement of such data [EU Data Protection Directive]. OJ L 281/31.

– 2000. Commission Decision 2000/519/EC of 26 July 2000 pursuant to Directive 95/46/EC of the European Parliament and of the Council on the adequate protection of personal data provided in Hungary (notified under document number C[2000] 2305). OJ L 215, 25/08/2000 at 4.

Gramm-Leach-Bliley Financial Services Modernization Act (GLBA). Pub. L. No. 106–102, 113 Stat. 1338 (1999).

Health Insurance Portability and Accountability Act of 1996. 21 August 1996. *Pub. L. No. 104–191*, 100 Stat. 1936.

Law of the People's Republic of China on the Protection of Minors. Adopted at the 21st meeting of the Standing Committee of the Seventh National People's Congress on 4 September 1991, promulgated by Order No. 50 of the president of the People's Republic of China on 4 September 1991 and effective as of 1 January 1992.

Loukidelis, David. 2004. *Privacy and the USA Patriot Act: Implications for British Columbia Public Sector Outsourcing*. Office of the Information and Privacy Commissioner. http://www.oipc.bc.ca/sector_public/archives/usa_patriot_act/pdfs/report/privacy-final%20summary.pdf (accessed 15 January 2008). McIsaac, Barbara, Rick Shields, and Kris Klein. 2005. *The Law of Privacy in Canada*. Toronto: Carswell.

Office of the Privacy Commissioner of Canada. 2004. "Your Privacy Responsibilities: Guide for Businesses and Organizations to Canada's Personal Information Protection and Electronic Documents Act." http://www.privcom.gc.ca/information/guide_e.asp (accessed 15 January 2008).

Organization for Economic Cooperation and Development (OECD). 1980. OECD *Guidelines on the Protection of Privacy and Transborder Flows of Personal Data*. http://www.oecd.org (accessed 15 January 2008).

Perrin, Stephanie. 2001. *Personal Information Protection and Electronic Documents Act: An Annotated Guide*. Toronto: Irwin Law.

Personal Information Protection and Electronic Documents Act (PIPEDA). RSC 2000, c. 5.

PIPEDA Case Summary #145. 2003. "Alleged Disclosure of Personal Information to a Third Party without Consent." http://www.privcom.gc.ca/cf-dc/2003/cf-dc_030401_2_e.asp (accessed 15 January 2008).

Swire, Peter P., and Robert E. Litan. 1998. *None of Your Business: World Data Flows, Electronic Commerce, and the European Privacy Directive*. Washington, DC: Brookings Institution.

Tang, Raymond. 10 June 2004. "Asian Privacy at the Crossroads." Paper presented to the "IAPP Truste Symposium: Privacy Futures," San Francisco.

Uniting and Strengthening America by Providing Appropriate Tools Required to Intercept and Obstruct Terrorism (USA PATRIOT) Act of 2001. Pub. L. No. 107–56, 115 Stat. 272 (26 October 2001).

Video Privacy Protection Act. USC, title 18, part 1, chapter 121, §2710.

CHAPTER FOUR

Davis, James A. 1990. *The Logic of Causal Order*. Newbury Park, CA: Sage.

Doherty, Joe, Volker Busch-Geertsema, Vita Karpuskiene, Jukka Korhonen, Eoin O'Sullivan, Ingrid Sahlin, Antonio Tosi, Agostino Petrillo, and Julia Wygnańska. 2008. "Homelessness and Exclusion: Regulating Public Space in European Cities." *Surveillance and Society* 5, no. 3: 290–314.

Gilliom, John. 2005. "Resisting Surveillance." *Social Text* 83, 23, no. 2: 71–83.

Lyon, David. 2007. *Surveillance Studies: An Overview*. Cambridge, UK: Polity Press.

Marx, Gary T. 2003. "A Tack in the Shoe: Neutralizing and Resisting the New Surveillance." *Journal of Social Issues* 59, no. 2: 369–90.

Scott, James C. 1985. *Weapons of the Weak: Everyday Forms of Peasant Resistance*. New Haven, CT: Yale University Press.

Shapiro, Michael J. 2005. "Every Move You Make: Bodies, Surveillance and Media." *Social Text* 83, 23, no. 2: 21–34.

Smith, Emily. 2006. "Comparing the Globalization of Personal Data Survey on Privacy and Surveillance to Alan Westin's Survey Results and the Privacy Dynamic." Background paper commissioned by the Globalization of Personal Data (GPD) project, Queen's University, Kingston, ON. http://www.sscqueens.org/intl_survey_background.

Westin, Alan F. 2003. "Social and Political Dimensions of Privacy." *Journal of Social Issues* 59, no. 2: 431–53.

PART 3.1

INTRODUCTION

Bennett, Colin J., and Charles D. Raab. 2006. *The Governance of Privacy: Policy Instruments in Global Perspective*. Cambridge, MA: MIT Press.

Electronic Privacy Information Center (EPIC). 2005. *Public Opinion on Privacy*. http://www.epic.org/privacy/survey (accessed 20 November 2009).

Gandy, Oscar H. 2003. "Public Opinion Surveys and the Formation of Privacy Policy." *Journal of Social Issues* 59, no. 2: 283–300.

Harper, Jim, and Solveig Singleton. 2001. *With a Grain of Salt: What Consumer Privacy Surveys Don't Tell Us*. Competitive Enterprise Institute. http://www.cel.org (accessed 20 November 2009).

Harris, Louis, and Associates. 1991. *Harris-Equifax Consumer Privacy Survey*. Atlanta, GA: Equifax Inc.

Westin, Alan F. 2000. "Intrusions: Privacy Tradeoffs in a Free Society." *Public Perspective* (November-December): 8–11.

CHAPTER FIVE

Barkema, Harry G., and Freek Vermeulen. 1997. "What Differences in the Cultural Backgrounds of Partners Are Detrimental for International Joint Ventures?" *Journal of International Business Studies* 28, no. 4: 845–64.

Factor Analysis. 2005. *SPSS Manual* (SPSS 14.0, release 14.0.1). Chicago: Statistical Package for the Social Sciences (SPSS).

Greene, William H. 1997. *Econometric Analysis*. 3rd ed. Upper Saddle River, NJ: Prentice-Hall.

Harris, Louis, and Alan F. Westin. 1991. *Harris-Equifax Consumer Privacy Survey 1991*. Atlanta: Equifax Inc.

Hofstede, Geert H. 1993. "Cultural Constraints in Management Theories." *Academy of Management Executive* 7, no. 1: 81–94.

Kogut, Bruce, and Harbir Singh. 1988. "The Effect of National Culture on the Choice of Entry Mode." *Journal of International Business Studies* 19: 411–32.

Margulis, Stephen T. 2003. "On the Status and Contribution of Westin's and Altman's Theories of Privacy." *Journal of Social Issues* 59, no. 2: 411–30.

Pope, Jennifer A. 2003. "Breaking Up Is Hard to Do: The Dissolution of Business Relationships in the Global Market Place." PhD diss., University of Texas-Pan American.

Reed, Russel. 1993. "Politics and Policies of National Economic Growth." PhD diss., Stanford University.

Smith, Emily. 2006. "Comparing the Globalization of Personal Data Survey on Privacy and Surveillance to Alan Westin's Survey Results and the Privacy Dynamic." Background paper commissioned by the Globalization of Personal Data (GPD) project, Queen's University, Kingston, ON. http://www.sscqueens.org/intl_survey_background (accessed 17 September 2006).

Westin, Alan F. 1970. *Privacy and Freedom.* New York: Atheneum.

– 2003. "Social and Political Dimensions of Privacy." *Journal of Social Issues* 59, no. 2: 431–53.

CHAPTER SIX

ABC News/*Washington Post.* 2006a. "Poll: Terrorism vs. Privacy." *ABCNEWS.com*, 10 January. http://abcnews.com/pollvault.html (accessed October 2006).

– 2006b. "Poll: Americans Skeptical of Islam and Arabs." *ABCNEWS.com*, 8 March. http://abcnews.com/pollvault.html (accessed October 2006).

– 2006c. "Poll: Phone-Records Surveillance Is Broadly Acceptable to Public." *ABCNEWS.com*, 12 May. http://abcnews.com/pollvault.html (accessed October 2006).

Arsenault, Amelia, and Manuel Castells. 2006. "Conquering the Minds, Conquering Iraq: The Social Production of Misinformation in the United States – a Case Study." *Information, Communication and Society* 9, no. 3: 284–307.

Bagdikian, Ben. 2004. *The New Media Monopoly.* Boston: Beacon Press.

Beck, Ulrich. 2000. *The Brave New World of Work.* New York: Polity Press.

Cauley, Leslie. 2006. "NSA Has Massive Database of American Calls." *USA Today*, 10 May. http://www.usatoday.com/news/washington/2006-05-10-nsa_x.htm (accessed November 2006).

Chanley, Virginia. 2002. "Trust in Government in the Aftermath of 9/11: Determinants and Consequences." *Political Psychology* 23, no. 3: 469–83.

CNN.com. 2006. "Bush: Leaving Iraq Now Would Be a 'Disaster.'" *CNN.com*, 21 August. http://www.cnn.com/2006/POLITICS/08/21/iraq.poll/index.html (accessed 21 August 2006).

Cook, Timothy, and Paul Gronke. 2005. "The Skeptical American: Revisiting the Meanings of Trust in Government and Confidence in Institutions." *The Journal of Politics* 67, no. 3: 784–803.

Cornell News. 2004. "Fear Factor: 44 Percent of Americans Queried in Cornell National Survey Favour Curtailing Some Civil Liberties for Muslim Americans." *Cornell News*, 17 December. http://www.news.cornell.edu/releases/Dec04/Muslim.Poll.bpf.html (accessed November 2006).

Curran, James. 2000. "Rethinking Media and Democracy." In James Curran and Michael Gurevitch, eds, *Mass Media and Society*, 3rd ed., 120–54. London: Arnold.

Electronic Privacy Information Center (EPIC). 2006. "The USA Patriot Act." http://www.epic.org/privacy/terrorism/usapatriot (accessed October 2006).

Epstein, William. 2004. "Cleavage in American Attitudes towards Social Welfare." *Journal of Sociology and Social Welfare* (December): 469–83.

Gerbner, George. 1998. "Cultivation Analysis: An Overview." *Mass Communication and Society* 1, nos 3–4: 175–94.

– Larry Gross, Michael Morgan, and Nancy Signorielli. 1994. "Growing Up with Television: The Cultivation Perspective." In J. Bryant and D. Zillman, eds, *Media Effects: Advances in Theory and Research*, 17–41. Hillsdale, NJ: Lawrence Earlbaum.

Goldberg, Michelle. 2003. "Osama University?" *Salon.com.* http://www.geocities.com/ivorytowersorg/OsamaUniversity.htm (accessed November 2004).

Gottlieb, Calvin C. 1996. "Privacy: A Concept Whose Time Has Come and Gone." In David Lyon and Elia Zureik, eds, *Computers, Surveillance, and Privacy*, 156–171. Minneapolis: University of Minnesota Press.

Harris Interactive. 2001. "Overwhelming Public Support for Increasing Surveillance Powers and, in Spite of Many Concerns about Potential Abuses, Confidence That These Powers Would Be Used Properly." *Harris Poll*, no. 49 (3 October). http://www.harrisinteractive.com/harris_poll/index.asp?PID=260 (accessed October 2006).

– 2002. "Homeland Security: Public Continues to Endorse a Broad Range of Surveillance Powers but Support Has Declined Somewhat since Last September." *Harris Poll*, no. 16 (3 April). http://www.harrisinteractive.com/harris_poll/index.asp?PID=293 (accessed October 2006).

– 2003. "Homeland Security: American Public Continues to Endorse a Broad Range of Proposals for Stronger Surveillance Powers, but Support Has Declined Somewhat." *Harris Poll*, no. 14 (10 March). http://www.harrisinteractive.com/harris_poll/index.asp?PID=362 (accessed October 2006).

– 2004a. "Strong and Continuing Support for Tough Measures to Prevent Terrorism." *Harris Poll*, no. 17 (5 March). http://www.harrisinteractive.com/harris_poll/index.asp?PID=446 (accessed October 2006).

– 2004b. "Public Perceptions of Likelihood of Future Terrorist Attack Leads to Continuing Support for Tough Surveillance Measures to Prevent Terrorism." *Harris Poll*, no. 73 (1 October). http://www.harrisinteractive.com/harris_poll/index.asp?PID=501 (accessed October 2006).

– 2006. "Belief that Iraq Had Weapons of Mass Destruction Has Increased Substantially." *Harris Poll*, no. 57 (21 July). http://harrisinteractive.com/harris_poll/index.asp?PID=684 (accessed October 2006).

Herman, Edward, and Noam Chomsky. 1988. *Manufacturing Consent: The Political Economy of the Mass Media*. New York: Pantheon Books.

Johnson, Chalmers. 2001. *Blowback: The Costs and Consequences of American Empire*. New York: Henry Holt.

– 2004. *The Sorrows of Empire: Militarism, Secrecy, and the End of the Republic*. New York: Henry Holt.

Karim, Karim. 2003. *Islamic Peril: Media and Global Violence*. New York: Black Rose.

Kellner, Douglas. 2005. *Media Spectacle and the Crisis of Democracy: Terrorism, War and Election Battles*. Boulder, CO: Paradigm.

Langer, Gary. 2002. "Trust in Government ... to Do What?" *Public Perspective* (July-August): 7–10.

– 2006. "NSA Polls: Do They Contradict Each Other?" *World Newser*, 14 May. http://blogs.abcnews.com/theworldnewser/2006/05/nsa_polls_do_th.html (accessed October 2006).

– and Daniel Merkle. 2006. "ABC News' Polling Methodology and Standards." ABC News. http://abcnews.go.com/US/PollVault/story?id=145373&page=1 (accessed October 2006).

Lustick, Ian. 2006. *Trapped in the War on Terror*. Philadelphia: University of Pennsylvania Press.

Lyon, David. 2003. *Surveillance after September 11*. Oxford, UK: Blackwell.

McAlister, Melani. 2001. *Epic Encounters: Culture, Media, and U.S. Interests in the Middle East, 1945–2000*. London: University of California Press.

McChesney, Robert. 2004. *The Problem of the Media: U.S. Communication Policy in the Twenty-First Century*. New York: Monthly Review Press.

McMurtry, John. 1998. *Unequal Freedoms: The Global Market as an Ethical System*. Toronto: Kumarian Press.

Moeller, Susan D. 2004. "Media Coverage of Weapons of Mass Destruction." Center for International and Strategic Studies at Maryland (CISSM), 9 March. http://www.pipa.org/articles/WMDstudy_full.pdf (accessed November 2009).

Mueller, John. 2006. "Is There a Terrorist Threat? The Myth of the Omnipresent Enemy." *Foreign Affairs* 85, no. 5: 2–8.

Murdock, Graham. 1973. "Political Deviance: The Press Presentation of a Militant Mass Demonstration." In Stanley Cohen and Jack Young, eds, *The Manufacture of News: A Reader*, 157–75. Beverly Hills: Sage.

Pew Research Center for the People and the Press. 2001. "Terror Coverage Boost News Media's Images: But Military Censorship Backed." Survey report, 28 November. http://people-press.org/reports/display.php3?ReportID=9 (accessed October 2006).

– 2003. "Religion and Consensus: Growing Number Says Islam Encourages Violence among Followers." Poll, 24 July. http://people-press.org/reports/display.php3?ReportID=189 (accessed October 2006).

– 2006. "No Rise in Civil Liberties Concerns." Poll, 11 January. http://people-press.org/reports/display.php3?ReportID=267 (accessed October 2006).

Philo, Greg. 2002. "Television News and Audience Understanding of War, Conflict and Disaster." *Journalism Studies* 3, no. 2: 173–86.

– and Mike Berry. 2004. *Bad News from Israel*. London: Pluto Press.

Risen, James, and Eric Lichtblau. 2005. "Bush Lets U.S. Spy on Callers without Courts." *New York Times*, 16 December. http://www.nytimes.com/2005/12/16/politics/16program.html (accessed October 2006).

Roy, Sara. 2005. "Strategizing Control of the Academy." *Thought and Action* (Fall): 147–62.

Said, Edward. 1994. *Culture and Imperialism*. New York: Vintage Books.

– 1997. *Covering Islam: How the Media and the Experts Determine How We See the Rest of the World*. New York: Vintage Books.

Schiller, Herbert. 1998. "Striving for Communication Dominance: A Half-Century Review." In Daya K. Thussu, ed., *Electronic Empires*, 17–26. London: Arnold.

Schudson, Michael. 2003. *The Sociology of News*. New York: Norton.

Steinbruner, John. 2004. "Foreword." In Susan D. Moeller, *Media Coverage of Weapons of Mass Destruction*, iii–iv. Center for International and Strategic Studies at Maryland (CISSM), 9 March. http://www.pipa.org/articles/WMDstudy_full.pdf (accessed November 2009).

University of Connecticut Center for Survey Research and Analysis. 2005. "University of Connecticut Releases New National Poll on the USA PATRIOT Act." 26 August.

Wallerstein, Immanuel. 2003. *The Decline of American Power: The U.S. in a Chaotic World*. New York: New Press.

CHAPTER SEVEN

Crutcher, Nicole, and Michelle Budak. 2006. *The Anti-Terrorism Act and Security Measures in Canada: Public Views, Impacts and Travel Experiences*. Report prepared for the Department of Justice Canada. http://www.justice.gc.ca/eng/pi/rs/rep-rap/2005/rr05_11/rr05_11.pdf (accessed 26 November 2009).

De Grandpré, Hugo. 2007. "Connaissance des institutions fédérales: Les Québécois font figure de cancres." *La Presse*, 13 September, A10.

Environics. 2006. *Backgrounder: Environics Research Group Poll for the Trudeau Foundation*. October.

EKOS. 1997. "Les Québécois ignorent l'existence de lois protégeant la vie privée." *Le Devoir*, 25 September.

Fournier, François. 2005. *Public Opinion in Quebec on Privacy Issues and Protection of Personal Data (1994–2004): A Report*. Centre for Bioethics, Institut de recherches cliniques de Montréal. http://www.sscqueens.org/node/78 (accessed 26 November 2009).

Gagnon, Katia, and Agnès Gruda. 2006. "Les Québécois plus réticents que l'ensemble des Canadiens aux signes religieux." *Le Devoir*, 22 September, A1.

Gouvernement du Québec. 1999. *Politique québécoise de cryptographie et d'identification électronique. Étude préparatoire. Rapport d'analyse descriptive*. http://www.stat.gouv.qc.ca/publications/hors-col/pdf/inforoute.pdf (accessed 26 November 2009).

Ipsos Reid. 2006. *Global Privacy of Data: International Survey*. Summary report commissioned by the Globalization of Personal Data (GPD) project, Queen's University, Kingston, ON. http://www.sscqueens.org/files/Ipsos_Report_Nov_2006.pdf (accessed 26 November 2009).

Léger et Léger. 2000. *Évaluation des perceptions de la population du Québec concernant une carte nationale d'identité optionnelle*.

Sciencetech and Gouvernement du Québec. 1999. *Les Québécois face aux inforoutes. Tendances et perceptions dans un contexte de transactions électroniques et d'identification*.

Sondagem. 1999. "Sondage éclair. Une carte pour voter." *L'Actualité*, February.

PART 3.2

CHAPTER EIGHT

Bennett, James C. 2004. *The Anglosphere Challenge*. Lanham, MD: Rowman and Littlefield.

European Opinion Research Group. 2003. *Data Protection*. Special Eurobarometer 196. European Commission.

Fenyo, Krisztina. 1997. "Gloomy Sunday: Are Hungarians the Gloomiest Nation On Earth?" http://www.phespirit.info/gloomysunday/article_02.htm (accessed 7 November 2009).

Fukuyama, Francis. 1995. *Trust: The Social Virtues and the Creation of Prosperity*. New York: Free Press.

Gallup Hungary. 1991. *Correlations of Opinions about Population Registering.* In Hungarian.

The Gallup Organization. 2008. *Data Protection in the European Union – Citizens' Perceptions.* Flash Eurobarometer Series 225. European Commission.

Hankiss, Elemér. 2007. "Borderland Situation and Transition: Possible Interpretations of the East-Central European Transformation." 2000 (February): http://www.ketezer.hu/menu4/2007_02/hankiss.html (accessed 7 November 2009). In Hungarian.

International Research Associates. 1997. *Information Technology and Data Privacy.* Eurobarometer 46.1. European Commission.

Ipsos Reid. 2006. *Global Privacy of Data: International Survey.* Summary report commissioned by the Globalization of Personal Data (GPD) project, Queen's University, Kingston, ON. http://www.sscqueens.org/files/Ipsos_Report_Nov_2006.pdf (accessed 7 November 2009).

Ipsos Szonda Hungary. 2004. "Executive Summary of the Hungarian Research." Report commissioned by Ipsos North America on behalf of the Globalization of Personal Data (GPD) project, Queen's University, Kingston, ON.

Majtényi, László. 1998. *The First Three Years of the Parliamentary Commissioner for Data Protection and Freedom of Information.* Office of the Parliamentary Commissioner for Data Protection and Freedom of Information, Budapest.

– 1999. *Annual Report of the Parliamentary Commissioner for Data Protection and Freedom of Information 1998.* Office of the Parliamentary Commissioner for Data Protection and Freedom of Information, Budapest.

Szabó, Máté D., and Iván Székely. 2005. "Privacy and Data Protection at the Workplace in Hungary." In Sjaak Nouwt and Berend R. de Vries, eds, *Reasonable Expectations of Privacy? Eleven Country Reports on Camera Surveillance and Workplace Privacy*, 249–84. IT and Law Series. The Hague: TMC Asser Press.

Székely, Iván. 1991. *Information Privacy in Hungary: Survey Report and Analysis.* Hungarian Institute for Public Opinion Research, Budapest.

– 2008. "Hungary." In Jim Rule and Graham Greenleaf, eds, *Global Privacy Protection: The First Generation*, 174–206. Cheltenham, UK, and Northampton, MA: Edward Elgar.

Vámos, Miklos. 1999. *Xenophobe's Guide to the Hungarians.* London: Oval Projects.

CHAPTER NINE

Anderson, Perry. 1976. *Lineages of the Absolutist State.* London: New Left Books.

Arendt, Hannah. 1951. *The Origins of Totalitarianism*. New York: Harcourt.

– 1970. *Men in Dark Times*. London: J. Cape.

Bigo, Didier. 2000. "When the Two Became One: Internal and External Securitization in Europe." In Morten Kelstrup and Michael Williams, eds, *International Relations Theory and the Politics of European Integration: Power, Security and Community*, 171–204. London: Routledge.

Birnbaum, Pierre. 1998. *La France Imaginée*. Paris: Fayard.

Ceyhan, Ayse. 2006. "Technologie et Sécurité: Une Gouvernance Libérale dans un Context d'Incertitudes." *Cultures et Conflits* 64: 11–33.

Foucault, Michel. 1979. *Discipline and Punish: The Birth of the Prison*. New York: Random House.

Giddens, Anthony. 1991. *Modernity and Self-Identity: Self and Society in the Late Modern Age*. Stanford, CA: Stanford University Press.

Hofstede, Geert. 1980. *Culture's Consequences: Comparing Values, Behaviors, Institutions and Organizations across Nations*. London: Sage.

Internet World Statistics. http://www.internetworldstats.com (accessed 7 December 2009).

Ipsos Reid. 2005. "Findings from the Pre-Survey Focus Groups: Summary Report for France." Commissioned by the Globalization of Personal Data (GPD) project, Queen's University, Kingston, ON. http://www.sscqueens.org/intl_survey_background (accessed 7 December 2009).

– 2006. *Global Privacy of Data: International Survey*. Summary report commissioned by the Globalization of Personal Data (GPD) project, Queen's University, Kingston, ON. http://www.sscqueens.org/intl_survey_background (accessed 7 December 2009).

Lemeire, Didier, and Christian Lennerz. 1998. *Selected Countries in the Spotlight: Recent Trends in Society and Economy*. http://www.lennerz.de/talk_orgaIII98.pdf (accessed 7 December 2009).

Levin, Avner, and Mary Jo Nicholson. 1998. "Privacy Law in the United States, the EU and Canada: The Allure of the Middle Ground." *University of Ottawa Law and Technology Journal* 2, no. 2: 357–95.

Lindsay, David. 2005. "An Exploration of the Conceptual Basis of Privacy and the Implications for the Future of Australian Privacy Law." *Melbourne University Law Review* 29, no. 1: 131–78.

Lyon, David. 2001. *Surveillance Society: Monitoring Everyday Life*. Buckingham, UK: Open University Press.

– 2003. *Surveillance after September 11*. Oxford, UK: Polity Press.

Martinais, Emmanuel, and Christian Bétin. 2004. "Social Aspects of the CCTV in France: The Case of the City of Lyons." *Surveillance and Society* 2, nos 2–3: 361–75.

Marx, Gary T. 1994. "The Declining Signification of Traditional Borders and the Appearance of New Borders in an Age of High Technology." Paper for the conference "Georg Simmel between Modernity and Postmodernity," Munich, Ludwig Maximillians Universidad.

Noiriel, Gérard. 1996. *The French Melting Pot, Immigration, Citizenship and National Identity*. Minneapolis: University of Minnesota Press.

– 2001. *État, Nation et Immigration: Vers une Histoire du Pouvoir*. Paris: Belin.

Notoriete de la CNIL et Niveau D'Information sur la Protection des Donnees Personnelles. 2006. TNS-Sofres Survey, 6–7 December.

Nissenbaum, Helen. 2004. "Privacy as Contextual Integrity." *Washington Law Review* 79, no. 1: 119–58.

Observatoire de la Sécurité. http://www.securitypoint.org/secpt/templates/LocalStartPageG2____3475.aspx (accessed 7 December 2009).

Observatoire des mobiles. http://www.lesmobiles.com (accessed 7 December 2009).

Piazza, Pierre. 2004. *Histoire de la carte d'identité*. Paris: Odile Jacob.

– 2006. "Les Résistances au Projet INES." *Cultures et Conflits* 64: 65–75.

Post, Robert. 2001. "Three Concepts of Privacy." *Georgetown Law Journal* 89 (June): 2087–98.

Public Opinion in Quebec on Privacy and Protection of Personal Data. 2005. Report prepared by François Foumer, Centre for Bioethics – Institut de Recherche Clinique de Montréal, 11 April.

Rosa, Ehrenreich. 2001. "Privacy and Power." *Georgetown Law Journal* 89, no. 6: 2047–62.

Rosen, Jeffrey. 2000. *The Unwanted Gaze: The Destruction of Privacy in America*. New York: Random House.

– 2004. "Continental Divide." *Legal Affairs*, September/October. http://www.legalaffairs.org/issues/September-October-2004/review_rosen_sepoct04.msp (accessed 7 December 2009).

– 2007. "Science and Technology: The Logic of Privacy; Personal Data." *Economist*, 6 January 2007.

Rule, James B. 2007. "Deux Parcours Divergents: Les Climats Politiques et l'Accessibilité des renseignements personnels." http://www.creis.sgdg.org/colloques%20creis (accessed 7 December 2009).

Scott, James. 1998. *Seeing Like a State: How Certain Schemes to Improve the Human Condition Have Failed*. New Haven, CT: Yale University Press.

Tilly, Charles. 1975. *The Formation of National States in Europe*. Princeton, NJ: Princeton University Press.

Walzer, Michael. 1983. *Spheres of Justice: A Defense of Pluralism*. New York: Basic Books.

Warren, Samuel D., and Louis D. Brandeis. 1890. "The Right to Privacy." *Harvard Law Review* 4, no. 5: 193–220.

Westin, Alan. 1967. *Privacy and Freedom*. New York: Atheneum.

Whitman, James Q. 2004. "The Two Western Cultures of Privacy: Dignity Versus Liberty." *Yale Law Journal* 113, no. 6: 1152–221.

Zureik, Elia. 2004. "Appendix A: Overview of Public Opinion Research Regarding Privacy." Globalization of Personal Data (GPD) project, Queen's University, Kingston, ON. http://www.sscqueens.org/research/intl_survey (accessed 20 November 2009).

– L. Lynda Harling Stalker, and Emily Smith. 2006. "Background Paper for the Globalization of Personal Data Project International Survey on Privacy and Surveillance." Commissioned by the Globalization of Personal Data (GPD) project, Queen's University, Kingston, ON. http://www.sscqueens.org/research/intl_survey (accessed 20 November 2009).

PART 3.3

INTRODUCTION

Bradsher, Keith. 2007. "An Opportunity for Wall Street in China's Surveillance Boom." *New York Times*, 11 September.

McDougall, Bonnie, ed. 2002. *Concepts of Privacy in China*. Leiden: E.J. Brill.

Miller, Daniel, and Don Slater. 2000. *The Internet: An Ethnographic Approach*. London: Berg.

Peerenboom, Randall. 2002. *China's Long March towards Rule of Law*. Cambridge, UK: Cambridge University Press.

CHAPTER TEN

Bellman, Steve, Eric Johnson, Stephen Korbin, and Gerald L. Loshe. 2004. "International Differences in Information Privacy Concerns: A Global Survey of Consumers." *Information Society* 20: 313–24.

Bradsher, Keith. 2007. "China Enacting a High-Tech Plan to Track People." *New York Times*, 19 August. http://www.nytimes.com (accessed 13 November 2009).

China Internet Network Information Centre (CNNIC). 1997. *CNNIC Statistical Report No. 1*. http://www.cnnic.net.cn/download/manual/en-reports/1.pdf (accessed 13 November 2009).

– 2006. *17th Statistical Survey Report on the Internet Development in China*. http://www.cnnic.net.cn/download/2006/17threport-en.pdf (accessed 13 November 2009).

– 2008. "Statistical Survey Report on the Internet Development in China." http://www.cnnic.cn/uploadfiles/pdf/2008/2/29/104126.pdf (accessed 13 November 2009).

Harwit, Eric. 2004. "Spreading Telecommunication to Developing Areas in China: Telephones, the Internet and the Digital Divide." *China Quarterly*: 1010–30.

Hofstede, Geert. 1991. *Cultures and Organizations: Software of the Mind.* London: McGraw-Hill.

Hutton, Will. 2007. *The Writing on the Wall: China and the West in the 21st Century.* London: Little, Brown.

International Telecommunications Union (ITU). 2009. "Asia and the Pacific." In *Information Society Statistical Profiles.* http://www.itu.int/dms_pub/ itu-d/opb/ind/D-IND-RPM.AP-2009-R1-PDF-E.pdf (accessed 13 November 2009).

Internet World Stats. http://www.internetworldstats.com/stats3.htm (accessed 13 November 2009).

Jingchun, Cao. 2005. "Protecting the Right to Privacy in China." *Victoria University of Wellington Law Review* 36, no. 3: 645–64.

Klein, Naomi. 2008. "China's All-Seeing Eye." *Rolling Stone*, 29 May. http://www.rollingstone.com/politics/story/20797485/chinas_allseeing_eye (accessed 13 November 2009).

Liang, Guo, and Chang Huili. 2006. *Surveillance and Privacy in Urban China.* Report submitted to the Globalization of Personal Data (GPD) project, Queen's University, Kingston, ON. http://www.sscqueens.org/files/China_ Report_March_07.pdf (accessed 5 October 2009).

Lui, Wei. 2005. "Privacy Issues in China." Background paper submitted to the Globalization of Personal Data (GPD) project, Queen's University, Kingston, ON. http://www.sscqueens.org/intl_survey_background (accessed 13 November 2009).

Millberg, Sandra J., Sandra J. Burke, and H.J. Kallman. 1995. "Values, Personal Information, Privacy and Regulatory Approaches." *Communications of the ACM* 38, no. 12: 64–74.

Milne, Helen V. 2006. "The Digital Divide: The Roles of Political Institutions in Technology Diffusion." *Comparative Political Studies* 39, no. 2: 176–99.

OpenNet Initiative. 2005. *Internet Filtering in China in 2004–2005: A Country Study.* http:// http://opennet.net/blog/2005/06/internet-filtering-china-2004–2005 (accessed 13 November 2009).

Organization for Economic Cooperation and Development (OECD). 2005. "China's Economy: Still Some Way to Go." OECD *Observer*, July. http://www. oecdobserver.org/news (accessed November 2007).

Sydney Morning News. 2007. "China, India Lead Strong Growth in Internet Users: Survey." 7 March. http://www.smh.com.au/news/Technology/India-China-lead-strong-growth-in-Internet-users-survey/2007/03/07/1173166736816 (accessed 13 November 2009).

Tsui, Lockman. 2003. "The Panopticon as the Antithesis of a Space of Freedom: Control and Regulation of the Internet in China." *China Information* 17, no. 2: 65–82.

Wu, Tao. 2007. "Urban-Rural Divide in China Continues to Widen." Gallup News Service. 28 March.

Yao-Huai, Lu. 2005. "Privacy and Data Privacy Issues in Contemporary China." *Ethics and Information Technology* 7: 7–15.

Zhu, Guobin. 1997. "The Right to Privacy: An Emerging Right in Chinese Law." *Statute Law Review* 18, no. 3: 208–14.

CHAPTER ELEVEN

Ariès, Philippe, and Georges Duby. 1990. *Historia de la Vida Privada.* Buenos Aires: Taurus.

Arraigada, Irma, and Lorena Godoy. 1999. *Seguridad ciudadana y violencia en América Latina: Diagnóstico y políticas en los años noventa.* Santiago de Chile: CEPAL División de Desarrollo Social.

Arteaga, Nelson. 2005. "The Future That Will Not Come: The Eradication of Poverty from the Mexican Federal Government's Viewpoint (2000–2006)." In Alberto Cimadore, ed., *The Poverty of the State*, 135–55. Buenos Aires: CLACSO Books.

Bellman, Steven, Eric J. Johnson, Stephen J. Kobrin, and Gerald L. Lohse. 2003. "International Differences in Information Privacy Concerns: Implications for the Globalization of Electronic Commerce." *Information Society* 20, no. 5: 313–24.

Caldeira, César. 2000. "El crimen organizado en Brasil." *Nueva Sociedad* 167: 99–113.

Castel, Robert. 2003. *Propiedad privada, propiedad social, propiedad de sí mismo: Conversaciones sobre la construcción del individuo moderno.* Argentina: Politeia.

Castells, Manuel. 1998. *La era de la información: El fin del milenio.* Madrid: Alianza Editorial.

de Araujo, Tarcisio, and Roberto Alves de Lima. 2005. "Public Employment Policies as Tools for the Reduction of Poverty and Inequality in Brazil." In Alberto Cimadore, Hartley Dean, and Jorge Siqueira, eds, *The Poverty of the State*, 179–99. Argentina: CLACSO Books.

de Mesquita, Neto, and Adriana Loche. 2005. "Las asociaciones entre la policía y la comunidad en Brasil." In Hugo Frühling and Joseph S. Tulchin, eds, *Crimen y violencia en América Latina*, 218–28. Colombia: FCE.

Dubet, Francois. 1994. *Sociologie de l'expérience*. Paris: Seuil.

Duby, Georges. 1989. "Prefacio a la historia de la vida privada." In Philippe Ariès and Georges Duby, eds, *Historia de la vida privada*: *Imperio Romano y antigüedad tardía*, vol. 1, 9–11. Buenos Aires: Taurus.

EKOS Research Associates. 2004. "Findings from the Pre-Survey Focus Groups: Canada." Summary report commissioned by the Globalization of Personal Data (GPD) project, Queen's University, Kingston, ON. http://www.sscqueens.org/intl_survey_background (accessed 2 December 2009).

Giddens, Anthony. 1991. *Modernity and Self-Identity*. Cambridge, UK: Polity Press.

González, Pablo. 1979. *Imperialismo y liberación: Una introducción a la historia contemporánea de América Latina*. Mexico: Siglo XXI.

Gouldner, Alvin. 1976. *The Dialectic of Ideology and Technology*. New York: Seabury Press.

Hofstede, Geert. 1980. *Culture's Consequences: International Differences in Work-Related Values*. Beverly Hills: Sage.

Introna, Lucas D. 1997. "Privacy and the Computer: Why We Need Privacy in the Information Society." *Metaphilosophy* 28, no. 3: 259–75.

Ipsos-Bimsa. 2004a. "A Brief Description of Privacy Issues in Mexico." Background report commissioned by the Globalization of Personal Data (GPD) project, Queen's University, Kingston, ON. http://www.sscqueens.org/intl_survey_background (accessed 2 December 2009).

– 2004b. "Findings from the Mexico Focus Groups." Report commissioned by the Globalization of Personal Data (GPD) project, Queen's University, Kingston, ON. http://www.sscqueens.org/intl_survey_background (accessed 2 December 2009).

– 2004c. "Mexico City Focus Group: Transcript Session 1." Report commissioned by the Globalization of Personal Data (GPD) project, Queen's University, Kingston, ON. http://www.sscqueens.org/intl_survey_background (accessed 2 December 2009).

– 2004d. "Mexico City Focus Group: Transcript Session 2." Report commissioned by the Globalization of Personal Data (GPD) project, Queen's University, Kingston, ON. http://www.sscqueens.org/intl_survey_background (accessed 2 December 2009).

Ipsos Insight France. 2005. "Findings from the Pre-Survey Focus Groups: Summary Report for France." Report commissioned by the Globalization of

Personal Data (GPD) project, Queen's University, Kingston, ON. http://www.sscqueens.org/intl_survey_background (accessed 2 December 2009).

Ipsos Opinion do Brasil. 2004a. "Findings from the Sao Paulo/Brazil Pre-Survey Focus Groups." Report commissioned by the Globalization of Personal Data (GPD) project, Queen's University, Kingston, ON. http://www.sscqueens.org/intl_survey_background (accessed 2 December 2009).

– 2004b. "São Paulo Brazil Focus Group Transcriptions: Citizens and Consumers." Report commissioned by the Globalization of Personal Data (GPD) project, Queen's University, Kingston, ON. http://www.sscqueens.org/intl_survey_background (accessed 2 December 2009).

– 2004c. "São Paulo Brazil Focus Group Transcriptions: Workers and Travellers." Report commissioned by the Globalization of Personal Data (GPD) project, Queen's University, Kingston, ON. http://www.sscqueens.org/intl_survey_background (accessed 2 December 2009).

Ipsos Reid. 2006. *Global Privacy of Data: International Survey*. Summary report commissioned by the Globalization of Personal Data (GPD) project, Queen's University, Kingston, ON. http://www.sscqueens.org/intl_survey_background (accessed 2 December 2009).

Lyon, David. 1994. *The Electronic Eye: The Rise of Surveillance Society*. Minneapolis: University of Minnesota Press.

– 2001. *Surveillance Society: Monitoring Everyday Life*. Philadelphia: Open University Press.

Pastor, Manuel, and Carol Wise. 1997. "State Policy, Distribution and Neoliberal Reform in Mexico." *Journal of Latin American Studies* 29, no. 2: 419–57.

Prost, Antoine. 1989. "Fronteras y espacios de lo privado." In *Historia de la vida privada: La vida privada en el siglo XX*, vol. 9, 13–153. Buenos Aires: Taurus.

Smith, Emily. 2005. "Privacy in Mexico." Background paper commissioned by the Globalization of Personal Data (GPD) project, Queen's University, Kingston, ON. http://www.sscqueens.org/intl_survey_background (accessed 2 December 2009).

Sosa, Raquel. 2004. "Pobreza, violencia y seguridad pública en los años neoliberales." In Raquel Sosa, ed., *Sujetos, víctimas y territorios de la violencia en América Latina*, 115–32. México: Universidad de la Ciudad de México.

Ward, Peter. 1993. "Social Welfare Policy and Political Opening in Mexico." *Journal of Latin American Studies* 25, no. 3: 613–28.

Wieviorka, Michel. 2004. *La violence*. Paris: Balland.

World Values Survey. 2005. "Encuesta Mundial de Valores: México." http://www.worldvaluessurvey.org (accessed 2 december 2009).

– 2006. "Fieldwork Report wvs – Brazil." http://www.worldvaluessurvey.org (accessed 2 december 2009).

Yurke, Shannon. 2005. "Privacy, Policy and Public Opinion in Brazil." Background paper commissioned by the Globalization of Personal Data (GPD) project, Queen's University, Kingston, ON. http://www.sscqueens.org/intl_survey_background (accessed 2 December 2009).

Zureik, Elia, L. Lynda Harling Stalker, and Emily Smith. 2006. "Background Paper for the Globalization of Personal Data Project International Survey on Privacy and Surveillance." Commissioned by the Globalization of Personal Data (GPD) project, Queen's University, Kingston, ON. http://www.sscqueens.org/intl_survey (accessed 2 December 2009).

PART 4.1

CHAPTER TWELVE

Agamben, Giorgio. 2005. *State of Exception*. Chicago: University of Chicago Press.

Angus Reid. 2004. http://www.angus-reid.com/polls/index.cfm/fuseaction/view-Item/itemID/5342 (accessed 23 November 2009).

Batson, Andrew. 2003. "China Begins Effort to Replace Citizen IDs with Digital Cards." *Wall Street Journal*, 12 August.

Bennett, Colin, and Charles Raab. 2003. *The Governance of Privacy*. London: Ashgate.

Bigo, Didier. 2006. "Security, Exception, Ban and Surveillance." In David Lyon, ed., *Theorizing Surveillance: The Panopticon and Beyond*, 46–68. Cullompton: Willan.

Chance, Clifford. 2004. *Information Resource on ID Cards*. London: Justice.

Fussell, Jim. 2001. "Group Classification on National ID Cards." http://www.preventgenocide.org/prevent/removing-facilitating-factors/IDcards/sources.htm (accessed 24 November 2009).

Gandy, Oscar. 2003. "Public Opinion Surveys and the Formation of Public Policy." *Journal of Social Issues* 59, no. 2: 283–99.

Information Privacy Commission (IPC). 2006. 7 *Laws of Privacy*. Toronto: IPC.

Isin, Engin, and Bryan Turner. 2007. "Investigating Citizenship: An Agenda for Citizenship Studies." *Citizenship Studies* 11, no. 1: 5–17.

Lui, Wei. 2005. "China Backgrounder." Paper commissioned by the Globalization of Personal Data (GPD) project, Queen's University, Kingston, ON. http://www.sscqueens.org/intl_survey_background (accessed 24 November 2009).

Lyon, David. 1993. "British ID Cards: The 'Unpalatable Logic' of European Integration?" *Political Quarterly* 62, no. 3: 377–85.

– 2003. *Surveillance after September 11*. Cambridge, UK: Polity Press.
– 2004. ID *Cards: Social Sorting by Database*. Oxford Internet Institute (OII) issue brief. http://www.oii.ox.ac.uk (accessed 24 November 2009).
– 2005. "The Border Is Everywhere: ID Cards, Surveillance and the Other." In Elia Zureik and Mark Salter, eds, *Global Surveillance and Policing*, 66–82. Cullompton, UK: Willan.
– 2009. *Identifying Citizens: ID Cards as Surveillance*. Cambridge, UK: Polity Press.
Margulis, Stephen. 1977. "Conceptions of Privacy: Current Status and Next Steps." *Journal of Social Issues* 33, no. 3: 5–21.
McLeod, Judi. 2006. "Company Working for China Secret Police to Issue Passports to Americans." http://www.canadafreepress.com/2006/cover030806.htm (accessed 24 November 2009).
Murakami Wood, David, David Lyon, and Kiyoshi Abe. 2007. "Surveillance in Urban Japan: A Critical Introduction." *Urban Studies* 44, no. 3: 551–68.
Pastor, Robert. 2006. "Mexico's Election Message to US." *Los Angeles Times*, 8 July. http://www.latimes.com/news/opinion/commentary/la-oe-pastor-8jul08,0,51027.story?coll=la-news-comment-opinions (accessed 24 November 2009).
Perri 6. 2005. "The Personal Information Economy." In Susanne Lace ed., *The Glass Consumer: Life in a Surveillance Society*, 17–44. Bristol, UK: Policy Press.
Piazza, Pierre. 2004. "Septembre 1921: La première carte d'identite de français et ses enjeux." *Geneses*, March, 76–89.
Roy, Jeffrey. 2006. "Privacy, Identity and Digital Policy." Research workshop presentation for the Globalization of Personal Data (GPD) project, Queen's University, Kingston, ON.
Schwartz, Ari. 2003. "Getting to Know All about You." *Chicago Tribune*, 23 August. http://www.chicagotribune.com/news/opinion/oped/chi-0208230299aug23.story (accessed 23 August 2003).
STMicroelectronics. 2006. "Spain Launches ID Card Based on STMicroelectronics' Secure Smart Card Chip." 9 October. http://www.st.com/stonline/stappl/press/news/year2006/t2079.htm (accessed 2 December 2009).
Surveillance Studies Network. 2006. *Report on the Surveillance Society*. London: Information Commissioner's Office (ICO).
Westin, Alan. 2003. "Social and Political Dimensions of Privacy." *Journal of Social Issues* 59, no. 2: 431–53.
Zureik, Elia, L. Lynda Harling Stalker, and Emily Smith. 2006. Background paper commissioned by the Globalization of Personal Data (GPD) project, Queen's University, Kingston, ON. http://www.sscqueens.org/research/intl_survey (accessed 24 November 2009).

CHAPTER THIRTEEN

Brown, David, and David Brook. 2003. "Biometrics: Implications and Applications for Citizenship and Immigration – Report on a Forum Hosted by Citizenship and Immigration Canada." Presented at Public Policy Forum, Ottawa, 7–8 October 2003. http://www.ppforum.com/ow/Biometrics-engcic.gc.ca/EnGLish/pdf/pub/biometrics.pdf (accessed 20 November 2009).

CBC. 2007. "Passport Delays to Worsen as U.S. Rules Come In." *CBC News*, 23 January. http://www.cbc.ca/canada/new-brunswick/story/2007/01/23/nb-uspassport.html (accessed 20 November 2009).

CTV. 2004. "Canadians Uneasy about Security-Rights Balance: Poll." *CTV.ca*, 9 February. http://www.ctv.ca/serv;let/ArticleNews/printstory/CTVNews/10762 89101731_6/?hub=CTVNewsCTVNewsAt11 (accessed 20 November 2009).

– 2005. "Canadians Split on Anti-Terror Measures: Poll." *CTV.ca*, 11 August. http://www.ctv.ca/servlet/ArticleNews/story/CTVNews/20050811/security_poll_050810?s_name=uselection2008&no_ads= (accessed 20 November 2009).

Delacourt, Susan. 2006. "Ottawa Takes 'Big Step' to Biometric ID." *Toronto Star*, 30 June. http://www.thestar.com/NASApp/cs/ContentServer?pagename=thestar/Layout/Article_Type1&call_pageid=971358637177&c=Article&cid=1151617836735 (accessed 15 August 2006).

EDS Canada, with Ipsos Reid. 2005. *EDS Canada Privacy and Identity Management Survey: White Paper – Summary of Results and Findings*. 31 January.

EKOS Research Associates. 2001. *Security, Sovereignty and Continentalism: Canadian Perspectives on September 11*. Commissioned by the *Toronto Star*, *La Presse*, and CBC/SRC, 27 September. http://www.ekos.com/admin/articles/27-sept-2001E.pdf (accessed 20 November 2009).

– 2003a. *Canadians' Views Towards a National ID Card and Biometrics*. Commissioned by Citizenship and Immigration Canada (CIC), 31 March.

– 2003b. *Public Opinion Concerning Biometrics and National ID Cards*. Commissioned by Citizenship and Immigration Canada (CIC) and presented to the Privacy Council Office.

Fournier, François. 2005. *Public Opinion in Quebec on Privacy Issues and Protection of Personal Data (1994–2004): A Report*. Centre for Bioethics, Institut de recherches cliniques de Montréal. http://www.sscqueens.org/intl_survey_background (accessed 20 November 2009).

Gandy, Oscar H., Jr. 2003. "Public Opinion Surveys and the Formation of Privacy Policy." *Journal of Social Issues* 59, no. 2: 283–300.

Government of Canada. 2004. *Public Opinion on Privacy Issues: Presentation to the ADM Privacy Committee*. Privy Council Office, May 2004.

Government of the United States, Department of State. 2006. "New Requirements for Travelers: Under the Western Hemisphere Travel Initiative." http://travel.state.gov/travel/cbpmc/cbpmc_2223.html (accessed 20 November 2009).

Homeland Security Western Hemisphere Travel Initiative. http://www.dhs.gov/xtrvlsec/crossingborders/gc_1156449786568.shtm (accessed 15 August 2006).

House of Commons, Canada. 2003. "A National Identity Card for Canada?" Interim Report of the Standing Committee on Citizenship and Immigration, MP Joe Fontana, chair, October 2003 [Standing Committee Interim Report]. http://192.197.82.11/infocomdoc/Documents/37/2/parlbus/commbus/house/reports/cimmrp06/cimmrp06-e.pdf (accessed 20 November 2009).

Ipsos Reid. 2003. *National ID Cards*. 7–9 October.

– with the *Globe and Mail* and CTV. 2004. "Almost Half (45%) Believe Police Have Gone 'Too Far' in Using Anti-Terrorism Powers." Press release, 8 February.

Ipsos Reid/*Globe and Mail*/CTV. 2001. "Majority (58%) Say Terrorism Threats Outweight the Protection of Individual Rights, Freedom and Due Process of Law." Press release, 5 October 2001.

Kapica, Jack. 2005. "Biometrics Make People Wary." *Globe and Mail*, 2 August. http://www.globetechnology.com/servlet/story/RTGAM.20050802.gtbiometrics0802/BNStory/Technology (accessed 2 August 2005).

Lysecki, Sarah. 2005. "Canadians Come Out in Support of Biometric Passports." *IT Business*, 2 August. http://www.itbusiness.ca/it/client/en/Home/News.asp?id=1819 (accessed 20 November 2009).

Singleton, Solveig, and Jim Harper. 2001. "With a Grain of Salt: What Consumer Privacy Surveys Don't Tell Us." http://www.cei.org/PDFs/with_a_grain_of_salt.pdf (accessed 20 November 2009).

The Strategic Counsel. 2005. "Terrorism and National Security." *Globe and Mail* and CTV, 7 August.

Workpermit.com. 2006. "Canadian Poll – Biometric Identification and Immigration in Favour." 4 October. http://www.workpermit.com/news/2006_10_04/canada/biometrics_immigration_opinion_poll.htm (accessed 20 November 2009).

Zureik, Elia. 2004. "Globalization of Personal Data Project International Survey Concept Paper." Queen's University, Kingston, ON. http://www.sscqueens.org/research/intl_survey (accessed 20 November 2009).

– with contributions from Karen Hindle. 2004. "Governance, Security and Technology: The Case of Biometrics." *Studies in Political Economy* 73 (Spring/Summer): 113–37.

– L. Lynda Harling Stalker, and Emily Smith. 2006. "Background Paper for the Globalization of Personal Data Project International Survey on Privacy and

Surveillance." Commissioned by the Globalization of Personal Data (GPD) project, Queen's University, Kingston, ON. http://www.sscqueens.org/research/intl_survey (accessed 20 November 2009).

CHAPTER FOURTEEN

Andal-Ancion, Angela, Phillip Cartwright, and George S. Yip. 2003. "The Digital Transformation of Traditional Business." MIT *Sloan Management Review* 44, no. 4: 34–41.

Arar Commision. 2006. *Report of the Events Relating to Maher Arar: Analysis and Recommendations*. http://www.pch.gc.ca/cs-kc/arar/Arar_e.pdf (accessed 4 December 2009).

Archick, Kristin. 2006. *US-EU Cooperation against Terrorism*. Washington, DC: Library of Congress, Congressional Research Service.

Coleman, Stephen. 2003. "The Future of the Internet and Democracy beyond Metaphors, towards Policy." In Organization for Economic Cooperation and Development (OECD), *Promise and Problems of E-Democracy: Challenges on Online Citizen Engagement*, 143–60. Paris: OECD, E-Government Project.

– 2006. "E-mail, Terrorism and the Right to Privacy." *Ethics and Information Technology* 8: 17–27.

– and Donald Norris. 2005. "A New Agenda for E-Democracy." *International Journal of Electronic Government Research* 1, no. 3: 69–82.

Dutta, Amit, and Kevin McCrohan. 2002. "Management's Role in Information Security in a Cyber Economy." *California Management Review* 45, no. 1: 67–87.

European Communities. 2005. *eGovernment in Spain*. http://ec.europa.eu/id-abc/servlets/Doc?id=21024 (accessed 3 December 2009).

Evans, Karen G. 2002. "Virtual Dialogue and Democratic Community." *The Transformative Power of Dialogue* 12: 157–77.

Gasco, Mila, and Jeffrey Roy. 2006. "E-Government and Multi-Level Governance: A Comparative Examination of Catalonia, Spain, and Ontario, Canada." *International Journal of E-Government Research* 2, no. 4: 57–75.

Geist, Michael. 2005. "The Three Stages of Canadian Privacy Law." http://www.michaelgeist.ca/resc/html_bkup/april112005.html (accessed 3 December 2009).

Gibbons, Roger. 2004. "Federalism and the Challenge of Electronic Portals." In E. Lynn Oliver and Larry Sanders, eds, *E-Government Reconsidered: Renewal of Governance for the Knowledge Age*, 33–42. Regina: Canadian Plains Research Center.

Henrich, Vincent C., and Albert N. Link. 2003. "Deploying Homeland Security Technology." *Journal of Technology Transfer* 28: 363–8.

Holden, Stephen. 2004. *Understanding Electronic Signatures: The Keys to e-Government*. Washington, DC: IBM Center for the Business of Government.

Holmes, Allan. 2005. "Riding the California Privacy Wave." *CIO Magazine*, 15 January. http://www.cio.com/article/1566/Riding_The_California_Privacy_Wave (accessed 3 December 2009).

Joshi, James B.D., Arif Ghafoor, and Walif G. Aref. 2002. "Security and Privacy Challenges of a Digital Government." In Ahmed K. Elmagarmid and William J. McIver, eds, *Advances in Digital Government – Technology, Human Factors and Policy*, 121–36. Boston: Kluwer Academic.

Kim, Soonhee, and Hyangsoo Lee. 2004. "Organizational Factors Affecting Knowledge Sharing Capabilities in E-government: An Empirical Study." In M.A. Wimmer, ed., *KMGov 2004, LNAI 3035*, 1–11. Seattle: International Federation for International Processing.

Lane, Greg, and Jeffrey Roy. 2006. "Security and Stability on the Electronic Highway: A Collaborative Challenge for Industry and Government." *Optimum Online* 36, no. 2: 45–54.

Lips, Miriam, John Taylor, and Joe Organ. 2006. "Electronic Government: New Forms of Authentication, Citizenship and Governance." Working paper. Oxford, UK: Oxford Internet Institute.

Lyon, David. 2004. "Surveillance Technologies: Trends and Social Implications." In Organization for Economic Cooperation and Development (OECD), *The Security Economy*, 126–48. Paris: OECD.

O'Harrow, Robert. 2005. *No Place to Hide*. New York: Free Press.

Prins, J.E.J., ed. 2001. *Designing E-Government: On the Crossroads of Technological Innovation and Institutional Change*. The Hague, Netherlands: Kluwer Law International.

Regan, P.M. 2004. "Old Issues, New Context: Privacy, Information Collection, and Homeland Security." *Government Information Quarterly* 21, no. 4: 481–97.

Reid, John. 2004. "Holding Governments Accountable by Strengthening Access to Information Laws and Information Management Practices." In E. Lynn Oliver and Larry Sanders, eds, *E-Government Reconsidered: Renewal of Governance for the Knowledge Age*, 79–88. Regina: Canadian Plains Research Center.

Roy, Jeffrey. 2005a. "Security, Sovereignty and Continental Interoperability: An Elusive Balance for Canada?" *Computers and Social Science Review* 22, no. 2: 1–17.

– 2005b. "Services, Security, Transparency and Trust: Government Online or Governance Renewal in Canada?" *International Journal of E-Government Research* 1, no. 1: 48–58.

– 2006. *E-Government in Canada: Transformation for the Digital Age*. Ottawa: University of Ottawa Press.

– 2007. "National Security Governance after Arar." *Options Politics* (March): 64–8.

Scholl, Hans. 2005. "Motives, Strategic Approach, Objectives and Focal Points in E-Government-Induced Change." *International Journal of E-Government Research* 1, no. 1: 59–78.

Uniting and Strengthening America by Providing Appropriate Tools Required to Intercept and Obstruct Terrorism (USA PATRIOT) Act. 2001. Pub. L. no. 107–56, 115 Stat. 272 (26 October).

Woodward, Val. 2003. "Participation the Community Work Way." *International Journal of Healthcare Technology and Management* 5, nos 1–2: 3–19.

PART 4.2

CHAPTER FIFTEEN

Acquisti, Alessandro, and Jens Grossklags. 2005. "Privacy and Rationality in Individual Decision Making." *Security and Privacy Magazine*, IEEE 3, no. 1: 26–33.

Burrows, Roger, and Nicholas Gane. 2006. "Geodemographics, Software and Class." *Sociology* 40, no. 5: 793–812.

Canadian Internet Policy and Public Interest Clinic (CIPPIC). 2006. *On the Data Trail: How Detailed Information about You Gets into the Hands of Organizations with Whom You Have No Relationship.* http://www.cippic.ca/documents/May1-06/DatabrokerReport.pdf (accessed 23 November 2009).

Danna, Anthony, and Oscar H. Gandy. 2002. "All That Glitters Is Not Gold: Digging beneath the Surface of Data Mining." *Journal of Business Ethics* 40: 373–86.

Deighton, John. 2005. "Consumer Identity Motives in the Information Age." In S. Ratneshwar and David Glen Mick, eds, *Inside Consumption: Consumer Motives, Goals and Desires*, 233–51. London: Routledge.

Dommeyer, Curt, and Barbara Gross. 2003. "What Consumers Know and What They Do: An Investigation of Consumer Knowledge, Awareness, and Use of Privacy Protection Strategies." *Journal of Interactive Marketing* 17, no. 2: 34–51.

EKOS Research Associates. 2004a. "Focus Group Findings: Toronto and Montreal." Report commissioned by the Globalization of Personal Data (GPD) project, Queen's University, Kingston, ON. http://www.sscqueens.org/intl_survey_background (accessed 23 November 2009).

– 2004b. "Focus Group Summary: Chicago." Report commissioned by the Globalization of Personal Data (GPD) project, Queen's University, Kingston, ON. http://www.sscqueens.org/intl_survey_background (accessed 23 November 2009).

– 2004c. "Focus Group Transcripts: Chicago." Commissioned by the Globalization of Personal Data (GPD) project, Queen's University, Kingston, ON. http://www.sscqueens.org/intl_survey_background (accessed 23 November 2009).

– 2004d. "Focus Group Transcripts: Toronto and Montreal." Commissioned by the Globalization of Personal Data (GPD) project, Queen's University, Kingston, ON. http://www.sscqueens.org/intl_survey_background (accessed 23 November 2009).

Evans, Martin. 1998. "From 1086 to 1984: Direct Marketing into the Millennium." *Marketing Intellegence and Planning* 16, no. 1: 56–67.

Gandy, Oscar H. 1993. *The Panoptic Sort: A Political Economy of Personal Information.* Boulder, CO: Westview.

Graeff, Timothy, and Susan Harmon. 2002. "Collecting and Using Personal Data: Consumers' Awareness and Concerns." *Journal of Consumer Marketing* 19, no. 4: 302–18.

Paul, Pamela. 2001. "Mixed Signals: When It Comes to Issues of Privacy, Consumers Are Fraught with Contradictions." *American Demographics* (July): 45–9.

Perri 6. 2005. "The Personal Information Economy: Trends and Prospects for Consumers." In Susanne Lace, ed., *The Glass Consumer: Life in a Surveillance Society*, 17–44. Bristol, UK: Polity Press.

Phelps, Joseph, Glen Nowak, and Elizabeth Ferrell. 2000. "Privacy Concerns and Consumer Willingness to Provide Personal Information." *Journal of Public Policy and Marketing* 19, no. 1: 27–41.

Rowley, Jennifer. 2005. "Customer Knowledge Management or Consumer Surveillance." *Global Business and Economics Review* 7, no. 1: 100–10.

Smith, Andrew, and Leigh Sparks. 2003. "Making Tracks: Loyalty Cards as Consumer Surveillance." *European Advances in Consumer Research* 6: 368–73.

– 2004. "All about Eve?" *Journal of Marketing Management* 20, nos 3–4: 363–85.

White, Tiffany Barnett. 2004. "Consumer Disclosure and Disclosure Avoidance." *Journal of Consumer Psychology* 14, nos 1–2: 41–51.

CHAPTER SIXTEEN

Act CLV of 1997 on Consumer Protection, Hungary. English version retrieved from the National Association for Consumer Protection in Hungary (OFE). http://www.ofe.hu (accessed 5 March 2007).

Blaikie, Norman. 2000. *Designing Social Research.* Cambridge, UK: Polity Press.

Cheung, Christy M.K., and Matthew K.O. Lee. 2006. "Understanding Consumer Trust in Internet Shopping: A Multidisciplinary Approach." *Journal of the American Society for Information Science and Technology* 54: 479–92.

Consumers International. 2000a. *Consumer Policy and Consumer Organisations in Central and Eastern Europe.* http://www.consumersinternational.org (accessed 5 March 2007).

– 2000b. *Balancing the Scales Part III: Consumer Protection in Greece and Spain.* http://www.consumersinternational.org (accessed 5 March 2007).

Cseres, Katalin. 2004. "The Hungarian Cocktail of Competition Law and Consumer Protection: Should It Be Dissolved?" *Journal of Consumer Policy* 27: 43–74.

EKOS Research Associates. 2005. "Findings from the Pre-Survey Focus Groups: Report for Spain." Commissioned by the Globalization of Personal Data (GPD) project, Queen's University, Kingston, ON.

Eurobarometer. 2003. "Consumer Protection in the EU." Special report no. 193. http://ec.europa.eu/public_opinion/archives/ebs/ebs_193_en.pdf (accessed 15 January 2009).

– 2004. "European Union Citizens and Access to Justice." Special report no. 195. http://ec.europa.eu/consumers/redress/reports_studies/eurobarometer_11-04_en.pdf (accessed 15 January 2009).

– 2006. "Consumer Protection in the Internal Market." Special report no. 252. http://ec.europa.eu/consumers/topics/eurobarometer_09-2006_en.pdf (accessed 15 January 2009).

European Commission, Working Party on the Protection of Individuals with Regard to the Processing of Personal Data. 1999. "Opinion 6/99 Concerning the Level of Personal Data Protection in Hungary." http://ec.europa.eu/justice_home/fsj/privacy/docs/wpdocs/1999/wp24en.pdf (accessed 15 January 2009).

European Commission, Consumer Affairs. 2007. "Out-of-Court Bodies in the Member States." Database. http://ec.europa.eu/consumers/redress/out_of_court/commu/database.htm (accessed 5 March 2007).

European Consumer Centre (ECC). 2003a. "The European Online Marketplace: Consumer Complaints – A Summary and Analysis of Consumer Complaints Reported to the European Consumer Centre Network." http://www.konsumenteuropa.se (accessed 15 January 2009).

– 2003b. "Realities of the European Online Marketplace – A Cross-Border E-Commerce Project by the European Consumer Centre's Network." http://www.konsumenteuropa.se (accessed 15 January 2009).

Gerring, John. 2007. *Case Study Research: Principles and Practices*. Cambridge, UK: Cambridge University Press.

Hirschman, Albert O. 1970. *Exit, Voice, and Loyalty: Responses to Decline in Firms, Organizations, and States*. Cambridge, MA: Harvard University Press.

Hoffman, Donna L., Thomas P. Novak, and Marcos A. Peralta. 1999. "Information Privacy in the Marketspace: Implications for the Commercial Uses of Anonymity on the Web." *The Information Society* 15: 129–39.

Hungarian Privacy Commissioner. http://abiweb.obh.hu/dpc/index.htm (accessed 5 March 2007).

Ipsos Insight France. 2005. "Findings from the Pre-Survey Focus Groups: Summary Report for France." Commissioned by the Globalization of Personal Data (GPD) project, Queen's University, Kingston, ON. http://www.sscqueens.org/intl_survey_background (accessed 24 February 2010).

Ipsos Szonda Hungary. 2004. "Executive Summary of the Hungarian Research." Report commissioned by Ipsos North America on behalf of the Globalization of Personal Data (GPD) project, Queen's University, Kingston, ON. http://www.sscqueens.org/intl_survey_background (accessed 24 February 2010).

Koehn, Daryl. 2003. "The Nature of and Conditions for Online Trust." *Journal of Business Ethics* 43: 3–19.

March, James G., and Johan P. Olsen. 1989. *Rediscovering Institutions*. New York: Free Press.

Metzger, Miriam J. 2006. "Effects of Site, Vendor, and Consumer Characteristics on Web Site Trust and Disclosure." *Communication Research* 33, no. 3: 155–79.

Organization for Economic Cooperation and Development (OECD). 2002. "Spain – Annual Report on Consumer Policy Developments 2002." http://www.oecd.org (accessed 15 January 2009).

Peters, Guy. 1996. "Political Institutions, Old and New." In Robert Goodin and Hans-Dieter Klingemann, eds, *A New Handbook of Political Science*, 205–20. Oxford, UK: Oxford University Press.

Princeton Survey Research Associates. 2002. "A Matter of Trust: What Users Want from Web Sites: Results of a National Survey of Internet Users for Consumer WebWatch." http://www.consumerwebwatch.org (accessed 15 January 2009).

Privacy International. 2003. "Privacy International & EPIC Privacy and Human Rights 2003 World Privacy Survey: Hungary." http://www.privacyinternational.org (accessed 15 January 2009).

Rezabakhsh, Behrang, Daniel Bornemann, Ursula Hansen, and Ulf Schrader. 2006. "Consumer Power: A Comparison of the Old Economy and the Internet Economy." *Journal of Consumer Policy* 29: 3–36.

Rose, Richard, and Wolfgang Seifert. 1995. "Materielle Lebensbedingungen und Einstellungen gegenüber Marktwirtschaft und Demokratie im Transformationsprozeß: Ostdeutschland und Osteuropa im Vergleich." In Hellmut Wollman, Helmut Wiesenthal, and Frank Bönker, eds, *Transformation sozialistischer gesellschaften: Am Ende des Anfangs*, 277–98. Opladen, Germany: Westdeutscher Verlag GmbH.

Sanches, Samy. 2005. "Sustainable Consumption à la française? Conventional, Innovative, and Alternative Approaches to Sustainability and Consumption in France." *Sustainability: Science, Practice, and Policy* 1, no. 1: http://ejournal.nbii.org/archives/vol1iss1/0410-010.sanches.html (accessed 15 November 2009).

Sculze, Reiner, and Hans Schulte-Nölke. 2003. "National Report: France." In Reiner Sculze and Hans Schulte-Nölke, eds, *Analysis of National Fairness Laws Aimed at Protecting Consumers in Relation to Commercial Practices*. Study commissioned by the Directorate-General for Health and Consumer

Protection of the European Commission (DG SANCO). http://ec.europa.eu/consumers/cons_int/safe_shop/fair_bus_pract/green_pap_comm/studies/unfair_practices_en.pdf (accessed 15 January 2009).

Streek, Wolfgang, and Kathleen Thelen. 2005. "Introduction: Institutional Change in Political Economies." In Wolfgang Streek and Kathleen Thelen, eds, *Beyond Continuity: Institutional Change in Advanced Political Economies*, 3–39. Oxford, UK: Oxford University Press.

CHAPTER SEVENTEEN

Alvim, Joaquim, and Roberto Filho. 2002. "Information Technology and Workplace Privacy: A Comparative Study: Part II: Information Technology and Workplace Privacy: The Brazilian Law." *Comparative Labor Law and Policy Journal* 23: 281–300.

American Management Association. 2005. *Electronic Monitoring and Surveillance Survey.* http://www.amanet.org/press/amanews/emso5.htm (accessed 18 December 2006).

Aranda, Javier. 2002a. "Information Technology and Workplace Privacy: A Comparative Study: Part II: National Studies: Information Technology and Workplace Privacy: The Spanish Law." *Comparative Labor Law and Policy Journal* 23: 431–70.

– 2002b. "Information Technology and Workplace Privacy: A Comparative Study: Part III: Recurring Questions of Comparative Law: The Role of Worker Representatives." *Comparative Labor Law and Policy Journal* 23: 533–4Arrêt 4164, Cour de Cassation – Chambre Sociale. 2001. http://www.courdecassation.fr/agenda/arrets/arrets/99-42942arr.htm (accessed 18 December 2006).

Article 29 – Data Protection Working Party. 2001. *Opinion 8/2001 on the Processing of Personal Data in the Employment Context.* http://www.garanteprivacy.it/garante/document?ID=1365969 (accessed 7 October 2009).

Bignami, Francesca. 2005. "Transgovernmental Networks vs. Democracy: The Case of the European Information Privacy Network." *Michigan Journal of International Law* 26: 807–68.

Brandeis, Louis, and Samuel Warren. 1890. "The Right to Privacy." *Harvard Law Review* 4: 193–220.

Brannen v. Kings Local School District Board of Education. 2001. 144 Ohio App. 3d 620.

Brazilian Constitution. http://webthes.senado.gov.br/web/const/const88.pdf (accessed 18 December 2006).

California Constitution. http://www.leginfo.ca.gov/const-toc.html (accessed 18 December 2006).

Cannataci, Joseph, and Jeanne Pia Mifsud-Bonnic. 2005. "Data Protection Comes of Age: The Data Protection Clauses in the European Constitutional Treaty." *Information and Communications Technology Law* 14, no. 5: 5–15.

Chinese Constitution. http://english.peopledaily.com.cn/constitution/constitution.html (accessed 18 December 2006).

Colb, Sherry. 2004. "A World without Privacy: Why Property Does Not Define the Limits of the Right against Unreasonable Searches and Seizures." *Michigan Journal of International Law* 102: 889–903.

Comparative Labor Law and Policy Journal 23. 2002.

Eastmond v. Canadian Pacific Railway. 2004. FC 852. http://privcom.gc.ca/cf-dc/2003/cf-dc_030123_e.asp (accessed 18 December 2006).

Eltis, Karen. 2004. "The Emerging American Approach to E-mail Privacy in the Workplace: Its Influence on Developing Caselaw in Canada and Israel: Should Others Follow Suit?" *Comparative Labor Law and Policy Journal* 24: 487–523.

European Union (EU) Draft Constitution. http://europa.eu.int/constitution/en/lstoc1_en.htm (accessed 18 December 2006).

Faleri, Claudia. 2002. "Information Technology and Workplace Privacy: A Comparative Study: Part III: Recurring Questions of Comparative Law: Public and Private Regulation." *Comparative Labor Law and Policy Journal* 23: 517–25.

Fisk, Catherine. 2006. "Privacy, Power, and Humiliation at Work: Re-Examining Appearance Regulation as an Invasion of Privacy." Duke Law School Legal Studies Paper No. 101. http://ssrn.com/abstract=893148 (accessed 18 December 2006).

Flint, Jason. 2004. "Internet and Email Monitoring in Spain: How Far Can Employers Go?" *International Company and Commercial Law Review* 15: 315–19.

French Civil Code. http://www.legifrance.gouv.fr/html/codes_traduits/code_civil_textA.htm (accessed 18 December 2006).

French Labour Code. http://lexinter.net/Legislation5/index.htm (accessed 23 November 2009).

Garrity v. John Hancock. 2002. 18 Industrial and Employment Relation Cases 981.

Globalization of Personal Data (GPD) 2006. *An International Survey on Privacy and Surveillance*. Funded by the Social Sciences and Humanities Research Council of Canada (SSHRCC), the Surveillance Project, Queen's University, Kingston, ON. http://www.sscqueens.org/research/intl_survey (accessed 23 November 2009).

Gomez-Arostegui, H. Tomas. 2005. "Defining Private Life under the European Convention on Human Rights by Referring to Reasonable Expectations." *California Western International Law Journal* 35: 153–202.

Greenleaf, Graham. 2008. "China Proposes Personal Information Protection Act 91:1." *Privacy Laws and Business International Newsletter* 91, no. 1: 1–6.

Hungarian Constitution. http://www.lectlaw.com/files/into5.htm (accessed 18 December 2006).

Isajiw, Peter. 2001. "Workplace E-mail Privacy Concerns: Balancing the Personal Dignity of Employees with the Propriety Interests of Employers." *Temple Environmental Law and Technology Journal* 20: 73–104.

Jeffery, Mark. 2002. "Information Technology and Workers' Privacy: A Comparative Study: Part I: Introduction." *Comparative Labor Law and Policy Journal* 23: 251–79.

Katz v. United States. 1967. 389 US 347.

Kerr, Orin. 2004a. "The Fourth Amendment and New Technologies: Constitutional Myths and the Case for Caution." *Michigan Law Review* 102: 801–88.

– 2004b. "Technology, Privacy, and the Courts: A Reply to Colb and Swire." *Michigan Law Review* 102: 933–43.

Kesan, Jay. 2002. "Cyber-Working or Cyber-Shirking? A First Principles Examination of Electronic Privacy in the Workplace." *Florida Law Review* 54: 290–332.

Koops, Bert-Jaap, and Leenes, Ronald. 2005. "Code and Privacy, or How Technology Is Slowly Eroding Privacy." In Egbert Dommering and Lodewijk Ascher, eds, *Coding Regulation: Essays on the Normative Role of Information Technology*, 1–60. The Hague, Netherlands: Asser Press.

Levin, Avner, and Mary Jo Nicholson. 2005. "Privacy Law in the United States, the EU and Canada: The Allure of the Middle Ground." *University of Ottawa Law and Technology Journal* 2, no. 2: 357–95.

– Mary Jo Nicholson, Mary Foster, and Tony Hernandez. 2006. *Under the Radar: The Employer Perspective on Workplace Privacy*. Toronto: Centre for the Study of Commercial Activity.

Lyon, David. 2001. *Surveillance Society: Monitoring Everyday Life*. Philadelphia, PA: Open University Press.

Mawdsley, Ralph. 2004. "The Law in Providing Education: School Board Control over Education and a Teacher's Right to Privacy." *St Louis University Public Law Review* 23: 609–33.

Mexican Constitution. http://www.gob.mx/wb/egobierno/egob_1917_Mexican_Constitution (accessed 18 December 2006).

Nouwt, Sjaak, Berend R. de Vries, and Corien Prins, eds. 2005. *Reasonable Expectations of Privacy? Eleven Country Reports on Camera Surveillance and Workplace Privacy*. The Hague, Netherlands: Asser Press.

O'Connor v. Ortega. 1987. 480 US 709.

Office of the Privacy Commissioner of Canada. 2006. *Use of Personal Information Collected by Global Positioning System Considered.* PIPEDA Case Summary

#2006–351. http://www.privcom.gc.ca/cf-dc/2006/351_20061109_e.asp (accessed 18 December 2006).

Oliver, Hazel. 2002. "Email and Internet Monitoring in the Workplace: Information Privacy and Contracting Out." *Industrial Law Journal* 31, no. 4: 321–52.

Rees, Phillip. 2003. "Hard to Put Your Finger On – Balancing Biometrics and Privacy." *Society for Computers and Law Magazine* 14, no. 4: 19–21.

Reinhard, Hans-Joachim. 2002. "Information Technology and Workplace Privacy: A Comparative Study: Part III: Recurring Questions of Comparative Law: Enforcement." *Comparative Labor Law and Policy Journal* 23: 527–32.

Rothstein, Lawrence. 2000. "Privacy or Dignity: Electronic Monitoring in the Workplace." *New York Law School Journal of International and Comparative Law* 19: 379–412.

Smyth v. Pillsbury. 1996. 924 F. Supp. 97 (ED Pa.).

Swire, Peter. 2004. "Katz is Dead. Long Live Katz." *Michigan Law Review* 102: 904–32.

Székely, Iván, and Mate Szabo. 2005. "Privacy and Data Protection at the Workplace in Hungary." In Sjaak Nouwt, Berend R. de Vries, and Corien Prins, eds, *Reasonable Expectations of Privacy? Eleven Country Reports on Camera Surveillance and Workplace Privacy,* 249–78. The Hague, Netherlands: Asser Press.

Thygeson v. US Bancorp. 2004. 34 Employee Benefits Cases 2097.

Vargas, Jorge. 2004. "Privacy Rights under Mexican Law: Emergence and Legal Configuration of a Panoply of New Rights." *Houston Journal of International Law* 27: 73–136.

Vigneau, Christophe. 2002a. "Information Technology and Workplace Privacy: A Comparative Study: Part II: National Studies: Information Technology and Workplace Privacy: The French Law." *Comparative Labor Law and Policy Journal* 23: 351–75.

– 2002b. "Information Technology and Workplace Privacy: A Comparative Study: Part III: Recurring Questions of Comparative Law: Regulatory Techniques." *Comparative Labor Law and Policy Journal* 23: 505–15.

Whitman, James. 2004. "The Two Western Cultures of Privacy: Dignity versus Liberty." *Yale Law Journal* 113: 1151–1221.

Zureik, Elia. 2002. "Theorizing Surveillance: The Case of the Workplace." In David Lyon, ed., *Surveillance as Social Sorting,* 31–56. New York: Routledge.

Zweig, David, Jane Webster, and Kristyn Scott. 2006. "Making the Decision to Monitor in the Workplace: Cybernetic Models and the Illusion of Control." In Gerard P. Hodgkinson and William H. Starbuck, eds, *The Oxford Handbook of Organizational Decision Making,* 116–33. Oxford, UK: Oxford University Press.

Index

actors: as citizens (*see also* citizenship), ix, 14–29, 55–7, 63, 64, 75–6, 77, 80–2, 87–100, 134–8, 147–9, 354–7,
as consumers (*see* consumers),
as travellers, 43, 100, 373,
as workers/employees, 106, 140–2, 149, 159–67, 182, 195, 200, 216–71, 221, 291, 328–45, 354–5
anti-Americanism, 161
antiterrorism, 15, 110, 163–4, 181–5, 238, 241, 270, 280, 284–6, 236,
legislation, ix, 15, 178, 188,
measures (*see also* post-9/11 surveillance), 111–25, 277,
technologies (*see also* surveillance: technologies), 171–2, 178

biometrics: attitudes and knowledge of/toward, 171, 178, 202, 217, 250, 259–63, 363
Bauman, Zygmunt, 1, 4
Bellman, Steven, 21, 205, 215, 219
Big Brother (George Orwell), 2, 164
border control regimes, 181, 189–90, 356

borders: and information sharing between (*see also* PIPEDA), 50–60, 65–6,
transgression of (*see also* Marx, Gary), 13
Brandeis, Louis, 330–1

cardification, 185
categorization (*see* social sorting)
citizenship, 189–92, 227, 233–5, 236, 243, 251, 252, 257–9
citizen versus state, 151
closed circuit television (CCTV): attitudes and knowledge of/toward, 73, 165, 178, 217, 239, 363, 371
collectivism versus individualism, 97, 203
consumers (*see also* actors), 104, 115, 354–5,
attitude toward personal information privacy, 15–18, 21, 23, 88, 92–4, 261–2,
behaviour, 310–11,
data as a commodity, 291, 297,
disclosure management, 302,
and Internet purchasing, 292–3, 310–19, 321–5, 378; trust,